Opposing Viewpoints in American History

SECOND EDITION

Volume 1: From Colonial Times to Reconstruction

Opposing Viewpoints in American History

VOLUME 1
FROM COLONIAL TIMES TO RECONSTRUCTION

William Dudley
VOLUME EDITOR

John C. Chalberg
CONSULTING EDITOR

GREENHAVEN PRESS
An imprint of Thomson Gale, a part of The Thomson Corporation

Detroit • New York • San Francisco • New Haven, Conn. • Waterville, Maine • London

Opposing Viewpoints in American History
Volume 1: From Colonial Times to Reconstruction

William Dudley, volume editor, and John C. Chalberg, consulting editor

LIBRARY OF CONGRESS CATALOGING-IN-PUBLICATION DATA

Opposing viewpoints in American history / William Dudley, volume editor; John C. Chalberg, consulting editor.
   v. cm.
   Includes bibliographical references and index.
   Contents: v. 1. From colonial times to Reconstruction – v. 2. From Reconstruction to the present.
   Audience: Grades 9–12.
   ISBN-13: 978-0-7377-3184-2 (v. 1 : lib. alk. paper) --
   ISBN-10: 0-7377-3184-2 (v. 1 : lib. alk. paper) --
   ISBN-13: 978-0-7377-3185-9 (v. 1 pbk. : alk. paper) --
   ISBN-10: 0-7377-3185-0 (v. 1 pbk. : alk. paper) --
   [etc.]
   1. United States -- History -- Sources -- Juvenile literature. I. Dudley, William, 1964–. II. Chalberg, John.
   E173.O7 2007
   973–dc22

2006024673

ISBN-13:

978-0-7377-3184-2
  (v. 1 : lib. alk. paper)
978-0-7377-3185-9
  (v. 1 : pbk. : alk. paper)

978-0-7377-3186-6
  (v. 2 : lib. alk. paper)
978-0-7377-3187-3
  (v. 2 : pbk. : alk. paper)

ISBN-10:

0-7377-3184-2
  (v. 1 : lib. alk. paper)
0-7377-3185-0
  (v. 1 : pbk. : alk. paper)

0-7377-3186-9
  (v. 2 : lib. : alk. paper)
0-7377-3187-7
  (v. 2 : pbk. : alk. paper)

Printed in the United States of America
10 9 8 7 6 5 4 3 2 1

Contents

Foreword

Educators have long sought ways to engage and interest students in American history. They have also tried to sharpen their students' critical thinking skills by teaching them how to effectively analyze and evaluate the material they read. *Opposing Viewpoints in American History* has been designed with both these objectives in mind.

Opposing Viewpoints in American History is an anthology of primary documents—the speeches, letters, articles, and other writings that are the raw material from which historians seek to understand and reconstruct the past. Assembled in two volumes (*Volume 1: From Colonial Times to Reconstruction* and *Volume 2: From Reconstruction to the Present*), these viewpoints trace American social, political, and diplomatic history from the time of the earliest European contact to the twenty-first century. The excerpts represent a wide spectrum of American voices, both the famous and the unfamiliar, expressing opinions on the critical issues of their times.

To help sustain student interest and stimulate critical thinking, primary documents in *Opposing Viewpoints in American History* are paired in a running debate format. This arrangement allows readers to compare and contrast opposing viewpoints on an issue. For example, readers can evaluate Thomas Paine's stirring call for American independence in *Common Sense* by comparing it with the tightly reasoned arguments of Loyalist Charles Inglis. Within these two volumes, early English settlers provide opposing views of life in the new colonies; Supreme Court justices clash over whether to extend civil rights to blacks and, over a hundred years later, debate the same issue in regard to World War II Japanese American internees. Franklin D. Roosevelt's call for a New Deal is complemented by Herbert Hoover's dire warnings about the harms of government meddling. A U.S. president and peace studies academic differ on how America should respond to the September 11, 2001, terrorist attacks. The paired structuring of sources found in *Opposing Viewpoints in American History* also reflects the important reality that American history itself has been a story of conflict and controversy. The birth of the nation was the result of a hotly debated decision to break from Great Britain, and Americans have continued to debate the meaning and direction of their nation ever since.

Along with primary documents, *Opposing Viewpoints in American History* includes several supplementary features intended to enhance the reader's understanding. Introductions and timelines supply basic historical background for each section of the two volumes. In addition, for each viewpoint the editors have provided essential biographical information about the author; a brief overview of the issue being debated; and questions designed to stimulate interest, reinforce comprehension, and encourage critical thinking. The combination of primary texts and background information make *Opposing Viewpoints in American History*, by itself or in conjunction with other American history textbooks, an effective way to teach and engage students in American history.

This second edition of *Opposing Viewpoints in American History* includes key viewpoints regarding the September 11 terrorist attacks and the Iraq War. In addition, bibliographies that accompany each pair of opposing viewpoints have been updated to include newly published material.

Thomas Jefferson once said that "difference of opinion leads to inquiry, and inquiry to truth"—a statement as valid today as in Jefferson's time. It is the editors' hope that this volume will challenge students to actively inquire into the "difference of opinion" found on the pages of America's history in order to better understand the nation's past.

Part 1
COLONIAL AMERICA (1582–1750)

CHRONOLOGY

Before 1600

August 3, 1492 Christopher Columbus begins first of six voyages to the New World.

August 1502 Spanish begin importing slaves into the New World from Africa.

September 8, 1565 Spaniards establish fort at St. Augustine, Florida.

Spring, 1580 Richard Hakluyt begins issuing a series of tracts urging Englishmen to engage in "western planting."

August 1585 First English colony in North America founded, under aegis of Walter Raleigh, at Roanoke, North Carolina.

September 1588 The English navy defeats the Spanish Armada, giving England control of the seas.

August 18, 1591 Roanoke settlement is found deserted.

1603

March 24 James I begins reign of Stuart monarchs in England.

1607

May 14 First permanent English colony is established at Jamestown, Virginia.

1608

Summer First permanent French colony in North America established at Quebec.

Summer Pilgrims leave England to seek refuge in Holland.

1609

Fall Dutch navigator Henry Hudson explores New York harbor.

1612

May Tobacco introduced into Virginia.

1614

April 5 Pocahontas, daughter of Native American leader Powhatan, marries Jamestown settler John Rolfe.

1619

July 30 First meeting of Virginia House of Burgesses.

August First blacks arrive in Virginia; their status is probably that of indentured servants.

1620

November Pilgrims arrive at Cape Cod, Massachusetts, and draft Mayflower Compact.

1622

March Members of Powhatan Confederacy attack English settlements in Virginia.

1624

May Charter of the Virginia Company revoked; Virginia becomes royal colony.

1629

September Colony of Massachusetts founded.

1630

April John Winthrop and 700 fellow Puritans arrive in Massachusetts.

1634

March 25 Colony of Maryland is established under George Calvert (Lord Baltimore).

1

1636

June Banished Puritan dissenter Roger Williams founds Rhode Island colony.

September 8 Harvard College founded in Massachusetts.

Summer First settlement in Connecticut is founded.

1637

May Pequot War in New England virtually wipes out the Pequot tribe.

November 7 Anne Hutchinson tried for heresy in Massachusetts and is banished.

1639

March First printing press set up in Cambridge, Massachusetts.

1640

November Charles I calls Parliament back into session; migration of Puritans to America decreases.

1642

August 22 English Civil War begins.

1644

April 18 Last concerted Indian attack in Virginia occurs.

1649

January 30 Charles I beheaded; 9-year reign of Puritan Oliver Cromwell in England begins.

April 21 Maryland establishes principle of religious toleration with its "Act Concerning Religion."

1653

September First Indian reservation established in Virginia.

1660

May 29 Charles II crowned king of England in Stuart restoration.

1660–1663

December Parliament passes a series of Navigation Acts to regulate trade.

1661

Fall Maryland defines slavery as lifelong, inheritable racial status; other colonies follow suit.

1663

March 24 Carolina colony founded.

1664

August England takes over New Amsterdam (renamed New York) from the Dutch.

1665

August Colony of New Jersey founded.

1675

June King Philip's War occurs in New England.

1676

September Bacon's Rebellion takes place against the royal government of Virginia.

1681

July 11 William Penn founds Pennsylvania colony.

1682

April 9 French explorer Sieur de La Salle claims Mississippi River area for Louis IV of France.

1685

February 6 Duke of York becomes King James II; establishes the Dominion of New England, dissolving existing legislative assemblies.

1688

November Glorious Revolution in England overthrows James II; William and Mary assume power as joint sovereign.

1689

May Leisler's rebellion takes place in New York against the architects of the Dominion of New England.

1689–1697

August King William's War fought between England and France in northern New England.

1691

October 7 New Massachusetts charter restores legislative body of Massachusetts General Court.

June 13 Spain establishes province of Texas.

1692

February 14 William and Mary College founded in Virginia.

June Salem witch trials take place.

1697

Fall Royal African Company's monopoly on the slave trade broken, allowing American competition.

1701

October 16 Yale College founded in Connecticut.

1701–1713

Fall Queen Anne's War fought between England and Spain.

1713

April 11 Treaty of Utrecht gives Nova Scotia and New-foundland to England.

1718

August 25 New Orleans founded by France.

1721

November 5 John Trenchard and Thomas Gordon's antimonarchical "Cato's Letters" begin publication in England.

1729

Fall Carolina is divided into North and South Carolina.

1730–1745

December The religious revival known as the Great Awakening sweeps across the colonies.

1733

January James Oglethorpe founds Georgia as colony without slavery.

May 17 Parliament passes the Molasses Act restricting access to British sugar islands in the West Indies.

1734

November 17 Trial of John Peter Zenger establishes that press criticism of government is not libelous if true.

1739

September 9 Stono slave rebellion in South Carolina quelled.

1744–1748

October King George's War fought between England and France; Fort Louisbourg in Nova Scotia is captured by Massachusetts colonists only to be returned to the French at the end of the war.

1746

October 22 College of New Jersey (Princeton) founded.

1747

November Boston mobs resist British navy's impressment of sailors.

1749

Spring French construct new fortresses in the Ohio Valley.

1750

June 24 Passage of Iron Act restricts colonists from engaging in metal processing.

PREFACE

On May 24, 1607, 105 Englishmen on three small ships completed a three-thousand-mile, five-month voyage by landing on a North American river peninsula about fifteen miles inland from the Atlantic Ocean. Their first act was to construct a fort to protect themselves from the native peoples in the region and the Spanish to the south. By January 1608, when a new ship landed with 120 new arrivals, almost two-thirds of the 105 original settlers had perished from malnutrition and disease. Another "starving time" in the winter of 1609–1610 reduced the population to 60; in the spring all survivors boarded a ship to return to England, only to be met at the mouth of the river by another ship from England with new supplies and colonists.

Such was the shaky founding of Jamestown, the first permanent English settlement in America. Over the next 150 years a steady stream of immigrants from England and other European countries followed the Jamestown colonists across the Atlantic Ocean to settle on what is now the eastern seaboard of the United States. These immigrants and their descendants were one of three groups of people whose destinies converged to be part of American colonial history—the others were the native inhabitants of America (who were largely displaced by the newcomers) and black Africans who came to America involuntarily as slaves.

AMERICA BEFORE JAMESTOWN

In 1607 perhaps 9 million people lived in what is now the United States of America. Their ancestors had migrated to North America from Asia perhaps as many as forty thousand years earlier, across a now-submerged land bridge connecting Siberia and Alaska. These people lived in more than two hundred separate groups and societies, ranging from small tribal bands of hunter-gatherers to large and complex agricultural societies. Some were organized into powerful political entities such as the Iroquois Confederacy; others lived in scattered small communities. Because most of these peoples did not use writing, there are almost no written records of their life and culture. Most of what is known about the early history of Native Americans is derived from oral tradition, archaeological evidence, and the reports of European explorers.

The relative isolation of the Western Hemisphere and its people from the rest of the globe ended with the voyage of Christopher Columbus in 1492. His voyage opened the way for other explorers, the establishment of colonies, and the migration of people from Europe and Africa to these lands.

EUROPEAN CONQUEST AND COLONIZATION

Columbus, an Italian-born navigator in the employ of Spain, was sailing westward in 1492 in search of a new trade route to India and the Far East. After thirty-three days at sea he landed on a small island east of the North American continent, which he named San Salvador. He mistakenly named the peoples he encountered there "Indians." In this and subsequent expeditions, Columbus explored much of the Gulf of Mexico and the Caribbean. Initially convinced he had discovered new lands in Asia, he was reluctant to admit he had come across a previously unknown continent. Nonetheless, his voyages sparked the attention of European rulers, who soon sent other explorers into what became known as the New World. One of them, Amerigo Vespucci, charted much of the eastern coastline from Mexico to Brazil beginning in 1497; it was his name that was ultimately given to the new lands of "America."

The early European explorers had two general objectives: to chart a trade route to Asia and to find gold. Toward both ends England sent John Cabot in 1497 and his son Sebastian eleven years later; they explored Newfoundland and the Atlantic coastline to its south. Explorers Giovanni da Verrazano and Jacques Cartier probed the coast of North America for France: Cartier ventured up the St. Lawrence River in search of a passage to Asia.

Spain and Portugal took the lead in establishing empires in the New World in the sixteenth century; by 1600 these two nations controlled most of what is now Central and South America. Spanish conquistadores discovered and quickly conquered the advanced Aztec and Inca civilizations in Mexico and Peru, respectively, in the process finding large sources of silver and some veins of gold. Spain soon established profitable colonies in these conquered territories, as well as in the Caribbean islands discovered by Columbus. Relying on native slave labor and, beginning in 1502, on African slave labor, the colonies sent great quantities of silver, gold, sugar, cocoa, and dyes back to Spain.

Spanish explorers also ventured into areas of North America, Hernando de Soto led an expedition in 1539–1543 that explored what is now the southeastern United States and crossed the Mississippi River. In 1540–1542 Francisco Vásquez de Coronado led an expedition that explored the Grand Canyon and ventured north into what is now Kansas. A third expedition led by Juan Rodriguez Cabrillo sailed along the California coastline in 1542–1543. None of these expeditions found riches comparable to what was found in Mexico and Peru. The only lasting settlement founded by Spain in North America during the sixteenth century was St. Augustine, Florida, a military outpost established in 1565 to protect Spanish shipping in the Caribbean.

European explorers had devastating effects on the Native Americans they encountered, with disease perhaps the single most important contributing factor. The populations of the New World had no immunity to such European diseases as smallpox, tuberculosis, and cholera. The native populations of the Caribbean islands where Columbus first landed were nearly extinct within a few decades. The population of Mexico dropped from about 25 million in 1519 to between 1 and 2 million by the early seventeenth century. Diseases were also spread to North America by de Soto and other explorers. The establishment of British colonies in Virginia and Massachusetts was facilitated by prior epidemics that had drastically reduced the local native populations.

ENGLAND AND THE NEW WORLD

While Spain was building an overseas empire in the 1500s, England was preoccupied with domestic affairs. King Henry VIII broke with the Roman Catholic Church in the 1530s, and for the next several decades Catholics battled Protestants for political control of England. Under the reign of Queen Elizabeth I (1558–1603), the Protestant Church of England was firmly established as the official national church. Protestantism and English nationalism were fused in the minds of many, especially after England's dramatic naval victory over Catholic Spain's "Invincible Armada" in 1588. Spain continued to be viewed as England's chief European rival, and many advisers to Queen Elizabeth argued that England needed its own colonies in the New World. Such colonies, they argued, would serve as bases from which to raid Spanish ships of gold and other riches and to control any potential westward passage to Asia—and they would lay the foundation for England's own empire.

In addition to political, military, and religious concerns, many supporters of English colonization advanced economic arguments. Elizabeth's reign was marked by the emergence of a wealthy and influential merchant class that was constantly searching for new markets for wool and other products. These merchants advocated the establishment of American colonies not only as a potential market for English goods, but as a source of raw materials as well. Such colonies, many argued, could also provide an outlet for England's exploding population, which grew from 3 million in 1550 to more than 4 million in

1600. The economic impact of such growth was aggravated by "enclosure"—the conversion of much of England's open farmland into fenced sheep pastures—which had resulted in the eviction of tenant farmers and an increase of England's landless and (some feared) idle and criminal population.

England's initial attempts to establish colonies in Newfoundland in 1583 and Roanoke Island (the Lost Colony) in 1587 both failed. Finally, in 1607, the Jamestown settlement was founded. In 1620 English religious refugees called Pilgrims established another settlement well north of Virginia in Plymouth, Massachusetts. They were followed a decade later by a much larger group of religious refugees, called Puritans, who had obtained a charter from King Charles I to establish the Massachusetts Bay Company with rights of settlement in what is now New England. The new and more populous settlement soon overshadowed the small Plymouth colony, which was eventually absorbed by Massachusetts in 1691. A quick look at the early history of America's first English colonies—Virginia and Massachusetts—suggests that the English had many different motives for colonizing America and that numerous controversies arose among them after they arrived in the New World.

GOALS OF THE TWO COLONIES

The Jamestown settlement had two important advantages over previous English efforts at colonization: The 1604 peace treaty between Great Britain and Spain reduced the danger of Spanish interference, and the use of a joint stock company (a new economic innovation) provided sufficient private financial backing for the colony. The Virginia Company of London obtained a charter from Elizabeth's successor, James I, granting them the right to establish a colony and govern it. The purpose of the Jamestown settlement was simple: to make money for its investors.

The stockholders of the Virginia Company hoped to profit quickly by finding precious metals and somewhat more slowly by cultivating mulberry trees (for silk production) and grapes. Many of the colonists were self-described "gentlemen" who expected to re-create an English society in which they would comprise a new noble class and in which others (including Indians) would do the work. All of these expectations proved illusory. No gold was found, despite a great amount of time and energy spent by the colonists in its pursuit. Efforts to develop land for cash crops were unsuccessful and aroused the suspicions and hostilities of the Native Americans residing in the area.

Virginia's first major economic breakthrough—and lure for large numbers of new settlers—was the successful cultivation and curing of tobacco. The breakthrough came too late for the Virginia Company, which was dissolved when Virginia was made a royal colony under the Crown's direct authority in 1624. By then the colony itself was well established and by 1627 was exporting five hundred thousand pounds of tobacco a year. The valuable crop proved to be a mixed blessing. Tobacco cultivation quickly exhausted the soil, causing settlers to move farther and farther west. Price fluctuations wreaked economic havoc on the colony. Finally, its cultivation required intensive labor, which was in short supply until the colony turned to black slavery later in the seventeenth century.

The Puritans who settled in New England had profoundly different concerns than the fortune seekers of Jamestown. Puritans were English Protestants who wished to "purify" the Church of England from what they regarded as dangerous vestiges of Roman Catholicism. Those Puritans who migrated to America sought not wealth, but the establishment of a pure and godly church and society in conformity with their beliefs. In part, they wanted to create a compelling example of true reform Christianity for those who remained behind in England.

The Puritans, like the Jamestown settlers, had mixed success in achieving their own goals. They established a system in which political control and social influence were limited to "visible saints"—those who could demonstrate that they had personally experienced God's grace. Only such church members could vote and participate in the colonial government (although church attendance was required of all, not all attenders could qualify as members). But at the same time Puritan leaders were compelled to wage wars against the native population and attack religious dissenters within their ranks.

CONTROVERSIES IN VIRGINIA AND MASSACHUSETTS

Most of the recorded disputes within Virginia revolved around economics and politics. In its earliest days the settlement was constantly riven by disagreements between its leaders, who sometimes resorted to martial law to compel their fellow Virginians to grow their own food, and settlers who resisted all efforts to take them away from searching for gold. The demands of the colonists for a greater say in their own affairs led to the creation in 1619 of the House of Burgesses, the first representative governmental assembly in America.

The cultivation of tobacco brought profits for only some in Virginia. By the mid-1600s the colony was beset by conflicts between the landless poor and an emerging economic and political elite. There were even fears among some that Virginia was replicating the social problems of England and that idleness and crime were undermining the colony. Economic and political divisions erupted in Bacon's Rebellion in 1676, the first major colonial rebellion against English authority. One solution to this persistent problem was the introduction of black slavery in the 1600s. (Africans had been captured and sold as slaves in Spanish and Portuguese New World colonies since the 1500s.) Not only did slavery provide a stable labor force, it also bridged class divisions between rich and poor whites who were united on the basis of race.

Unlike the Virginians, the main controversies that divided the Massachusetts Puritans revolved around religious issues. Puritan ministers and leaders sought levels of political and religious conformity that proved unattainable. As a result, religious dissenters were put on trial and banished, or, in the case of Roger Williams, simply encouraged to depart. During the second half of the seventeenth century another kind of dissent proved to be even more insidious: religious indifference. Puritan ministers preached warning sermons ("jeremiads") pleading with their followers to disregard worldly concerns and return to the faith of their forefathers. Devastating Indian attacks in 1675 (King Philip's War) and a disastrous Boston fire in 1679 were seen as signs of God's displeasure with the Puritans. By the end of the century controversy over witchcraft, especially in Salem in 1692, was also tearing the Puritan world apart.

COLONISTS AND NATIVE AMERICANS

King Philip's War of 1675–1676 was one of many conflicts that beset both the Virginia and Massachusetts colonies. The relationship between the Jamestown settlers and the local Powhatan Confederacy of Indian tribes was tense from the beginning and exploded into a major war in 1622 when Indians in a surprise attack killed 347 settlers. The Virginia authorities responded by declaring a policy of "perpetual enmity" toward the Indians and began periodic military expeditions that destroyed Indian villages and food supplies, reduced the Indian population, and drove survivors farther westward. Another Indian uprising in 1641 resulted in the death of 500 settlers but failed to stop the growth of the colony. Thirty years later in New England, Metacom (a Wampanoag Indian leader known to the English as King Philip) led well-armed tribesmen in an attack on fifty-two of New England's ninety towns in retaliation for the execution of three of his people, destroying twelve towns and killing 600 colonists. But in the end Metacom was killed and the Wampanoags defeated.

A NEW LIFE

The colonies of Virginia and Massachusetts were soon joined by others. Some, such as New York and Maryland, were the domains of English proprietors who received land grants from the Crown. Others, such as Connecticut and Rhode Island, were formed by colonists who were dissatisfied with existing colonies and who moved to create their own. The colonists created societies that combined ideas brought over from England with experiences in the new environment of America. Left largely to their own devices by the remote English government, the American colonies evolved in ways divergent from their ruling country—a development that would cause new controversies and ultimately result in independence from England in 1776.

ORIGINS OF ENGLISH SETTLEMENT

Viewpoint 1A

National and Economic Reasons to Colonize the New World (1585)

Richard Hakluyt

INTRODUCTION *During the long reign (1558–1603) of Queen Elizabeth I, England was on the sidelines of the European rush to colonize the New World following Christopher Columbus's 1492 voyage. Spain, on the other hand, created an empire of profitable colonies in South America and the Caribbean Sea. Ships from Spain's colonies laden with gold and silver made Spain the envy of other European nations. Portugal established a colony in what is now Brazil. France sent explorers up the St. Croix River in an attempt to find a trade route to Asia, established fur trading posts, and laid claims to much of North America. England sponsored several exploring expeditions, but its colonizing efforts were limited to small fishing settlements off the coast of North America and failed attempts at colonizing Newfoundland in 1583 and Roanoke Island (off what is now North Carolina) in 1587.*

A growing number of Englishmen began to promote the idea that England needed to establish colonies in the New World to compete with Spain and other nations. The following is taken from a 1585 treatise by Richard Hakluyt the elder, a prominent English lawyer who became interested in overseas colonization in the 1570s (his cousin, Richard Hakluyt the younger, also was a noted colonization promoter). The following excerpt lists thirty-one reasons ("Inducements") why England should begin colonizing efforts in the New World. Although he mentions the spread of Protestant Christianity as a reason for settlement, many of Hakluyt's arguments dwell on strategic and economic benefits for England, including trade opportunities and the ability to provide employment for England's poor.

What commodities does Hakluyt believe could be cultivated in America? Why do you think Hakluyt placed religion first on his list of "Inducements?" How does Hakluyt anticipate dealing with native peoples in the New World?

1. The glory of God by planting of religion among those infidels.

2. The increase of the force of the Christians.

3. The possibility of the enlarging of the dominions of the Queen's Most Excellent Majesty, and consequently of her honour, revenues, and of her power by this enterprise.

4. An ample vent [market] in time to come of the woollen cloths of England, especially those of the coarsest sorts, to the maintenance of our poor, that else starve or become burdensome to the realm; and vent also of sundry our commodities upon the tract of that firm land, and possibly in other regions from the northern side of that main.

5. A great possibility of further discoveries of other regions from the north part of the same land by sea, and of unspeakable honour and benefit that may rise upon the same by the trades to ensue in Japan, China, and Cathay, etc.

6. By return thence, this realm shall receive (by reason of the situation of the climate, and by reason of the excellent soil) woad, oil, wines, hops, salt, and most or all the commodities that we receive from the best parts of Europe, and we shall receive the same better cheap than now we receive them, as we may use the matter.

7. Receiving the same thence, the navy, the human strength of this realm, our merchants and their goods, shall not be subject to arrest of ancient enemies and doubtful friends as of late years they have been.

8. If our nation do not make any conquest there but only use traffic and change of commodities, yet, by means the country is not very mighty but divided into petty kingdoms, they shall not dare to offer us any great annoy but such as we may easily revenge with sufficient chastisement to the unarmed people there.

9. Whatsoever commodities we receive by the Steelyard Merchants, or by our own merchants from Eastland, be it flax, hemp, pitch, tar, masts, clapboard, wainscot, or such-like; the like good[s] may we receive from the north and north-east part of that country near unto Cape Breton, in return for our coarse woollen cloths, flannels, and rugs fit for those colder regions.

10. The passage to and fro is through the main ocean sea, so as we are not in danger of any enemy's coast.

TRADE OPPORTUNITIES

11. In the voyage we are not to cross the burnt zone [tropics], nor to pass through frozen seas encumbered with ice and fogs, but in temperate climate at all times of the year; and it requireth not, as the East Indies voyage

Richard Hakluyt, "Inducements to the Liking of the Voyage Intended Towards Virginia in 40. and 42. Degrees," from *The Original Writings and Correspondence of the Two Richard Hakluyts*, edited by E.G.R. Taylor (London: Hakluyt Society, 1935).

doth, the taking in of water in divers places, by reason that it is to be sailed in five or six weeks; and by the shortness the merchant may yearly make two returns (a factory [trade center] once being erected there), a matter in trade of great moment.

12. In this trade by the way, in our pass to and fro, we have in tempests and other haps all the ports of Ireland to our aid and no near coast of any enemy.

13. By this ordinary trade we may annoy the enemies to Ireland and succour the Queen's Majesty's friends there, and in time we may from Virginia yield them whatsoever commodity they now receive from the Spaniard; and so the Spaniards shall want the ordinary victual that heretofore they received yearly from thence, and so they shall not continue trade, nor fall so aptly in practice against this government as now by their trade thither they may.

14. We shall, as it is thought, enjoy in this voyage either some small islands to settle on or some one place or other on the firm land to fortify for the safety of our ships, our men, and our goods, the like whereof we have not in any foreign place of our traffic, in which respect we may be in degree of more safety and more quiet.

15. The great plenty of buff [buffalo or wild ox] hides and of many other sundry kinds of hides there now presently to be had, the trade of whale and seal fishing and of divers other fishings in the great rivers, great bays, and seas there, shall presently defray the charge in good part or in all of the first enterprise, and so we shall be in better case than our men were in Russia, where many years were spent and great sums of money consumed before gain was found.

16. The great broad rivers of that main that we are to enter into, so many leagues navigable or portable into the mainland, lying so long a tract with so excellent and so fertile a soil on both sides, do seem to promise all things that the life of man doth require and whatsoever men may wish that are to plant upon the same or to traffic in the same.

17. And whatsoever notable commodity the soil within or without doth yield in so long a tract, that is to be carried out from thence to England, the same rivers so great and deep do yield no small benefit for the sure, safe, easy, and cheap carriage of the same to shipboard, be it of great bulk or of great weight.

18. And in like sort whatsoever commodity of England the inland people there shall need, the same rivers do work the like effect in benefit for the incarriage of the same aptly, easily, and cheaply.

19. If we find the country populous and desirous to expel us and injuriously to offend us, that seek but just and lawful traffic, then, by reason that we are lords of navigation and they not so, we are the better able to defend ourselves by reason of those great rivers and to annoy them in many places.

20. Where there be many petty kings or lords planted on the rivers' sides, and [who] by all likelihood maintain the frontiers of their several territories by wars, we may by the aid of this river join with this king here, or with that king there, at our pleasure, and may so with a few men be revenged of any wrong offered by any of them; or may, if we will proceed with extremity, conquer, fortify, and plant in soils most sweet, most pleasant, most strong, and most fertile, and in the end bring them all in subjection and to civility.

21. The known abundance of fresh fish in the rivers, and the known plenty of fish on the sea-coast there, may assure us of sufficient victual in spite of the people, if we will use salt and industry.

22. The known plenty and variety of flesh of divers kinds of beasts at land there may seem to say to us that we may cheaply victual our navies to England for our returns, which benefit everywhere is not found of merchants.

23. The practice of the people of the East Indies, when the Portugals came thither first, was to cut from the Portugals their lading of spice; and hereby they thought to overthrow their purposed trade. If these people shall practise the like, by not suffering [allowing] us to have any commodity of theirs without conquest which requireth some time), yet may we maintain our first voyage thither till our purpose come to effect by the sea-fishing on the coasts there and by dragging for pearls, which are said to be on those parts: and by return of those commodities the charges in part shall be defrayed; which is a matter of consideration in enterprises of charge.

EMPLOYING ENGLAND'S POOR

24. If this realm shall abound too too much with youth, in the mines there of gold (as that of Chisea and Saguenay), of silver, copper, iron, etc., may be an employment to the benefit of this realm; in tilling of the rich soil there for grain and in planting of vines there for wine or dressing of those vines which grow there naturally in great abundance; olives for oil; orange trees, lemons, figs and almonds for fruit; woad, saffron, and madder for dyers: hops for brewers: hemp, flax; and in many such other things, by employment of the soil, our people void of sufficient trades may be honestly employed, that else may become hurtful at home.

25. The navigating of the seas in the voyage, and of the great rivers there, will breed many mariners for service and maintain much navigation.

26. The number of raw hides there of divers kinds of beasts, if we shall possess some island there or settle on the firm, may presently employ many of our idle people in

divers several dressings of the same, and so we may return them to the people that cannot dress them so well, or into this realm, where the same are good merchandise, or to Flanders, etc., which present gain at the first raiseth great encouragement presently to the enterprise.

27. Since great waste woods be there of oak, cedar, pine, walnuts, and sundry other sorts, many of our waste people may be employed in making of ships, hoys, busses [types of ships], and boats, and in making of rosin, pitch, and tar, the trees natural for the same being certainly known to be near Cape Breton and the Bay of Menan, and in many other places thereabout.

28. If mines of white or grey marble, jet, or other rich stone be found there, our idle people may be employed in the mines of the same and in preparing the same to shape, and, so shaped, they may be carried into this realm as good ballast for our ships and after serve for noble buildings.

We shall not only receive many precious commodities.... but also shall in time find ample vent of the labour of our poor people at home.

---

29. Sugar-canes may be planted as well as they are now in the South of Spain, and besides the employment of our idle people, we may receive the commodity cheaper and not enrich infidels or our doubtful friends, of whom now we receive that commodity.

30. The daily great increase of wools in Spain, and the like in the West Indies, and the great employment of the same into cloth in both places, may move us to endeavour, for vent of our cloth, new discoveries of peopled regions where hope of sale may arise; otherwise in short time many inconveniences may possibly ensue.

INCREDIBLE THINGS MAY FOLLOW

31. This land that we purpose to direct our course to, lying in part in the 40th degree of latitude, being in like heat as Lisbon in Portugal doth, and in the more southerly part, as the most southerly coast of Spain doth, may by our diligence yield unto us, besides wines and oils and sugars, oranges, lemons, figs, raisins, almonds, pomegranates, rice, raw silks such as come from Granada, and divers commodities for dyers, as anil and cochineal, and sundry other colours and materials. Moreover, we shall not only receive many precious commodities besides from thence, but also shall in time find ample vent of the labour of our poor people at home, by sale of hats, bonnets, knives, fish-hooks, copper kettles, beads, looking-glasses, bugles, and a thousand kinds of other wrought wares that in short time may be brought in use among the people of that country, to the great relief of the multitude of our poor people and to the wonderful enriching of this realm. And in time, such league and intercourse may arise between our stapling seats there, and other ports of our Northern America, and of the islands of the same, that incredible things, and by few as yet dreamed of, may speedily follow: tending to the impeachment of our mighty enemies and to the common good of this noble government.

The ends of this voyage are these:

1. To plant Christian religion.
2. To traffic.
3. To conquer.

Or, to do all three.

Viewpoint 1B

Religious Reasons to Colonize the New World (1629)

John Winthrop (1588–1649)

INTRODUCTION *The first two lasting English settlements in what is now the United States were at Jamestown, Virginia, 1607, and Plymouth, Massachusetts, 1620. Jamestown was sponsored by the Virginia Company of London, a joint-stock corporation whose investors (some of whom settled in Jamestown) hoped to make a quick profit from the colony. The leaders of the Plymouth colony—the Pilgrims—as well as the Puritans who settled close by in Massachusetts in subsequent years, had different motives.*

The Puritans and Pilgrims were religious people who were dissatisfied with the pace of Protestant reform in the Church of England, the official established church that all English people were then obliged to support. Under Queen Elizabeth I and her successor, King James I, the Church of England was closely linked to the royal government. Many Puritans came to America to avoid being persecuted for their beliefs and to create a new society that harmonized with their conceptions of true Christianity. A passionate summary of Puritan motives comes from the following viewpoint, excerpted from a 1629 pamphlet by John Winthrop. Winthrop, one of the wealthiest and most distinguished of the Puritan settlers, served as governor of the Massachusetts Bay Colony for thirteen of his nineteen years in America following his migration in 1630. In his 1629 pamphlet he argues that the true Christian church is hopelessly corrupt in England and that the faith can be preserved only by creating a new society in the New World. Puritan settlers were not to be adventurers seeking their fortune or the desperately poor seeking employment, but rather people inspired by God to practice their faith free of the constraints of the Church of England.

How do Winthrop's views of religion and of God expressed here differ from those expressed by Richard Hakluyt in the opposing viewpoint? What comments does Winthrop make about Jamestown? Hakluyt was writing to persuade government officials, while Winthrop is hoping to attract fellow settlers; how much might their differences in their arguments be attributed to the fact that their essays are aimed at different audiences?

Reasons to be considered for justifying the undertakers of the intended plantation in New England and for encouraging such whose hearts God shall move to join with them in it.

First, it will be a service to the church of great consequence to carry the gospel into those parts of the world, to help on the coming in of fullness of the Gentiles, and to raise a bulwark against the kingdom of anti-Christ which the Jesuits labor to rear up in those parts.

RESCUING THE CHURCH

2. All other churches of Europe are brought to desolation, and our sins, for which the Lord begins already to frown upon us, do threaten us fearfully, and who knows but that God hath provided this place to be a refuge for many whom he means to save out of the general calamity. And seeing the church hath no place left to fly into but the wilderness, what better work can there be than to go before and provide tabernacles and food for her, against she cometh thither?

3. This land grows weary of her inhabitants, so as man who is the most precious of all creatures is here more vile and base than the earth we tread upon, and of less price among us than a horse or a sheep; masters are forced by authority to entertain servants, parents to maintain their own children. All towns complain of the burthen of their poor, though we have taken up many unnecessary, yea unlawful, trades to maintain them. And we use the authority of the law to hinder the increase of people, as urging the execution of the state against cottages and inmates, and thus it is come to pass that children, servants, and neighbors (especially if the[y] be poor) are counted the greatest burthen, which if things were right it would be the chiefest earthly blessing.

4. The whole earth is the Lord's garden, and He hath given it to the sons of men with a general condition, Gen. 1:28, "Increase and multiply, replenish the earth and subdue it," which was again renewed to Noah. The end is double moral and natural: that man might enjoy the fruits

From *Reasons to be Considered for Justifying the Undertakers of the Intended Plantation in New England* by John Winthrop. (Proceedings, vol. 8, Massachusetts Historical Society, 1864–65).

of the earth, and God might have his due glory from the creature. Why then should we stand here striving for places of habitation (many men spending as much labor and cost to recover or keep sometimes an acre or two of land as would procure them many hundred as good or better in an other country) and in the meantime suffer a whole continent as fruitful and convenient for the use of man to lie waste without any improvement?

5. We are grown to that height of intemperance in all excess of riot, as no man's estate almost will suffice to keep sail with his equals, and he who fails herein must live in scorn and contempt. Hence it comes that all arts and trades are carried in that deceitful and unrighteous course, as it is almost impossible for a good and upright man to maintain his charge and live comfortably in any of them.

———◼———

If any such who are known to be godly, and live in wealth and prosperity here, shall forsake all this to join themselves to this church, . . . it will be an example of great use . . . to give more life to the faith of God's people in their prayers for the plantation.

———◼———

6. The fountains of learning and religion are so corrupted (as beside the unsupportable charge of the education) most children (even the best wits and fairest hopes) are perverted, corrupted, and utterly overthrown by the multitude of evil examples and the licentious government of those seminaries, where men strain at gnats and swallow camels, use all severity for maintenance of capes and other complements, but suffer all ruffian-like fashion and disorder in manners to pass uncontrolled.

7. What can be a better work and more honorable and worthy a Christian than to help raise and support a particular church while it is in the infancy, and to join his forces with such a company of faithful people as by a timely assistance may grow strong and prosper, and for want of it may be put to great hazard, if not wholly ruined.

8. If any such who are known to be godly, and live in wealth and prosperity here, shall forsake all this to join themselves to this church, and to run a hazard with them of a hard and mean condition, it will be an example of great use both for removing the scandal of worldly and sinister respects which is cast upon the adventurers, to give more life to the faith of God's people in their prayers for the plantation, and to encourage others to join the more willingly in it.

9. It appears to be a work of God for the good of His church, in that He hath disposed the hearts of so many of His wise and faithful servants (both ministers and others)

not only to approve of the enterprise but to interest themselves in it, some in their persons and estates, others by their serious advice and help otherwise. And all by their prayers for the welfare of it, Amos 3. The Lord revealeth His secrets to His servants the prophets; it is likely He hath some great work in hand which He hath revealed to His prophets among us, whom He hath stirred up to encourage His servants to this plantation, for He doth not use to seduce His people by His own prophets but commits that office to the ministry of false prophets and lying spirits. . . .

OBJECTIONS AND REPLIES

Objection 1: We have no warrant to enter upon that land which hath been so long possessed by others.

Answer 1: That which lies common and hath never been replenished or subdued is free to any that will possess and improve it, for God hath given to the sons of men a double right to the earth: there is a natural right and a civil right. The first right was natural when men held the earth in common, every man sowing and feeding where he pleased, and then as men and the cattle increased they appropriated certain parcels of ground by enclosing, and peculiar manurance, and this in time gave them a civil right. . . . And for the natives in New England, they enclose no land, neither have any settled habitation, nor any tame cattle to improve the land by, and so have no other but a natural right to those countries. So as if we leave them sufficient for their use, we may lawfully take the rest, there being more than enough for them and us.

Secondly, we shall come in with a good leave of the Natives, who find benefit already by our neighborhood and learn of us to improve part to more use than before they could do the whole. And by this means we come in by valuable purchase, for they have of us that which will yield them more benefit than all the land which we have from them.

Thirdly, God hath consumed the Natives with a great plague in those parts so as there be few inhabitants left.

Objection 2: It will be a great wrong to our church to take away the good people, and we shall lay it the more open to the judgment feared.

Answer 1: The departing of good people from a country doth not cause a judgment but foreshew it, which may occasion such as remain to turn from their evil ways that they may prevent it, or to take some other course that they may escape it.

Secondly, such as go away are of no observation in respects of those who remain, and they are likely to do more good there than here. And since Christ's time, the church is to be considered as universal without distinction of countries, so as he who doeth good in any one place serves the church in all places in regard of the unity.

Thirdly, it is the revealed will of God that the gospel should be preached to all nations, and though we know not whether those barbarians will receive it at first or not, yet it is a good work to serve God's providence in offering it to them; and this is fittest to be done by God's own servants, for God shall have glory by it though they refuse it, and there is good hope that the posterity *shall by this means be gathered into Christ's sheepfold.* . . .

Objection 4: The ill success of other plantations may tell us what will become of this.

Answer 1: None of the former sustained any great damage but Virginia; which happened through their own sloth and security.

2. The argument is not good, for thus it stands: some plantations have miscarried, therefore we should not make any. It consists in particulars and so concludes nothing. We might as well reason thus: many houses have been burnt by kilns, therefore we should use none; many ships have been cast away, therefore we should content ourselves with our home commodities and not adventure men's lives at sea for those things that we might live without; some men have been undone by being advanced to great places, therefore we should refuse our preferment, etc.

3. The fruit of any public design is not to be discerned by the immediate success; it may appear in time that former plantations were all to good use.

4. There were great and fundamental errors in the former which are like to be avoided in this, for first their main end was carnal and not religious; secondly, they used unfit instruments—a multitude of rude and misgoverned persons, the very scum of the people; thirdly, they did not establish a right form of government.

FOR FURTHER READING

Francis J. Bremer, *John Winthrop: America's Forgotten Founding Father*. New York: Oxford University Press, 2003.

Stephen Greenblatt, *Marvelous Possessions: The Wonders of the New World*. Chicago: University of Chicago Press, 1991.

Peter C. Mancall, ed., *Envisioning America: English Plans for the Colonization of North America, 1580–1640*. Boston: Bedford Books of St. Martin's Press, 1995.

David B. Quinn, North America from Earliest Discovery to First Settlements: The Norse Voyages to 1612. New York: Harper & Row, 1975.

Alan Taylor, *American Colonies: The Settling of North America*. New York: Penguin, 2001.

The complete text of Richard Hakluyt's *Inducements* can be found in Peter C. Mancall, ed., *Envisioning America: English Plans for the Colonization of North America, 1580–1640*. Boston: Bedford Books of St. Martin's Press, 1995. The complete text of Winthrop's sermon can be found online at the web site of the Winthrop Society at http://www.winthropsociety.org/doc-reasons.php.

Virginia Is an Abundant New Paradise (1613)

Alexander Whitaker (1585–1617?)

INTRODUCTION *Jamestown, the first enduring English settlement in the New World, was financed by the Virginia Company of London, a private joint-stock company. Much of the historical record of Jamestown comes from company records and publications. The company's efforts to recoup its expenses and make a profit in its venture were jeopardized in Jamestown's early years as reports of hardship and starvation reached England. In order to attract additional investors and settlers, the company published several pamphlets describing the resources of the new land of "Virginia" and the riches to be attained there. The following viewpoint is one example of such writing; it is excerpted (with modernized spelling) from a 1613 pamphlet published by the Virginia Company and written by Alexander Whitaker, a minister who had arrived in the new colony in 1611. Whitaker was motivated to move to America to preach Christianity to the Indians, according to William Crashaw, a minister who stayed in England and who wrote the preface to Whitaker's pamphlet. Little else is known about Whitaker other than a 1617 letter from Samuel Argall, the colony's deputy governor, stating that the young minister had drowned.*

What Virginia resources does Whitaker describe? What major questions and problems about the new colony does he address? What are his concluding arguments for urging people not to give up on Jamestown?

The whole continent of Virginia, situate within the degrees of 34 and 47, is a place beautified by God with all the ornaments of nature and enriched with His earthly treasures. That part of it which we already possess, beginning at the Bay of Chesapeake and stretching itself in northerly latitude to the degrees of 39 and 40, is interlined with seven most goodly rivers, the least whereof is equal to our river of Thames; and all these rivers are so nearly joined as that there is not very much distance of dry good between either of them, and those several mainlands are everywhere watered with many veins or creeks of water, which sundry ways do overthwart the land and make it almost navigable from one river to the other. The commodity [advantage] whereof to those that shall inhabit this land is infinite in respect of the speedy and easy transportation of goods from one river to the other. I cannot better manifest it unto you but in advising you to consider whether the water or land hath been more beneficial to the Low Countries; but here we shall have the commodity both of water and land more ready, with less charge and labour, than hath been bestowed by them in turning land into water....

Alexander Whitaker, "Good News from Virginia" (London: Virginia Company of London, 1613).

HEALTH AND CLIMATE

The air of the country (especially about Henrico and upward) is very temperate and agreeth well with our bodies. The extremity of summer is not so hot as Spain nor the cold of winter so sharp as the frosts of England. The spring and harvest are the two longest seasons and most pleasant; the summer and winter are both but short. The winter is for the most part dry and fair but the summer watered often with many great and sudden showers of rain, whereby the cold of winter is warmed and the heat of summer cooled. Many have died with us heretofore through their own filthiness and want of bodily comforts for sick men; but now very few are sick among us: not above three persons amongst all the inhabitants of Henrico. I would to God our souls were no sicker than our bodies and that other of God's blessings were as general and common as the bodily health. I have seen it by experience and dare boldly affirm it that sickness doth more rage in England quarterly than here yearly. I doubt [fear] that hereafter, when our hospital or guest house is built up, you hear of many more cut off by the sword of justice (unless the better people be sent over) than perished by the diseases of the country.

THE NATIVE INHABITANTS

The natural people of the land are generally such as you heard of before: a people to be feared of those that come upon them without defensive armour, but otherwise faint-hearted (if they see their arrows cannot pierce) and easy to be subdued. Shirts of mail or quilted cotton are the best defence against them. There is but one or two of their petty kings that for fear of us have desired our friendship, and those keep good quarter with us, being very pleasant amongst us and (if occasion be) serviceable unto us. Our eldest friends be Pipsco and Chopoke, who are our overthwart neighbours at Jamestown and have been friendly to us in our great want. The other is the werowance of Chesapeake, who but lately traded with us peaceably. If we were once the masters of their country and they stood in fear of us (which might with few hands employed about nothing else be in short time brought to pass), it were an easy matter to make them willingly to forsake the Devil, to embrace the faith of Jesus Christ, and to be baptized. Besides, you cannot easily judge how much they would be available to us in our discoveries of the country, in our buildings and plantings and quiet provision for ourselves, when we may peaceably pass from place to place without need of arms or guard.

NATURAL RESOURCES

The means for our people to live and subsist here of themselves are many and most certain, both for beasts, birds, fish, and herbs. The beasts of the country are for the most part wild: as lions, bears, wolves, and deer; foxes, black and red: raccoons; beavers: possums; squirrels; wildcats, whose skins are of great price; and muskrats, which yield musk as the muskcats do. There be two kinds of beasts among these most strange: one of them is the female possum, which will let forth her young out of her belly and take them up into her belly again at her pleasure without hurt to herself; neither think this to be a traveller's tale but the very truth, for Nature hath framed her fit for that service: my eyes have been witness unto it and we have sent of them and their young ones into England. The other strange-conditioned creature is the flying squirrel, which, through the help of certain broad flaps of skin growing on each side of her forelegs, will fly from tree to tree twenty or thirty paces at one flight and more, if she have the benefit of a small breath of wind. Besides these, since our coming hither we have brought both kine, goats, and hogs, which prosper well and would multiply exceedingly if they might be provided for.

Let now the fear of starving hereafter, or of any great want, dishearten your valiant minds from coming to a place of so great plenty.

This country besides is replenished with birds of all sorts, which have been the best sustenance of flesh which our men have had since they came; also eagles and hawks of all sorts, amongst whom are osprey, fishing hawk, and the cormorant. The woods be everywhere full of wild turkeys, which abound and will run as swift as a greyhound. In winter our fields be full of cranes, herons, pigeons, partridges, and blackbirds; the rivers and creeks be overspread everywhere with water-fowl of the greatest and least sort, as swans, flocks of geese and brants, duck and mallard, sheldrakes, divers, etc., besides many other kinds of rare and delectable birds whose names and natures I cannot yet recite; but we want the means to take them.

The rivers abound with fish both great and small. The sea-fish come into our rivers in March and continue until the end of September; great schools of herrings come in first; shads, of it great bigness, and rock fish, follow them. Trouts, bass, flounders, and other dainty fish come in before the other be gone; then come multitudes of great sturgeons, whereof we catch many and should do more but that we want good nets answerable to the breadth and depth of our rivers: besides our channels are so foul in the bottom with great logs and trees that we often break our nets upon them. I cannot reckon

nor give proper names to the divers kinds of fresh fish in our rivers. I have caught with mine angle [fishhook] pike, carp, eel, perches of six several kinds, crayfish, and the torope or little turtle, besides many smaller kinds.

DO NOT FEAR STARVATION
Wherefore, since God hath filled the elements of earth, air, and waters with His creatures, good for our food and nourishment, let not the fear of starving hereafter, or of any great want, dishearten your valiant minds from coming to a place of so great plenty. If the country were ours and means for the taking of them (which shortly I hope shall be brought to pass), the all of these should be ours; we have them now but we are fain to fight for them; then should we have them without that trouble. Fear not, then, to want food but only provide means to get it here. We have store of wild-fowl in England, but what are they better for them that cannot come by them, wanting means to catch them? Even such is and hath been our case heretofore.

But even these are not all the commodities which we may find here: for the earth will yield much more fruit to our industrious labours, as hath been proved by the corn and other things which we have planted this last year.... Our English seeds thrive very well here, as peas, onions, turnips, cabbages, coleflowers, carrots, thyme, parsley, hyssop, marjoram, and many other whereof I have tasted and eaten.

What should I name unto you the divers sorts of trees, sweet woods, and physical [medicinal] plants: the divers kinds of oaks and walnut trees; the pines, pitch-trees, soap-ashes trees, sassafras, cedar, ash, maple cypress, and many more which I daily see and admire at the beauty and riches which God hath bestowed upon this people that yet know not how to use them.

BE NOT DISCOURAGED
Wherefore, you (right wise and noble adventurers of Virginia) whose hearts God hath stirred up to build Him a temple, to make Him an house, to conquer a kingdom for Him here: be not discouraged with those many lamentable assaults that the Devil hath made against us: he now rageth most because he knoweth his kingdom is to have a short end. Go forward boldly and remember that you fight under the banner of Jesus Christ, that you plant His kingdom Who hath already broken the serpent's head. God may defer His temporal reward for a season, but be assured that in the end you shall find riches and honour in this world and blessed immortality in the world to come. And you, my brethren, my fellow labourers, send up your earnest prayers to God for His church in Virginia, that, since His harvest here is great but the labourers few, He would thrust forth labourers into His harvest. And pray also for me that the

ministration of His Gospel may he powerful and effectual by me, to the salvation of many and advancement of the kingdom of Jesus Christ, to whom, with the Father and the Holy Spirit, be all honour and glory forevermore.

Amen.

Viewpoint 2B

Virginia Is Not a New Paradise (1624)

Richard Ffrethorne (dates unknown)

INTRODUCTION *A stark counterpoint to the glowing reports of life in Virginia published by the Virginia Company of London is found in the following viewpoint, a 1623 letter from a Virginia colonist to his parents in England. Richard Ffrethorne came to Virginia an indentured servant, bound to work for a planter for a fixed period of time (probably four years). The letter describes the lack of food and harsh conditions Ffrethorne faced in his small settlement ten miles from Jamestown, and helps to explain why by 1624 four out of five Virginia colonists had perished. The letter also includes accounts of Indian attacks. Historians know little about Richard Ffrethorne other than the information found here.*

How do Ffrethorne's descriptions of Virginia's food resources and Indian inhabitants differ from those of Alexander Whitaker, author of the opposing viewpoint? Ffrethorne was in debt for his voyage to America; is this a focus of complaint in his letter?

Loveing and kind father and mother my most humble duty remembred to you hopeing in God of your good health, as I my selfe am at the makeing hereof, this is to let you understand that I your Child am in a most heavie Case by reason of the nature of the Country is such that it Causeth much sicknes, as the scurvie and the bloody flix, and divers other diseases, wch maketh the bodie very poore, and Weake, and when wee are sicke there is nothing to Comfort us; for since I came out of the ship, I never at[e] anie thing but pease, and loblollie (that is water gruell) as for deare or venison I never saw anie since I came into this land, ther is indeed some foule, but Wee are not allowed to goe, and get it, but must Worke hard both earelie, and late for a messe of water gruell, and a mouthfull of bread, and beife, a mouthfull of bread for a pennie loafe must serve for 4 men wch is most pitifull if you did knowe as much as I, when people crie out day, and night, Oh that they were in England without their lymbes and would not care to loose anie lymbe to bee in England againe, yea though they beg from doore to doore, for wee live in feare of the Enimy [Indians] everie hower, yet wee have had a Combate with them on the Sunday before Shrovetyde, and wee

Reprinted from *The Records of the Virginia Company of London*, edited by Susan Kingsbury, vol. 4 (Washington, DC: GPO, 1935).

tooke two alive, and make slaves of them, but it was by pollicie, for wee are in great danger, for our Plantācon is very weake, by reason of the dearth, and sicknes, of our Companie, for wee came but Twentie for the marchaunts, and they are halfe dead Just; and wee looke everie hower When two more should goe, yet there came some for other men yet to live with us, of which ther is but one alive, and our Leiftenant is dead, and his ffather, and his brother, and there was some 5 or 6 of the last yeares 20 of wch there is but 3 left, so that wee are faine to get other men to plant with us, and yet wee are but 32 to fight against 3000 if they should Come, and the nighest helpe that Wee have is ten miles of us, and when the rogues ouvercame this place last, they slew 80 Persons how then shall wee doe for wee lye even in their teeth, they may easilie take us but that God is mercifull, and can save with few as well as with many; as he shewed to Gilead and like Gilead's Souldiers if they lapt water, wee drinkee water wch is but Weake.

And I have nothing to Comfort me, nor ther is nothing to be gotten here but sicknes, and death, except that one had money to lay out in some thinges for profit; But I have nothing at all, no not a shirt to my backe, but two Ragges nor no Clothes, but one poore suite, nor but one paire of shooes, but one paire of stockins, but one Capp, but two bands, my Cloke is stollen by one of my owne fellowes, and to his dying hower would not tell mee what he did with it but some of my fellows saw him have butter and beife out of a ship, wch my Cloke I doubt [fear] paid for, so that I have not a penny, nor a a penny Worth to helpe me to either spice, or sugar, or strong Waters, without the wch one cannot live here, for as strong beare [beer] in England doth fatten and strengthen them so water here doth wash and weaken theis here, onelie keepe life and soule togeather, but I am not halfe a quarter so strong as I was in England, and all is for want of victualls, for I doe protest unto you, that I have eaten more in day at home then I have allowed me here for a Weeke, you have given more then my dayes allowance to a beggar at the doore; and if Mr. Jackson had not releived me, I should bee in a poore Case, but he like a ffather and shee like a loveing mother doth still helpe me, for when wee goe up to James Towne that is 10 myles of us, there lie all the ships that Come to the land, and there they must deliver their goods, and when wee went up to Towne as it may bee on Moonedaye, at noone, and come there by night, then load the next day by noone, and goe home in the afternoone, and unload, and then away againe in the night, and bee up about midnight then if it rayned, or blowed never so hard wee must lye in the boate on the water, and have nothing but alitle bread, for when wee go into the boate wee have a loafe allowed to two men, and it is all if we staid there 2 dayes, wch is hard, and must lye all that while in the boate, but that Goodman Jackson pityed me & made me a Cabbin to lye in always when I come up, and he would give me some poore Jacks home with me wch Comforted mee more then pease, or water gruell. Oh they bee verie godlie folkes, and love me verie well, and will doe anie thing for me, and he much marvailed that you would send me a servant to the Companie, he saith I had beene better knockd on the head, and Indeede so I fynd it now to my greate greif and miserie, and saith, that if you love me you will redeeme me suddenlie, for wch I doe Intreate and begg, and if you cannot get the marchaunts to redeeme me for some little money then for God's sake get a gathering or intreat some good folks to lay out some little Sum of moneye, in meale, and Cheese and butter, and beife, anie eating meate will yeald great profit, oile and vyniger is verie good, but ffather ther is greate losse in leakinge, but for God's sake send beife and Cheese and butter or the more of one sort and none of another, but if you sent Cheese it must bee very old Cheese, and at the Chesmongers you may buy good Cheese for two-pence farthing or halfepenny that will be liked verie well, but if you send Cheese you must have a Care how you packe it in barrells, and you must put Coopers Chips betweene everie Cheese, or els the heat of the hold will rott them, and looke whatsoever you send me be it never so much looke what I make of it I will deale trulie with you I will send it over, and begg the profit to redeeme me, and if I die before it Come I have intreated Goodman Jackson to send you the worth of it, who hath promised he will; If you send you must direct your letters to Goodman Jackson, at James Towne a Gunsmith. (you must set downe his frayt) because there bee more of his name there; good ffather doe not forget me, but have mercie and pittye my miserable Case. I know if you did but see me you would weepe to see me, for I have but one suite, but it is a strange one, it is very well guarded, wherefore for God's sake pittie me, I pray you to remember my love my love to all my ffreinds, and kindred. I hope all my Brothers and Sisters are in good health, and as for my part I have set downe my resolucon that certainelie Wilbe, that is, that the Answeare of this letter wilbee life or death to me, therefore good ffather send as soone as you can, and if you send me anie thing let this bee the marke.

ROT

Richard Ffrethorne

Martyns Hundred.

FOR FURTHER READING

Dorothy and Thomas Hoobler, *Captain John Smith: Jamestown and the Birth of the American Dream.* Hoboken, NJ: John Wiley & Sons, 2006.

James Horn, *A Land As God Made It: Jamestown And The Birth Of America.* New York: Basic Books, 2005.

Edmund S. Morgan, *American Slavery, American Freedom: The Ordeal of Colonial Virginia.* New York: W.W. Norton, 1995.

Edward D. Neill, *History of the Virginia Company of London.* La Crosse, WI: Brookhaven, 2001.

The complete original texts of the both the Whitaker and Frethorne documents can be found online at the Virtual Jamestown project at http://etext.lib.virginia.edu/etcbin/jamestown-browse?id=J1024 (Whitaker) and http://etext.lib.virginia.edu/etcbin/jamestown-browse?id=J1012 (Ffrethorne).

CONTACT AND CONFLICT WITH NATIVE AMERICANS

Viewpoint 3A

Indians and Colonists Should Live in Peace (1609)

Powhatan (ca. 1550–1618)

INTRODUCTION *Powhatan (also called Wahunsonacock) was the leader of a group of Indian tribes that lived in what is now the state of Virginia, and was thus one of the first Indian leaders to have extensive contact with European colonists in North America. The following viewpoint is taken from a 1609 speech Powhatan made to John Smith, the leader of the English settlement of Jamestown. Smith recorded Powhatan's call for peaceful relations between the two peoples, including his remarks on the importance of the Indians' providing food to help Jamestown settlers survive. Despite occasional skirmishes and confrontations, the Indians of the Powhatan Confederacy and the English settlers maintained a general truce until 1622 (a truce aided in part by the marriage of Powhatan's daughter, Pocahontas, to English settler John Rolfe in 1614).*

What benefits of peaceful relations for both colonists and Indians does Powhatan list? What dangers does he say might threaten the settlers if they fail to deal peacefully with him and his tribe?

I am now grown old, and must soon die; and the succession must descend, in order, to my brothers. *Opitchapan, Opekankanough,* and *Catataugh,* and then to my two sisters, and their two daughters. I wish their experience was equal to mine; and that your love to us might not be less than ours to you. Why should you take by force that from us which you can have by love? Why should you destroy us, who have provided you with food? What can you get by war? We can hide our provisions, and fly into the woods; and then you must consequently famish by wronging your friends. What is the cause of your jealousy? You see us unarmed, and willing to supply your wants, if you will come in a friendly manner, and

From *Biography and History of the Indians of North America* by Samuel Drake. 8th ed. Boston: Antiquarian Bookstore, 1841.

not with swords and guns, as to invade an enemy. I am not so simple, as not to know it is better to eat good meat, lie well, and sleep quietly with my women and children; to laugh and be merry with the English; and, being their friend, to have copper, hatchets, and whatever else I want, than to fly from all, to lie cold in the woods, feed upon acorns, roots, and such trash, and to be so hunted, that I cannot rest, eat, or sleep. In such circumstances, my men must watch, and if a twig should but break, all would cry out, "*Here comes Captain Smith;* " and so, in this miserable manner, to end my miserable life; and, Captain *Smith*, this *might* be soon your fate too, through your rashness and unadvisedness. I, therefore, exhort you to peaceable councils; and, above all, I insist that the guns and swords, the cause of all our jealousy and uneasiness, be removed and sent away.

Indians Should Be Conquered and Exterminated (1622)

Virginia Company of London/Edward Waterhouse

INTRODUCTION *A few years after the death of American Indian leader Powhatan (see viewpoint 3A), his brother Opekankanough (Opachankana), the new leader of the Powhatan Confederacy, launched a surprise attack on English settlements in and around Jamestown, Virginia. The 1622 assault, one of the first major conflicts between English colonists and American Indians, was in part a response to continuing seizures of Indian land by the colonists. The attackers killed 347 Jamestown residents (including John Rolfe, the widower of Powhatan's daughter Pocahontas) and destroyed many houses and farms before they were stopped. The following viewpoint contains an account of the violence and its ramifications for the colonization of Virginia. It was written by Edward Waterhouse, secretary to the Virginia Company of London, the outfit that had sponsored the Jamestown settlement. The document was produced in part to explain why the colony had yet to show any profit for its investors.*

How do the Virginia Company officials characterize the Indians? How does this account compare with the company's earlier optimistic writing on Virginia, as presented in Viewpoint 2A?

That all men may see the impartial ingenuity of this discourse, we freely confess, that the country is not so good, as the natives are bad, whose barbarous selves need more cultivation then the ground itself, being more overspread with incivility and treachery, than that with briars. For the land, being tilled and used well by us, deceive not our expectation but rather exceeded it

Reprinted from *The Records of the Virginia Company of London,* edited by Susan Kingsbury, vol. 3 (Washington, DC: GPO, 1933).

far, being so thankful as to return a hundred for one. But the savages, though never a nation used so kindly upon so small desert, have instead of that harvest which our pains merited, returned nothing but briars and thorns, pricking even to death many of their benefactors. Yet doubt we not, but that as all wickedness is crafty to undo itself, so these also have more wounded themselves than us, God Almighty making way for severity there, where a fair gentleness would not take place. The occasion whereof thus I relate from thence.

The last May there came a letter from Sir Francis Wiat [Wyatt] Governor in Virginia, which did advertise that when in November last [1621] he arrived in Virginia and entered upon his government, he found the country settled in a peace (as all men there thought), sure and unviolable, not only because it was solemnly ratified and sworn, but as being advantageous to both parts; to the savages as the weaker, under which they were safely sheltered and defended; to us, as being the easiest way then thought to pursue and advance our projects of buildings, plantings, and effecting their conversion by peaceable and fair means. And such was the conceit [conception] of firm peace and amity as that there was seldom or never a sword worn. . . . The plantations of particular adventurers and planters were placed scatteringly and stragglingly as a choice vein of rich ground invited them, and the further from neighbors held the better. The houses generally set open to the savages, who were always friendly entertained at the tables of the English, and commonly lodged in their bedchambers. The old planters (as they thought now come to reap the benefit of their long travels) placed with wonderful content upon their private lands, and their familiarity with the natives, seeming to open a fair gate for their conversion to Christianity.

A SURPRISE ATTACK

The country being in this estate, an occasion was ministered of sending to Opachankano, the King of these savages, about the middle of March last [1622], what time the messenger returned back with these words from him, that he held the peace concluded so firm as the sky should sooner fall than it dissolve. Yea, such was the treacherous dissimulation of that people who then had contrived our destruction, that even two days before the massacre, some of our men were guided through the woods by them in safety. . . . Yea, they borrowed our own boats to convey themselves across the river (on the banks of both sides whereof all our plantations were) to consult of the devilish murder that ensued, and of our utter extirpation, which God of His mercy (by the means of themselves converted to Christianity) prevented. And as well on the Friday morning (the fatal day) the twenty-second of March, as also in the evening, as on other days before, they came unarmed into our houses, without bows or arrows, or other weapons, with deer, turkey, fish, fur, and other provisions to sell and trade with us for glass, beads, and other trifles. Yet in some places, they sat down at breakfast with our people at their tables, whom immediately with their own tools and weapons either laid down, or standing in their houses, they basely and barbarously murdered, not sparing either age or sex, man, woman, or child, so sudden in their cruel execution that few or none discerned the weapon or blow that brought them to destruction. In which manner they also slew many of our people then at their several work and husbandries in the fields, and without their houses, some in planting corn and tobacco, some in gardening, some in making brick, building, sawing, and other kinds of husbandry, they well knowing in what places and quarters each of our men were, in regard of their daily familiarity and resort to us for trading and other negotiations, which the more willingly was by us continued and cherished for the desire we had of effecting that great masterpiece of works, their conversion. And by this means that fatal Friday morning, there fell under the bloody and barbarous hands of that perfidious and inhuman people, contrary to all laws of God and men, of nature and nations, three hundred forty seven men, women, and children, most by their own weapons. And not being content with taking away life alone, they fell after again upon the dead, making as well as they could, a fresh murder, defacing, dragging, and mangling the dead carcasses into many pieces, and carrying some parts away in derision, with base and brutish triumph....

That the slaughter had been universal, if God had not put it into the heart of an Indian belonging to one Perry to disclose it, who living in the house of one Pace, was urged by another Indian his brother (who came the night before and lay with him) to kill Pace. Telling further that by such an hour in the morning a number would come from different places to finish the execution, who failed not at the time, Perry's Indian rose out of his bed and revealed it to Pace, that used him as a son. And thus the rest of the colony that had warning given them by this means was saved. Such was (God be thanked for it) the good fruit of an infidel converted to Christianity. For though three hundred and more of ours died by many of these pagan infidels, yet thousands of ours were saved by the means of one of them alone which was made a Christian. Blessed be God forever, whose mercy endureth forever....

LESSONS OF THE MASSACRE

Thus have you seen the particulars of this massacre, wherein treachery and cruelty have done their worst to us, or rather to themselves; for whose understanding is so shallow, as not to perceive that this must needs be

for the good of the plantation after, and the loss of this blood to make the body more healthful, as by these reasons may be manifest.

First, because betraying innocence never rests unpunished....

Secondly, because our hands, which before were tied with gentleness and fair usage, are now set at liberty by the treacherous violence of the savages, not untying the knot, but cutting it. So that we, who hitherto have had possession of no more ground than their waste, and our purchase at a valuable consideration to their own contentment gained, may now, by right of war and law of nations, invade the country, and destroy them who sought to destroy us. Whereby we shall enjoy their cultivated places, possessing the fruits of others' labors. Now their cleared grounds in all their villages (which are situated in the fruitfulest places of the land) shall be inhabited by us, whereas heretofore the grubbing of woods was the greatest labor.

The way of conquering them is much more easy than of civilizing them by fair means, for they are a rude, barbarous, and naked people.

Thirdly, because those commodities which the Indians enjoyed as much or rather more than we, shall now also be entirely possessed by us. The deer and other beasts will be in safety, and infinitely increase, which heretofore not only in the general huntings of the King, but by each particular Indian were destroyed at all times of the year, without any difference of male, dame, or young.

There will be also a great increase of wild turkeys, and other weighty fowl, for the Indians never put difference of destroying the hen, but kill them whether in season or not, whether in breeding time, or sitting on their eggs, or having new hatched, it is all one to them....

Fourthly, because the way of conquering them is much more easy than of civilizing them by fair means, for they are a rude, barbarous, and naked people, scattered in small companies, which are helps to victory, but hindrance to civility. Besides that, a conquest may be of many, and at once; but civility is in particular and slow, the effect of long time, and great industry. Moreover, victory of them may be gained many ways: by force, by surprise, by famine in burning their corn, by destroying and burning their boats, canoes, and houses, by breaking their fishing wares, by assailing them in their huntings, whereby they get the greatest part of their sustenance in winter, by pursuing and chasing them with our horses and bloodhounds to draw after them, and mastiffs to tear them.

FOR FURTHER READING

Frederic W. Gleach, *Powhatan's World and Colonial Virginia: A Conflict of Cultures* Lincoln: University of Nebraska Press, 2000.

Francis Jennings, *The Invasion of America: Indians, Colonialism, and the Cant of Conquest.* Chapel Hill: University of North Carolina Press, 1975.

Karen Ordahl Kupperman, *Settling with the Indians: The Meeting of English and Indian Cultures in America, 1580–1640.* Totowa, NJ: Rowman and Littlefield, 1980.

Helen C. Rountree, *Pocahontas, Powhatan, Opechancanough: Three Indian Lives Changed By Jamestown.* Richmond: University Press of Virginia, 2005.

Bernard W. Sheehan, *Savagism & Civility: Indians and Englishmen in Colonial Virginia.* New York: Cambridge University Press, 1980.

Camila Townsend, *Pocahontas and the Powhatan Dilemma.* New York: Hill and Wang, 2005.

Viewpoint 4A

A Puritan Missionary's Account of Indians (1646)

John Eliot (1604–1690)

INTRODUCTION *A Puritan who migrated to the Massachusetts Bay Colony in 1631, John Eliot was a minister at Roxbury, a community close to Boston. In the 1640s he learned the Algonquian language from an Indian servant and began missionary work among the Native Americans—work that he continued until his death. Widely known both in America and in England as the "Apostle to the Indians," Eliot translated the Bible into the Algonquian language, founded numerous villages where "praying Indians" could learn English handicrafts and laws as well as Christian teachings, and wrote numerous pamphlets and tracts about his missionary work. The following viewpoint is taken from a pamphlet first published in London in 1646. It provides his descriptions of Native Americans and his efforts to convert them to Christianity. Part of the pamphlet's purpose was to gather financial support from England for his missionary work.*

What assumptions about European and American cultures does Eliot demonstrate? What reasons does he give for optimism in his missionary work among the Indians?

Methinks now that it is with the Indians as it was with our New English ground when we first came over—there was scarce any man that could believe that English grain would grow, or that the plow could do

John Eliot, "The Day-Breaking, If Not the Sun-Rising, of the Gospell with the Indians in New-England." (Massachusetts Historical Society, *Collections*, Vol. 3.)

any good in this woody and rocky soil. And thus they continued in this supine unbelief for some years, till experience taught them otherwise; and now all see it to be scarce inferior to Old English tillage, but bears very good burdens. So we have thought of our Indian people, and, therefore, have been discouraged to put plow to such dry and rocky ground, but God, having begun thus with some few, it may be they are better soil for the gospel than we can think.

I confess I think no great good will be done till they be more civilized. But why may not God begin with some few to awaken others by degrees? Nor do I expect any great good will be wrought by the English (leaving secrets to God, although the English surely begin and lay the first stones of Christ's kingdom and temple among them), because God is wont ordinarily to convert nations and peoples by some of their own countrymen who are nearest to them and can best speak, and, most of all, pity their brethren and countrymen. But yet, if the least beginnings be made by the conversion of two or three, it is worth all our time and travails, and cause of much thankfulness for such seeds, although no great harvests should immediately appear....

We see the Spirit of God working mightily upon the hearts of these natives in an ordinary way.

HOPEFUL BEGINNINGS

The observations I have gathered by conversing with them are such as these:

1. That none of them . . . derided God's messenger: Woe unto those English that are grown bold to do that which Indians will not—heathens dare not.

2. That there is need of learning in ministers who preach to Indians, much more [than] to Englishmen and gracious Christians, for these had sundry philosophical questions which some knowledge of the arts must help to give answer to; and without which these would not have been satisfied. Worse than Indian ignorance has blinded their eyes that renounce learning as an enemy to gospel ministries.

3. That there is no necessity of extraordinary gifts nor miraculous signs always to convert heathens . . . for we see the Spirit of God working mightily upon the hearts of these natives in an ordinary way, and I hope will, they being but a remnant, the Lord using to show mercy to the remnant. For there be but few that are left alive from the plague and pox, which God sent into those

parts; and, if one or two can understand, they usually talk of it as we do of news—it flies suddenly far and near, and truth scattered will rise in time, for ought we know.

4. If Englishmen begin to despise the preaching of faith and repentance and humiliation for sin, yet the poor heathens will be glad of it and it shall do good to them; for so they are and so it begins to do. The Lord grant that the foundation of our English woe be not laid in the ruin and contempt of those fundamental doctrines of faith, repentance, humiliation for sin, etc., but rather relishing the novelties and dreams of such men as are surfeited with the ordinary food of the Gospel of Christ. Indians shall weep to hear faith and repentance preached, when Englishmen shall mourn, too late, that are weary of such truths.

5. That the deepest estrangements of man from God is no hindrance to His grace nor to the spirit of grace; for what nation or people ever so deeply degenerated since Adam's fall as these Indians, and yet the Spirit of God is working upon them? . . .

CREATING A CHRISTIAN INDIAN TOWN

We have cause to be very thankful to God who has moved the hearts of the General Court to purchase so much land for them to make their town in which the Indians are much taken with. And it is somewhat observable that, while the court were considering where to lay out their town, the Indians (not knowing of anything) were about that time consulting about laws for themselves, and their company who sit down with Waaubon [a local Christian Indian leader]. There were ten of them: two of them are forgotten.

Their laws were these:

1. That if any man be idle a week, at most a fortnight, he shall pay 5s [shillings].
2. If any unmarried man shall lie with a young woman unmarried, he shall pay 20s.
3. If any man shall beat his wife, his hands shall be tied behind him and [he shall be] carried to the place of justice to be severely punished.
4. Every young man, if not another's servant and if unmarried, he shall be compelled to set up a wigwam and plant for himself, and not live shifting up and down to other wigwams.
5. If any woman shall not have her hair tied up but hang loose or be cut as men's hair, she shall pay 5s.
6. If any woman shall go with naked breasts, [she] shall pay 2s. 6d [2 shillings 6 pence].
7. All those men that wear long locks shall pay 5s.
8. If any shall kill their lice between their teeth, they shall pay 5s. This law, though ridiculous to English ears, yet tends to preserve cleanliness among Indians.

It is wonderful in our eyes to understand by these two honest Indians [helpers of Eliot] what prayers Waaubon and the rest of them use to make, for he that preaches to them professes he never yet used any of their words in his prayers, from whom otherwise it might be thought that they had learned them by rote. One is this:

Amanaomen Jehovah tahassen metagh.

(Take away Lord my stony heart.)

Another:

Chechesom Jehovah kekowhogkew.

(Wash Lord my soul.)

Another:

(Lord lead me, when I die, to heaven.)

These are but a taste. They have many more, and these more enlarged than thus expressed, yet what are these but the sprinklings of the spirit and blood of Christ Jesus in their hearts?

And it is no small matter that such dry, barren, and long-accursed ground should yield such kind of increase in so small a time. I would not readily commend a fair day before night, nor promise much of such kind of beginnings, in all persons, nor yet in all of these, for we know the profession of very many is but a mere paint, and their best graces nothing but mere flashes and pangs, which are suddenly kindled and as soon go out and are extinct again. Yet God, does not usually send His plow and seeds-man to a place but there is at least some little piece of good ground, although three to one be naught. And methinks the Lord Jesus would never have made so fit a key for their locks, unless He had intended to open some of their doors, and so to make way for His coming in. He that God has raised up and enabled to preach unto them is a man (you know) of a most sweet, humble, loving, gracious, and enlarged spirit, whom God hath blessed, and surely will still delight in and do good by.

Viewpoint 4B

A Puritan Captive's Account of Indians (1682)

Mary Rowlandson (ca. 1637–ca. 1711)

INTRODUCTION *Mary Rowlandson was the author of one of the most popular and widely read books published during the colonial era—an account of her three-month captivity by Indians in 1676. She was captured during King Philip's War, a conflict in which Metacom (called King Philip by the English) led the last major challenge to white settlement in New England.*

Rowlandson was the wife of Joseph Rowlandson, a Puritan minister in Lancaster, a small village on the western frontier in Massachusetts. On February 10, 1676, while her husband was traveling to Boston, a band of Indians attacked and burned the village and took many captives, including Mary Rowlandson and her three children. The youngest soon died of wounds sustained during the initial attack. For almost three months Rowlandson was held prisoner; on May 2 she was released for a sizable ransom. She was shortly thereafter reunited with her husband and surviving children. Little is known of her later life, aside from a second marriage after her first husband's death in 1678.

Her book, first published in 1682, was the first of many "captivity narratives"—popular accounts of white settlers (often women) surviving against great odds the experience of being taken by "savage" Indians. It is noteworthy for its descriptions of capture and imprisonment, its ruminations on suffering and God's power and its descriptions of Indian life. It also provides evidence of changing Puritan attitudes toward Native Americans. In the relatively peaceful decades before 1675, many Puritans viewed the Indians as unbelievers who needed to be taught Christianity by missionaries such as John Eliot. After the shock of King Philip's War, Indians—including those who professed Christianity and who lived in missionary-sponsored communities—came to be seen as enemies who needed to be exterminated.

How does Rowlandson describe the actions of the "praying Indians" she encounters? How did the experience affect her religious faith? What observations does she make concerning the English army sent to fight the Indians?

On the tenth of February 1675 [1676 in modern reckoning] came the Indians with great numbers upon Lancaster. Their first coming was about sunrising. Hearing the noise of some guns, we looked out; several houses were burning and the smoke ascending to heaven. There were five persons taken in one house; the father and the mother and a sucking child they knocked on the head; the other two they took and carried away alive.... Another there was who running along was shot and wounded and fell down; he begged of them his life, promising them money (as they told me), but they would not hearken to him but knocked him in [the] head, stripped him naked, and split open his bowels.... Thus these murderous wretches went on, burning and destroying before them....

My eldest sister [Elizabeth] being yet in the house and seeing those woeful sights, the infidels hailing mothers one way and children another and some wallowing in their blood, and her elder son telling her that her son William was dead and myself was wounded, she said, "And, Lord, let me die with them." Which was no

From *The Soveraignty and Goodness of God... Being a Narrative of the Captivity and Restauration of Mrs. Mary Rowlandson* (Cambridge, 1682).

sooner said, but she was struck with a bullet and fell down dead over the threshold. I hope she is reaping the fruit of her good labors, being faithful to the service of God in her place.... But to return: the Indians laid hold of us, pulling me one way and the children another, and said, "Come go along with us." I told them they would kill me. They answered, if I were willing to go along with them they would not hurt me....

I had often before this said that if the Indians should come I should choose rather to be killed by them than taken alive, but when it came to the trial, my mind changed; their glittering weapons so daunted my spirit that I chose rather to go along with those (as I may say) ravenous beasts than that moment to end my days. And that I may the better declare what happened to me during that grievous captivity, I shall particularly speak of the several removes we had up and down the wilderness.

THE FIRST REMOVE

Now away we must go with those barbarous creatures with our bodies wounded and bleeding and our hearts no less than our bodies. About a mile we went that night up upon a hill within sight of the town where they intended to lodge. There was hard by a vacant house (deserted by the English before for fear of the Indians). I asked them whether I might not lodge in the house that night, to which they answered, "What, will you love English men still?" This was the dolefullest night that ever my eyes saw. Oh, the roaring and singing and dancing and yelling of those black creatures in the night, which made the place a lively resemblance of hell. And as miserable was the waste so close unto my spirit that it was easy for me to see how righteous it was with God to cut the thread of my life and cast me out of His presence forever. Yet the Lord still showed mercy to me and upheld me, and as He wounded me with one hand, so He healed me with the other....

DEATH OF A CHILD

Nine days I sat upon my knees with my babe in my lap till my flesh was raw again; my child being even ready to depart this sorrowful world, they bade me carry it out to another wigwam (I suppose because they would not be troubled with such spectacles), whither I went with a heavy heart, and down I sat with the picture of death in my lap. About two hours in the night my sweet babe like a lamb departed this life on Feb. 18, 1675 [1676], it being about six years and five months old. It was nine day from the first wounding in this miserable condition without any refreshing of one nature or other except a little cold water. I cannot but take notice how at another time I could not bear to be in the room where any dead person was, but now the case is changed; I must and could lie down by my dead babe side by side all the night after. I have thought since of the wonderful goodness of God to me in preserving me in the use of my reason and senses in that distressed time that I did not use wicked and violent means to end my own miserable life.

In the morning when they understood that my child was dead, they sent for me home to my master's wigwam. (By my master in this writing must be understood Quanopin who was a sagamore and married [to] King Philip's wife's sister, not that he first took me, but I was sold to him by another Narragansett Indian who took me when first I came out of the garrison.) I went to take up my dead child in my arms to carry it with me, but they bid me let it alone. There was no resisting, but go I must and leave it. When I had been at my master's wigwam, I took the first opportunity I could get to go look after my dead child. When I came, I asked them what they had done with it. Then they told me it was upon the hill. Then they went and showed me where it was, where I saw the ground was newly digged, and there they told me they had buried it. There I left that child in the wilderness and must commit it and myself also in this wilderness condition to Him who is above all....

THE EIGHTH REMOVE

On the morrow morning we must go over the river, i.e. Connecticot, to meet with King Philip....

We traveled on till night, and in the morning we must go over the river to Philip's crew. When I was in the canoe, I could not but be amazed at the numerous crew of pagans that were on the bank on the other side. When I came ashore, they gathered all about me, I sitting alone in the midst. I observed they asked one another questions and laughed and rejoiced over their gains and victories. Then my heart began to fail and I fell a-weeping, which was the first time to my remembrance that I wept before them. Although I had met with so much affliction and my heart was many times ready to break, yet could I not shed one tear in their sight but rather had been all this while in a maze and like one astonished. But now I may say as Psal. 137:1, "By the rivers of Babylon there we sat down; yea, we wept when we remembered Zion." There one of them asked me why I wept: I could hardly tell what to say, yet I answered they would kill me. "No," said he, "none will hurt you." Then came one of them and gave me two spoonfuls of meal to comfort me, and another gave me half a pint of peas which was more worth than many bushels at another time. Then I went to see King Philip. He bade me come in and sit down and asked me whether I would smoke it (a usual compliment nowadays among saints and sinners), but this no way suited me. For though I had formerly used tobacco, yet I had left it ever since I was first taken. It seems to be a bait the devil lays to make men lose their precious time. I remember with shame how formerly when I had taken two or three pipes I was presently ready for another, such a bewitching thing it is. But I thank God He has now given me power over it; surely there are many who may be better employed than to lie sucking a stinking tobacco pipe.

Now the Indians gather their forces to go against Northampton. Overnight one went about yelling and hooting to give notice of the design, whereupon they fell to boiling of groundnuts and parching of corn (as many as had it) for their provision, and in the morning away they went. During my abode in this place Philip spoke to me to make a shirt for his boy, which I did, for which he gave me a shilling. I offered the money to my master, but he bade me keep it, and with it I bought a piece of horseflesh. Afterwards he asked me to make a cap for his boy, for which he invited me to dinner. I went, and he gave me a pancake about as big as two fingers; it was made of parched wheat, beaten and fried in bear's grease, but I thought I never tasted pleasanter meat in my life. There was a squaw who spoke to me to make a shirt for her *sannup* [husband], for which he gave me a piece of bear. Another asked me to knit a pair of stockings, for which she gave me a quart of peas. I boiled my peas and bear together and invited my master and mistress to dinner, but the proud gossip [i.e., companion], because I served them both in one dish, would eat nothing except one bit that he gave her upon the point of his knife....

THE TREACHERY OF PRAYING INDIANS

Then came Tom and Peter [Christian Indians] with the second letter from the [Massachusetts authorities] about the captives. Though they were Indians, I got them by the hand and burst out into tears; my heart was so full that I could not speak to them, but recovering myself, I asked them how my husband did and all my friends and acquaintances. They said they [were] all very well but melancholy....

When the letter was come, the sagamores met to consult about the captives and called me to them to inquire how much my husband would give to redeem me. When I came, I sat down among them as I was wont to do as their manner is. Then they bade me stand up and said they were the General Court. They bid me speak when I thought he would give. Now knowing that all we had was destroyed by the Indians, I was in a great strait. I thought if I should speak of but a little, it would be slighted and hinder the matter; if of a great sum, I knew not where it would be procured. Yet at a venture, I said twenty pounds yet desired them to take less, but they would not hear of that but sent that message to

Boston that for twenty pounds I should be redeemed. It was a praying Indian that wrote their letter for them. . . .

There was another praying Indian who, when he had done all the mischief that he could, betrayed his own father into the English hands thereby to purchase his own life. Another praying Indian was at Sudbury fight, though, as he deserved, he was afterward hanged for it. There was another praying Indian so wicked and cruel as to wear a string about his neck strung with Christians' fingers. Another praying Indian, when they went to Sudbury fight, went with them and had his squaw also with him with her papoose at her back. . . .

On Tuesday morning they called their General Court (as they call it) to consult and determine whether I should go home or no. And they all as one man did seemingly consent to it that I should go home except Philip who would not come among them.

OBSERVATIONS

But before I go any further, I would take leave to mention a few remarkable passages of providence which I took special notice of in my afflicted time.

1. Of the fair opportunity lost in the long march a little after the fort fight when our English army was so numerous and in pursuit of the enemy and so near as to take several and destroy them, and the enemy in such distress for food that our men might track them by their rooting in the earth for groundnuts while they were flying for their lives. I say that then our army should want provision and be forced to leave their pursuit and return homeward. And the very next week the enemy came upon our town like bears bereft of their whelps or so many ravenous wolves, rending us and our lambs to death. But what shall I say? God seemed to leave His people to themselves and order all things for His own holy ends. . . .

4. It was thought if their corn were cut down they would starve and die with hunger, and all their corn that could be found was destroyed, and they driven from that little they had in store into the woods in the midst of winter. And yet how to admiration did the Lord preserve them for His holy ends and the destruction of many still amongst the English! Strangely did the Lord provide for them that I did not see (all the time I was among them) one man, woman, or child die with hunger. Though many times they would eat that that a hog or dog would hardly touch, yet by that God strengthened them to be a scourge to His people.

The chief and commonest food was groundnuts. They eat also nuts and acorns, artichokes, lily roots, groundbeans, and several other weeds and roots that I know not.

They would pick up old bones and cut them to pieces at the joints, and if they were full of worms and maggots, they would scald them over the fire to make the vermin come out and then boil them and drink up the liquor and then beat the great ends of them in a mortar and so eat them. They would eat horses' guts and ears, and all sorts of wild birds which they could catch; also bear, venison, beaver, tortoise, frogs, squirrels, dogs, skunks, rattlesnakes, yea, the very bark of trees, besides all sorts of creatures and provision which they plundered from the English. I can but stand in admiration to see the wonderful power of God in providing for such a vast number of our enemies in the wilderness where there was nothing to be seen but from hand to mouth. . . .

5. Another thing that I would observe is the strange providence of God in turning things about when the Indians [were] at the highest and the English at the lowest. I was with the enemy eleven weeks and five days, and not one weeks passed without the fury of the enemy and some desolation by fire and sword upon one place or other. They mourned (with their black faces) for their own losses, yet triumphed and rejoiced in their inhuman and many times devilish cruelty to the English. They would boast much of their victories, saying that in two hours' time they had destroyed such a captain and his company in such a place, and boast how many towns they had destroyed; and then scoff and say they had done them a good turn to send them to heaven so soon. Again they would say this summer that they would knock all the rogues in the head, or drive them into the sea, or make them fly the country, thinking surely Agag-like, "The bitterness of death is past." Now the heathen begins to think all is their own, and the poor Christians' hopes to fail (as to man), and now their eyes are more to God, and their hearts sigh heavenward and to say in good earnest, "Help Lord, or we perish." When the Lord had brought His people to this that they saw no help in anything but Himself, then He takes the quarrel into His own hand, and though they [the Indians] had made a pit in their own imaginations as deep as hell for the Christians that summer, yet the Lord hurled themselves into it. And the Lord had not so many ways before to preserve them, but now He hath as many to destroy them.

FOR FURTHER READING

Christopher Castiglia, *Bound and Determined: Captivity, Culture-Crossing, and White Womanhood.* Chicago: University of Chicago Press, 1996.

Kathryn Derounian-Stodula, ed., *Women's Indian Captivity Narratives.* New York: Penguin, 1998.

Pauline Turner Strong, *Captive Selves, Captivating Others: The Politics and Poetics of Colonial American Captivity Narratives.* Boulder, CO: Westview Press, 1999.

George E. Tinker, *Missionary Conquest: The Gospel and Native American Cultural Genocide.* Minneapolis: Fortress Press, 1993.

Ola Elizabeth Winslow, *John Eliot, Apostle to the Indians.* Boston: Houghton Mifflin, 1968.

The complete text of Rowlandson's narrative can be found at Project Gutenberg at http://www.gutenberg.org.

RELIGIOUS DISPUTES IN THE NEW WORLD

Viewpoint 5A

The Colonies Should Allow Religious Toleration (1657)

Edward Hart and Citizens of Flushing

INTRODUCTION *The following viewpoint is taken from one of the earliest recorded demands for religious toleration in American history. It involves one of the main targets of religious persecution in the American colonies, the Quakers. Founded by George Fox in England in 1646, the Quaker movement emphasized the importance of individual religious conscience and rejected the doctrines and formalism of the Roman Catholic Church, the Church of England, and the established Puritan and Anglican churches in the American colonies. (Instead of church services, they held meetings at private homes.) Like the Puritans, Quakers found themselves persecuted in England and sought to practice their faith in the American colonies, only to be frequently harassed there as well.*

Among the places Quakers were persecuted was the Dutch colony of New Netherlands (later New York). In 1657 a group of residents of the town of Flushing (Vlissengen) drafted and delivered a call for religious freedom to colonial governor Peter Stuyvesant. Stuyvesant had issued edicts establishing the Dutch Reformed Church as the official church of the colony and forbidding anyone from hosting a Quaker meeting, and had gone so far as to fine and banish a Flushing resident, Henry Townsend, for hosting such a meeting. The Flushing Remonstrance, written by town clerk Edward Hart and signed by him and other citizens, argues that such rules harm both religion and government and violate the town's own charter, which granted Flushing the right "to have and Enjoy the Liberty of Conscience." They urged religious toleration for different Christian sects, Jews, and "Independents." Stuyvesant was unmoved by their plea and later deported another Flushing resident, John Bowne, back to Holland for hosting a Quaker meeting. However, Bowne was able to convince the Dutch West India Colony in Holland to acquit him and permit him to return in triumph to New Netherlands with a letter from Holland establishing religious tolerance in the colony.

What religious arguments do the petitioners make in support of religious tolerance? How do they justify breaking the civil law as decreed by Stuyvesant?

To Governor Stuyvesant December 27, 1657
Right Honorable,

You have been pleased to send up unto us a certain prohibition or command that we should not receive or entertain any of those people called Quakers because they are supposed to be by some, seducers of the people. For our part we cannot condemn them in this case, neither can we stretch out our hands against them, to punish, banish or persecute them for out of Christ God is a consuming fire, and it is a fearful thing to fall into the hands of the living God.

We desire therefore in this case not to judge least we be judged, neither to condemn least we be condemned, but rather let every man stand and fall to his own Master. We are bound by the law to do good unto all men, especially to those of the household of faith. And though for the present we seem to be unsensible of the law and the law giver, yet when death and the law assault us, if we have our advocate to seek, who shall plead for us in this case of conscience betwixt God and our own souls; the powers of this world can neither attack us, neither excuse us, for if God justify who can condemn and if God condemn there is none can justify.

SCRIPTURAL AND CIVIL LAW

And for those jealousies and suspicions which some have of them, that they are destructive unto magistracy and minssereye [ministry], that can not be, for the magistrate hath the sword in his hand and the minister hath the sword in his hand, as witness those two great examples which all magistrates and ministers are to follow, Moses and Christ, whom God raised up maintained and defended against all the enemies both of flesh and spirit; and therefore that which is of God will stand, and that which is of man will come to nothing. And as the Lord hath taught Moses or the civil power to give an outward liberty in the state by the law written in his heart designed for the good of all, and can truly judge who is good, who is civil, who is true and who is false, and can pass definite sentence of life or death against that man which rises up against the fundamental law of the States General; so he hath made his ministers a savor of life unto life, and a savor of death unto death.

The law of love, peace and liberty in the states extending to Jews, Turks, and Egyptians, as they are considered the sons of Adam, which is the glory of the outward state of Holland, so love, peace and liberty, extending to all in Christ Jesus, condemns hatred, war and bondage. And because our Savior saith it is impossible but that offenses will come, but woe unto him by whom they cometh, our desire is not to offend one of

Excerpted from *Remonstrance of the Inhabitants of the Town of Flushing to Governor Stuyvesant*, by Edward Hart (New York: New York Historical Records, 1657).

his little ones, in whatsoever form, name or title he appears in, whether Presbyterian, Independent, Baptist or Quaker, but shall be glad to see anything of God in any of them, desiring to doe unto all men as we desire all men should do unto us, which is the true law both of Church and State; for our Savior saith this is the law and the prophets.

ALL RELIGIONS WILL BE TOLERATED

Therefore, if any of these said persons come in love unto us, we cannot in conscience lay violent hands upon them, but give them free egress and regress unto our town, and houses, as God shall persuade our consciences. And in this we are true subjects both of Church and State, for we are bound by the law of God and man to do good unto all men and evil to no man. And this is according to the patent and charter of our Town, given unto us in the name of the States General, which we are not willing to infringe, and violate, but shall hold to our patent and shall remain, your humble subjects, the inhabitants of [Flushing].

Viewpoint 5B

Religious Toleration Is Unwise (1647)

Nathaniel Ward (1578–1662)

INTRODUCTION *The Puritans of Massachusetts had left England because they wanted to practice their religion free of the established Church of England. But their vision of creating a "Bible Commonwealth" in Massachusetts did not include tolerating Quakers and other religious nonconformists who did not respect the authority of the Puritan clergy. Religious dissenters were fined, flogged, banished, and in some cases executed. The following viewpoint in defense of such practices is taken from a pamphlet by Nathaniel Ward, a minister who had been excommunicated from the Church of England for his views, and who had come to America and became a longtime minister at Ipswich, Massachusetts. Ward argues that the state and the church should work together to enforce Christian orthodoxy (as he conceives it) and that tolerating different religions—and different forms of Christianity—creates confusion and spreads false religious teachings. Ward's book, defending the practices of Massachusetts, was published under a pseudonym in England in 1647.*

What sort of reports about the American colonies is Ward responding to? What are the dangers he sees in religious tolerance for individuals and the community? How does he characterize opponents of his position?

First, such as have given or taken any unfriendly reports of us New-English, should do well to recollect

Excerpted from *The Simple Cobbler of Aggawamm in America* (London, 1647).

themselves. We have been reputed a colluvies [slapdash collection] of wild opinionists, swarmed into a remote wilderness to find elbow-room for our fanatic doctrines and practices: I trust our diligence past, and constant sedulity [diligence] against such persons and courses, will plead better things for us. I dare take upon me, to be the herald of New England so far, as to proclaim to the world, in the name of our colony, that all Familists, Antinomians, Anabaptists [Protestant sects], and other enthusiasts shall have free liberty to keep away from us, and such as will come to be gone as fast as they can, the sooner the better.

Secondly, I dare aver, that God doth no where in his word tolerate Christian States, to give tolerations to such adversaries of his Truth, if they have power in their hands to suppress them. . . .

TOLERATION IS NEITHER A CHRISTIAN NOR CIVIC VIRTUE

Not to tolerate things merely indifferent to weak consciences, argues a conscience too strong: pressed uniformity in these, causes much disunity: To tolerate more than indifference, is not to deal indifferently with God: He that doth it, takes his scepter out of his hand, and bids him stand by. Who hath to do to institute religion but God. The power of all religion and ordinances, lies in their purity: their purity in their simplicity: then are mixtures pernicious. I lived in a city, where a Papist [Roman Catholic] preached in one church, a Lutheran in another, a Calvinist in a third—a Lutheran one part of the day, a Calvinist the other, in the same pulpit: the religion of that place was but motley and meager, their affections leopard-like. . . .

That State is wise, that will improve all pains and patience rather to compose, than tolerate differences in Religion. There is no divine truth, but hath much celestial fire in it from the spirit of truth: nor no irreligious untruth, without its proportion of antifire from the spirit of error to contradict it: the zeal of the one, the virulency of the other, must necessarily kindle combustions. Fiery diseases seated in the spirit, embroil the whole frame of the body: others more external and cool, are less dangerous. They which divide in religion, divide in God; they who divide in him, divide beyond Genus Generalissimum [logical term referring to a supreme category], where there is no reconciliation, without atonement—that is, without uniting in him, who is one, and in his truth, which is also one. . . .

And prudent are those Christians, that will rather give what may be given, than hazard all by yielding nothing. To sell all peace of country, to buy some peace of conscience unseasonably, is more avarice than thrift, imprudence than patience: they deal not equally, that set any Truth of God at such a rate; but they deal wisely that will stay till the market is fallen. . . .

MORE ERRORS IN TOLERATION

Concerning Tolerations I may further assert....

He that is willing to tolerate any religion, or discrepant way of religion, besides his own, unless it be in matters merely indifferent, either doubts of his own, or is not sincere in it.

He that is willing to tolerate any unsound opinion, that his own may also be tolerated, though never so sound, will for a need hang God's Bible at the Devil's girdle.

Every toleration of false religions, or opinions hath as many errors and sins in it, as all the false religions and opinions it tolerates, and one sound one more.

There is no rule given by God for any State to give an affirmative toleration to any false religion.

ON LIBERTY OF CONSCIENCE

That State that will give liberty of conscience in matters of religion, must give liberty of conscience and conversation in their moral laws, or else the fiddle will be out of tune, and some of the strings crack.

He that will rather make an irreligious quarrel with other religions than try the truth of his own by valuable arguments, and peaceable sufferings; either his religion, or himself is irreligious.

Experience will teach churches and Christians, that it is far better to live in a State united, though a little corrupt, than in a State, whereof some part is incorrupt, and all the rest divided....

There is no rule given by God for any State to give an affirmative toleration to any false religion, or opinion whatsoever; they must connive in some cases, but may not concede in any....

That if the State of England shall either willingly tolerate, or weakly connive at such courses, the church of that kingdom will sooner become the Devil's dancing-school, than God's temple: ...And what pity it is, that that country which hath been the staple of truth to all Christendom, should now become the aviary of errors to the whole world, let every fearing heart judge.

I take liberty of conscience to be nothing but a freedom from sin, and error....And liberty of error nothing but a prison for conscience. Then small will be the kindness of a State to build such prisons for their subjects.

ONLY ONE TRUE RELIGION

The scripture saith, there is nothing makes free but truth, and truth faith, there is no truth but one: If the States of

the world would make it their summ-operous care to preserve this one truth in its purity and authority it would ease you of all other political cares. I am sure Satan makes it his grand, if not only task, to adulterate truth; falsehood is his sole scepter, whereby he first ruffled, and ever since ruined the world....

There is talk of an universal toleration, I would talk as loud as I could against it, did I know what more apt and reasonable sacrifice England could offer to God for his late performing all his heavenly truths then an universal toleration of all hellish errors, or how they shall make an universal reformation, but by making Christ's academy the Devil's university....

It is said, that men ought to have liberty of their conscience, and that it is persecution to debar them of it: I can rather stand amazed then reply to this: it is an astonishment to think that the brains of men should be parboiled in such impious ignorance; Let all the wits under the heavens lay their heads together and find an assertion worse than this (one excepted) I will petition to be chosen the universal Idiot of the world.

FOR FURTHER READING

James P. Byrd, *The Challenge of Roger Williams: Religious Liberty, Violent Persecution, and the Bible.* Macon, GA: Mercer University Press, 2002.

Thomas D. Hamm, *The Quakers in America.* New York: Columbia University Press, 2003.

Alf J. Mapp, *The Faiths of Our Fathers: What America's Founders Really Believed.* Lanham, MD: Rowman & Littlefield, 2003.

Stephen J. Stein, *Communities of Dissent: A History of Alternative Religions in America.* New York: Oxford University Press, 2003.

Viewpoint 6A
A Defense of the Salem Witch Trials (1692)
Cotton Mather (1663–1728)

INTRODUCTION *The Salem witchcraft trials were one of the most infamous episodes in American colonial history. In early 1692 some children in Salem, a village in Massachusetts close to Boston, accused three women of bewitching them. Charges and countercharges followed, and in June of that year witchcraft trials were authorized by the colonial governor, William Phips. Over the next few months the special court appointed by Phips tried, convicted, and executed nineteen people in witchcraft in the largest such proceeding in American history (one other person was tortured to death after refusing to enter a plea of guilty or not guilty). Amid growing criticism and doubts over the witch trails, Phips turned to Cotton Mather, Boston's leading minister and author of several books and sermons on witches, to defend the Salem proceedings. The result was* The Wonders of the Invisible World, *published in*

October 1692. This viewpoint contains excerpts of Mather's tract defending the Salem witch trials.

Mather begins by arguing that the Devil must be unhappy with the "People of God" settling what used to be the "Devil's Territories" in America, and that witches were perhaps part of a Satanic effort to disrupt or destroy the New England colonies. He then cites the records of court clerk Stephen Sewall to examine the trials of some of the Salem people convicted of witchcraft (one trial account is featured in this excerpt). Some historians have argued that Mather was selective in his choice of trials to examine. Mather had been among a group of ministers who argued against reliance on "spectral evidence"—testimony that a spirit resembling the accused had been seen tormenting a victim—as sole grounds for conviction of witchcraft. In Wonders *Mather chose to focus on the cases least affected by such evidence.*

What special position is held by New England and its people, according to Mather? What beliefs concerning witches and their powers are displayed by his writings and by the trial reports?

The *New-Englanders* are a People of God settled in those, which were once the *Devil's* Territories; and it may easily be supposed that the Devil was exceedingly disturbed, when he perceived such a People here accomplishing the Promise of old made unto our Blessed Jesus, *That He should have the Utmost parts of the Earth for his Possession.* . . . I believe, that never were more *Satanical Devices* used for the Unsetling of any People under the Sun, than what have been Employ'd for the Extirpation of the *Vine* which God has here *Planted, Casting out the Heathen, and preparing a Room Before it, and causing it to take deep Root, and fill the Land, so that it sent its Boughs unto the* Atlantic *Sea* Eastward, *and its Branches unto the* Connecticut *River* Westward, *and the Hills were covered with the shadows thereof.* But, All those Attempts of Hell, have hitherto been Abortive, many an *Ebenezer* [place of worship] has been Erected unto the Praise of God, by his Poor People here; and, *Having obtained Help from God, we continue to this Day.* Wherefore the Devil is now making one Attempt more upon us; an Attempt more Difficult, more Surprizing, more snarl'd with unintelligible Circumstances than any that we have hitherto Encountred; an Attempt so *Critical,* that if we get well through, we shall soon enjoy *Halcyon* Days with all the *Vultures* of hell *Trodden under our Feet.* He has wanted his *Incarnate Legions* to Persecute us, as the People of God have in the other Hemisphere been Persecuted: he has therefore drawn forth his more *Spiritual* ones to make an Attacque upon us. We have been advised by some Credible Christians yet alive, that a Malefactor,

From *The Wonders of the Invisible World* by Cotton Mather (Boston, 1692).

accused of *Witchcraft* as well as *Murder,* and Executed in this place more than Forty Years ago, did then give Notice of, *An Horrible* Plot *against the Country by* Witchcraft, *and a Foundation of* Witchcraft *then laid, which if it were not seasonably discovered, would probably Blow up, and pull down all the Churches in the Country.* And we have now with Horror seen the *Discovery* of such a *Witchcraft!* An Army of *Devils* is horribly broke in upon the place which is the *Center,* and after a sort, the *First-born* of our *English* Settlements: and the Houses of the Good People there are fill'd with the doleful Shrieks of their Children and Servants, Tormented by Invisible Hands, with Tortures altogether preternatural. After the Mischiefs there Endeavoured, and since in part Conquered, the terrible Plague, of *Evil Angels,* hath made its Progress into some other places, where other Persons have been in like manner Diabolically handled. These our poor Afflicted Neighbours, quickly after they become *Infected* and *Infested* with these *Dæmons,* arrive to a Capacity of Discerning those which they conceive the *Shapes* of their Troublers; and notwithstanding the Great and Just Suspicion, that the *Dæmons* might Impose the *Shapes* of Innocent Persons in their *Spectral Exhibitions* upon the Sufferers, (which may perhaps prove no small part of the *Witch-Plot* in the issue) yet many of the Persons thus Represented; being Examined, several of them have been Convicted of a very Damnable *Witchcraft:* yea, more than one *Twenty* have *Confessed,* that they have Signed unto a *Book,* which the Devil show'd them, and Engaged in his Hellish Design of *Bewitching,* and *Ruining* our Land. *We* know not, at least *I* know not; how far the *Delusions* of Satan may be Interwoven into some Circumstances of the *Confessions;* but one would think, all the Rules of Understanding Humane Affairs are at an end, if after so many most Voluntary Harmonious *Confessions,* made by Intelligent Persons of all Ages, in sundry Towns, at several Times, we must not Believe the *main strokes* wherein those *Confessions* all agree: especially when we have a thousand preternatural Things every day before our eyes, wherein the *Confessors* do acknowledge their Concernment, and give Demonstration of their being so Concerned. If the Devils now can strike the minds of men with any *Poisons* of so fine a Composition and Operation, that Scores of Innocent People shall Unite, in *Confessions* of a Crime, which we see actually committed, it is a thing prodigious, beyond the Wonders of the former Ages, and it threatens no less than a sort of a Dissolution upon the World. Now, by these *Confessions* 'tis Agreed, *That* the Devil has made a dreadful Knot of *Witches* in the Country, and by the help of *Witches* has dreadfully increased that Knot: *That* these *Witches* have driven a Trade of Commissioning their *Confederate Spirits,* to do all sorts of Mischiefs to the Neighbours, whereupon there have ensued such Mischievous consequences upon the Bodies and Estates of the Neighbourhood, as could not otherwise be accounted for: yea, *That* at prodigious *Witch-Meetings*, the Wretches have proceeded so far, as to Concert and Consult the Methods of Rooting out the Christian Religion from this Country, and setting up instead of it, perhaps a more gross *Diabolism*, than ever the World saw before. . . .

THE SALEM TRYALS

For my own part, I was not present at any of them [Salem witch trials]; nor ever had I any Personal prejudice at the Persons thus brought upon the Stage; much less at the Surviving Relations of those Persons, with and for whom I would be as hearty a Mourner as any Man living in the World: *The Lord Comfort them!* But having received a Command so to do, I can do no other than shortly relate the chief *Matters of Fact*, which occur'd in the Tryals of some that were Executed, in an Abridgment Collected out of the *Court-Papers* on this occasion put into my hands. You are to take the *Truth*, just as it was; and the Truth will hurt no good Man. . . .

The Trial of Martha Carrier, at the Court of Oyer and Terminer, Held by Adjournment at Salem, August 2, 1692

Martha Carrier was Indicted for the bewitching certain Persons, according to the Form usual in such Cases, pleading *Not Guilty*, to her Indictment; there were first brought in a considerable number of the bewitched Persons; who not only made the Court sensible of an horrid Witchcraft committed upon them, but also deposed. That it was *Martha Carrier*, or her Shape, that grievously tormented them, by Biting, Pricking, Pinching and Choaking of them. It was further deposed, That while this *Carrier* was on her Examination, before the Magistrates, the Poor People were so tortured that every one expected their Death upon the very spot, but that upon the binding of *Carrier* they were eased. Moreover the Look of *Carrier* then laid the Afflicted People for dead; and her Touch, if her Eye at the same time were off them, raised them again: Which Things were also now seen upon her Tryal. And it was testified, That upon the mention of some having their Necks twisted almost round, by the Shape of this *Carrier*, she replyed, *Its no matter though their Necks had been twisted quite off.*

2. Before the Tryal of this Prisoner, several of her own children had frankly and fully confessed, not only that they were Witches themselves, but that this their Mother had made them so. This Confession they made with great Shews of Repentance, and with much Demonstration of Truth. They related Place, Time, Occasion; they gave an account of Journeys, Meetings and Mischiefs by them performed, and were very credible in what they said. Nevertheless, this Evidence was not produced against the Prisoner at the Bar, inasmuch as there was other Evidence enough to proceed upon. . . .

5. *John Rogger* also testified, That upon threatning words of this malicious *Carrier*, his Cattle would be strangely bewitched; as was more particularly then described.

6. *Samuel Preston* testify'd, that about two years ago, having some difference with *Martha Carrier*, he lost a *Cow* in a strange Preternatural unusual manner; and about a month after this, the said *Carrier*, having again some difference with him, she told him; *He had lately lost a Cow, and it should not be long before he lost another*; which accordingly came to pass; for he had a thriving and well-kept *Cow*, which without any known cause quickly fell down and dy'd.

7. *Phebe Chandler* testify'd, that about a Fortnight before the apprehension of *Martha Carrier*, on a Lordsday while the Psalm was singing in the *Church*, this *Carrier* then took her by the shoulder and shaking her, asked her, *where she lived:* she made her no Answer, although as *Carrier*, who lived next door to her Fathers House, could not in reason but know who she was.

Quickly after this, as she was at several times crossing the Fields, she heard a voice, that she took to be *Martha Carriers*, and it seem'd as if it was over her head. The voice told her, *she should within two or three days be poisoned*. Accordingly, within such a little time, one half of her right hand, became greatly swollen, and very painful; as also part of her Face: whereof she can give no account how it came. It continued very bad for some dayes: and several times since, she has had a great pain in her breast; and been so seized on her leggs, that she has hardly heen able to go. She added, that lately, going well to the House of God, *Richard*, the son of *Martha Carrier*, look'd very earnestly upon her, and immediately her hand, which had formerly been poisoned, as is above-said, began to pain her greatly, and she had a strange Burning at her stomach; but was then struck deaf, so that she could not hear any of the prayer, or singing, till the two or three last words of the Psalm.

8. One *Foster*, who confessed her own share in the Witchcraft for which the Prisoner stood indicted, affirm'd, that she had seen the prisoner at some of their *Witch-meetings*, and that it was this *Carrier*, who perswaded her to be a Witch. She confessed, that the Devil carry'd them on a pole, to a Witch-meeting; but the pole broke, and she hanging about *Carriers neck*, they both fell down, and she then received an hurt by the Fall, whereof she was not at this very time recovered.

9. One *Lacy*, who likewise confessed her share in this Witchcraft, now testify'd, that she and the prisoner were once Bodily present at a *Witch-meeting in Salem Village*; and that she knew the prisoner to be a Witch, and to have been at a Diabolical sacrament; and that the prisoner was the undoing of her, and her Children, by enticing them into the snare of the Devil.

10. Another *Lacy*, who also confessed her share in this Witchcraft, now testify'd, that the prisoner was at the *Witch-meeting*, in *Salem Village*, where they had Bread and Wine Administred unto them.

11. In the time of this prisoners Trial, one *Susanna Sheldon*, in open Court had her hands Unaccountably ty'd together with a wheel-band, so fast that without cutting, it could not be loosed: It was done by a *Spectre*, and the Sufferer affirm'd, it was the *Prisoners*.

Memorandum. This rampant Hag, *Martha Carrier*, was the person, of whom the Confessions of the Witches, and of her own children among the rest, agreed, That the Devil had promised her, she should be Queen *of Heb.* . . .

DELIVERANCE FROM EVIL

If a Drop of *Innocent Blood* should be shed, in the Prosecution of the *Witchcrafts* among us, how unhappy are we! For which cause, I cannot express myself in better terms, than those of a most Worthy Person, who lives near the present Center of these things. *The Mind of God in these matters, is to be carefully lookt into, with due Circumspection, that Satan deceive as not with his Devices, who transforms himself into an Angel of Light, and may pretend justice and yet intend mischief.* But on the other side, if the storm of Justice do now fall only on the Heads of those guilty *Witches* and *Wretches* which have defiled our Land. *How Happy!*

The Execution of some that have lately Dyed, has been immediately attended, with a strange Deliverance of some, that had lain for many years, in a most sad Condition, under, they knew not whose *evil hands*. As I am abundantly satisfy'd. That many of the Self-Murders committed here, have been the effects of a Cruel and Bloody *Witchcraft*, letting fly *Demons* upon the miserable *Seneca's*; thus, it has *been* admirable unto me to see, how a Devilish *Witchcraft*, sending Devils upon them, has driven many poor people to *Despair*, and persecuted their minds, with such Buzzes of *Atheism* and *Blasphemy* as has made them even run *distracted with Terrors.* And some long *Bow'd* down under such a *spirit of Infirmity*, have been marvelously Recovered upon the death of the Witches.

An Attack on the Salem Witch Trials (1692)
Thomas Brattle (1658–1713)

INTRODUCTION *Although the 1692 witch trials in Salem, Massachusetts, had significant public support, many were deeply disturbed by the proceedings. One critic was Thomas Brattle, a prominent Boston merchant. Educated at Harvard College, Brattle had interests in science and mathematics as well as commerce. He was liberal in his political and religious*

beliefs and opposed Puritan orthodoxy. The following viewpoint is taken from a letter Brattle wrote to an unknown English clergyman in which he attacks the procedures used in the Salem witch trials, including their reliance on testimony and confessions of supposed witches and victims. The letter was not officially published in Brattle's day, but is believed by historians to have been widely circulated, allowing Brattle to discreetly make his views of the witchcraft trials known. Governor William Phips suspended the proceedings in October 1692. In all, several hundred people were accused of witchcraft, fifty-five confessed, and twenty put to death.

Does Brattle express belief in the Devil and in witchcraft? How do his views of confessions of witchcraft differ from those of Cotton Mather, author of the opposing viewpoint? What does Brattle find most disturbing about the Salem trials?

I am very open to communicate my thoughts unto you, and in plain terms to tell you what my opinion is of the Salem proceedings.

First, as to the method which the Salem justices do take in their examinations, it is truly this: A warrant being issued out to apprehend the persons that are charged and complained of by the afflicted children, as they are called; said persons are brought before the justices, the afflicted being present. The justices ask the apprehended why they afflict those poor children; to which the apprehended answer, they do not afflict them. The justices order the apprehended to look upon the said children, which accordingly they do; and at the time of that look (I dare not say *by* that look, as the Salem gentlemen do), the afflicted are cast into a fit. The apprehended are then blinded, and ordered to touch the afflicted; and at that touch, though not *by* the touch (as above), the afflicted ordinarily do come out of their fits. The afflicted persons then declare and affirm that the apprehended have afflicted them; upon which the apprehended persons, though of never so good repute, are forthwith committed to prison on suspicion for witchcraft. . . .

I cannot but condemn this method of the justices, of making this touch of the hand a rule to discover witchcraft; because I am fully persuaded that it is sorcery, and a superstitious method, and that which we have no rule for, either from reason or religion. . . .

SUPERSTITION AND MOCKERY

This Salem philosophy some men may call the new philosophy; but I think it rather deserves the name of Salem superstition and sorcery, and it is not fit to be named in a land of such light as New England is. I think the matter

From Thomas Brattle's letter dated 8 October 1692 to an unknown clergyman in England (Massachusetts Historical Society, *Collections*, vol. 5)

might be better solved another way; but I shall not make any attempt that way further than to say that these afflicted children, as they are called, do hold correspondence with the devil, even in the esteem and account of the Salem gentlemen; for when the black man, *i.e.*, say these gentlemen, the devil, does appear to them, they ask him many questions, and accordingly give information to the inquirer; and if this is not holding correspondence with the devil, and something worse, I know not what is....

Second, with respect to the confessors, as they are improperly called, or such as confess themselves to be witches (the second thing you inquire into in your letter), there are now about fifty of them in prison, many of which I have again and again seen and heard; and I cannot but tell you that my faith is strong concerning them, that they are deluded, imposed upon, and under the influence of some evil spirit, and therefore unfit to be evidences, either against themselves or anyone else. I now speak of one sort of them, and of others afterward.

CONTRADICTORY TESTIMONY

These confessors, as they are called, do very often contradict themselves, as inconsistently as is usual for any crazed, distempered person to do. This the Salem gentlemen do see and take notice of; and even the judges themselves have, at some times, taken these confessors in flat lies, or contradictions, even in the courts; by reason of which one would have thought that the judges would have frowned upon the said confessors, discarded them, and not minded one tittle of anything that they said. But instead thereof, as sure as we are men, the judges vindicate these confessors and salve their contradictions by proclaiming that the devil takes away their memory and imposes upon their brain. If this reflects anywhere, I am very sorry for it. I can but assure you that, upon the word of an honest man, it is truth, and that I can bring you many credible persons to witness it, who have been eye and ear witnesses to these things.

These confessors, then, at least some of them, even in the judges' own account, are under the influence of the devil; and the brain of these confessors is imposed upon by the devil, even in the judges' account. But now, if, in the judges' account, these confessors are under the influence of the devil, and their brains are affected and imposed upon by the devil so that they are not their own men, why then should these judges, or any other men, make such account of, and set so much by, the words of these confessors, as they do? In short, I argue thus:

If the devil does actually take away the memory of them at some times, certainly the devil, at other times, may very reasonably be thought to affect their fancies, and to represent false ideas to their imagination. But,

now, if it be thus granted that the devil is able to represent false ideas (to speak vulgarly) to the imaginations of the confessors, what man of sense wilt regard the confessions, or any of the words, of these confessors?

The great cry of many of our neighbors now is— What, will you not believe the confessors? Will you not believe men and women who confess that they have signed to the devil's book? that they were baptized by the devil; and that they were at the mock sacrament once and again? What! will you not believe that this is witchcraft, and that such and such men are witches, although the confessors do own and assert it?

Thus, I say, many of our good neighbors do argue; but methinks they might soon be convinced that there is nothing at all in all these their arguings, if they would but duly consider of the premises....

IGNORANCE OF HUMAN NATURE

Some of the Salem gentlemen are very forward to censure and condemn the poor prisoner at the bar because he sheds no tears; but such betray great ignorance in the nature of passion, and as great heedlessness as to common passages of a man's life. Some there are who never shed tears; others there are that ordinarily shed tears upon light occasions, and yet for their lives cannot shed a tear when the deepest sorrow is upon their hearts. And who is there that knows not these things? Who knows not that an ecstasy of joy will sometimes fetch tears, when as the quite contrary passion will shut them close up? Why then should any be so silly and foolish as to take an argument from this appearance? But this is by the by. In short, the prisoner at the bar is indicted for sorcery and witchcraft acted upon the bodies of the afflicted. Now, for the proof of this, I reckon that the only pertinent evidences brought in are the evidences of the said afflicted.

It is true that over and above the evidences of the afflicted persons there are many evidences brought in against the prisoner at the bar; either that he was at a witch meeting; or that he performed things which could not be done by an ordinary natural power; or that she sold butter to a sailor, which, proving bad at sea, and the seamen exclaiming against her, she appeared, and soon after there was a storm, or the like. But what if there were ten thousand evidences of this nature; how do they prove the matter of indictment? And if they do not reach the matter of indictment, then I think it is clear that the prisoner at the bar is brought in guilty and condemned, merely from the evidences of the afflicted persons....

I cannot but admire that the justices, whom I think to be well-meaning men, should so far give ear to the devil, as merely upon his authority, to issue out their warrants and apprehend people. Liberty was evermore accounted the great privilege of an Englishman; but certainly, if the devil will be heard against us and his testimony taken, to the seizing and apprehending of us, our liberty vanishes, and we are fools if we boast of our liberty. Now, that the justices have thus far given ear to the devil, I think may be mathematically demonstrated to any man of common sense. And for the demonstration and proof hereof, I desire, only, that these two things may be duly considered, viz.:

1. That several persons have been apprehended purely upon the complaints of these afflicted, to whom the afflicted were perfect strangers, and had not the least knowledge of [them] imaginable, before they were apprehended.

2. That the afflicted do own and assert, and the justices do grant, that the devil does inform and tell the afflicted the names of those persons that are thus unknown unto them. Now these two things being duly considered, I think it will appear evident to anyone that the devil's information is the fundamental testimony that is gone upon in the apprehending of the aforesaid people.

If I believe such or such an assertion as comes immediately from the minister of God in the pulpit, because it is the Word of the everliving God, I build my faith on God's testimony; and if I practise upon it, this my practice is properly built on the Word of God; even so in the case before us.

If I believe the afflicted persons as informed by the devil, and act thereupon, this my act may properly be said to be grounded upon the testimony or information of the devil. And now, if things are thus, I think it ought to be for a lamentation to you and me, and all such as would be accounted good Christians.

If any should see the force of this argument, and upon it say (as I heard a wise and good judge once propose) that they know not but that God Almighty, or a good spirit, does give this information to these afflicted persons, I make answer thereto and say that it is most certain that it is neither Almighty God, nor yet any good spirit, that gives this information; and my reason is good, because God is a God of truth, and the good spirits will not lie; whereas these informations have several times proved false, when the accused were brought before the afflicted.

FOR FURTHER READING

Paul Boyer and Stephen Nissenbaum, eds., *Salem-Village Witchcraft: A Documentary Record of Local Conflict in Colonial New England*. Belmomt, CA: Wadsworth, 1972.

Carol F. Karlsen, *The Devil in the Shape of a Woman*. New York: W.W. Norton, 1987.

Bryan F. LeBeau, *The Story of the Salem Witch Trials*. Saddle River, NJ: Prentice-Hall, 1998.

Laura Marvel, ed. *The Salem Witch Trials: At Issue in History*. San Diego: Greenhaven, 2003.

The complete texts of both Cotton Mather's book and Thomas Brattle's letter can be found at the Electronic Text Center of the University of Virginia library. The respective URLs are http://etext.virginia.edu/toc/modeng/public/Bur4Nar.html (Mather) and http://etext.virginia.edu/etcbin/toccer-new2?id=BurNarr.sgm&images=images/modeng&data=/texts/english/modeng/parsed&ta g=public&part=2&division=div1 (Brattle).

Viewpoint 7A

The Great Awakening Is a Welcome Religious Revival (1743)

An Assembly of Pastors of Churches in New England

INTRODUCTION *For several decades beginning in the 1720s, a religious revival, later called the Great Awakening, swept the American colonies. Traveling preachers such as George Whitefield and Gilbert Tennent, as well as some Puritan ministers such as Jonathan Edwards, emphasized the importance of an emotional commitment to Christianity and stirred the religious passions of thousands. Flamboyant preaching, speaking in tongues, lively singing, and dramatic conversions were all part of these religious gatherings. The traveling evangelists often left in their wake divisions between new converts and those who looked at the emotionalism of the phenomenon with suspicion. In New England, the Great Awakening stirred debate over whether this religious movement helped the colonies live up to their Puritan heritage or represented a dangerous diversion. The following viewpoint is taken from a statement of New England ministers who convened in July 1743 and who decided to support the Great Awakening and those affected by the religious revival. The ministers do caution against deviations from Puritan orthodoxy, including Antinomianism (the belief that personal revelations from God supersede human laws and church teachings), and Arminianism (the belief that humans can accept or reject salvation independent of God's will). In general, however, the ministers conclude that the revival and the behaviors it has inspired are the work of God.*

What positive aspects of the Great Awakening do the ministers describe? Judging from their listings of possible religious errors people might fall into, how do you think their views may have been affected by concern over their position in the community as ministers?

When Christ is pleased to come into his church in a plentiful effusion of his Holy Spirit, by whose powerful influences the ministration of the word is attended with

From *The Testimony and Advice of an Assembly of Pastors of Churches in New England, at a Meeting in Boston, July 7, 1743, Occasioned by the Late Happy Revival of Religion in Many parts of the Land.*

uncommon success, salvation-work carried on in an eminent manner, and his kingdom, which is within men, and consists in righteousness and peace and joy in the Holy Ghost, is notably advanced, this is an event which, above all others, invites the notice and bespeaks the praises of the Lord's people, and should be declared abroad for a memorial of the divine grace; as it tends to confirm the divinity of a despised gospel, and manifests the work of the Holy Spirit in the application of redemption, which too many are ready to reproach. . . .

But if it is justly expected of all who profess themselves the disciples of Christ, that they should openly acknowledge and rejoice in a work of this nature, wherein the honor of their divine Master is so much concerned; how much more is it to be looked for from those who are employed in the ministry of the Lord Jesus, and so stand in a special relation to him, as servants of his household, and officers in his kingdom! These stand as watchmen upon the walls of Jerusalem; and it is their business not only to give the alarm of war when the enemy is approaching, but to sound the trumpet of praise when the King of Zion cometh, in a meek triumph, having salvation.

For these and other reasons, we, whose names are hereunto annexed, pastors of churches in New England, met together in Boston, July 7, 1743, think it our indispensable duty, (without judging or censuring such of our brethren as cannot at present see things in the same light with us,) in this open and conjunct manner to declare, to the glory of sovereign grace, our full persuasion, either from what we have seen ourselves, or received upon credible testimony, that there has been a happy and remarkable revival of religion in many parts of this land, through an uncommon divine influence; after a long time of great decay and deadness, and a sensible and very awful withdraw of the Holy Spirit from his sanctuary among us.

Though the work of grace wrought on the hearts of men by the word and Spirit of God, and which has been more or less carried on in the church from the beginning, is always the same for substance, and agrees, at one time and another, in one place or person and another, as to the main strokes and lineaments of it, yet the present work appears to be remarkable and extraordinary.

PROOF OF GOD'S WORK

On account of the numbers wrought upon. We never before saw so many brought under soul concern, and with distress making the inquiry, What must we do to be saved? And these persons of all characters and ages. *With regard to the suddenness and quick progress of it.* Many persons and places were surprised with the gracious visit together, or near about the same time; and the

heavenly influence diffused itself far and wide like the light of the morning. *Also in respect of the degree of operation*, both in a way of terror and in a way of consolation; attended in many with unusual bodily effects. . . .

As to those whose inward concern has occasioned extraordinary outward distresses, the most of them, when we came to converse with them, were able to give, what appeared to us, a rational account of what so affected their minds; viz., a quick sense of their guilt, misery, and danger; and they would often mention the passages in the sermons they heard, or particular texts of Scripture, which were set home upon them with such a powerful impression. And as to such whose joys have carried them into transports and extasies, they in like manner have accounted for them, from a lively sense of the danger they hoped they were freed from, and the happiness they were now possessed of; such clear views of divine and heavenly things, and particularly of the excellencies and loveliness of Jesus Christ, and such sweet tastes of redeeming love, as they never had before. The instances were very few in which we had reason to think these affections were produced by visionary or sensible representations, or by any other images than such as the Scripture itself presents unto us.

And here we think it not amiss to declare, that in dealing with these persons, we have been careful to inform them, that the nature of conversion does not consist in these passionate feelings; and to warn them not to look upon their state safe, because they have passed out of deep distress into high joys, unless they experience a renovation of nature, followed with a change of life, and a course of vital holiness. Nor have we gone into such an opinion of the bodily effects with which this work has been attended in some of its subjects, as to judge them any signs that persons who have been so affected, were then under a saving work of the Spirit of God. No; we never so much as called these bodily seizures, convictions; or spake of them as the immediate work of the Holy Spirit. Yet we do not think them inconsistent with a work of God upon the soul at that very time; but judge that those inward impressions which come from the Spirit of God, those terrors and consolations of which he is the author, may, according to the natural frame and constitution which some persons are of, occasion such bodily effects; and therefore that those extraordinary outward symptoms are not an argument that the work is delusive, or from the influence and agency of the evil spirit.

With respect to numbers of those who have been under the impressions of the present day, we must declare there is good ground to conclude they are become real Christians; the account they give of their conviction and consolation agreeing with the standard of the Holy Scriptures, corresponding with the experiences of the saints, and evidenced by the external fruits of holiness in their lives; so that they appear to those who have the nearest access to them, as so many epistles of Christ, written, not with ink, but by the Spirit of the living God, attesting to the genuineness of the present operation, and representing the excellency of it. . . .

Thus we have freely declared our thoughts as to the work of God, so remarkably revived in many parts of this land. And now, we desire to bow the knee in thanksgiving to the God and Father of our Lord Jesus Christ, that our eyes have seen and our ears heard such things. And while these are our sentiments, we must necessarily be grieved at any accounts sent abroad, representing this work as all enthusiasm, delusion and disorder.

WARNINGS OF SATAN'S DEVICES

Indeed, it is not to be denied, that in some places many irregularities and extravagances have been permitted to accompany it, which we would deeply lament and bewail before God, and look upon ourselves obliged, for the honor of the Holy Spirit, and of his blessed operations on the souls of men, to bear a public and faithful testimony against; though at the same time it is to be acknowledged with much thankfulness, that in other places, where the work has greatly flourished, there have been few, if any, of these disorders and excesses. But who can wonder, if at such a time as this, Satan should intermingle himself, to hinder and blemish a work so directly contrary to the interests of his own kingdom? Or if, while so much good seed is sowing, the enemy should be busy to sow tares? We would therefore, in the bowels of Jesus, beseech such as have been partakers of this work, or are zealous to promote it, that they be not ignorant of Satan's devices; that they watch and pray against errors and misconduct of every kind, lest they blemish and hinder that which they desire to honor and advance. Particularly,

That they do not make secret impulses on their minds, without a due regard to the written word, the rule of their duty: a very dangerous mistake, which, we apprehend, some in these times have gone into. That to avoid Arminianism, they do not verge to the opposite side of Antinomianism; while we would have others take good heed to themselves, lest they be by some led into, or fixed in, Arminian tenets, under the pretense of opposing Antinomian errors. That laymen do not invade the ministerial office, and under a pretense of exhorting, set up preaching; which is very contrary to gospel order, and tends to introduce errors and confusion into the church. That ministers do not invade the province of others, and in ordinary cases preach in another's parish without his knowledge, and against his consent; nor encourage raw and indiscreet young candidates, in rushing into particular places, and preaching publicly or privately, as some have done, to the no small disrepute and damage of the work in places where it once promised

to flourish. Though at the same time we would have ministers show their regard to the spiritual welfare of their people, by suffering them to partake of the gifts and graces of able, sound and zealous preachers of the word, as God in his providence may give opportunity therefor; being persuaded God has in this day remarkably blessed the labors of some of his servants who have travelled in preaching the gospel of Christ. That people beware of entertaining prejudices against their own pastors, and do not run into unscriptural separations. That they do not indulge a disputatious spirit, which has been attended with mischievous effects; nor discover a spirit of censoriousness, uncharitableness, and rash judging the state of others than which scarce any thing has more blemished the work of God amongst us. And while we would meekly exhort both ministers and Christians, so far as is consistent with truth and holiness, to follow the things that make for peace; we would most earnestly warn all sorts of persons not to despise these outpourings of the Spirit, lest a holy God be provoked to withhold them, and instead thereof, to pour out upon this people the vials of his wrath, in temporal judgments and spiritual plagues; and would call upon every one to improve this remarkable season of grace, and put in for a share of the heavenly blessings so liberally dispensed.

Viewpoint 7B

The Great Awakening Has Led to Harmful Religious Zealotry (1742)

Charles Chauncy (1705–1787)

INTRODUCTION *The Great Awakening—the religious revival movement that swept the American colonies in the middle of the eighteenth century—often caused many divisions within communities and their churches. Congregations split between factions of the newly converted (the New Lights) and those who looked on the emotional displays of the Great Awakening with suspicion (the Old Lights). Revivalist preacher Gilbert Tennent called most practicing clergy "dead formalists" who were not true Christians. Some ministers responded by barring Tennent and other preachers from speaking in their churches, and accusing them of being charlatans, deceivers, or even workers of the devil. A prominent clerical critic of the Great Awakening was Charles Chauncy, a minister of the First Church in Boston. In the following viewpoint, taken from a sermon published in Boston in 1742, Chauncy describes the harms of religious "enthusiasm" engendered by the Great Awakening. Like many other detractors, Chauncy criticized the emotionalism and mysticism of the movement, which he felt displaced reason and learning.*

How does Chauncey describe "enthusiasm" and contrast it with "the proper work of the Spirit"? The Great Awakening was noteworthy for increasing the involvement of women, slaves, and the uneducated poor in religious life; some historians have argued that Chauncy's views reflect his class position as a conservative upper-class white male. What, if anything, do you find in the viewpoint to support this argument?

I shall take occasion to discourse to you upon the following Particulars.

I. I shall give you some account of Enthusiasm, in its nature and influence.

II. Point you to a rule by which you may judge of persons, whether they are under the influence of Enthusiasm.

III. Say what may be proper to guard you against this unhappy turn of mind.

The whole will then be follow'd with some suitable Application.

The Enthusiast. . . . fancies himself immediately inspired by the Spirit of God, when all the while, he is under no other influence than that of an over-heated imagination.

I am in the first place, to give you some account of Enthusiasm. And as this a thing much talk'd of at present, more perhaps than at any other time that has pass'd over us, it will not be tho't unseasonable, if I take some pains to let you into a true understanding of it.

The word, from its Etymology, carries in it a good meaning, as signifying inspiration from God: in which sense, the prophets under the old testament, and the apostles under the new, might properly be called Enthusiasts. For they were under a divine influence, spake as moved by the Holy Ghost, and did such things as can be accounted for in no way, but by recurring to an immediate extraordinary power, present with them.

THE BAD SIDE OF ENTHUSIASM

But the word is more commonly used in a bad sense, as intending an imaginary, not a real inspiration: according to which sense, the Enthusiast is one, who has a conceit of himself as a person favoured with the extraordinary presence of the Deity. He mistakes the workings of his own passions for divine communications, and fancies himself immediately inspired by the Spirit of God, when all the while, he is under no other influence than that of an over-heated imagination.

The cause of this enthusiasm is a bad temperament of the blood and spirits; 'tis properly a disease, a sort

From *Enthusiasm Described and Caution'd Against*, by Charles Chauncy (Boston, 1742).

of madness: And there are few; perhaps none at all, but are subject to it, tho' none are so much in danger of it as those, in whom melancholy is the prevailing ingredient in their constitution. In these it often reigns; and sometimes to so great a degree, that they are really beside themselves, acting as truly by the blind impetus of a wild fancy, as tho' they had neither reason nor understanding.

And various are the ways in which their enthusiasm discovers itself.

Sometimes, it may be seen in their countenance. A certain wildness is discernable in their general look and air; especially when their imaginations are mov'd and fired.

Sometimes, it strangely loosens their tongues, and gives them such an energy, as well as fluency and volubility in speaking, as they themselves, by their utmost efforts, can't so much as imitate, when they are not under the enthusiastick influence.

Sometimes, it affects their bodies, throws them into convulsions and distortions, into quakings and tremblings. This was formerly common among the people called Quakers. I was myself, when a Lad, an eye witness to such violent agitations and foamings, in a boisterous female speaker, as I could not behold but with surprize and wonder.

Sometimes, it will unaccountably mix itself with their conduct, and give it such a tincture of that which is freakish or furious, as none can have an idea of, but those who have seen the behaviour of a person in a phrenzy.

Sometimes, it appears in their imaginary peculiar intimacy with heaven. They are, in their own opinion, the special favourites of God, have more familiar converse with him than other good men, and receive immediate, extraordinary communications from him. The tho'ts, which suddenly rise up in their minds, they take for suggestions of the Spirit; their very fancies are divine illuminations; nor are they strongly inclin'd to any thing, but 'tis an impulse from God, a plain revelation of his will.

And what extravagances, in this temper of mind, are they not capable of, and under the specious pretext too of paying obedience to the authority of God? Many have fancied themselves acting by immediate warrant from heaven, while they have been committing the most undoubted wickedness. There is indeed scarce any thing so wild, either in speculation or practice, but they have given into it: They have, in many instances, been blasphemers of God, and open disturbers of the peace of the world.

AGAINST ALL REASON

But in nothing does the enthusiasm of these persons discover it self more, than in the disregard they express to the Dictates of reason. They are above the force of argument, beyond conviction from a calm and sober address to their understandings. As for them, they are distinguish'd persons; God himself speaks inwardly and immediately to their souls. "They see the light infused into their understandings, and cannot be mistaken; 'tis clear and visible there, like the light of bright sunshine; shews it self and needs no other proof but its own evidence. They feel the hand of God moving them within, and the impulses of his Spirit; and cannot be mistaken in what they feel. Thus they support themselves, and are sure reason hath nothing to do with what they see and feel. What they have a sensible experience of, admits no doubt, needs no probation." And in vain will you endeavour to convince such persons of any mistakes they are fallen into. They are certainly in the right, and know themselves to be so. They have the Spirit opening their understandings and revealing the truth to them. They believe only as he has taught them: and to suspect they are in the wrong is to do dishonour to the Spirit; 'tis to oppose his dictates, to set up their own wisdom in opposition to his, and shut their eyes against that light with which he has shined into their souls. They are not therefore capable of being argued with; you had as good reason with the wind. . . .

This is the nature of Enthusiasm, and this its operation, in a less or greater degree, in all who are under the influence of it. 'Tis a kind of religious Phrenzy, and evidently discovers it self to be so, whenever it rises to any great height. . . .

GUARDING AGAINST ENTHUSIASM

But as the most suitable guard against the first tendencies towards enthusiasm, let me recommend to you the following words of counsel.

1. Get a true understanding of the proper work of the Spirit; and don't place it in those things wherein the gospel does not make it to consist. The work of the Spirit is different now from what it was in the first days of christianity. Men were then favored with the extraordinary presence of the Spirit. He came upon them in miraculous gifts and powers; as a spirit of prophecy, of knowledge, of revelation, of tongues, of miracles: But the Spirit is not now to be expected in these ways. His grand business lies in preparing men's minds for the grace of God, by true humiliation, from an apprehension of sin, and the necessity of a Saviour; then in working in them faith and repentance, and such a change as shall turn them from the power of sin and satan unto God; and in fine, by carrying on the good work he has begun in them; assisting them in duty, strengthening them against temptation, and in a word, preserving them blameless thro' faith unto salvation: And all this he does by the word and prayer, as the great means in the accomplishment of these purposes of mercy.

Herein, in general, consists the work of the Spirit. It does not lie in giving men private revelations, but in opening their minds to understand the publick ones contained in the scripture. It does not lie in sudden impulses and impressions, in immediate calls and extraordinary missions. Men mistake the business of the Spirit, if they understand by it such things as these. And 'tis, probably, from such unhappy mistakes, that they are at first betrayed into enthusiasm. Having a wrong notion of the work of the Spirit, 'tis no wonder if they take the uncommon sallies of their own minds for his influences.

You cannot, my brethren, be too well acquainted with what the bible makes the work of the Holy Ghost, in the affair of salvation: And if you have upon your minds a clear and distinct understanding of this, it will be a powerful guard to you against all enthusiastical impressions.

2. Keep close to the scripture, and admit of nothing for an impression of the Spirit, but what agrees with that unerring rule. Fix it in your minds as a truth you will invariably abide by, that the bible is the grand test, by which every thing in religion is to be tried; and that you can, at no time, nor in any instance, be under the guidance of the Spirit of God, much less his extraordinary guidance, if what you are led to, is inconsistent with the things there revealed, either in point of faith or practice. And let it be your care to compare the motions of your minds, and the workings of your imaginations and passions, with the rule of God's word. And see to it, that you be impartial in this matter: Don't make the rule bend to your pre-conceiv'd notions and inclinations; but repair to the bible, with a mind dispos'd, as much as may be, to know the truth as it lies nakedly and plainly in the scripture it self. And whatever you are moved to, reject the motion, esteem it as nothing more than a vain fancy, if it puts you upon any method of thinking, or acting, that can't be evidently reconcil'd with the revelations of God in his word. . . .

MAKE USE OF REASON

3. Make use of the Reason and Understanding God has given you. This may be tho't an ill-advis'd direction, but 'tis as necessary as either of the former. Next to the scripture, there is no greater enemy to enthusiasm, than reason. 'Tis indeed impossible a man shou'd be an enthusiast, who is in the just exercise of his understanding; and 'tis because men don't pay a due regard to the sober dictates of a well inform'd mind, that they are led aside by the delusions of a vain imagination. Be advised then to shew yourselves men, to make use of your reasonable powers; and not act as the horse or mule, as tho' you had no understanding.

'Tis true, you must not go about to set up your own reason in opposition to revelation: Nor may you entertain a tho't of making reason your rule instead of scripture. The bible, as I said before, is the great rule of religion, the grand test in matters of salvation: But then you must use your reason in order to understand the bible: Nor is there any other possible way, in which, as a reasonable creature, you shou'd come to an understanding of it. . . .

4. You must not lay too great stress upon the workings of your passions and affections. These will be excited, in a less or greater degree, in the business of religion: And 'tis proper they shou'd. The passions, when suitably mov'd, tend mightily to awaken the reasonable powers, and put them upon a lively and vigorous exercise. And this is their proper use: And when address'd to, and excited to this purpose, they may be of good service: whereas we shall mistake the right use of the passions, if we place our religion only or chiefly, in the heat and fervour of them. . . .

REAL, SOBER RELIGION

There is such a thing as real religion, let the conduct of men be what it will; and 'tis, in its nature, a sober, calm, reasonable thing: Nor is it an objection of any weight against the sobriety or reasonableness of it, that there have been enthusiasts, who have acted as tho' it was a wild, imaginary business. We should not make our estimate of religion as exhibited in the behaviour of men of a fanciful mind; to be sure, we should not take up an ill opinion of it, because in the example they give of it, it don't appear so amiable as we might expect. This is unfair. We shou'd rather judge of it from the conduct of men of a sound judgment; whose lives have been such a uniform, beautiful transcript of that which is just and good, that we can't but think well of religion, as display'd in their example.

FOR FURTHER READING

Edward M. Griffin, *Old Brick: Charles Chauncy of Boston, 1705–1787.* Minneapolis: University of Minnesota Press, 1980.

Alan Heimert and Perry Miller, eds., *The Great Awakening.* Indianapolis: Bobbs-Merrill, 1967.

Frank Lambert, *Inventing the "Great Awakening."* Princeton, NJ: Princeton University Press, 2001.

Mark A. Noll, *The Rise of Evangelicalism: The Age of Edwards, Whitefield, and the Wesleys.* Downer's Grove, IL: InterVarsity Press, 2004.

The complete original text of both the New England pastors' statement and Charles Chauncy's sermon can be found at Gale's Eighteenth Century Collections Online (document numbers CW119875094 and CW3320607149).

LABOR IN COLONIAL AMERICA
Viewpoint 8A
Poor Europeans Should Come to America as Indentured Servants (1666)
George Alsop (c. 1636–1673)

INTRODUCTION *A significant problem facing Virginia, Maryland, and other American colonies in the 1600s and 1700s was a shortage of labor. One answer devised by the Virginia Company was indentured servitude, a system by which impoverished people in England and other countries agreed to bind themselves for a fixed period of labor in exchange for passage to America. The exact contractual agreements and conditions of service varied depending on the master and local laws. However, servants were often treated harshly and many died before their terms of service were over. The lot of survivors also varied. In the 1600s Maryland law entitled ex-servants to claim fifty acres of land (if they could afford to have the land surveyed), and many did become landowners. Virginia law only required ex-servants to receive a new suit of clothes and a year's supply of corn; many servants there became destitute laborers. Some people compared indentured servitude to slavery.*

The following viewpoint is taken from a 1666 book published in England; its purpose was in all likelihood to encourage people to settle in America as indentured servants. The author, George Alsop, an indentured servant himself in Maryland who eventually returned to England for health reasons, paints an idealized picture of life in the colony.

What beliefs does Alsop express about human equality and justice? How does he say indentured servitude has improved his own life?

As there can be no Monarchy without the Supremacy of a King and Crown, nor no King without Subjects, nor any Parents without it be by the fruitful off-spring of Children; neither can there be any Masters, unless it be by the inferior Servitude of those that dwell under them, by a commanding enjoyment: And since it is ordained from the original and superabounding wisdom of all things, That there should be Degrees and Diversities amongst the Sons of men, in acknowledging of a Superiority from Inferiors to Superiors; the Servant with a reverent and befitting Obedience is as liable to this duty in a measurable performance to him whom he serves, as the loyalest of Subjects to his Prince. Then since it is a common and ordained Fate, that there must be Servants as well as Masters, and that good Servitudes are those

From *A Character of the Province of Mary-Land* by George Alsop (London, 1666), as reprinted in *Narratives of Early Maryland*, edited by Clayton Colman Hal (New York: Scribner, 1910).

Colledges of Sobriety that checks in the giddy and wild-headed youth from his profuse and uneven course of life, by a limited constrainment, as well as it otherwise agrees with the moderate and discreet Servant: Why should there be such an exclusive Obstacle in the minds and unreasonable dispositions of many people, against the limited time of convenient and necessary Servitude, when it is a thing so requisite, that the best of Kingdoms would be unhing'd from their quiet and well setled Government without it. . . .

There is no truer Emblem of Confusion either in Monarchy or Domestick Governments, then when either the Subject, or the Servant, strives for the upper hand of his Prince, or Master, and to be equal with him, from whom he receives his present subsistance: Why then, if Servitude be so necessary that no place can be governed in order, nor people live without it, this may serve to tell those which prick up their ears and bray against it, That they are none but Asses, and deserve the Bridle of a strict commanding power to reine them in: For I'me certainly confident, that there are several Thousands in most Kingdoms of Christendom, that could not at all live and subsist, unless they had served some prefixed time, to learn either some Trade, Art, or Science, and by either of them to extract their present livelihood.

Then methinks this may stop the mouths of those that will undiscreetly compassionate them that dwell under necessary Servitudes; for let but Parents of an indifferent capacity in Estates, when their Childrens age by computation speak them seventeen or eighteen years old, turn them loose to the wide world, without a seven years working Apprenticeship (being just brought up to the bare formality of a little reading and writing) and you shall immediately see how weak and shiftless they'le be towards the maintaining and supporting of themselves; and (without either stealing or begging) their bodies like a Sentinel must continually wait to see when their Souls will be frighted away by the pale Ghost of a starving want.

Then let such, where Providence hath ordained to live as Servants, either in England or beyond Sea, endure the prefixed yoak of their limited time with patience, and then in a small computation of years, by an industrious endeavour, they may become Masters and Mistresses of Families themselves. And let this be spoke to the deserved praise of Mary-Land, That the four years I served there were not to me so slavish, as a two years Servitude of a Handicraft Apprenticeship was here in London; *Volenti enim nil difficile* [Nothing is difficult to the willing]: Not that I write this to seduce or delude any, or to draw them from their native soyle, but out of a love to my Countrymen, whom in the general I wish well to. . . .

The Servants here in Mary-Land of all Colonies. . . have the least cause to complain, either for strictness of Servitude, want of Provisions, or need of Apparel.

They whose abilities cannot extend to purchase their own transportation over into Mary-Land, (and surely he that cannot command so small a sum for so great a matter, his life must needs be mighty low and dejected) I say they may for the debarment of a four years sordid liberty, go over into this Province and there live plentiously well. And what's a four years Servitude to advantage a man all the remainder of his dayes, making his predecessors happy in his sufficient abilities, which he attained to partly by the restrainment of so small a time?

Now those that commit themselves unto the care of the Merchant to carry them over, they need not trouble themselves with any inquisitive search touching their Voyage; for there is such an honest care and provision made for them all the time they remain aboard the Ship, and are sailing over, that they want for nothing that is necessary and convenient.

The Merchant commonly before they go aboard the Ship, or set themselves in any forwardness for their Voyage, has Conditions of Agreements drawn between him and those that by a voluntary consent become his Servants, to serve him, his Heirs or Assigns, according as they in their primitive acquaintance have made their bargain, some two, some three, some four years; and whatever the Master or Servant tyes himself up to here in England by Condition, the Laws of the Province will force a performance of when they come there: Yet here is this Priviledge in it when they arrive, If they dwell not with the Merchant they made their first agreement withall, they may choose whom they will serve their prefixed time with; and after their curiosity has pitcht on one whom they think fit for their turn, and that they may live well withall, the Merchant makes an Assignment of the Indenture over to him whom they of their free will have chosen to be their Master, in the same nature as we here in England (and no otherwise) turn over Covenant Servants or Apprentices from one Master to another. Then let those whose chaps are always breathing forth those filthy dregs of abusive exclamations, which are Lymbeckt from their sottish and preposterous brains, against this Country of Mary-Land, saying, That those which are transported over thither, are sold in open Market for Slaves, and draw in Carts like Horses; which is so damnable an untruth, that if they should search to the very Center of Hell, and enquire for a Lye of the most antient and damned stamp, I confidently believe they could not find one to parallel this: For know, That the Servants here in Mary-Land of all Colonies, distant or remote Plantations, have the least cause to complain, either for strictness of Servitude, want of Provisions, or need of Apparel: Five dayes and a half in the Summer weeks is the alotted time that they work in; and for two months, when the Sun predominates in the highest pitch of his heat, they claim an antient and customary Priviledge, to repose themselves three hours in the day within the house, and this is undeniably granted to them that work in the Fields.

In the Winter time, which lasteth three months (*viz.*) December, January, and February, they do little or no work or imployment, save cutting of wood to make good fires to sit by, unless their Ingenuity will prompt them to hunt the Deer, or Bear, or recreate themselves in Fowling, to slaughter the Swans, Geese, and Turkeys (which this Country affords in a most plentiful manner:) For every Servant has a Gun, Powder and Shot allowed him, to sport him withall on all Holidayes and leasurable times, if he be capable of using it, or be willing to learn.

Viewpoint 8B

Poor Europeans Should Not Come to America as Indentured Servants (1754)

Gottlieb Mittelberger (dates unknown)

INTRODUCTION *Many of the people who migrated to the American colonies were indentured servants—people who paid for their passage by pledging themselves to be servants for a set period of time. The following viewpoint is taken from an account by Gottlieb Mittelberger, a German schoolmaster and organist who lived in America as an indentured servant from 1750 to 1754. His account describes the hardships of both the Atlantic voyage and life in America.*

Mittelberger's description of the indentured servant's life is much more negative than that of George Alsop (see viewpoint 8A). The differences between the two viewpoints can be attributed in part to differing times and circumstances. Alsop's account was written a century earlier at a time when most indentured servants came from England and settled in the Chesapeake colonies of Virginia and Maryland. In the eighteenth century the majority of servants came from non-English ethnic backgrounds, including German, Dutch, and Scotch-Irish, and most landed in Pennsylvania and neighboring colonies. Many, called "redemptioners," were at the mercy of the sea captains who paid for their passage to America and who sold them as servants to the highest bidder at the port of arrival.

How do the conditions of the sea voyage and American life described by Mittelberger differ from those depicted by George Alsop, author of the opposing viewpoint?

What are some aspects of American life that Mittelberger finds most objectionable?

Both in Rotterdam and in Amsterdam the people are packed densely, like herrings so to say, in the large sea vessels. One person receives a place of scarcely 2 feet width and 6 feet length in the bedstead, while many a ship carries four to six hundred souls, not to mention the innumerable implements, tools, provisions, water-barrels and other things which likewise occupy much space.

On account of contrary winds it takes the ships sometimes 2, 3 and 4 weeks to make the trip from Holland to Kaupp [Cowes] in England. But when the wind is good, they get there in 8 days or even sooner. Everything is examined there and the custom-duties paid, whence it comes that the ships ride thee 8, 10 to 14 days and even longer at anchor, till they have taken in their full cargoes. During that time every one is compelled to spend his last remaining money and to consume his little stock of provisions which had been reserved for the sea; so that most passengers, finding themselves on the ocean where they would be in greater need of them, must greatly suffer from hunger and want. Many suffer want already on the water between Holland and Old England.

THE LONG VOYAGE

When the ships have for the last time weighed their anchors near the city of Kaupp in Old England, the real misery begins with the long voyage. For from there the ships, unless they have good wind, must often sail 8, 9, 10 to 12 weeks before they reach Philadelphia. But even with the best wind the voyage lasts 7 weeks.

But during the voyage there is on board these ships terrible misery, stench, fumes, horror, vomiting, many kinds of sea-sickness, fever, dysentery, headache, heat, constipation, boils, scurvy, cancer, mouth-rot, and the like, all of which come from old and sharply salted food and meat, also from very bad and foul water, so that many die miserably.

Add to this want of provisions, hunger, thirst, frost, heat, dampness, anxiety, want, afflictions and lamentations, together with other trouble, as . . . the lice abound so frightfully, especially on sick people, that they can be scraped off the body. The misery reaches the climax when a gale rages for 2 or 3 nights and days, so that every one believes that the ship will go to the bottom with all human beings on board. In such a visitation the people cry and pray most piteously. . . .

Many sigh and cry: "Oh, that I were at home again, and if I had to lie in my pig-sty!" Or they say: "O God, if I only had a piece of good bread, or a good fresh drop of water." Many people whimper, sigh and cry piteously for their homes; most of them get home-sick. Many hundred

From *Journey to Pennsylvania in the Year 1750 and Return to Germany in the Year 1754* by Gottlieb Mittelberger, trans. By Carl Theo. Eben (Philadelphia: John Joseph McVey, 1898.

people necessarily die and perish in such misery, and must be cast into the sea, which drives their relatives, or those who persuaded them to undertake the journey, to such despair that it is almost impossible to pacify and console them. . . .

Children from 1 to 7 years rarely survive the voyage. I witnessed . . . misery in no less than 32 children in our ship, all of whom were thrown into the sea. The parents grieve all the more since their children find no resting-place in the earth, but are devoured by the monsters of the sea. . . .

That most of the people get sick is not surprising, because, in addition to all other trials and hardships, warm food is served only three times a week, the rations being very poor and very little. Such meals can hardly be eaten, on account of being so unclean. The water which is served out on the ships is often very black, thick and full of worms, so that one cannot drink it without loathing, even with the greatest thirst. Toward the end we were compelled to eat the ship's biscuit which had been spoiled long ago; though in a whole biscuit there was scarcely a piece the size of a dollar that had not been full of red worms and spiders' nests. . . .

ARRIVAL IN AMERICA

At length, when, after a long and tedious voyage, the ships come in sight of land, so that the promontories can be seen, which the people were so eager and anxious to see, all creep from below on deck to see the land from afar, and they weep for joy, and pray and sing, thanking and praising God. The sight of the land makes the people on board the ship, especially the sick and the half dead, alive again, so that their hearts leap within them; they shout and rejoice, and are content to bear their misery in patience, in the hope that they may soon reach the land in safety. But alas!

When the ships have landed at Philadelphia after their long voyage, no one is permitted to leave them except those who pay for their passage or can give good security; the others, who cannot pay, must remain on board the ships till they are purchased, and are released from the ships by their purchasers. The sick always fare the worst, for the healthy are naturally preferred and purchased first; and so the sick and wretched must often remain on board in front of the city for 2 or 3 weeks, and frequently die, whereas many a one, if he could pay his debt and were permitted to leave the ship immediately, might recover and remain alive. . . .

———————■———————

Who therefore wishes to earn his bread in a Christian and honest way, . . . let him do so in his own country and not in America; for he will not fare better in America.

———————■———————

The sale of human beings in the market on board the ship is carried on thus: Every day Englishmen, Dutchmen, and High-German people come from the city of Philadelphia and other places, in part from a great distance, say 20, 30, or 40 hours away, and go on board the newly arrived ship that has brought and offers for sale passengers from Europe, and select among the healthy persons such as they deem suitable for their business, and bargain with them how long they will serve for their passage money, which most of them are still in debt for. When they have come to an agreement, it happens that adult persons bind themselves in writing to serve 3, 4, 5, or 6 years for the amount due by them, according to their age and strength. But very young people, from 10 to 15 years, must serve till they are 21 years old.

Many parents must sell and trade away their children like so many head of cattle; for if their children take the debt upon themselves, the parents can leave the ship free and unrestrained; but as the parents often do not know where and to what people their children are going, it often happens that such parents and children, after leaving the ship, do not see each other again for many years, perhaps no more in all their lives. . . .

HARD WORK

Work and labor in this new and wild land are very hard and manifold, and many a one who came there in his old age must work very hard to his end for his bread. I will not speak of young people. Work mostly consists in cutting wood, felling oak-trees, rooting out, or as they say there, clearing large tracts of forest. Such forests, being cleared, are then laid out for fields and meadows. From the best hewn wood, fences are made around the new fields; for there all meadows, orchards and fruit-fields are surrounded and fenced in with planks made of thickly-split wood, laid one above the other, as in zigzag lines, and within such enclosures, horses, cattle, and sheep are permitted to graze. Our Europeans, who are purchased, must always work hard, for new fields are constantly laid out; and so they learn that stumps of oak-trees are in America certainly as hard as in Germany. In this hot land they fully experience in their own persons what God has imposed on man for his sin and disobedience; for in Genesis we read the words: In the sweat of thy brow shalt thou eat bread. Who therefore wishes to earn his bread in a Christian and honest way, and cannot earn it in his fatherland otherwise than by the work of his hands, let him do so in his own country and not in America; for he will not fare better in America. However hard he may be compelled to work in his fatherland, he will surely find it quite as hard, if not harder, in the new country. Besides, there is not only the long and arduous journey lasting half a year, during which he has to suffer, more than with the hardest work; he has also spent about 200 florins which no one will refund to him. If he has so much money, it will slip out of his hands; if he has it not, he must work his debt off as a slave and poor serf. Therefore let every one stay in his own country and support himself and his family honestly. Besides I say that those who suffer themselves to be persuaded and enticed away by the man-thieves, are very foolish if they believe that roasted pigeons will fly into their mouths in America or Pennsylvania without their working for them.

FOR FURTHER READING

Clifford L. Alderman, *Colonists for Sale: The Story of Indentured Servants in America*. New York: Macmillan, 1975.

David W. Galson, *White Servitude in Colonial America: An Economic Analysis*. New York: Cambridge University Press, 1981.

Daniel Meaders, *Dead or Alive: Fugitive Slaves and White Indentured Servants Before 1830*. New York: Garland, 1993.

Sharon V. Salinger, *"To Serve Thee Well and Faithfully": Labor and Indentured Servants in Pennsylvania, 1682–1800*. New York: Cambridge University Press, 1987.

The complete text of Alsop's book can be found at the web site of the Early Americas Digital Archive at http://narcissus.umd.edu:8080/eada/html/display.jsp?docs=alsop_character.xml&action=show.

Viewpoint 9A

Slavery Is Immoral (1700)

Samuel Sewall (1652–1730)

INTRODUCTION *The economies of many of the American colonies rested on a foundation of raising and selling cash crops, especially tobacco in Virginia and Maryland and rice in South Carolina. However, successful cultivation of these crops required intensive labor—something in short supply in the thinly populated colonies. Pressing captured Indians to work proved unsuccessful, in part because many Indians quickly succumbed to diseases brought over from Europe. Indentured servitude (see viewpoints 8A and 8B) formed in its wake an impoverished white underclass of former servants—a development that often caused political instability and violence.*

A lasting solution to the colonies' labor shortage was finally found by importing black Africans as slaves. Since the early 1500s, Africans had been captured and transported to Spanish, Portuguese, and (later) British colonies in South America and the Carribean. Although blacks were present in Virginia as early as 1619, it was not until the 1680s that they began to replace the white indentured servants as the main source of labor in Virginia, South Carolina, and other colonies. Unlike indentured servants, black slaves were bound for life and lacked all legal and political rights. Their different skin color made escape much more difficult. By 1700 slavery was legal in all English

colonies in America and Africans (mostly slaves) accounted for 15 percent of the population in southern colonies. Although legal in New England, slavery was not as widespread as in colonies farther south.

Although slavery did establish itself as a lasting solution to the colonies' labor shortage problem, its morality did not go unquestioned in colonial times. The following viewpoint is taken from one of the earliest antislavery pamphlets published in America. The author, Samuel Sewall, was a Massachusetts Superior Court judge who became involved in a legal dispute involving a black slave owned by another judge. Sewall wanted the judge to honor a contract calling for the slave's release. In defense of his position, Sewall wrote and circulated a pamphlet attacking slavery, The Selling of Joseph, *that was published in Boston in 1700.*

What objections does Sewall have to slavery? Why might he use Biblical citations to support his views? Does Sewall exhibit racial prejudice in this viewpoint? Explain your answer.

Forasmuch *as Liberty is in real value next unto* Life: *None ought to part with it themselves, or deprive others of it, but upon most mature consideration.*

The Numerousness of Slaves at this Day in the Province, and the Uneasiness of them under their Slavery, hath put many upon thinking whether the Foundation of it be firmly and well laid; so as to sustain the Vast Weight that is built upon it. It is most certain that all Men, as they are the Sons of *Adam*, are Co-heirs, and have equal Right unto Liberty, and all other outward Comforts of Life. God *hath given the Earth [with all its commodities] unto the Sons of Adam, Psal.,* 115, 16. *And hath made of one Blood all Nations of Men, for to dwell on all the face of the Earth, and hath determined the Times before appointed, and the bounds of their Habitation: That they should seek the Lord. Forasmuch then as we are the Offspring of* God. &c. *Acts* 17, 26, 27, 29. . . . So that Originally, and Naturally, there is no such thing as Slavery. *Joseph* was rightfully no more a Slave to his Brethren, than they were to him; and they had no more Authority to *Sell* him, than they had to *Slay* him. . . .

And all things considered, it would conduce more to the Welfare of the Province, to have White Servants for a Term of Years, than to have Slaves for Life. Few can endure to hear of a Negro's being made free; and indeed they can seldom use their Freedom well; yet their continual aspiring after their forbidden Liberty, renders them Unwilling Servants. And there is such a disparity in their Conditions, Colour, and Hair, that they can never embody with us, & grow up in orderly Families, to the Peopling of the Land; but still remain in our

From *The Selling of Joseph: A Memorial* by Samuel Sewall, Boston, 1700 (Massachusetts Historical Society, *Proceedings*, vol. 7, 1864).

Body Politick as a kind of extravasat Blood. Moreover it is too well known what Temptations Masters are under, to connive at the Fornication of their Slaves; lest they should be obliged to find them Wives, or pay their Fines. It seems to be practically pleaded that they might be lawless; 'tis thought much of, that the Law should have satisfaction for their Thefts, and other Immoralities; by which means, *Holiness to the Lord* is more rarely engraven upon this sort of Servitude. It is likewise most lamentable to think, how in taking Negroes out of *Africa*, and selling of them here, That which God has joined together, Men do boldly rend asunder; Men from their Country, Husbands from their Wives, Parents from their Children. How horrible is the Uncleanness, Mortality, if not Murder, that the Ships are guilty of that bring great Crouds of these miserable Men and Women. Men thinks when we are bemoaning the barbarous Usage of our Friends and Kinsfolk in *Africa*, it might not be unreasonable to enquire whether we are not culpable in forcing the *Africans* to become Slaves amongst ourselves. And it may be a question whether all the Benefit received by *Negro* Slaves will balance the Accompt of Cash laid out upon them; and for the Redemption of our own enslaved Friends out of *Africa*. Besides all the Persons and Estates that have perished there.

OBJECTIONS AND ANSWERS

Obj. 1. *These Blackamores are of the Posterity of Cham, and therefore are under the Curse of Slavery. Gen. 9, 25, 26, 27.*

Ans. Of all Offices, one would not beg this; viz. Uncall'd for, to be an Executioner of the Vindictive Wrath of God; the extent and duration of which is to us uncertain. If this ever was a Commission; How do we know but that it is long since out of Date? Many have found it to their Cost, that a Prophetical Denunciation of Judgment against a Person or People, would not warrant them to inflict that evil. If it would, *Hazael* might justify himself in all he did against his master, and the *Israelites* from 2 *Kings* 8, 10, 12.

But it is possible that by cursory reading, this Text may have been mistaken. For *Canaan* is the Person Cursed three times over, without the mentioning of *Cham*. Good Expositors suppose the Curse entailed on him, and that this Prophesie was accomplished in the Extirpation of the *Canaanites*, and in the Servitude of the *Gibeonites*. . . . *Whereas* the Blackamores are not descended of *Canaan*, but of *Cush. Psal.* 68, 31. *Princes shall come out of Egypt* [Mizraim]. *Ethiopia* [Cush] *shall soon stretch out her hands unto God.* Under which Names, all *Africa* may be comprehended; and their Promised Conversion ought to be prayed for. *Jer.* 13, 23. *Can the Ethiopian change his Skin?* This shows that Black Men are the Posterity of *Cush.* Who time out of mind have been distinguished by their Colour. . . .

Obj. 2. *The Nigers are brought out of a Pagan Country, into places where the Gospel is preached.*

Ans. Evil must not be done, that good may come of it. The extraordinary and comprehensive Benefit accruing to the Church of God, and to *Joseph* personally, did not rectify his Brethren's Sale of him.

Obj. 3. *The Africans have Wars one with another: Our Ships bring lawful Captives taken in those wars.*

Ans. For aught is known, their Wars are much such as were between *Jacob's* Sons and their Brother *Joseph.* If they be between Town and Town; Provincial or National: Every War is upon one side Unjust. An Unlawful War can't make lawful Captives. And by receiving, we are in danger to promote, and partake in their Barbarous Cruelties. I am sure, if some Gentlemen should go down to the [town of] *Brewsters* to take the Air, and Fish: And a stronger Party from *Hull* should surprise them, and sell them for Slaves to a Ship outward bound; they would think themselves unjustly dealt with; both by Sellers and Buyers. And yet 'tis to be feared, we have no other Kind of Title to our *Nigers. Therefore all things whatsoever ye would that men should do to you, do you even so to them: for this is the Law and the Prophets. Matt.* 7, 12.

Obj. 4. Abraham *had Servants bought with his Money and born in his House.*

Ans. Until the Circumstances of *Abraham's* purchase be recorded, no Argument can be drawn from it. In the mean time, Charity obliges us to conclude, that He knew it was lawful and good.

It is Observable that the *Israelites* were strictly forbidden the buying or selling one another for Slaves. *Levit.* 25. 39. 46. *Jer.* 34. 8–22. And God gages His Blessing in lieu of any loss they might conceit they suffered thereby, *Deut.* 15. 18. And since the partition Wall is broken down, inordinate Self-love should likewise be demolished. God expects that Christians should be of a more Ingenuous and benign frame of Spirit. Christians should carry it to all the World, as the *Israelites* were to carry it one towards another. And for Men obstinately to persist in holding their Neighbours and Brethren under the Rigor of perpetual Bondage, seems to be no proper way of gaining Assurance that God has given them Spiritual Freedom. Our Blessed Saviour has altered the Measures of the ancient Love Song, and set it to a most Excellent New Tune, which all ought to be ambitious of Learning. *Matt.* 5. 43. 44. *John* 13. 34. These *Ethiopians*, as black as they are, seeing they are the Sons and Daughters of the First *Adam*, the Brethren and Sisters of the Last Adam, and the Offspring of God; They ought to be treated with a Respect agreeable.

Slavery Is Moral (1701)

John Saffin (1632–1710)

INTRODUCTION *John Saffin was a wealthy landowner and Massachusetts judge. In 1700 he became embroiled in a legal dispute when he refused to give a black slave in his possession his freedom. He viewed Samuel Sewall's tract* The Selling of Joseph, a Memorial *(see viewpoint 9A) as a personal affront, and in 1701 published a reply defending the institution of slavery (and his own actions as a slaveowner). The tract, reprinted here, is notable in that many of its arguments appear repeatedly in later proslavery literature.*

How does Saffin respond to Samuel Sewall's "Objections" to slavery? What beliefs does Saffin express about equality? What beliefs does he express about blacks?

That Honourable and Learned Gentleman, the Author of a Sheet, Entituled, *The Selling of Joseph, A Memorial,* seems from thence to draw this conclusion, that because the Sons of *Jacob* did very ill in selling their Brother *Joseph* to the *Ishmaelites,* who were Heathens, therefore it is utterly unlawful to Buy and Sell Negroes, though among Christians; which Conclusion I presume is not well drawn from the Premises, nor is the case parallel; for it was unlawfull for the *Israelites* to sell their Brethren upon any account, or pretence whatsoever during life. But it was not unlawful for the Seed of *Abraham* to have Bond men, and Bond women either born in their House, or bought with their Money, as it is written of *Abraham, Gen.* 14.14 & 21.10 & *Exod.* 21.16 & *Levit.* 25.44, 45, 46 v. After the giving of the Law: And in *Josh.* 9.23.

DIFFERENT ORDERS OF MEN

To speak a little to the Gentleman's first Assertion: *That none ought to part with their Liberty themselves, or deprive others of it but upon mature consideration*; a prudent exception, in which he grants, that upon some consideration a man may be deprived of his Liberty. And then presently in his next Position or Assertion he denies it, *viz.: It is most certain, that all men as they are the Sons of* Adam *are Coheirs, and have equal right to Liberty, and all other Comforts of Life,* which he would prove out of *Psal.* 115.16. *The Earth hath he given to the Children of Men.* True, but what is all this to the purpose, to prove that all men have equal right to Liberty, and all outward comforts of this life; which Position seems to invert the Order that God hath set in the World, who hath Ordained different degrees and orders of men, some to be High and Honourable, some to be Low and Despicable; some to

be Monarchs, Kings, Princes and Governours, Masters and Commanders, others to be Subjects, and to be Commanded; Servants of sundry sorts and degrees, bound to obey; yea, some to be born Slaves, and so to remain during their lives, as hath been proved. Otherwise there would be a meer parity among men, contrary to that of the Apostle; I *Cor. 12 from the 13 to the 26 verse,* where he sets forth (by way of comparison) the different sorts and offices of the Members of the Body, indigitating that they are all of use, but not equal, and of like dignity. So God hath set different Orders and Degrees of Men in the World, both in Church and Common weal. Now, if this Position of parity should be true, it would then follow that the ordinary Course of Divine Providence of God in the World should be wrong, and unjust, (which we must not dare to think, much less to affirm) and all the sacred Rules, Precepts and Commands of the Almighty which he hath given the Son of Men to observe and keep in their respective Places, Orders and Degrees, would be to no purpose; which unaccountably derogate from the Divine Wisdom of the most High, who hath made nothing in vain, but hath Holy Ends in all his Dispensations to the Children of men.

In the next place, this worthy Gentleman makes a large Discourse concerning the Utility and Conveniency to keep the one, and inconveniency of the other; respecting white and black Servants, which conduceth most to the welfare and benefit of this Province: which he concludes to be white men, who are in many respects to be preferred before Blacks; who doubts that? doth it therefore follow, that it is altogether unlawful for Christians to buy and keep Negro Servants (for this is the Thesis) but that those that have them ought in Conscience to set them free, and so lose all the money they cost (for we must not live in any known sin) this seems to be his opinion; but it is a Question whether it ever was the Gentleman's practice? But if he could perswade the General Assembly to make an Act, That all that have Negroes, and do set them free, shall be Re imbursed out of the Publick Treasury, and that there shall be no more Negroes brought into the Country; 'tis probable there would be more of his opinion; yet he would find it a hard task to bring the Country to consent thereto; for then the Negroes must be all sent out of the Country, or else the remedy would be worse than the Disease; and it is to be feared that those Negroes that are free, if there be not some strict course taken with them by Authority, they will be a plague to this Country....

Our Author doth further proceed to answer some Objections of his own flaming, which he supposes some might raise.

Object. 1. *That these Blackamores are of the Posterity of Cham, and therefore under the Curse of Slavery. Gen.* 9.25, 26, 27. That which the Gentleman seems to deny, saying, *they were the Seed of Canaan that were Cursed,* etc.

From *A Brief and Candid Answer to a Late Printed Sheet Entituled "The Selling of Joseph"* by John Saffin (Boston, 1701), as reprinted in *Notes on the History of Slavery in Massachusetts* by George H. Moore (New York: D. Appleton, 1866).

Ans. Whether they were so or not, we shall not dispute: this may suffice, that not only the seed of *Cham* or *Canaan*, but any lawful Captives of other Heathen Nations may be made Bond men as hath been proved.

Obj. 2. That the Negroes are brought out of Pagan Countreys into places where the Gospel is Preached. To which he Replies, *that we must not doe Evil that Good may come of it.*

Ans. To which we answer, That it is no Evil thing to bring them out of their own Heathenish Country, where they may have the Knowledge of the True God, be Converted and Eternally saved.

AFRICAN WARS

Obj. 3. The Affricans have Wars one with another; our Ships bring lawful Captives taken in those Wars.

To which our Author answer Conjecturally, and Doubtfully, *for aught we know,* that which may or may not be; which is insignificant, and proves nothing. He also compares the Negroes Wars, one Nation with another, with the Wars between *Joseph* and his Brethren. But where doth he read of any such War? We read indeed of a Domestick Quarrel they had with him, they envyed and hated *Joseph;* but by what is Recorded, he was meerly passive and meek as a Lamb. This Gentleman farther adds, *That there is not any War but is unjust on one side.* etc. Be it so, what doth that signify: We read of lawful Captives taken in the Wars, and lawful to be Bought and Sold without contracting the guilt of the *Agressors;* for which we have the example of *Abraham* before quoted; but if we must stay while both parties Warring are in the right, there would be no lawful Captives at all to be Bought; which seems to be rediculous to imagine, and contrary to the tenour of Scripture, and all Humane Histories on that subject.

Obj. 4. Abraham had Servants bought with his Money, and born in his House. Gen. 14.14. To which our worthy Author answers, *until the Circumstances of Abraham's purchase be recorded, no Argument can be drawn from it.*

Ans. To which we Reply, this is also Dogmatical, and proves nothing. He farther adds. *In the mean time Charity Obliges us to conlude, that he knew it was lawful and good.* Here the gentleman yields the case; for if we are in Charity bound to believe *Abraham's* practice, in buying and keeping *Slaves* in his house to be lawful and good: then it follows, that our imitation of him in this his Moral Action, is as warrantable as that of his Faith; *who is the Father of all them that believe. Rom.* 4.16. . . .

By the Command of God . . . , we may keep Bond men, and use them in our Service.

And after a Serious Exhortation to us all to Love one another according to the Command of Christ. *Math.* 5.43, 44. This worthy Gentleman concludes with this Assertion, *That these Ethiopeans as Black as they are, seeing they are the Sons and Daughters of the first* Adam; *the Brethren and Sisters of the Second Adam, and the Offspring of God; we ought to treat them with a respect agreeable.*

LOVING ALL PEOPLE EQUALLY IS IMPOSSIBLE

Ans. We grant it for a certain and undeniable verity, That all Mankind are the Sons and Daughters of *Adam,* and the Creatures of God: But it doth not therefore follow that we are bound to love and respect all men alike; this under favour we must take leave to deny; we ought in charity, if we see our Neighbour in want, to relieve them in a regular way, but we are not bound to give them so much of our Estates, as to make them equal with our selves, because they are our Brethren, the Sons of *Adam,* no, not our own natural Kinsmen: We are Exhorted *to do good unto all, but especially to them who are of the Houshold of Faith, Gal.* 6.10. And we are to love, honour and respect all men according to the gift of God that is in them: I may love my Servant well, but my Son better; Charity begins at home, it would be a violation of common prudence, and a breach of good manners, to treat a Prince like a Peasant. And this worthy Gentleman would deem himself much neglected, if we should show him no more Defference than to an ordinary Porter: And therefore these florid expressions, the Sons and Daughters of the First *Adam,* the Brethren and Sisters of the Second *Adam,* and the Offspring of God, seem to bemisapplied to import and insinuate, that we ought to tender Pagan Negroes with all love, kindness, and equal respect as to the best of men.

By all which it doth evidently appear both by Scripture and Reason, the practice of the People of God in all Ages, both before and after the giving of the Law, and in the times of the Gospel, that there were Bond men, Women and Children commonly kept by holy and good men, and improved in Service; and therefore by the Command of God, *Lev.* 24:44, and their venerable Example, we may keep Bond men, and use them in our Service still; yet with all candour, moderation and Christian prudence, according to their state and condition consonant to the Word of God.

THE NEGROES' CHARACTER
Cowardly and cruel are those Blacks *Innate,*
Prone to Revenge, Imp of inveterate hate.
He that exasperates them, soon espies
Mischief and Murder in their very eyes.

Libidinous, Deceitful, False and Rude,
The Spume Issue of Ingratitude.
The Premises consider'd, all may tell,
How near good Joseph *they are parallel.*

FOR FURTHER READING

Ira Berlin, *Many Thousands Gone: The First Two Centuries of Slavery in North America.* Cambridge, MA: The Belknap Press of Harvard University Press, 1998.

Winthrop Jordan, *White over Black: American Attitudes Toward the Negro, 1550–1812*, New York: Norton, 1977.

T. Benson Strandness, *Samuel Sewall: A Puritan Portrait.* East Lansing: Michigan State University Press, 1967.

Larry Tise, *Proslavery: A History of the Defense of Slavery in America, 1701–1840.* Athens, University of Georgia Press, 1987.

Betty Wood, *The Origins of American Slavery: Freedom and Bondage in the English Colonies.* New York: Hill and Wang, 1997.

Part 2
FORGING A NEW NATION (1750–1800)

CHRONOLOGY

1754

May Governor of Virginia sends militia under George Washington into Ohio Valley to challenge French expansion.

June Albany Congress held by delegates of six colonies to discuss defense; Benjamin Franklin drafts Albany Plan of Union.

1754–1763

Winter French and Indian War takes place.

1760

October 25 George III becomes king of Great Britain.

1763

February 10 France cedes North American territories to England in Treaty of Paris.

May Chief Pontiac of Ottawa tribe leads Indian attacks in Great Lakes region.

October 7 Great Britain declares territory west of Appalachians off limits to American colonization.

1765

March 22 Stamp Act becomes law.

May Patrick Henry attacks Stamp Act at meeting of Virginia House of Burgesses.

August Riots against Stamp Act take place in Boston.

October 5 Stamp Act Congress meets to protest Stamp Act.

1766

March 18 Parliament repeals Stamp Act and passes Declaratory Act asserting Parliament's supremacy over colonial affairs.

1767

July 2 Quartering Act and Townshend Duties passed.

1768

August Boston merchants adopt colonies' first nonimportation agreement against British goods.

October British soldiers stationed in Boston.

1769

July 16 First permanent European settlement in California established by Fr. Junipero Serra at San Diego.

1770

March 5 Boston Massacre occurs.

April Townsend Duties repealed, colonists lift trade embargo.

1771

May 16 North Carolina farmers known as Regulators, rebelling against North Carolina governor William Tryon, defeated at Battle of Alamance Creek.

1773

December 16 Boston Tea Party colonists objecting to tea tax dump English tea into Boston harbor.

1774

March Parliament passes Coercive Acts (Intolerable Acts).

September First Continental Congress convenes in Philadelphia; delegates approve Suffolk Resolves, declaring "murderous" Intolerable Acts unconstitutional.

1775

April 14 First American slavery abolition society organized in Pennsylvania.

April 19 Battles of Lexington and Concord between American militia and British troops occur; Boston placed under siege by colonists.

May Second Continental Congress convenes.

1776

January Thomas Paine's pamphlet *Common Sense* published.

March 17 British troops evacuate Boston.

July 2 First colonial statute granting woman's suffrage passed in New Jersey; remains in effect until reversed in 1807.

July 4 Continental Congress approves Declaration of Independence.

1777

October 4 Washington defeated in Battle of Germantown. Continental Army spends winter at Valley Forge.

October 17 General Horatio Gates scores a major American victory in Battle of Saratoga.

November 17 Continental Congress approves Articles of Confederation.

1778

February 6 France and U.S. sign treaty of alliance.

July–November Joseph Brant leads Iroquois attacks against American settlers in New York and Pennsylvania.

1781

March 1 Articles of Confederation become effective following Maryland's ratification.

October 17 British general Charles Cornwallis surrenders to combined American-French force at Yorktown.

1783

May 30 First daily American newspaper, *Pennsylvania Evening Post*, begins publication.

September 3 Peace treaty signed by U.S. and Great Britain.

Summer *The American Speller* by Noah Webster published.

1784

January Economic depression begins.

March Virginia surrenders to Congress its territory northwest of Ohio River.

June 26 Spain closes New Orleans to American shipping.

1785

May Ordinance of 1785 creates system for surveying and selling western lands.

1786

January 1 Virginia enacts statute for religious freedom drafted by Thomas Jefferson.

August Shays's Rebellion erupts in western Massachusetts.

1787

January Shays's Rebellion routed by Massachusetts militia.

May 25 Constitutional Convention opens at Philadelphia.

July 13 Enactment of Northwest Ordinance determines government of lands north of Ohio River.

September 17 Constitutional Convention completed; delegates sign Constitution and send to states for ratification.

1788

May *The Federalist* by James Madison, Alexander Hamilton, and John Jay published in book form.

June 21 Constitution goes into effect as New Hampshire becomes ninth state to ratify.

1789

March First Congress under Constitution convenes in New York.

April 30 George Washington inaugurated in New York as first president of United States.

September 25 Bill of Rights approved by both houses of Congress.

November 21 North Carolina ratifies Constitution and enters Union.

1790

January 9 Alexander Hamilton submits "Report on the Public Credit" to Congress.

1791

March 4 Vermont enters Union as fourteenth state.

December 12 Bank of United States opens.

December 15 Bill of Rights becomes law with Virginia's ratification.

1792

Winter Federalists and Democratic Republicans emerge as opposing political parties.

June 1 Kentucky enters Union.

December 5 Washington reelected president.

1793

April Eli Whitney invents cotton gin.

May Washington's administration proclaims U.S. neutral in war between Great Britain and France.

1794

August U.S. defeats Miami Indians at Battle of Fallen Timbers in Ohio Valley; subsequent treaty cedes substantial new lands to U.S.

1795

June Senate ratifies Jay Treaty with Great Britain.

October Pinckney's Treaty secures Mississippi navigation rights from Spain.

1796

June 1 Tennessee enters Union.

September Washington's Farewell Address published.

December 7 John Adams elected president.

1797

March 4 John Adams inaugurated president.

1798

June–July Congress passes Alien and Sedition Acts in effort to suppress dissent.

1798–1800

July 11 U.S. and France fight Quasi-War.

PREFACE

Relations between Great Britain and its thirteen American colonies began to break down in the mid-1700s, as British efforts to tighten control were resisted by colonists accustomed to running their own affairs. Disputes over taxation and other issues eventually turned into war in April 1775, with the Americans deciding on July 4, 1776, to declare independence. That bold (and disputed) decision was just the beginning of a significant series of turning points and challenges facing the Americans. In the quest to become a new and independent nation the former colonists defeated the world's mightiest military empire in battle, negotiated alliances with other nations, coped with the economic dislocations of war and independence, replaced the colonial governments with new state constitutions, and created a new national constitution and national government. Throughout this time the American people strongly disagreed about many issues concerning the break with Great Britain and on what kind of new nation should be created once independence was declared.

THE MATURING AMERICAN COLONIES

By the middle of the eighteenth century the thirteen British colonies were well on their way to becoming established and mature societies. The population of the colonies tripled from 330,000 in 1714 to 1 million in 1744, and continued to double every twenty-six years. The major factors in the population growth were America's large families and low mortality rates (relative to Europe). Colonial women averaged eight children and forty-two grandchildren. Another important factor was immigration, which became less English-centered in the eighteenth century. From 1713 to 1753 the colonies absorbed 350,000 immigrant newcomers, including approximately 65,000 Germans, 65,000 "Scotch-Irish" (Scottish Presbyterians who had settled in Northern Ireland), and 33,000 Irish. Immigrants also came from France, the Netherlands, and other countries. The largest single group of newcomers were the 140,000 Africans brought to America as slaves.

Many of the new immigrants settled in the Piedmont region along the eastern slope of the Appalachian Mountains. In contrast to 1713, when most colonists lived within fifty miles of the Atlantic coast, one-third of the colonists in 1753 lived and farmed in the Piedmont. The average standard of living of the colonists equaled that of England and exceeded that found in Scotland and Ireland. Literacy was widespread in America, especially in the northern colonies.

BRITISH RULE IN THE 1700S

To govern this realm, Great Britain (created by the 1707 union of England and Scotland) relied on two London-based institutions: a Privy Council to review and sometimes veto colonial laws and a Board of Trade to regulate and enforce British trading rules designed to enrich Great Britain. These governing bodies, however, often received scant attention from the British government and were thus often ineffectual.

In addition to these institutions, Great Britain was represented in the colonies by colonial governors. Appointed in eleven of the thirteen colonies by the British monarch or colonial proprietors, governors in turn appointed the council, or upper house of the colonial legislature, and had the official power to veto legislation and to call or dismiss legislative sessions. However, the governors depended on the colonial assemblies for their salaries. In most colonies in the 1700s the lower house of the colonial assemblies, the only representative instrument of the colonists, grew increasingly assertive in using their control over governors' salaries. They forced governors to sign laws opposed in England and in general governed as they saw fit. In two colonies, Rhode Island and Connecticut, the assembly actually elected the governor.

By the 1760s the leaders of the colonies came to believe that, as Englishmen, they possessed certain fundamental rights of self-government that could not be rescinded. On the other hand, British authorities held that colonial self-government was a mere privilege that could be rescinded unilaterally by the Crown or Parliament.

THE FRENCH AND INDIAN WAR

A pivotal event in the relationship between Great Britain and the colonies was the French and Indian War (known in Europe as the Seven Years' War). Part of a larger conflict fought in Europe, India, and elsewhere, the war from the American colonists' perspective was the culmination of a long struggle between Great Britain and France for control of North America. In 1749 France began construction of a chain of forts in the Ohio Valley in territory claimed by both Great Britain and France. Despite early defeats of Virginia militia (commanded by George Washington) and British troops by the French and their Indian allies, Great Britain eventually prevailed. In the 1763 Treaty of Paris, Great Britain acquired all French territory on the North American continent.

Ironically, Britain's defeat of France planted the seeds for eventual American independence. Free from the need for protection from the French threat, colonists in America were emboldened to pursue an independent course. In addition, the immense debt Great Britain had incurred to pay the costs of the French and Indian War convinced members of the British Parliament to attempt to tighten their control and raise revenues from the colonists— actions which soon sparked protest in the colonies.

TAXES AND PROTEST

Beginning in 1763 the British Parliament, at the urging of King George III, passed a series of laws designed to raise revenues from the thirteen colonies and to strengthen British control over them. Parliament voted to maintain a standing army in America, mandated that colonists provide British soldiers with living quarters and supplies, and proclaimed that colonists may not settle west of the Appalachian Mountains until treaties with the Native Americans there could be made. The 1764 Sugar Act strengthened enforcement of laws against trade between the colonies and non-British Caribbean islands. The 1764 Currency Act restricted the ability of colonial assemblies to create paper money.

The single most objectionable act, in the minds of many colonists, was the 1765 Stamp Act, which imposed a tax on all legal documents, pamphlets, almanacs, business licenses, and other items. Many Americans, noting that they had no representatives in Parliament, adopted the slogan of "no taxation without representation." Colonists organized economic boycotts against British goods. Secret clubs called Sons of Liberty engaged in violence and threats of violence to prevent enforcement of the Stamp Act. The Virginia Assembly, led by Patrick Henry, passed resolutions against taxation by the British Parliament. Representatives of nine colonies met in October 1765 in the Stamp Act Congress and petitioned Parliament to repeal the measure. Parliament repealed the Stamp Act in 1766 but also passed a resolution affirming parliamentary authority over the colonies "in all cases whatsoever."

Parliament again asserted its tax authority in 1767 by passing the Townshend Acts, which created import duties on several British goods. Again the colonists protested, pamphlets and newspapers decried the measure, and a boycott of British goods was organized. Parliament backed down and repealed the taxes but refused to cede the principle of its authority to tax by retaining a small tax on tea. This tax, coupled with British efforts to give a British trading company a monopoly in the American tea trade, inspired perhaps the most significant single act of colonial tax resistance: the 1773 Boston Tea Party, in which a group of colonists boarded British ships in Boston Harbor and threw the tea overboard.

The disputes over taxes reflected a deeper division over political authority. The British held that all parts of the British Empire had to yield to the ultimate authority of Parliament, whether they elected members to it or not (many cities in Great Britain, for instance, did not send members to Parliament). But many colonists held that although the colonies should maintain loyalty to the Crown, political authority in the colonies lay with each colonial assembly. Many Americans cited English political writers, such as John Locke, Thomas Gordon, and Joseph Priestley, to justify their views.

THE INTOLERABLE ACTS

Parliament responded to the Boston Tea Party by passing a series of measures designed to punish Massachusetts. Known in America as the Intolerable Acts, these included closing the port of Boston, requiring the quartering of additional British troops, and increasing the powers of the governor. In an unrelated action (but quickly linked to these punitive measures by many concerned Americans), Parliament passed the Quebec Act to govern its Canadian territories. This act nullified the western land claims of several American colonies by extending the boundaries of Quebec south to the Ohio River and west to the Mississippi.

Leaders in several colonies had by this time established "committees of correspondence" and other political organizations to communicate with each other and to act collectively. In September 1774 the trend toward political union took a further step with the convention of the First Continental Congress in Philadelphia, a gathering of delegates for the purpose of formulating a united colonial response to the Intolerable Acts. Elected by colonial assemblies, many of which were meeting without authorization from the colonial governor, and at other extralegal meetings, few delegates at this time supported American independence; the goal was to express and gain redress for grievances against Great Britain. They expressed these grievances in a petition to King George III that attacked virtually all of Parliament's actions since 1763. The delegates resolved to boycott imported British goods and adjourned after determining to meet again in May 1775 if their concerns had not been addressed.

THE DECISION FOR INDEPENDENCE

When the Second Continental Congress convened as planned on May 10, 1775, the first battles of the Revolutionary War had already been fought. British troops sent from Boston to capture military supplies had exchanged fire with Massachusetts militia (called minutemen) in Lexington and Concord on April 19. By April 20 an army of twenty thousand New England patriots was besieging the British garrison in Boston.

The Second Continental Congress continued to debate independence. King George III declared the colonies in a state of rebellion in December 1775. In January 1776 Thomas Paine's pamphlet *Common Sense* was published and sold thousands of copies. Paine's arguments convinced many Americans of the need for a total break from Great Britain. On July 2 the Continental Congress adopted the resolution "that these United Colonies are, and, of right, ought to be, free and independent states." On July 4 they passed the Declaration of Independence, penned by Thomas Jefferson, to explain to the world the reasons for their decision for independence and war.

THE REVOLUTIONARY WAR

The American Revolution had three interrelated components. First, it was a military confrontation between Great Britain and the colonies. It was also a continuation of the struggles between Great Britain and France, with France allying itself with the Americans to avenge defeat in previous wars with Britain. Lastly, the American Revolution was a civil war, with the American population divided between supporters of Great Britain (loyalists) and supporters of independence.

The military confrontation seemed a mismatch. On one side was the British Empire with the powerful British navy and one of the world's leading professional armies. The population of the British Isles in 1776 was 11.5 million, compared to 2.5 million colonists (of which a third were either loyalists or slaves). The armed forces the colonies were able to muster lacked training, experienced officers, naval support, equipment, and money. The Continental Army led by George Washington was defeated repeatedly by British forces in the early years of the war. However, the Americans did have the advantage of fighting on their home territory. The British were fighting in unfamiliar and often unfriendly circumstances and had to be equipped and supplied from abroad. Washington was able to achieve his underlying objective of keeping his forces together and prolonging the war until the British no longer wished to fight.

Diplomacy played a major role in the American Revolution, as many European nations, envious and fearful of Great Britain's worldwide power, took various steps to ensure British defeat and American victory. The most significant of these nations was France. Eager for British defeat, the French government secretly supplied much of the munitions used by the Americans in the first years of the war. In 1778, following American victory in Saratoga, New York, France openly allied itself with the rebelling colonies. French naval and armed forces were instrumental in the Battle of Yorktown in 1781, the last major battle of the war and one of the few outright victories for the Americans.

The Revolutionary War was in some respects a civil war. Many of the colonists remained loyal to Great Britain or were indifferent. The British had planned to enlist the help of loyalists (or Tories), who totaled about a quarter of the American population. Loyalists were drawn from all social ranks and classes, ranging from prominent landowners to African slaves and members of ethnic and religious minorities. Nevertheless, the effectiveness of loyalists in helping the British was hampered by three factors: the vigilant actions of the local patriot (Whig) militia, the cruelty of many English soldiers toward the American populace, and the decision of about one hundred thousand loyalists to flee the country during the Revolutionary War.

THE STATE CONSTITUTIONS AND THE ARTICLES OF CONFEDERATION

While the military battles, the diplomatic maneuverings, and the clashes between Whigs and loyalists proceeded, the new United States of America attempted to create a government. All thirteen former colonies had formulated and passed new state constitutions before the Revolutionary War was over. Most of these constitutions included guarantees of civil liberties, including freedom of speech, religion, and the press; many extended suffrage to most white male taxpayers. Meanwhile the Continental Congress, without formal and defined powers, took on more of the trappings and duties of a national government: It created and supplied the Continental Army (with George Washington as commander in chief), issued paper currency, established a post office, and oversaw diplomatic efforts. In 1777 the national body approved the Articles of Confederation. Ratified by all the states by 1781, the Articles formalized some of the powers Congress was already using and created a central government—but a government sharply limited in its powers to tax American citizens or directly regulate the states. Sovereignty and political authority remained with the states and the colonial assemblies that governed them—a deliberate decision by Americans who did not want independence from Britain only to be ruled by a new, large, remote, and potentially tyrannical government.

The major legislative achievements of the Confederation Congress were the Land Ordinance in 1785 and the Northwest Ordinance in 1787. These laws provided for the orderly surveying, sale, and governing of the western territories. The Northwest Ordinance was notable for establishing the principle that these territories should eventually enter the Union as states fully equal to the original thirteen and for banning slavery in the new territories.

POSTWAR PROBLEMS

Great Britain formally recognized American independence in the Treaty of Paris in 1783, in which the United States also gained western territory bordered by Canada to the north, Florida to the south, and the Mississippi River to the west. However, the new nation of nine hundred thousand square miles and three million people faced several significant difficulties. An economic depression hit the new nation in 1784, aggravated by the loss of trading privileges with the British West Indies and of British naval protection against North African pirates. Commerce was also hurt by Spain's closure of the Mississippi River to American goods and by the fact that each state set its own tariff rate (the national government under the Articles of Confederation had no authority to regulate trade). The Confederation Congress, unable to levy taxes, could neither support its issued currency nor meet payments on domestic or foreign debt. Diplomacy faltered because the national government was unable to enforce any obligations it entered into with foreign nations. State laws and taxes pitted debtors against creditors. Shays's Rebellion, in which Massachusetts farmers in 1786 violently resisted tax and debt collection, alarmed many Americans fearful of anarchy. Congress also proved unable to respond to conflicts between Native Americans and the rapidly increasing number of white settlers moving west. Attempts to amend the Articles fell short of the required unanimous consent of the states.

In May 1787 leading American figures gathered in Philadelphia to devise a replacement for the Articles of Confederation. The result of their deliberations was the U.S. Constitution. The Philadelphia meeting had been proposed in 1786 at an earlier convention, called by Virginia to discuss problems of interstate commerce. The delegates of the Philadelphia convention, which included such noted national figures as George Washington, Benjamin Franklin, and James Madison, decided to go beyond merely revising the Articles of Confederation by devising a whole new system of government.

The document they created differed from the Articles of Confederation in several important respects. It created a national government with powers to tax and regulate commerce, whose laws would be held supreme over conflicting state laws. States would be forbidden from conducting foreign policy, coining money, or setting tariff rates. Unlike the Articles of Confederation, which concentrated legislative, judicial, and executive functions in Congress, the Constitution established three separate branches of government. In the Confederation Congress each state had one vote; the Constitution, in a crucial compromise, created a divided legislature in which each state had two votes in the Senate, but votes relative to its population in the House of Representatives.

RATIFICATION OF
THE CONSTITUTION

Many Americans had been generally satisfied with the government under the Articles of Confederation and were highly suspicious of this attempt to create a new and more powerful central government. The ratification of the Constitution—a step that required the approval of special ratifying conventions by nine of the thirteen states—was marked by an intense public controversy that featured hundreds of newspaper articles and pamphlets debating the merits and demerits of the Constitution. Opponents of the Constitution—termed anti-federalists—criticized the creation of what they viewed as a potentially tyrannical government with supremacy over the states. Many criticized the lack of a bill of rights. In Massachusetts and other states, passage was secured after supporters of the Constitution (federalists) pledged to immediately amend the Constitution by adding a bill of rights. Due in large part to this promise, the Constitution was successfully ratified in 1788. The new Congress passed ten amendments (drafted largely by James Madison) in 1789; they were ratified in 1791 and are known today as the Bill of Rights.

EARLY DOMESTIC AND FOREIGN
POLICY DISPUTES

The first government under the new Constitution assembled in New York City in 1789. George Washington, the nation's first president, took care to appoint to his administration people who had supported the Constitution. Yet this did not prevent divisions within America's government and Washington's administration over important public policy decisions involving foreign policy and finance. Relations with France, Great Britain, and Spain were difficult, especially after those three nations went to war with each other in 1793. The people Washington appointed, especially Secretary of the Treasury Alexander Hamilton and Secretary of State Thomas Jefferson, differed over which nation to support, as well as such issues as the creation of a national bank and the funding of the national debt.

Two political camps emerged within Washington's administration. One, led by Hamilton, advocated a strong and vigorous national government and generally backed Great Britain in foreign policy. The other, led by Jefferson and James Madison, then a member of the House of Representatives, advocated a weaker central government and favored France in foreign disputes. The differences signaled the emergence of opposing political parties—the Federalists, led by Hamilton, and the Democratic-Republicans, led by Jefferson. This development was something the makers of the Constitution did not anticipate. Political parties were bitterly attacked by George Washington in his Farewell Address in 1796. Their emergence clearly shows that the momentous decision for independence, the victorious war with Great Britain, and the successful creation of the Constitution did not mark the end of political controversy within the United States.

THE DECISION TO BREAK FROM GREAT BRITAIN

Viewpoint 10A

Parliament Is Abusing the Rights of Americans (1764)

Stephen Hopkins (1707–1785)

INTRODUCTION *Between 1763 and 1765 the British Parliament passed a series of controversial laws meant to recover costs from the French and Indian War. Among these laws were trade regulations and the Stamp Act, a direct tax colonists had to pay on legal documents, pamphlets, and newspapers. The following viewpoint is excerpted from one of the many pamphlets written at this time protesting these new British policies. The author, Stephen Hopkins, was then the colonial governor of Rhode Island. Unlike the governors of most other colonies, who were appointed by the colony's proprietor or by the king or queen of England, Rhode Island's governor was elected by members of its colonial assembly.*

The Rights of Colonists Examined was highly acclaimed and reprinted several times in the colonies and in Great Britain. In it Hopkins argues that Americans share with the citizens of Great Britain the same rights and liberties protected by the British constitution (the fundamental rights and freedoms that had evolved in English common law over the previous centuries). Hopkins asserts that recent British actions such as the Stamp Act jeopardize those rights. Leading colonists organized political protests and economic boycotts against the Stamp Act; Parliament repealed the controversial tax in 1766.

Hopkins did not originally advocate American independence from Great Britain. By 1776, however, he had changed his mind and was one of the signers of the Declaration of Independence.

How does Hopkins define liberty? What is it about taxes that he finds objectionable? What appeal does he make to the British Parliament?

Liberty is the greatest blessing that men enjoy, and slavery the heaviest curse that human nature is capable of.—This being so, makes it a matter of the utmost importance to men, which of the two shall be their portion.

Absolute liberty is, perhaps, incompatible with any kind of government.—The safety resulting from society, and the advantage of just and equal laws, hath caused men to forego some part of their natural liberty, and submit to government. This appears to be the most rational account of its beginning; although, it must be confessed, mankind have by no means been agreed about it. Some have found its origin in the divine appointment; others have thought it took its rise from power; enthusiasts have dreamed that dominion was founded in grace. Leaving these points to be settled [in the future], we will consider the British constitution, as it at present stands, on revolution principles; and from thence endeavor to find the measure of the magistrate's power and the people's obedience.

This glorious constitution, the best that ever existed among men, will be confessed by all, to be founded by compact, and established by consent of the people. By this most beneficent compact, British subjects are governed only agreeable to laws to which themselves have some way consented; and are not to be compelled to part with their property, but as it is called for by the authority of such laws. The former, is truly liberty; the latter is really to be possessed of property, and to have something that may be called one's own.

THE RIGHTS OF COLONISTS

On the contrary, those who are governed at the will of another, or of others, and whose property may be taken from them by taxes, or otherwise, without their own consent, and against their will, are in the miserable condition of slaves. "For liberty solely consists in an independency upon the will of another; and by the name of slave, we understand a man who can neither dispose of his person or goods, but enjoys all at the will of his master," says [Algernon] Sidney, on government. These things premised, whether the British American colonies, on the continent, are justly entitled to like privileges and freedom as their fellow subjects in Great Britain are, shall be the chief point examined. In discussing this question, we shall make the colonies in New England, with whose rights we are best acquainted, the rule of our reasoning; not in the least doubting but all the others are justly entitled to like rights with them.

New England was first planted by adventurers, who left England, their native country, by permission of King Charles the First; and, at their own expense, transported themselves to America, with great risk and difficulty settled among savages, and in a very surprising manner formed new colonies in the wilderness. Before their departure, the terms of their freedom, and the

From *The Rights of Colonists Examined* by Stephen Hopkins (Providence, RI: 1764). Reprinted in *Records of the Colony of Rhode Island and the Providence Plantations*, vol. 6, edited by John R. Bartlett (Providence, 1861).

relation they should stand in to the mother country, in their emigrant state, were fully settled; they were to remain subject to the King, and dependent on the kingdom of Great Britain. In return, they were to receive protection, and enjoy all the rights and privileges of free-born Englishmen.

THE COLONIAL CHARTERS

This is abundantly proved by the charter given to the Massachusetts colony, while they were still in England, and which they received and brought over with them, as the authentic evidence of the conditions they removed upon. The colonies of Connecticut and Rhode Island, also, afterwards obtained charters from the crown, granting them the like ample privileges. By all these charters, it is in the most express and solemn manner granted, that these adventurers, and their children after them for ever, should have and enjoy all the freedom and liberty that the subjects in England enjoy; that they might make laws for their own government, suitable to their circumstances not repugnant to, but as near as might be, agreeable to the laws of England; that they might purchase lands, acquire goods, and use trade for their advantage, and have an absolute property in whatever they justly acquired. These, with many other gracious privileges, were granted them by several kings; and they were to pay, as an acknowledgment to the crown, only one-fifth part of the ore of gold and silver, that should at any time be found in the said colonies, in lieu of, and full satisfaction for, all dues and demands of the crown and kingdom of England upon them.

There is not any thing new or extraordinary in these rights granted to the British colonies; the colonies from all countries, at all times, have enjoyed equal freedom with the mother state. Indeed, there would be found very few people in the world, willing to leave their native country, and go through the fatigue and hardship of planting in a new uncultivated one, for the sake of losing their freedom. They who settle new countries, must be poor; and, in course, ought to be free. Advantages, pecuniary or agreeable, are not on the side of emigrants; and surely they must have something in their stead....

EQUAL LIBERTY

If it were possible a doubt could yet remain, in the most unbelieving mind, that these British colonies are not every way justly and fully entitled to equal liberty and freedom with their fellow subjects in Europe, we might show, that the parliament of Great Britain, have always understood their rights in the same light.

By an act passed in the thirteenth year of the reign of his late majesty King George the Second, entitled an act for naturalizing foreign protestants, &c.; and by another act passed in the twentieth year of the same reign, for nearly the same purposes, by both which it is enacted and ordained, "that all foreign protestants, who had inhabited, and resided for the space of seven years, or more, in any of his majesty's colonies, in America," might, on the conditions therein mentioned, be naturalized and thereupon should "be deemed, adjudged and taken to be his majesty's natural born subjects of the kingdom of Great Britain, to all intents, constructions and purposes, as if they, and every one of them, had been, or were born within the same." No reasonable man will here suppose the parliament intended by these acts to put foreigners, who had been in the colonies only seven years, in a better condition than those who had been born in them, or had removed from Britain thither, but only to put these foreigners on an equality with them; and to do this, they are obliged to give them all the rights of natural born subjects of Great Britain.

From what hath been shown, it will appear beyond a doubt, that the British subjects in America, have equal rights with those in Britain; that they do not hold those rights as a privilege granted them, nor enjoy them as a grace and favor bestowed; but possess them as an inherent indefeasible right, as they, and their ancestors, were free-born subjects, justly and naturally entitled to all the rights and advantages of the British constitution....

We believe no good reason can be given, why the colonies should not ... inquire, what right the parliament of Great Britain have to tax them.

UNFAIR TAXES

The resolution of the house of commons, ... asserting their rights to establish stamp duties, and internal taxes, to be collected in the colonies without their own consent, hath much more, and for much more reason, alarmed the British subjects in America, than any thing that had ever been done before. These resolutions, carried into execution, the colonies cannot help but consider as a manifest violation of their just and long enjoyed rights. For it must be confessed by all men, that they who are taxed at pleasure by others, cannot possibly have any property, can have nothing to be called their own; they who have no property, can have no freedom, but are indeed reduced to the most abject slavery; are in a condition far worse than countries conquered and made tributary; for these have only a fixed sum to pay, which they are left to raise among themselves, in the way that they may think most equal and easy; and having paid the stipulated sum, the debt is discharged, and what is left is their own. This is much more tolerable than to be taxed at the mere will of others, without any bounds, without any stipulation and agreement, contrary to their consent, and against their will. . . .

But it will be said, that the monies drawn from the colonies by duties, and by taxes, will be laid up and set apart to be used for their future defence. This will not at all alleviate the hardship, but serves only more strongly to mark the servile state of the people. Free people have ever thought, and always will think, that the money necessary for their defence, lies safest in their own hands, until it be wanted immediately for that purpose. To take the money of the Americans, which they want continually to use in their trade, and lay it up for their defence, at a thousand leagues distance from them, when the enemies they have to fear, are in their own neighborhood, hath not the greatest probability of friendship or of prudence. . . . We believe no good reason can be given, why the colonies should not modestly and soberly inquire, what right the parliament of Great Britain have to tax them. We know such inquiries, by a late letter writer, have been branded with the little epithet of *mushroom policy;* and he insinuates, that for the colonies to pretend to claim any privileges, will draw down the resentment of the parliament on them—Is the defence of liberty become so contemptible, and pleading for just rights so dangerous? Can the guardians of liberty be thus ludicrous? Can the patrons of freedom be so jealous and so severe? If the British house of commons are rightfully possessed of a power to tax the colonies in America, this power must be vested in them by the British constitution, as they are one branch of the great legislative body of the nation; as they are the representatives of all the people in Britain, they have, beyond doubt, all the power such a representation can possibly give; yet, great as this power is, surely it cannot exceed that of their constituents. And can it possibly be shown that the people in Britain have a sovereign authority over their fellow subjects in America? Yet such is the authority that must be exercised in taking peoples' estates from them by taxes, or otherwise, without their consent.

If the colonies are not taxed by parliament, are they therefore exempted from bearing their proper share in the necessary burdens of government? This by no means follows. Do they not support a regular internal government in each colony, as expensive to the people here, as the internal government of Britain is to the people there? Have not the colonies here, at all times when called upon by the crown, raised money for the public service, done it as cheerfully as the parliament have done on like occasions? Is not this the most easy, the most natural, and most constitutional way of raising money in the colonies? What occasion then to distrust the colonies? What necessity to fall on an invidious and unconstitutional method, to compel them to do what they have ever done freely? Are not the people in the colonies as loyal and dutiful subjects as any age or nation ever produced? And are they not as useful to the kingdom, in this remote quarter of the world, as their fellow subjects are who dwell in Britain? The parliament, it is confessed, have power to regulate the trade of the whole empire; and hath it not full power, by this means, to draw all the money and all the wealth of the colonies into the mother country, at pleasure? What motive, after all this, can remain, to induce the parliament to abridge the privileges, and lessen the rights of the most loyal and dutiful subjects; subjects justly entitled to ample freedom, who have long enjoyed, and not abused or forfeited their liberties; who have used them to their own advantage, in dutiful subserviency to the orders and interests of Great Britain? Why should the gentle current of tranquillity, that has so long run with peace through all the British states, and flowed with joy and with happiness in all her countries, be at last obstructed, be turned out of its true course, into unusual and winding channels, by which many of those states must be ruined; but none of them can possibly be made more rich or more happy? . . .

FAITHFUL SUBJECTS

We finally beg leave to assert, that the first planters of these colonies were pious christians; were faithful subjects; who, with a fortitude and perseverance little known, and less considered, settled these wild countries, by God's goodness, and their own amazing labors; thereby added a most valuable dependence to the crown of Great Britain; were ever dutifully subservient to her interests; so taught their children, that not one has been disaffected to this day; but all have honestly obeyed every royal command, and cheerfully submitted to every constitutional law; have as little inclination as they have ability, to throw off their dependency; have carefully avoided every offensive measure, and every interdicted manufacture; have risked their lives as they have been ordered, and furnished their money when it has been called for; have never been troublesome or expensive to the mother country; have kept due order, and supported a regular government; have maintained peace, and practiced christianity; and in all conditions, and in every relation, have demeaned [conducted] themselves as loyal, as dutiful, and as faithful subjects ought; and that no kingdom or state hath, or ever had, colonies more quiet, more obedient, or more profitable, than these have ever been.

May the same divine goodness, that guided the first planters, protected the settlements, inspired kings to be gracious, parliaments to be tender, ever preserve, ever support our present gracious King; give great wisdom to his ministers, and much understanding to his parliaments; perpetuate the sovereignty of the British constitution, and the filial dependency and happiness of all the colonies.

Viewpoint 10B

Parliament Is Not Abusing the Rights of Americans (1765)

Martin Howard (ca. 1720–1781)

INTRODUCTION *In February 1765 a pamphlet was published sharply attacking Stephen Hopkins's tract* The Rights of Colonists Examined, *in which the Rhode Island governor asserted that American colonists had the same political rights as Englishmen (see viewpoint 10A). The anonymous author purported to be a gentleman from Halifax, Nova Scotia, but was in fact Martin Howard, a Newport, Rhode Island, resident and a political opponent of Hopkins. In his pamphlet, excerpted here, Howard sharply attacks both Hopkins's writing style and his arguments. Howard asserts that the political rights of colonists are limited by the colonial charters, and he refutes Hopkins's contention that Americans share equal rights with the English. His sympathies toward Great Britain known (despite the use of a pseudonym in this instance), Howard was forced to flee Rhode Island after being attacked by mobs during the August 1765 Stamp Act riots.*

What distinctions does Howard make between personal and political rights? How does he respond to the argument that colonists cannot be taxed by Parliament without representation in that body? How popular does Howard believe to be his own views in the colonies?

My Dear Sir,

I thank you very kindly for the pamphlets and newspapers you was so obliging as to send me. I will, according to your request, give you a few miscellaneous strictures on that pamphlet, wrote by Mr. *H—p—s*, your governor, entitled *The Rights of Colonies Examined....*

The Rights of Colonies Examined is a labored, ostentatious piece, discovers its author to be totally unacquainted with style or diction, and eagerly fond to pass upon the world for a man of letters....

However disguised, polished, or softened the expression of this pamphlet may seem, yet everyone must see that its professed design is sufficiently prominent throughout, namely, to prove *that the colonies have rights independent of, and not controllable by the authority of Parliament.* It is upon this dangerous and indiscreet position I shall communicate to you my real sentiments....

——————■——————

The colonists have no rights independent of their charters.

——————■——————

From *A Letter from a Gentleman at Halifax, to His Friend in Rhode Island, Containing Remarks upon a Pamphlet Entitled "The Rights of Colonists Examined"* by Martin Howard.

PERSONAL AND POLITICAL RIGHTS

The several New England charters ascertain, define, and limit the respective rights and privileges of each colony, and I cannot conceive how it has come to pass that the colonies now claim any other or greater rights than are therein expressly granted to them. I fancy when we speak or think of the rights of freeborn Englishmen, we confound those rights which are personal with those which are political: there is a distinction between these which ought always to be kept in view.

Our personal rights, comprehending those of life, liberty, and estate, are secured to us by the common law, which is every subject's birthright, whether born in Great Britain, on the ocean, or in the colonies; and it is in this sense we are said to enjoy all the rights and privileges of Englishmen. The political rights of the colonies or the powers of government communicated to them are more limited, and their nature, quality, and extent depend altogether upon the patent or charter which first created and instituted them. As individuals, the colonists participate of every blessing the English constitution can give them: as corporations created by the crown, they are confined within the primitive views of their institution. Whether, therefore, their indulgence is scanty or liberal can be no cause of complaint; for when they accepted of their charters they tacitly submitted to the terms and conditions of them.

The colonies have no rights independent of their charters; they can claim no greater than those give them; by those the Parliamentary jurisdiction over them is not taken away, neither could any grant of the King abridge that jurisdiction, because it is founded upon common law, as I shall presently show, and was prior to any charter or grant to the colonies: every Englishman, therefore, is subject to this jurisdiction, and it follows him wherever he goes. It is of the essence of government that there should be a supreme head, and it would be a solecism in politics to talk of members independent of it.

With regard to the jurisdiction of Parliament, I shall endeavor to show that it is attached to every English subject wherever he be, and I am led to do this from a clause in page nine of His Honor's pamphlet, where he says "That the colonies do not hold their rights as a privilege granted them, nor enjoy them as a grace and favor bestowed, but possess them as an inherent, indefeasible right." This postulatum cannot be true with regard to political rights, for I have already shown that these are derived from your charters, and are held by force of the King's grant; therefore these inherent, indefeasible rights, as His Honor calls them, must be personal ones, according to the distinction already made. Permit me to say that inherent and indefeasible as these rights may be, the jurisdiction of Parliament over every English subject is equally as inherent and indefeasible: that both have grown out of the same stock, and that if we avail ourselves of the one we must submit to and acknowledge the other.

It might here be properly enough asked, Are these personal rights self-existent? Have they no original some? I answer, They are derived from the constitution of England, which is the common law; and from the same fountain is also derived the jurisdiction of Parliament over us.

BRITISH COMMON LAW

But to bring this argument down to the most vulgar apprehension: The common law has established it as a rule or maxim that the plantations are bound by British acts of Parliament if particularly named; and surely no Englishman in his senses will deny the force of a common law maxim. . . .

Can we claim the common law as an inheritance, and at the same time be at liberty to adopt one part of it and reject the other? Indeed we cannot. The common law, pure and indivisible in its nature and essence; cleaves to us during our lives and follows us from Nova Zembla to Cape Horn; and therefore, as the jurisdiction of Parliament arises out of and is supported by it, we may as well renounce our allegiance or change our nature as to be exempt from the jurisdiction of Parliament. Hence it is plain to me that in denying this jurisdiction we at the same time take leave of the common law, and thereby, with equal temerity and folly, strip ourselves of every blessing we enjoy as Englishmen: a flagrant proof, this, that shallow drafts in politics and legislation confound and distract us, and that an extravagant zeal often defeats its own purposes.

TAXATION AND REPRESENTATION

I am aware that the foregoing reasoning will be opposed by the maxim "That no Englishman can be taxed but by his own consent or by representatives."

It is this dry maxim, taken in a literal sense and ill understood, that, like the song of "Lillibullero," has made all the mischief in the colonies; and upon this the partisans of the colonies' rights chiefly rest their cause. I don't despair, however, of convincing you that this maxim affords but little support to their argument when rightly examined and explained.

It is the opinion of the House of Commons, and may be considered as a law of Parliament, that they are the representatives of every British subject, wheresoever he be. In this view of the matter, then, the aforegoing maxim is fully vindicated in practice, and the whole benefit of it, in substance and effect, extended and applied to the *colonies*. Indeed the maxim must be considered in this latitude, for in a literal sense or construction it ever was,

and ever will be, impracticable. Let me ask, Is the Isle of Man, Jersey, or Guernsey represented? What is the value or amount of each man's representation in the kingdom of Scotland, which contains near two millions of people, and yet not more than three thousand have votes in the election of members of Parliament? . . .

Suppose that this Utopian privilege of representation should take place. I question if it would answer any other purpose but to bring an expense upon the colonies, unless you can suppose that a few American members could bias the deliberations of the whole British legislature. In short, this right of representation is but a phantom, and if possessed in its full extent would be of no real advantage to the colonies. . . .

I could further urge the danger of innovations. Every change in a constitution in some degree weakens its original frame, and hence it is that legislators and statesmen are cautious in admitting them. The goodly building of the British constitution will be best secured and perpetuated by adhering to its original principles. Parliaments are not of yesterday; they are as ancient as our Saxon ancestors. Attendance in Parliament was originally a duty arising from a tenure of lands, and grew out of the feudal system, so that the privilege of sitting in it is territorial and confined to Britain only. Why should the beauty and symmetry of this body be destroyed and its purity defiled by the unnatural mixture of representatives from every part of the British dominions? *Parthians, Medes, Elamites, and the dwellers of Mesopotamia, etc.*, would not, in such a case, speak the same language. What a heterogeneous council would this form? What a monster in government would it be? In truth, my friend, the matter lies here: the freedom and happiness of every British subject depends not upon his share in elections but upon the sense and virtue of the British Parliament, and these depend reciprocally upon the sense and virtue of the whole nation. When virtue and honor are no more, the lovely frame of our constitution will be dissolved. Britain may one day be what Athens and Rome now are; but may Heaven long protract the hour!

The jurisdiction of Parliament being established, it will follow that this jurisdiction cannot be apportioned; it is transcendent and entire, and may levy internal taxes as well as regulate trade. There is no essential difference in the rights: a stamp duty is confessedly the most reasonable and equitable that can be devised, yet very far am I from desiring to see it established among us; but I fear the shaft is sped and it is now too late to prevent the blow. . . .

Believe me, my friend, it gives me great pain to see so much ingratitude in the colonies to the mother country, whose arms and money so lately rescued them from a French government. I have been told that some have gone so far as to say that they would, as things are, prefer such a government to an English one. Heaven knows I have but little malice in my heart, yet, for a moment, I ardently wish that these spurious, unworthy sons of Britain could feel the iron rod of a Spanish inquisitor or a French farmer of the revenue; it would indeed be a punishment suited to their ingratitude.

The dispute between Great Britain and the colonies consists of two parts: first, the jurisdiction of Parliament, and, secondly, the exercise of that jurisdiction. His Honor hath blended these together, and nowhere marked the division between them. The first I have principally remarked upon. As to the second, it can only turn upon the expediency or utility of those schemes which may, from time to time, be adopted by Parliament relative to the colonies. Under this head, I readily grant, they are at full liberty to remonstrate, petition, write pamphlets and newspapers without number, to prevent any improper or unreasonable imposition. Nay, I would have them do all this with that spirit of freedom which Englishmen always have, and I hope ever will, exert; but let us not use our liberty for a cloak of maliciousness. Indeed I am very sure the loyalty of the colonies has ever been irreproachable; but from the pride of some and the ignorance of others the cry against mother country has spread from colony to colony; and it is to be feared that prejudices and resentments are kindled among them which it will be difficult ever thoroughly to soothe or extinguish. It may become necessary for the supreme legislature of the nation to frame some code, and therein adjust the rights of the colonies with precision and certainty, otherwise Great Britain will always be teased with new claims about liberty and privileges.

I have no ambition in appearing in print, yet if you think what is here thrown together is fit for the public eye you are at liberty to publish it. I the more cheerfully acquiesce in this because it is with real concern I have observed that, notwithstanding the frequent abuse poured forth in pamphlets and newspapers against the mother country, not one filial pen in America hath as yet been drawn, to my knowledge, in her vindication.

FOR FURTHER READING

Bernard Bailyn, *The Ideological Origins of the American Revolution.* Enlarged ed. Cambridge, MA: Belknap Press of Harvard University Press, 1992.

Pauline Maier, *From Resistance to Revolution: Colonial Radicals and the Development of American Opposition to Britain, 1765–1776.* New York: W.W. Norton, 1991.

Edmund S. Morgan and Helen M. Morgan, *The Stamp Act Crisis: Prologue to Revolution.* Chapel Hill: University of North Carolina Press, 1995.

Andrew Stephen Walmsley, *Thomas Hutchinson and the Origins of the American Revolution.* New York: New York University Press, 1999.

Gordon S. Wood, *The American Revolution: A History.* New York: Modern Library, 2003.

The Hopkins viewpoint can be found at Gale's Eighteenth Century Collections Online, Document Number: CW3307764120

Viewpoint 11A

America Must Seek Independence of Great Britain (1776)

Thomas Paine (1737–1809)

INTRODUCTION *By the end of 1775, British and American forces had engaged in violent clashes in New England and Canada, and King George III had declared the colonies to be in a state of rebellion. Yet many colonists, including influential members of the Continental Congress, were not ready to contemplate the final step of full independence from Great Britain. Many people still professed loyalty to the king.*

Perhaps the single document most influential in persuading the American people that independence was necessary was a pamphlet first published in Philadelphia on January 10, 1776. It was quickly reprinted throughout the colonies and sold an estimated 120,000 copies over the next three months. The pamphlet was Common Sense *and the author was Thomas Paine, an impoverished writer who had moved from Great Britain to America in 1774 after a checkered career as a corset maker, customs inspector, and schoolmaster. Following the battles of Lexington and Concord in April 1775, he began to advocate total independence from Great Britain. In the following excerpts from* Common Sense, *Paine attacks the British monarchy and argues the case for independence in forthright language that many Americans found convincing.*

What economic arguments for American independence does Paine make? Why is independence inevitable, in his opinion? Which of Paine's arguments do you find most convincing? Which do you find least convincing? Why?

In the following pages I offer nothing more than simple facts, plain arguments, and common sense: and have no other preliminaries to settle with the reader, than that he will divest himself of prejudice and prepossession, and suffer his reason and his feelings to determine for themselves: that he will put on, or rather that he will not put off the true character of a man, and generously enlarge his views beyond the present day.

Volumes have been written on the subject of the struggle between England and America. Men of all ranks have embarked in the controversy, from different motives, and with various designs; but all have been ineffectual, and the period of debate is closed. Arms as the last resource decide the contest; the appeal [to arms] was the

From *Common Sense* by Thomas Paine (Philadelphia, 1776).

choice of the King, and the Continent has accepted the challenge. . . .

A GREAT CAUSE

The Sun never shined on a cause of greater worth. 'Tis not the affair of a City, a County, a Province or a Kingdom; but of a Continent—of at least one eighth part of the habitable Globe. 'Tis not the concern of a day, a year, or an age; posterity are virtually involved in the contest, and will be more or less affected even to the end of time by the proceedings now. Now is the seed time of Continental union, faith, and honour. The least fracture now, will be like a name engraved with the point of a pin on the tender rind of a young oak; the wound will enlarge with the tree, and posterity read it in full grown characters.

By referring the matter from argument to arms, a new era for politics is struck—a new method of thinking hath arisen. All plans, proposals, &c. prior to the 19th of April, i.e. to the commencement of hostilities, are like the almanacks of the last year; which tho' proper then, are superceded and useless now. Whatever was advanced by the advocates on either side of the question then, terminated in one and the same point, viz. a union with Great Britain; the only difference between the parties, was the method of effecting it; the one proposing force, the other friendship; but it hath so far happened that the first hath failed, and the second hath withdrawn her influence. . . .

I have heard it asserted by some, that as America hath flourished under her former connection with Great Britain, that the same connection is necessary towards her future happiness and will always have the same effect—Nothing can be more fallacious than this kind of argument:—we may as well assert that because a child hath thrived upon milk, that it is never to have meat, or that the first twenty years of our lives is to become a precedent for the next twenty. But even this is admitting more than is true, for I answer, roundly, that America would have flourished as much, and probably much more had no European power taken any notice of her. The commerce by which she hath enriched herself are the necessaries of life, and will always have a market while eating is the custom of Europe.

But she has protected us say some. That she hath engrossed us is true, and defended the Continent at our expence as well as her own is admitted; and she would have defended Turkey from the same motive viz. the sake of trade and dominion.

ANCIENT PREJUDICES

Alas! we have been long led away by ancient prejudices and made large sacrifices to superstition. We have boasted the protection of Great Britain, without considering, that

her motive was *interest* not *attachment*; that she did not protect us from *our enemies* on *our account*, but from *her enemies* on *her own account*, from those who had no quarrel with us on any *other account*, and who will always be our enemies on the *same account*. Let Britain wave [waive] her pretensions to the Continent, or the Continent throw off the dependance, and we should be at peace with France and Spain were they at war with Britain.

I challenge the warmest advocate for reconciliation, to shew, a single advantage for this Continent can reap, by being connected with Great Britain.

But Britain is the parent country say some. Then the more shame upon her conduct. Even brutes do not devour their young, nor savages make war upon their families; wherefore the assertion if true, turns to her reproach; but it happens not to be true, or only partly so, and the phrase, *parent* or *mother country*, hath been jesuitically adopted by the King and his parasites, with a low papistical design of gaining an unfair bias on the credulous weakness of our minds. Europe and not England is the parent country of America. This new World hath been the asylum for the persecuted lovers of civil and religious liberty from *every part* of Europe. Hither have they fled, not from the tender embraces of the mother, but from the cruelty of the monster; and it is so far true of England, that the same tyranny which drove the first emigrants from home, pursues their descendants still.

In this extensive quarter of the Globe, we forget the narrow limits of three hundred and sixty miles (the extent of England) and carry our friendship on a larger scale; we claim brotherhood with every European Christian, and triumph in the generosity of the sentiment. . . .

I challenge the warmest advocate for reconciliation, to shew, a single advantage that this Continent can reap, by being connected with Great Britain. I repeat the challenge, not a single advantage is derived. Our corn will fetch its price in any market in Europe and our imported goods must be paid for by them where we will.

But the injuries and disadvantages we sustain by that connection, are without number, and our duty to mankind at large, as well as to ourselves, instruct us to renounce the alliance: because any submission to, or dependence on Great Britain, tends directly to involve this Continent in European wars and quarrels. As Europe is our market for trade, we ought to form no political connection with any part of it. 'Tis the true interest of

America, to steer clear of European contentions, which she never can do, while by her dependance on Britain, she is made the makeweight in the scale of British politics.

Europe is too thickly planted with Kingdoms, to be long at peace, and whenever a war breaks out between England and any foreign power, the trade of America goes to ruin, *because of her connection with Britain.* The next war may not turn out like the last, and should it not, the advocates for reconciliation now, will be wishing for separation then, because neutrality in that case, would be a safer convoy than a man of war. Every thing that is right or reasonable pleads for separation. The blood of the slain, the weeping voice of nature cries, 'Tis Time To Part. Even the distance at which the Almighty hath placed England and America, is a strong and natural proof, that the authority of the one over the other, was never the design of Heaven....

The authority of Great Britain over this Continent is a form of Government which sooner or later must have an end: And a serious mind can draw no true pleasure by looking forward, under the painful and positive conviction, that what he calls "the present constitution," is merely temporary. As parents, we can have no joy, knowing that this government is not sufficiently lasting to ensure any thing which we may bequeath to posterity: And by a plain method of argument, as we are running the next generation into debt, we ought to do the work of it, otherwise we use them meanly and pitifully....

THOSE WHO ADVOCATE RECONCILIATION

Though I would carefully avoid giving unnecessary offence, yet I am inclined to believe, that all those who espouse the doctrine of reconciliation, may be included within the following descriptions. Interested men who are not to be trusted, weak men who cannot see, prejudiced men who will not see, and a certain set of moderate men who think better of the European world than it deserves; and this last class, by an ill-judged deliberation, will be the cause of more calamities to this Continent, than all the other three.

It is the good fortune of many to live distant from the scene of present sorrow; the evil is not sufficiently brought to their doors to make them feel the precariousness with which all American property is possessed. But let our imaginations transport us for a few moments to Boston [where British forces were then under siege by the Continental Army]; that seat of wretchedness will teach us wisdom, and instruct us for ever to renounce a power in whom we can have no trust. The inhabitants of that unfortunate city who but a few months ago were in ease and affluence, have now no other alternative than to stay and starve, or turn out to beg. Endangered

by the fire of their friends if they continue within the city, and plundered by government if they leave it. In their present condition they are prisoners without the hope of redemption, and in a general attack for their relief, they would be exposed to the fury of both armies....

'Tis repugnant to reason, to the universal order of things; to all examples from former ages, to suppose, that this Continent can long remain subject to any external power. The most sanguine in Britain doth not think so. The utmost stretch of human wisdom cannot at this time compass a plan, short of separation, which can promise the Continent even a year's security. Reconciliation is *now* a fallacious dream....

Every quiet method for peace hath been ineffectual. Our prayers have been rejected with disdain; and hath tended to convince us that nothing flatters vanity or confirms obstinacy in Kings more than repeated petitioning—and nothing hath contributed more, than that very measure, to make the Kings of Europe absolute....

As to government matters 'tis not in the power of Britain to do this Continent justice: the business of it will soon be too weighty and intricate to be managed with any tolerable degree of convenience, by a power so distant from us, and so very ignorant of us; for if they cannot conquer us, they cannot govern us. To be always running three or four thousand miles with a tale or a petition, waiting four or five months for an answer, which when obtained requires five or six more to explain it in, will in a few years be looked upon as folly and childishness—There was a time when it was proper, and there is a proper time for it to cease.

Small islands not capable of protecting themselves are the proper objects for government to take under their care: but there is something very absurd, in supposing a Continent to be perpetually governed by an island. In no instance hath nature made the satellite larger than its primary planet, and as England and America with respect to each other reverse the common order of nature, it is evident they belong to different systems. England to Europe: America to itself.

I am not induced by motives of pride, party or resentment to espouse the doctrine of separation and independance; I am clearly, positively, and conscientiously persuaded that 'tis the true interest of this Continent to be so; that every thing short of that is mere patchwork, that it can afford no lasting felicity,—that it is leaving the sword to our children, and shrinking back at a time, when a little more, a little farther, would have rendered this Continent the glory of the earth....

No man was a warmer wisher for reconciliation than myself, before the fatal 19th of April 1775, but the moment the event of that day was made known, I rejected the hardened, sullen tempered Pharoah of England for ever; and disdain the wretch, that with the pretended title of Father of his people can unfeelingly hear of their slaughter, and composedly sleep with their blood upon his soul.

IF RECONCILIATION WERE TO HAPPEN

But admitting that matters were now made up, what would be the event? I answer, the ruin of the Continent. And that for several reasons.

First. The powers of governing still remaining in the hands of the King, he will have a negative over the whole legislation of this Continent: and as he hath shewn himself such an inveterate enemy to liberty, and discovered such a thirst for arbitrary power; is he, or is he not, a proper man to say to these Colonies, *You shall make no laws but what I please.* And is there any inhabitant in America so ignorant, as not to know, that according to what is called the *present constitution,* that this Continent can make no laws but what the King gives leave to; and is there any man so unwise, as not to see, that (considering what has happened) he will suffer no laws to be made here, but such as suit his purpose. We may be as effectually enslaved by the want of laws in America, as by submitting to laws made for us in England. After matters are made up (as it is called) can there be any doubt, but the whole power of the crown will be exerted to keep this Continent as low and humble as possible? Instead of going forward, we shall go backward, or be perpetually quarrelling or ridiculously petitioning.—We are already greater than the King wishes us to be, and will he not hereafter endeavour to make us less. To bring the matter to one point, is the power who is jealous of our prosperity, a proper power to govern us? Whoever says *no* to this question is an *Independant,* for independancy means no more than whether we shall make our own laws, or, whether the King, the greatest enemy this Continent hath, or can have, shall tell us, *there shall be no laws but such as I like.* . . .

Secondly—That as even the best terms which we can expect to obtain, can amount to no more than a temporary expedient, or a kind of government by guardianship, which can last no longer than till the Colonies come of age, so the general face and state of things in the interim will be unsettled and unpromising. Emigrants of property will not choose to come to a country whose form of government hangs but by a thread, and who is every day tottering on the brink of commotion and disturbance. And numbers of the present inhabitants would lay hold of the interval to dispose of their effects, and quit the Continent.

But the most powerful of all arguments is, that nothing but independance i.e. a Continental form of government, can keep the peace of the Continent and preserve it inviolate from civil wars. I dread the event of a reconciliation with Britain now, as it is more than probable, that it will be followed by a revolt some where or other, the consequences of which may be far more fatal than all the malice of Britain. . . .

Oye that love mankind! Ye that dare oppose not only the tyranny but the tyrant, stand forth! Every spot of the old world is over-run with oppression. Freedom hath been hunted round the Globe. Asia and Africa have long expelled her. Europe regards her like a stranger, and England hath given her warning to depart. O! receive the fugitive, and prepare in time an asylum for mankind.

Viewpoint 11B

America Must Reconcile with Great Britain (1776)

Charles Inglis (1734–1816)

INTRODUCTION *Thomas Paine's 1776 tract* Common Sense *inspired the writing of pamphlets rebutting its arguments for American independence. The following viewpoint is taken from one such pamphlet, written by Charles Inglis. Inglis, born in Ireland, first arrived in Pennsylvania in 1755 as a missionary to the Mohawk Indians. Ordained as an Anglican clergyman in 1758 and assigned to Trinity Church in New York City in 1764, Inglis was a prolific writer of essays who consistently opposed American independence. Inglis's 1776 pamphlet,* The True Interest of America Impartially Stated, in Certain Strictures on a Pamphlet Intitled Common Sense, *begins by listing the advantages Inglis believes the colonies would derive from reconciling with Great Britain. He goes on to list the disadvantages and calamities he believes would result from pursuing independence. Inglis was banished to England in 1783 because of his Loyalist views; he later moved to the Canadian province of Nova Scotia and served as its Anglican bishop.*

What advantages would America gain by remaining under British colonial rule, according to Inglis? What disasters does Inglis predict would befall an independent America? How would you summarize the main differences between the beliefs of Inglis and Thomas Paine, author of the opposing viewpoint?

I think it no difficult matter to point out many advantages which will certainly attend our reconciliation and connection with Great Britain on a firm, constitutional plan. I shall select a few of these; and, that their importance may be more clearly discerned, I shall afterward point out some of the evils which inevitably must attend our separating from Britain and declaring for independency. On each article I shall study brevity.

From *The True Interest of America Impartially Stated, in Certain Strictures on a Pamphlet Intitled Common Sense,* by Charles Inglis (Philadelphia, 1776).

PREVENTING WAR

1. By a reconciliation with Britain, a period would be put to the present calamitous war, by which so many lives have been lost, and so many more must be lost if it continues. This alone is an advantage devoutly to be wished for. This author [Thomas Paine] says: "The blood of the slain, the weeping voice of nature cries, 'Tis time to part." I think they cry just the reverse. The blood of the slain, the weeping voice of nature cries: It is time to be reconciled; it is time to lay aside those animosities which have pushed on Britons to shed the blood of Britons: it is high time that those who are connected by the endearing ties of religion, kindred, and country should resume their former friendship and be united in the bond of mutual affection, as their interests are inseparably united.

2. By a reconciliation with Great Britain, peace—that fairest offspring and gift of heaven—will be restored. In one respect peace is like health—we do not sufficiently know its value but by its absence. What uneasiness and anxiety, what evils has this short interruption of peace with the parent state brought on the whole British Empire! Let every man only consult his feelings—I except my antagonist—and it will require no great force of rhetoric to convince him that a removal of those evils and a restoration of peace would be a singular advantage and blessing.

3. Agriculture, commerce, and industry would resume their wonted vigor. At present, they languish and droop, both here and in Britain; and must continue to do so while this unhappy contest remains unsettled.

AMERICA'S TRADE

4. By a connection with Great Britain, our trade would still have the protection of the greatest naval power in the world. England has the advantage, in this respect, of every other state, whether of ancient or modern times. Her insular situation, her nurseries for seamen, the superiority of those seamen above others—these circumstances, to mention no other, combine to make her the first maritime power in the universe—such exactly is the power whose protection we want for our commerce. To suppose, with our author, that we should have no war were we to revolt from England is too absurd to deserve a confutation. I could just as soon set about refuting the reveries of some brainsick enthusiast. Past experience shows that Britain is able to defend our commerce and our coasts; and we have no reason to doubt of her being able to do so for the future.

5. The protection of our trade, while connected with Britain, will not cost us a *fiftieth* part of what it must cost were we ourselves to raise a naval force sufficient for the purpose.

6. While connected with Great Britain, we have a bounty on almost every article of exportation; and we may be better supplied with goods by her than we could elsewhere. What our author says is true, "that our imported goods must be paid for, buy them where we will"; but we may buy them dearer, and of worse quality, in one place than another. The manufactures of Great Britain confessedly surpass any in the world, particularly those in every kind of metal, which we want most; and no country can afford linens and woolens of equal quality cheaper.

7. When a reconciliation is effected, and things return into the old channel, a few years of peace will restore everything to its pristine state. Emigrants will flow in as usual from the different parts of Europe. Population will advance with the same rapid progress as formerly, and our lands will rise in value.

These advantages are not imaginary but real. They are such as we have already experienced; and such as we may derive from a connection with Great Britain for ages to come. Each of these might easily be enlarged on, and others added to them; but I only mean to suggest a few hints. . . .

CONSEQUENCES OF INDEPENDENCE

Let us now, if you please, take a view of the other side of the question. Suppose we were to revolt from Great Britain, declare ourselves independent, and set up a republic of our own—what would be the consequence? I stand aghast at the prospect; my blood runs chill when I think of the calamities, the complicated evils that must ensue, and may be clearly foreseen—it is impossible for any man to foresee them all.

Our author cautiously avoids saying anything of the inconveniences that would attend a separation. He does not even suppose that any inconvenience would attend it. Let us only declare ourselves independent, break loose from Great Britain, and, according to him, a paradisiacal state will follow! But a prudent man will consider and weigh matters well before he consents to such a measure—when on the brink of such a dreadful precipice, he must necessarily recoil and think of the consequences before he advances a step forward. Supposing then we declared for independency, what would follow? I answer:

1. All our property throughout the continent would be unhinged; the greatest confusion and most violent convulsions would take place. It would not be here as it was in England at the Revolution in 1688. That Revolution was not brought about by a defeasance or disannulling the right of succession. James II, by abdicating the throne, left it vacant for the next in succession; accordingly, his eldest daughter and her husband stepped in. Every other matter went on in the usual, regular way; and the constitution, instead of being dissolved, was

strengthened. But in case of our revolt, the old constitution would be totally subverted. The common bond that tied us together, and by which our property was secured, would be snapped asunder. It is not to be doubted but our Congress would endeavor to apply some remedy for those evils; but, with all deference to that respectable body, I do not apprehend that any remedy in their power would be adequate, at least for some time. I do not choose to be more explicit; but I am able to support my opinion.

2. What a horrid situation would thousands be reduced to who have taken the oath of allegiance to the King; yet, contrary to their oath as well as inclination, must be compelled to renounce that allegiance or abandon all their property in America! How many thousands more would be reduced to a similar situation, who, although they took not that oath, yet would think it inconsistent with their duty and a good conscience to renounce their sovereign. I dare say these will appear trifling difficulties to our author; but, whatever he may think, there are thousands and thousands who would sooner lose all they had in the world, nay, life itself, than thus wound their conscience. A declaration of independency would infallibly disunite and divide the colonists.

WAR WILL LEAD TO RUIN

3. By a declaration for independency, every avenue to an accommodation with Great Britain would be closed; the sword only could then decide the quarrel; and the sword would not be sheathed till one had conquered the other.

The importance of these colonies to Britain need not be enlarged on—it is a thing so universally known. The greater their importance is to her, so much the more obstinate will her struggle be not to lose them. The independency of America would, in the end, deprive her of the West Indies, shake her empire to the foundation, and reduce her to a state of the most mortifying insignificance. Great Britain, therefore, must, for her own preservation, risk everything, and exert her whole strength to prevent such an event from taking place. This being the case.

4. Devastation and ruin must mark the progress of this war along the seacoast of America. Hitherto, Britain has not exerted her power. Her number of troops and ships of war here at present is very little more than she judged expedient in time of peace—the former does not amount to 12,000 men—nor the latter to 40 ships, including frigates. Both she and the colonies hoped for and expected an accommodation; neither of them has lost sight of that desirable object. The seas have been open to our ships; and, although some skirmishes have unfortunately happened, yet a ray of hope still cheered

both sides that peace was not distant. But, as soon as we declare for independent, every prospect of this kind must vanish. Ruthless war, with all its aggravated horrors, will ravage our once happy land; our seacoasts and ports will be ruined, and our ships taken. Torrents of blood will be spilled, and thousands reduced to beggary and wretchedness.

This melancholy contest would last till one side conquered. Supposing Britain to be victorious; however high my opinion is of British generosity, I should be exceedingly sorry to receive terms from her in the haughty tone of a conqueror. Or supposing such a failure of her manufactures, commerce, and strength, that victory should incline to the side of America; yet, who can say, in that case, what extremities her sense of resentment and self-preservation will drive Great Britain to? For my part, I should not in the least be surprised if, on such a prospect as the independency of America, she would parcel out this continent to the different European powers. Canada might be restored to France, Florida to Spain, with additions to each; other states also might come in for a portion. Let no man think this chimerical or improbable. The independency of America would be so fatal to Britain that she would leave nothing in her power undone to prevent it. I believe as firmly as I do my own existence that, if every other method failed, she would try some such expedient as this to disconcert our scheme of independency; and let any man figure to himself the situation of these British colonies, if only Canada were restored to France!

5. But supposing once more that we were able to cut off every regiment that Britain can spare or hire, and to destroy every ship she can send, that we could beat off any other European power that would presume to intrude upon this continent; yet, a republican form of government would neither suit the genius of the people nor the extent of America. . . .

A BLESSED COUNTRY

America is far from being yet in a desperate situation. I am confident she may obtain honorable and advantageous terms from Great Britain. A few years of peace will soon retrieve all her losses. She will rapidly advance to a state of maturity whereby she may not only repay the parent state amply for all past benefits but also lay under the greatest obligations.

America, till very lately, has been the happiest country in the universe. Blessed with all that nature could bestow with the profusest bounty, she enjoyed, besides, more liberty, greater privileges than any other land. How painful is it to reflect on these things, and to look forward to the gloomy prospects now before us! But it is not too late to hope that matters may mend. By prudent management her former happiness may again return;

and continue to increase for ages to come, in a union with the parent state.

However distant humanity may wish the period, yet, in the rotation of human affairs, a period may arrive when (both countries being prepared for it) some terrible disaster, some dreadful convulsion in Great Britain may transfer the seat of empire to this Western Hemisphere—where the British constitution, like the Phoenix from its parent's ashes, shall rise with youthful vigor and shine with redoubled splendor.

But if America should now mistake her real interest—if her sons, infatuated with romantic notions of conquest and empire, ere things are ripe, should adopt this republican's scheme—they will infallibly destroy this smiling prospect. They will dismember this happy country, make it a scene of blood and slaughter, and entail wretchedness and misery on millions yet unborn.

FOR FURTHER READING

Edward Countryman, *The American Revolution.* New York: Hill and Wang, 2003.

Eric Foner, *Tom Paine and Revolutionary America.* New York: Oxford University Press, 1976.

David McCullough, *1776,* New York: Simon & Schuster, 2005.

Mary Beth Norton, *Liberty's Daughters: The Revolutionary Experience of American Women, 1750–1800.* Boston: Little, Brown, 1980.

Leslie Upton, *Revolutionary vs. Loyalist.* Waltham, MA: Blaisdell, 1968.

REVOLUTIONARY WAR
Viewpoint 12A
War Against the British Is Not Justified (1776)
The Ancient Testimony and Principles of the People Called Quakers

INTRODUCTION *The following viewpoint is taken from a tract published in January 1776 following a Philadelphia meeting of Quakers, a religious group that traditionally opposed all war. Although American independence had not been formally declared, significant hostilities between British and American soldiers had already broken out, including clashes between British troops and American militia in Massachusetts and a failed American invasion of Canada led by General Benedict Arnold. The pamphlet, excerpted here, expresses opposition to war and violence and calls on the colonists to maintain what the writers describe as a happy connection to Great Britain. John Pemberton (1727–1795), who as clerk to the meeting signed his name to the pamphlet, was imprisoned in September 1777 because of his suspected Loyalist views. He was pardoned by George Washington in April 1778.*

Whom do the Quakers blame for recent violent events? What alternatives to violence do they propose?

A religious concern for our friends and fellow subjects of every denomination, and more especially for those of all ranks, who, in the present commotions, are engaged in publick employments and stations, induces us earnestly to beseech every individual in the most solemn manner, to consider the end and tendency of the measures they are promoting; and on the most impartial enquiry into the state of their minds, carefully to examine whether they are acting in the fear of God, and in conformity to the precepts and doctrine of our Lord Jesus Christ, whom we profess to believe in, and that by him alone we expect to be saved from our sins.

The calamities and afflictions which now surround us should, as we apprehend, affect every mind with the most awful considerations of the dispensations of Divine Providence to mankind in general in former ages, and that as the sins and iniquities of the people subjected them to grievous sufferings, the same causes still produce the like effects.

PEACE AND PLENTY

The inhabitants of these provinces were long signally favoured with peace and plenty: Have the returns of true thankfulness been generally manifest? Have integrity and godly simplicity been maintained, and religiously regarded? Hath a religious care to do justly, love mercy, and walk humbly, been evident? Hath the precept of Christ, to do unto others as we would they should do unto us, been the governing rule of our conduct? Hath an upright impartial desire to prevent the slavery and oppression of our fellow-men, and to restore them to their natural right, to true christian liberty, been cherished and encouraged? Or have pride, wantonness, luxury, profaneness, a partial spirit, and forgetfulness of the goodness and mercies of God, become lamentably prevalent? Have we not, therefore, abundant occasion to break off from our sins by righteousness, and our iniquities by shewing mercy to the poor; and with true contrition and abasement of soul, to humble ourselves, and supplicate the Almighty Preserver of men, to shew favour, and to renew unto us a state of tranquillity and peace?

[Christ's] spirit ever leads to seek for . . . every opportunity of promoting peace and reconciliation.

It is our fervent desire that this may soon appear to be the pious resolution of the people in general, of all

From *The Ancient Testimony and Principles of the People Called Quakers Renewed, with Respect to the King and Government, and Touching the Commotions Now Prevailing in These and Other Parts of America* (Philadelphia, 1776).

ranks and denominations: then may we have a well grounded hope, that wisdom from above, which is pure, peaceable, and full of mercy and good fruits, will preside and govern in the deliberations of those who, in these perilous times, undertake the transaction of the most important public affairs; and that by their steady care and endeavours, constantly to act under the influences of this wisdom, those of inferior stations will be incited diligently to pursue those measures which make for peace, and tend to the reconciliation of contending parties, on principles dictated by the spirit of Christ, who "came not to destroy men's lives, but to save them." Luke ix. 56.

We are so fully assured that these principles are the most certain and effectual means of preventing the extreme misery and desolations of wars and bloodshed, that we are constrained to intreat all who profess faith in Christ, to manifest that they really believe in him, and desire to obtain the blessings he pronounced to the makers of peace, Mat. v. 9.

His spirit ever leads to seek for and improve every opportunity of promoting peace and reconciliation; and constantly to remember, that as we really confide in him, he can, in his own time, change the hearts of all men in such manner, that the way to obtain it hath been often opened, contrary to every human prospect or expectation. . . .

JUST SUBORDINATION TO THE KING

The peculiar evidence of divine regard manifested to our ancestors, in the founding and settlement of these provinces, we have often commemorated, and desire ever to remember with true thankfulness and reverent admiration.

When we consider—That at the time they were persecuted and subjected to severe sufferings, as a people unworthy of the benefits of religious or civil society, the hearts of the king and rulers, under whom they thus suffered, were inclined to grant them these fruitful countries, and entrust them with charters of very extensive powers and privileges.—That on their arrival here, the minds of the natives were inclined to receive them with great hospitality and friendship, and to cede to them the most valuable part of their land on very easy terms.—That while the principles of justice and mercy continued to preside, they were preserved in tranquility and peace, free from the desolating calamities of war; and their endeavours were wonderfully blessed and prospered; so that the saying of the wisest of kings was signally verified to them, "When a man's ways please the Lord, he maketh even his enemies to be at peace with him." Prov. xvi. 7.

The benefits, advantages, and favour, we have experienced by our dependence on, and connection with, the kings and government, under which we have enjoyed this happy state, appear to demand from us the greatest circumspection, care, and constant endeavours, to guard against every attempt to alter, or subvert, that dependence and connection.

The scenes lately presented to our view, and the prospect before us, we are sensible, are very distressing and discouraging. And though we lament that such amicable measures, as have been proposed, both here and in England, for the adjustment of the unhappy contests subsisting, have not yet been effectual; nevertheless, we should rejoice to observe the continuance of mutual peaceable endeavours for effecting a reconciliation; having grounds to hope that the divine favour and blessing will attend them. . . .

May we therefore firmly unite in the abhorrence of all such writings and measures, as evidence a desire and design to break off the happy connection we have heretofore enjoyed with the kingdom of Great Britain, and our just and necessary subordination to the king, and those who are lawfully placed in authority under him; that thus the repeated solemn declarations made on this subject, in the addresses sent to the king on behalf of the people of America in general, may be confirmed, and remain to be our firm and sincere intentions to observe and fulfil.

Viewpoint 12B

War Against the British Is Justified (1775)

John Carmichael (1728–1785)

INTRODUCTION *John Carmichael, a Presbyterian minister serving in Chester County, Pennsylvania, began preaching and writing against British taxes and other actions in the colonies in the late 1760s. On June 4, 1775—less than two months after the April 1775 battles of Lexington and Concord—he preached a sermon to a company of Chester County militia in Lancaster, Pennsylvania. The sermon was later reprinted in a widely circulated pamphlet, from which the following viewpoint is excerpted. Carmichael argues that wars against oppressors are sometimes justified and that British actions against the colonies make violent resistance necessary. Carmichael's writings and sermons persuaded most members of his congregation to join the American cause. He later addressed the Continental Congress and was a frequent visitor to George Washington's Continental Army during the war.*

What moral arguments does Carmichael make concerning violence? What does he say should be done about pacifists and other opponents of revolution?

At a time when the unjust storm of ministerial wrath is discharging itself, in a cruel and ignominious manner, on the noble, patriotic, brave people of the ancient,

From *A Self-Defensive War Is Lawful* by John Carmichael (Philadelphia: John Dean, 1775).

loyal, important colony of the Massachusetts-Bay, in New-England;—at a time when all the other colonies in North-America, like the true children of a *free-born family*, are roused to some just resentment of such insults, on their natural and legal rights, taking each other as by the hand, and uniting by the invincible chains of love, friendship, and interest, are determined to support this their elder sister colony, now suffering so gloriously in the common cause, or *sink* together;—at a time when the alarm is sounding from east to west, over this vast continent of North-America, to arms! to arms!—in short, at a time when the minds of *all* are in such a ferment, that they can be scarce composed to hear any subject, but what may have some reference to the present times;—it is but reasonable to suppose, that even the Minister of the *Prince of Peace*, whose business for ordinary is neither *war* or *politicks*, in such a situation, being member of civil society, and interested like other men would improve the times, by adopting their public instructions, to the best service of the people, and not offensive or displeasing to God; whose holy word is a blessed directory in every emergency.

It is also but reasonable to suppose, that every judicious, sober American, being now reduced to the dreadful alternative, either to take up arms, apparently against that very government, which he was wont to revere, and under which he expected protection for both life and property; or submit tamely to the galling yoke of *perpetual slavery*, I say, it is supposable, that every such Christian American soldier will be all ear to wholesome instructions, relative to his present duty....

DISCERNING THE CIRCUMSTANCES THAT JUSTIFY WAR

Although war is in itself a very great evil, and one of those sore judgments, by which a holy God punishes the world for sin, therefore to be deprecated, and avoided as much as possible; yet is, at times, by reason of certain circumstances, so unavoidable, that it is our duty to enter into it....

SELF-PRESERVATION

It is certainly evident, wherever we turn our eyes, on any part of the whole creation of God, that the principle of self-love or self-preservation, or the desire of existence, is deeply engraved on the nature of every creature....

The little industrious bee is furnished by her Creator with a sting, to preserve for her own use her sweet honey, the fruit of her toil and industry.

The ox has his horns; and the horse his teeth and hoofs.—The deer her feet for flight, and the fowls their wings to escape danger and preserve themselves. And shall man, the noblest creature in his lower world, be destitute of this necessary principle! which we see engraved by instinct on the irrational creation: Man is blest with

reason to direct his enquiries, in search of happiness. His maker God allows him to seek to be as happy as he possibly can, both in this life and the life to come. But since man is a fallen, sinful creature, he has lost his true road to happiness—and can never find it, until his Maker points it out to him in the Holy Bible. Here we are taught how to conduct both in the civil and religious life: We are certain the scriptures allow us to defend ourselves in the best manner we can against an enemy.

Therefore, such passages, as would seem to speak a different language; such as those already quoted, must be understood, in a consistency with this great law of nature; as well as consistent with other parts of scripture. For Christ came not to make void, or destroy the law, but to fulfil—when therefore we are forbid to shed blood, or to kill; it is innocent blood is meant—but this doth not forbid to execute a murderer. The divine law requires, that a murderer should be executed, and forbids to take a ransom for his life.

———◼———

That a self-defensive war is lawful,
I will prove from the conduct
of Jesus Christ himself.

———◼———

Also, when a body of wicked people join together, or a nation unite, to fall upon and destroy without any just cause an innocent people: The insulted, or invaded people are then to unite together to oppose, expel and punish the guilty invaders—as in Judges v, 23. *Curse ye Meroz, (said the Angel of the Lord) curse ye bitterly the inhabitants thereof: Because they came not to the help of the Lord, against the mighty.* And Jeremiah xlviii, 10. *Cursed be he that doth the work of the Lord deceitfully; and cursed be he that keepeth back his sword from blood:* And in Luke xxii, 36. Jesus Christ told his Disciples to arm themselves against approaching danger.—*And he that hath no sword let him sell his garment and buy one....*

Also, it must of course follow, that where our blessed Lord enjoins us, when smote on the one cheek, to turn the other also, he does not mean to forbid us to use lawful and proper means of self-preservation. But the meaning must be as the phrase is proverbial, that we should at no time discover a revengeful or unforgiving disposition; but should be ready to put up with a good deal of ill-usage, before we would create disturbance,—yea that we should do any thing consistent with our own safety. Again, where our Lord enjoins us to love our enemies—he can't possibly mean that we should love them better than ourselves—that we should put it in the enemy's power to kill us, when we had it in our power to save our own life, by killing the enemy. I say, this cannot be the meaning; for that exposition will thwart the original first great law of self-preservation. The meaning therefore must be, that we do not cherish a spirit of hatred towards the enemies, and would be willing to be reconciled again—and would be desirous, the enemy would be convinced of his evil sentiment against us, that we might be again on friendly terms,—that we can be sincere in our prayer to God, to bring such a desirable event to pass. Again,

That a self-defensive war is lawful, I will prove from the conduct of Jesus Christ himself. If civil government is necessary to self-preservation, and war is necessary, at times, in government, as has been already proved; then it will follow, that those who support civil government, do support war, and so of consequence approve of war. But Jesus Christ did pay his tribute money, to the Emperor Tiberius, Matthew xvii, 27. And those who are acquainted with the life of Tiberius Caesar know that he had frequent wars. . . .

I think I have now proved, from the light of nature, from the reason of things—from the Old and New-Testament, as well as from the example of Christ and his Apostles, that a self-defensive war is lawful. . . .

It is also equally unfair, to say, *Let us stand still and see the salvation of God*; for if this proves any thing, it proves too much, it proves that we are to use no means at all, for why to use lawful means in our power one time, and not another; we must therefore neither plow or sow; build, raise stock, or do any thing in the use of means, *but stand still and see the salvation of God*: But our reason is given us to use it in a proper manner, to preserve our own lives and the lives of others, as God's servants, in a state of probation in this world; and God will reward every one finally, according to his works; when we have no means in our power, we honor God to trust him, as Israel at the Red-Sea, and in the wilderness;— but when means are in our power, and we do not use them, we then tempt God, and rebel against his government, which he exercises over the world, in the way of free and moral agency.

DO NOT PERSECUTE PACIFISTS

Therefore for these people, to argue as they do now, when they are among other societies,—who they know will preserve the state from slaughter or slavery, in the use of lawful means, as has been now proved, is vastly disingenuous, and will undoubtedly subject their opinions to this censure, that it is a sanctuary of sloth—for greed— cowardice &c.—*for it is easy to stay at home and earn money, to what it is to spend money and expose life, to protect and defend the worldling coward;—it is easy to pay money, to what it is to be slain in battle*, &c. But after all that has been said, I am myself so warm an advocate for the sacred rights of conscience, that if these people will not be

convinced of their duty; can not get their eyes open; they are to be pitied, but not persecuted. I beg of all, for God and conscience sake, to let them alone, if they will not in these terrible times, draw the sword *for* Liberty and their Country; surely they will not *against* Liberty and their Country; and if we can do with them, we can without them: O then, let there be no disturbance on that head! But should any of these inoffensive guiltless anti-warriors be detected in assisting Gage or his army with provisions, &c. for lucre or any other motive whatever conscience could not apologize for them but ought to be dealt with accordingly.

FOR FURTHER READING

Jack P. Greene and J.R. Pole, eds., *A Companion to the American Revolution.* Malden, MA: Blackwell, 2004.

Robert Gross, *The Minutemen and Their World.* New York: Hill and Wang, 1976.

Arthur J. Mekeel, *The Relation of the Quakers to the American Revolution.* Washington, DC: University Press of America, 1979.

Gary B. Nash, *The Unknown American Revolution: The Unruly Birth of Democracy and the Struggle to Create America.* New York: Penguin, 2005.

Viewpoint 13A
American Soldiers Should Act Together to Ensure Their Own Welfare (1783)
John Armstrong (1758–1843)

INTRODUCTION *By early 1783 the end of the Revolutionary War was at hand as Great Britain and the United States were negotiating terms of peace. However, at the encampment of Newburgh, north of New York City, there existed rumblings within the Continental Army over the failure of Congress to deliver pay, food rations, and promised pensions. In March 1783 two anonymous letters circulated among the Continental Army. One called for a mass meeting of officers. The other, excerpted here, expressed complaints about the army's treatment at the hands of Congress and suggested that after they disband they will have no leverage in obtaining what has been promised them. The letter closes by suggesting that members of the Continental Army refuse to disband and disarm in the event or peace, but instead boldly demand that the federal government fulfill its obligations. The anonymous author is believed to have been John Armstrong, a major and aide to General Horatio Gates. Armstrong later served as a United States senator and minister to France.*

How does the author begin his letter? What questions does he believe army officers should be asking? What courses of action does he recommend?

From *A Collection of Papers, Relative to Half-Pay and Commutation of Half-Pay, Granted by Congress to the Officers of the Army* (Fishkill, 1783), reprinted in *American History Told by Contemporaries*, Albert B. Hart, ed., New York: Macmillan, 1901.

TO THE OFFICERS OF THE ARMY.

Gentlemen,

A FELLOW-SOLDIER, whose interest and affections bind him strongly to you, whose past sufferings have been as great, and whose future fortunes may be as desperate as yours—would beg leave to address you.

Age has its claims, and rank is not without its pretensions to advise; but though unsupported by both, he flatters himself, that the plain language of sincerity and experience, will neither be unheard nor unregarded.

Like many of you, he loved private life, and left it with regret.—He left it, determined to retire from the field, with the necessity that called him to it, and not till then,—not till the enemies of his country, the slaves of power and the hirelings of injustice, were compelled to abandon their schemes, and acknowledge America as terrible in arms, as she had been humble in remonstrance.—With this object in view, he has long shared in your toils, and mingled in your dangers,—he has felt the cold hand of poverty, without a murmur, and has seen the insolence of wealth, without a sigh.—But too much under the direction of his wishes, and sometimes weak enough to mistake desire for opinion, he has till lately, very lately, believed in the justice of his country.—He hoped that as the clouds of adversity scattered, and as the sunshine of peace and better fortune broke in upon us,—the coldness and severity of government would relax, and that more than justice, that gratitude, would blaze forth upon those hands, which had upheld her, in the darkest stages of her passage, from impending servitude, to acknowledged independence.

But faith has its limits as well as temper, and there are points, beyond which neither can be stretched without sinking into cowardice, or plunging into credulity. . . .

Can you then consent to be the only sufferers by this revolution,—and retiring from the field, grow old in poverty, wretchedness, and contempt?

After a pursuit of seven long years, the object for which we set out, is at length brought within our reach.—Yes, my friends, that suffering courage of yours, was active once; it has conducted the United States of America, through a doubtful and a bloody war—it has placed her in the chair of independency, and peace returns again to bless—Whom? A country willing to redress your wrongs, cherish your worth, and reward your services?—A country courting your return to private life, with tears of gratitude and smiles of admiration?—

longing to divide with you that independency which your gallantry has given, and those riches which your wounds have preserved?—Is this the case? Or is it rather a country that tramples upon your rights, disdains your cries, and insults your distresses?—have you not more than once suggested your wishes, and made known your wants to Congress (wants and wishes which gratitude and policy should have anticipated, rather than evaded); and have you not lately, in the meek language of entreating memorials, begged from their justice what you could no longer expect from their favour? How have you been answered?

If this then be your treatment, while the swords you wear are necessary for the defence of America, what have you to expect from peace; when your voice shall sink, and your strength dissipate by division—when those very swords, the instruments and companions of your glory, shall be taken from your sides, and no remaining mark of military distinction left, but your wants, infirmities and scars.—Can you then consent to be the only sufferers by this revolution,—and retiring from the field, grow old in poverty, wretchedness and contempt?—Can you consent to wade through the vile mire of dependency, and owe the miserable remnant of that life to charity, which has hitherto been spent in honor?

But if your spirits should revolt at this, if you have sense enough to discover, and spirit sufficient to oppose tyranny, under whatever garb it may assume—whether it be the plain coat of republicanism—or the splendid robe of royalty;—if you have yet learned to discriminate, between a people and a cause—between men and principles,—awake, attend to your situation, and redress yourselves. If the present moment be lost, every future effort is in vain—your threats then, will be as empty, as your entreaties now. I would advise you therefore, to come to some final opinion, of what you can bear and what you will suffer. If your determination be in any proportion to your wrongs—carry your appeal from the justice to the fears of government. Change the milk and water stile of your last memorial.—Assume a bolder tone, decent, but lively, spirited and determined;—and suspect the man who would advise to more moderation, and longer forbearance. Let two or three men, who can feel as well as write, be appointed to draw up your last remonstrance (for I would no longer give it the sueing, soft, unsuccessful epithet of memorial). Let it represent in language, that will neither dishonour you by its rudeness, nor betray you by its fears—what has been promised by Congress, and what has been performed—how long and how patiently you have suffered—how little you have asked, and how much of that little has been denied.

That in any political event, the army has its alternative.—If peace, that nothing shall separate you from your arms but death.—If war, that courting the auspices, and inviting the direction of your illustrious leader, you will retire to some yet unsettled country, smile in your turn, "and mock when their fear cometh on."—But let it represent also, that should they comply with the request of your late memorial, it would make you more happy, and them more respectable.—That while the war should continue, you would follow their standard in the field,—and that when it came to an end, you would withdraw into the shade of private life, and give the world another subject of wonder and applause—an army victorious over its enemies—victorious over itself.

American Soldiers Should Act in the Nation's Interest (1783)

George Washington (1732–1799)

INTRODUCTION *George Washington was appointed commander in chief of the Continental Army in 1775; he stayed in that position until December 1783, after the Revolutionary War had successfully ended with American independence. One of the main challenges he faced throughout the conflict was discontent within his own ranks. In March 1783 Washington called a special meeting to respond to concerns raised by an anonymous letter suggesting that military officers take drastic action against Congress to get their promised pay and pensions. Washington viewed the idea as a strong threat to the creation of America's new republic. The following viewpoint is excerpted from Washington's address to officers under his command in which he strongly condemned any action to withhold their services or otherwise coerce America's civilian government, and promised that they would eventually receive just treatment from Congress. Washington was able to win officers to his view. His 1783 retirement from the Continental Army to private life was short: he served as America's first president from 1789 to 1797.*

What comments does Washington make about the author of viewpoint 13A? What does he appeal to in asking military officers to reject any plan to act against Congress?

Gentlemen:

By an anonymous summons, an attempt has been made to convene you together. How inconsistent with the rules of propriety! How unmilitary! And how subversive of all order and discipline, let the good sense of the Army decide.

In the moment of this summons, another anonymous production was sent into circulation, addressed more to the feelings and passions than to the reason and judgment of the Army. The author of the piece is entitled to much credit for the goodness of his pen, and I could wish he had as much credit for the rectitude of

From John Marshall, *The Life of George Washington, etc. etc.* 2nd ed., Philadelphia, 1848.

his heart; for, as men see through different optics and are induced by the reflecting faculties of the mind to use different means to attain the same end, the author of the address should have had more charity than to mark for suspicion the man who should recommend moderation and longer forbearance—or, in other words, who should not think as he thinks and acts as he advises. But he had another plan in view, in which candor and liberality of sentiment, regard to justice, and love of country have no part; and he was right to insinuate the darkest suspicion to effect the blackest design.

That the address is drawn with great art and is designed to answer the most insidious purposes; that it is calculated to impress the mind with an idea of premeditated injustice in the sovereign power of the United States, and rouse all those resentments which must unavoidably flow from such a belief; that the secret mover of this scheme (whoever he may be) intended to take advantage of the passions while they were warmed by the recollection of past distresses, without giving time for cool, deliberative thinking, and that composure of mind which is so necessary to give dignity and stability to measures is rendered too obvious, by the mode of conducting the business, to need other proof than a reference to the proceedings.

Thus much, gentlemen, I have thought it incumbent on me to observe to you, to show upon what principles I opposed the irregular and hasty meeting which was proposed to have been held on Tuesday last, and not because I wanted a disposition to give you every opportunity consistent with your own honor and the dignity of the Army to make known your grievances. If my conduct heretofore has not evinced to you that I have been a faithful friend to the Army, my declaration of it at this time would be equally unavailing and improper. But as I was among the first who embarked in the cause of our common country; as I have never left your side one moment but when called from you on public duty; as I have been the constant companion and witness of your distresses, and not among the last to feel and acknowledge your merits; as I have ever considered my own military reputation as inseparably connected with that of the Army; as my heart has ever expanded with joy when I have heard its praises, and my indignation has arisen when the mouth of detraction has been opened against it, it can *scarcely be supposed*, at this late stage of the war, that I am indifferent to its interests. But how are they to be promoted? The way is plain, says the anonymous addresser.

This dreadful alternative, of either deserting our Country . . . or turning our arms against it . . . has something so shocking in it that humanity revolts at the idea.

A DREADFUL PLAN

If war continues, remove into the unsettled country; there establish yourselves and leave an ungrateful country to defend itself. But who are they to defend? Our wives, our children, our farms, and other property which we leave behind us, or, in this state of hostile separation, are we to take the two first (the latter cannot be removed) to perish in a wilderness, with hunger, cold, and nakedness?

If peace takes place, never sheath your swords, says he, until you have obtained full and ample justice. This dreadful alternative, of either deserting our country in the extremest hour of her distress or turning our arms against it (which is the apparent object, unless Congress can be compelled into instant compliance), has something so shocking in it that humanity revolts at the idea. My God! What can this writer have in view, by recommending such measures? Can he be a friend to the Army? Can he be a friend to this country? Rather, is he not an insidious foe? Some emissary, perhaps, from New York, plotting the ruin of both by sowing the seeds of discord and separation between the civil and military powers of the continent? And what a compliment does he pay to our understandings when he recommends measures in either alternative, impracticable in their nature?

But here, gentlemen, I will drop the curtain, because it would be as imprudent in me to assign my reasons for this opinion as it would be insulting to your conception to suppose you stood in need of them. A moment's reflection will convince every dispassionate mind of the physical impossibility of carrying either proposal into execution. . . .

With respect to the advice given by the author, to suspect the man who shall recommend moderate measures and longer forbearance, I spurn it, as every man who regards that liberty and reveres that justice for which we contend undoubtedly must; for if men are to be precluded from offering their sentiments on a matter which may involve the most serious and alarming consequences that can invite the consideration of mankind, reason is of no use to us—the freedom of speech may be taken away and, dumb and silent, we may be led, like sheep, to the slaughter.

FAITH IN CONGRESS

I cannot, in justice to my own belief and what I have great reason to conceive is the intention of Congress, conclude this address without giving it as my decided opinion that that honorable body entertains exalted sentiments of the services of the Army; and, from a full conviction of its merits and sufferings, will do it complete justice. That their endeavors to discover and establish funds for this purpose have been unwearied, and will not cease till they have succeeded, I have not a doubt.

But like all other large bodies where there is a variety of different interests to reconcile, their deliberations are slow. Why then should we distrust them, and, in consequence of that distrust, adopt measures which may cast a shade over that glory which has been so justly acquired, and tarnish the reputation of an Army which is celebrated through all Europe for its fortitude and patriotism? And for what is this done? To bring the object we seek nearer? No! Most certainly, in my opinion, it will cast it at a greater distance. . . .

Let me entreat you, gentlemen, on your part, not to take any measures which, viewed in the calm light of reason, will lessen the dignity and sully the glory you have hitherto maintained. Let me request you to rely on the plighted faith of your country, and place a full confidence in the purity of the intentions of Congress; that, previous to your dissolution as an Army they will cause all your accounts to be fairly liquidated, as directed in their resolutions, which were published to you two days ago, and that they will adopt the most effectual measures in their power to render ample justice to you for your faithful and meritorious services. And let me conjure you, in the name of our common country, as you value your own sacred honor, as you respect the rights of humanity, and as you regard the military and national character of America, to express your utmost horror and detestation of the man who wishes, under any specious pretenses, to overturn the liberties of our country, and who wickedly attempts to open the floodgates of civil discord and deluge our rising empire in blood.

FOR FURTHER READING

Bruce Chadwick, *George Washington's War: The Forging of a Revolutionary Leader and the American Presidency.* Naperville, IL: Sourcebooks, 2005.

Joseph J. Ellis, *His Excellency: George Washington.* New York: Alfred A. Knopf, 2004.

Thomas J. Fleming, *Liberty! The American Revolution.* New York: Viking, 1997.

Both Armstrong's letter and Washington's reply can be read and found at http://www.earlyamerica.com/earlyamerica/milestones/newburgh/index.html.

CREATING A NEW GOVERNMENT

Viewpoint 14A

A Strong National Government Is Necessary to Ensure the Nation's Survival (1783)

George Washington (1732–1799)

INTRODUCTION *As American independence became a reality in 1783, political debate turned towards the social and political future of the new nation, consisting of thirteen new states united by the Articles of Confederation. In one of his last acts as commander in chief of the Continental Army, George Washington wrote a letter in 1783 to the state governors in which he announced his intention to retire to private life and described some of his ideas about government and America's future. He contended that the choices America's citizens made now could determine whether the new nation would be "respectable and prosperous, or contemptible and miserable." A main point Washington wanted to raise was the danger of states going their separate ways and effectively dissolving the Union—a prospect he considered dangerous both to national survival and to the well-being of the American people. The necessity for greater national unity was a prime motivation for the Philadelphia Convention of 1787—a meeting Washington chaired, and which created the U.S. Constitution to replace the Articles of Confederation.*

Why might Washington want to address state governors in his letter? What advantages does Washington perceive the new nation possessing? What four elements does he deem critical?

The citizens of America, placed in the most enviable condition as the sole lords and proprietors of a vast tract of continent, comprehending all the various soils and climates of the world and abounding with all the necessaries and conveniences of life, are now, by the late satisfactory pacification, acknowledged to be possessed of absolute freedom and independency. They are, from this period, to be considered as the actors on a most conspicuous theater, which seems to be peculiarly designated by Providence for the display of human greatness and felicity. Here they are not only surrounded with everything which can contribute to the completion of private and domestic enjoyment, but Heaven has crowned all its other blessings by giving a fairer opportunity for political happiness than any other nation has ever been favored with. Nothing can illustrate these observations more forcibly than a recollection of the happy conjuncture of times and circumstances under which our republic assumed its rank among the nations.

The foundation of our empire was not laid in the gloomy age of ignorance and superstition but at an epoch when the rights of mankind were better understood and more clearly defined than at any former period. The researches of the human mind, after social happiness, have been carried to a great extent; the treasures of knowledge, acquired by the labors of philosophers, sages, and legislators through a long succession of years, are laid open for our use; and their collected wisdom may be happily applied in the establishment of our forms of

From John Marshall, *The Life of George Washington, etc. etc.* 2nd ed., Philadelphia, 1848.

government. The free cultivation of letters, the unbounded extension of commerce, the progressive refinement of manners, the growing liberality of sentiment, and, above all, the pure and benign light of revelation have had a meliorating influence on mankind and increased the blessings of society. At this auspicious period, the United States came into existence as a nation; and, if their citizens should not be completely free and happy, the fault will be entirely their own.

A TEST FOR AMERICANS

Such is our situation, and such are our prospects; but notwithstanding the cup of blessing is thus reached out to us; notwithstanding happiness is ours, if we have a disposition to seize the occasion and make it our own; yet it appears to me there is an option still left to the United States of America, that it is in their choice, and depends upon their conduct, whether they will be respectable and prosperous, or contemptible and miserable, as a nation. This is the time of their political probation; this is the moment when the eyes of the whole world are turned upon them; this is the moment to establish or ruin their national character forever; this is the favorable moment to give such a tone to our federal government as will enable it to answer the ends of its institution; or this may be the ill-fated moment for relaxing the powers of the Union, annihilating the cement of the Confederation, and exposing us to become the sport of European politics, which may play one state against another, to prevent their growing importance and to serve their own interested purposes. For, according to the system of policy the states shall adopt at this moment, they will stand or fall; and by their confirmation or lapse, it is yet to be decided whether the Revolution must ultimately be considered as a blessing or a curse—a blessing or a curse not to the present age alone, for with our fate will the destiny of unborn millions be involved. . . .

FOUR NECESSARY ELEMENTS

There are four things which, I humbly conceive, are essential to the well-being, I may even venture to say to the existence, of the United States as an independent power.

First, an indissoluble union of the states under one federal head.

Second, a sacred regard to public justice.

Third, the adoption of a proper peace establishment; and,

Fourth, the prevalence of that pacific and friendly disposition among the people of the United States which will induce them to forget their local prejudices and policies; to make those mutual concessions which are requisite to the general prosperity; and, in some instances, to sacrifice their individual advantages to the interest of the community.

These are the pillars on which the glorious fabric of our independency and national character must be supported. Liberty is the basis; and whoever would dare to sap the foundation, or overturn the structure, under whatever specious pretext he may attempt it, will merit the bitterest execration and the severest punishment which can be inflicted by his injured country.

On the three first articles I will make a few observations, leaving the last to the good sense and serious consideration of those immediately concerned.

Under the first head, although it may not be necessary or proper for me, in this place, to enter into a particular disquisition on the principles of the Union, and to take up the great question which has been frequently agitated—whether it be expedient and requisite for the states to delegate a larger proportion of power to Congress or not—yet it will be a part of my duty, and that of every true patriot, to assert without reserve, and to insist upon, the following positions: That, unless the states will suffer Congress to exercise those prerogatives they are undoubtedly invested with by the constitution, everything must very rapidly tend to anarchy and confusion. That it is indispensable to the happiness of the individual states that there should be lodged somewhere a supreme power to regulate and govern the general concerns of the confederated republic, without which the Union cannot be of long duration. That there must be a faithful and pointed compliance, on the part of every state, with the late proposals and demands of Congress, or the most fatal consequences will ensue. That whatever measures have a tendency to dissolve the Union, or contribute to violate or lessen the sovereign authority, ought to be considered as hostile to the liberty and independency of America, and the authors of them treated accordingly. And lastly, that unless we can be enabled, by the concurrence of the states, to participate of the fruits of the Revolution and enjoy the essential benefits of civil society, under a form of government so free and uncorrupted, so happily guarded against the danger of oppression as has been devised and adopted by the Articles of Confederation, it will be a subject of regret that so much blood and treasure have been lavished for no purpose, that so many sufferings have been encountered without a compensation, and that so many sacrifices have been made in vain.

Many other considerations might here be adduced to prove that, without an entire conformity to the spirit of the Union, we cannot exist as an independent power. It will be sufficient for my purpose to mention but one or two which seem to me of the greatest importance.

It is only in our united character, as an empire, that our independence is acknowledged, that our power can be regarded, or our credit supported, among foreign nations. The treaties of the European powers with the United States of America will have no validity on a dissolution of the Union. We shall be left nearly in a state of nature; or we may find, by our own unhappy experience, that there is a natural and necessary progression from the extreme of anarchy to the extreme of tyranny, and that arbitrary power is most easily established on the ruins of liberty abused to licentiousness.

FOR FURTHER READING

Bruce Chadwick, *George Washington's War: The Forging of a Revolutionary Leader and the American Presidency*. Naperville, IL: Sourcebooks, 2005.

Joseph J. Ellis, *His Excellency: George Washington*. New York: Alfred A. Knopf, 2004.

Thomas J. Fleming, *Liberty! The American Revolution*. New York: Viking, 1997.

Viewpoint 14B
Strong State Governments Are Maintaining Freedom and Prosperity (1787)
James Winthrop (1752–1821)

INTRODUCTION *The Articles of Confederation, ratified by the former colonies in 1781, formed the basis of the national government of the United States for several years. Under the Articles Congress had the power to declare war and enter into foreign alliances, but it had little power to raise taxes, make laws, or create a national economic or trade policy. Political leaders met in Philadelphia in 1787 and came up with a new blueprint for national government—the Constitution—which then had to be ratified by the states. The following viewpoint is taken from a 1787 newspaper article arguing that such a new Constitution was not needed and that the new nation was indeed prospering under its current weak central government. The author, "Agrippa," is believed by most historians to be James Winthrop, a librarian and teacher at Harvard University.*

What argument does Winthrop make about the governments of large states. What objections does he have to the proposed Constitution and its "consolidation" of the states?

Having considered some of the principal advantages of the happy form of government under which it is our peculiar good fortune to live, we find by experience, that it is the best calculated of any form hitherto invented,

Massachusetts Gazette (Boston), December 3, 1787, reprinted in *American History Told by Contemporaries*, Albert B. Hart, ed., New York: Macmillan, 1901.

to secure to us the rights of our persons and of our property, and that the general circumstances of the people shew an advanced state of improvement never before known. We have found the shock given by the war in a great measure obliterated, and the publick debt contracted at that time to be considerably reduced in the nominal sum. The Congress lands are fully adequate to the redemption of the principal of their debt, and are selling and populating very fast. The lands of this state, at the west, are, at the moderate price of eighteen pence an acre worth near half a million pounds in our money. They ought, therefore, to be sold as quick as possible. An application was made lately for a large tract at that price, and continual applications are made for other lands in the eastern part of the state. Our resources are daily augmenting.

We find, then, that after the experience of near two centuries our separate governments are in full vigour. They discover, for all the purposes of internal regulation, every symptom of strength, and none of decay. The new system is, therefore, for such purposes, useless and burdensome.

It is impossible for one code of laws to suit Georgia and Massachusetts.

Let us now consider how far it is practicable consistent with the happiness of the people and their freedom. It is the opinion of the ablest writers on the subject, that no extensive empire can be governed upon republican principles, and that such a government will degenerate to a despotism, unless it be made up of a confederacy of smaller states, each having the full powers of internal regulation. This is precisely the principle which has hitherto preserved our freedom. No instance can be found of any free government of considerable extent which has been supported upon any other plan. Large and consolidated empires may indeed dazzle the eyes of a distant spectator with their splendour, but if examined more nearly are always found to be full of misery. The reason is obvious. In large states the same principles of legislation will not apply to all the parts. The inhabitants of warmer climates are more dissolute in their manners, and less industrious, than in colder countries. A degree of severity is, therefore, necessary with one which would cramp the spirit of the other. We accordingly find that the very great empires have always been despotick. They have indeed tried to remedy the inconveniences to which the people were exposed by local regulations; but these contrivances have never answered the end. The laws not being made by the people, who felt the inconveniences, did not suit their circumstances. It is under such tyranny

that the Spanish provinces languish, and such would be our misfortune and degradation, if we should submit to have the concerns of the whole empire managed by one legislature. To promote the happiness of the people it is necessary that there should be local laws; and it is necessary that those laws should be made by the representatives of those who are immediately subject to the want of them. By endeavouring to suit both extremes, both are injured.

AGAINST CONSOLIDATION

It is impossible for one code of laws to suit Georgia and Massachusetts. They must, therefore, legislate for themselves. Yet there is, I believe, not one point of legislation that is not surrendered in the proposed plan. Questions of every kind respecting property are determinable in a continental court, and so are all kinds of criminal causes. The continental legislature has, therefore, a right to make rules *in all cases* by which their judicial courts shall proceed and decide causes. No rights are reserved to the citizens. The laws of Congress are in all cases to be the supreme law of the land, and paramount to the constitutions of the individual states. The Congress may institute what modes of trial they please, and no plea drawn from the constitution of any state can avail. This new system is, therefore, a consolidation of all the states into one large mass, however diverse the parts may be of which it is to be composed. The idea of an uncompounded republick, on an average, one thousand miles in length, and eight hundred in breadth, and containing six millions of white inhabitants all reduced to the same standard of morals, of habits, and of laws, is in itself an absurdity, and contrary to the whole experience of mankind. The attempt made by Great-Britain to introduce such a system, struck us with horrour, and when it was proposed by some theorists that we should be represented in parliament, we uniformly declared that one legislature could not represent so many different interests for the purposes of legislation and taxation. This was the leading principle of the revolution, and makes an essential article in our creed. All that part, therefore, of the new system, which relates to the internal government of the states, ought at once to be rejected.

FOR FURTHER READING

Keith L. Dougherty, *Collective Action under the Articles of Confederation.* New York: Cambridge University Press, 2001.

Christopher M. Duncan, *The Anti-Federalists and Early American Political* Thought. DeKalb: Northern Illinois University Press, 1995.

David C. Hendrickson, *Peace Pact: The Lost World of the American Founding.* Lawrence: University Press of Kansas, 2003.

Robert W. Hoffert, *A Politics of Tensions: The Articles of Confederation and American Political Ideas.* Niwot: University Press of Colorado, 1992.

Viewpoint 15A

A Republic Must Be Small and Uniform to Survive (1787)

"Brutus"

INTRODUCTION *The U.S. Constitution was written by delegates meeting in a special convention in Philadelphia from May to September 1787. The product of the Constitutional Convention, which then had to be ratified by the states, faced widespread debate. Numerous pamphlets and newspaper articles were published as federalists (supporters of the Constitution) sparred with anti-federalists. The following viewpoint is taken from the first of sixteen articles by "Brutus" published in the* New York Journal *between October 1787 and April 1788 and widely reprinted elsewhere. Some historians have suggested that the author was Robert Yates (1738–1801), a New York delegate to the Constitutional Convention who refused to sign the Constitution.*

"Brutus" criticizes the proposed Constitution for greatly centralizing the powers of the national government. He argues that republican government has proved practical only in communities where the population was manageably small and homogeneous, unlike that of America. Many anti-federalist writers like "Brutus" argued that the size and diversity of America's population meant that a national regime could not effectively govern without sacrificing the personal liberties Americans valued.

What arguments and reasons does the author use to support the idea that free republics only exist in small areas? Which, if any, of his predictions have come true?

The first question that presents itself on the subject is, whether a confederated government be the best for the United States or not? Or in other words, whether the thirteen United States should be reduced to one great republic, governed by one legislature, and under the direction of one executive and judicial; or whether they should continue thirteen confederated republics, under the direction and controul of a supreme federal head for certain defined national purposes only?

This enquiry is important, because, although the government reported by the convention does not go to a perfect and entire consolidation, yet it approaches so near to it, that it must, if executed, certainly and infallibly terminate in it. . . .

CAN A NATION BE LARGE AND FREE?

It is here taken for granted, that all agree in this, that whatever government we adopt, it ought to be a free

From an editorial by "Brutus" that appeared in the October 18, 1787, *New York Journal.*

one; that it should be so framed as to secure the liberty of the citizens of America, and such an one as to admit of a full, fair, and equal representation of the people. The question then will be, whether a government thus constituted, and founded on such principles, is practicable, and can be exercised over the whole United States, reduced into one state?

If respect is to be paid to the opinion of the greatest and wisest men who have ever thought or wrote on the science of government, we shall be constrained to conclude, that a free republic cannot succeed over a country of such immense extent, containing such a number of inhabitants, and these encreasing in such rapid progression as that of the whole United States. Among the many illustrious authorities which might be produced to this point, I shall content myself with quoting only two. The one is the baron [Charles-Louis] de Montesquieu, spirit of laws, chap. xvi. vol. I [book VIII]. "It is natural to a republic to have only a small territory, otherwise it cannot long subsist. In a large republic there are men of large fortunes, and consequently of less moderation; there are trusts too great to be placed in any single subject; he has interest of his own; he soon begins to think that he may be happy, great and glorious, by oppressing his fellow citizens; and that he may raise himself to grandeur on the ruins of his country. In a large republic, the public good is sacrificed to a thousand views; it is subordinate to exceptions, and depends on accidents. In a small one, the interest of the public is easier perceived, better understood, and more within the reach of every citizen; abuses are of less extent, and of course are less protected." Of the same opinion is the marquis Beccarari [Cesare di Beccaria].

History furnishes no example of a free republic, any thing like the extent of the United States. The Grecian republics were of small extent; so also was that of the Romans. Both of these, it is true, in process of time, extended their conquests over large territories of country; and the consequence was, that their governments were changed from that of free government to those of the most tyrannical that ever existed in the world.

Not only the opinion of the greatest men, and the experience of mankind, are against the idea of an extensive republic, but a variety of reasons may be drawn from the reason and nature of things, against it. In every government, the will of the sovereign is the law. In despotic governments, the supreme authority being lodged in one, his will is law, and can be as easily expressed to a large extensive territory as to a small one. In a pure democracy the people are the sovereign, and their will is declared by themselves; for this purpose they must all come together to deliberate, and decide. This kind of government cannot be exercised, therefore, over a country of any considerable extent; it must be confined to a single city, or at least limited to such bounds as that the people can conveniently assemble, be able to debate, understand the subject submitted to them, and declare their opinion concerning it.

THE CONSENT OF THE PEOPLE

In a free republic, although all laws are derived from the consent of the people, yet the people do not declare their consent by themselves in person, but by representatives, chosen by them, who are supposed to know the minds of their constituents, and to be possessed of integrity to declare this mind.

In every free government, the people must give their assent to the laws by which they are governed. This is the true criterion between a free government and an arbitrary one. The former are ruled by the will of the whole, expressed in any manner they may agree upon; the latter by the will of one, or a few. If the people are to give their assent to the laws, by persons chosen and appointed by them, the manner of the choice and the number chosen, must be such, as to possess, be disposed, and consequently qualified to declare the sentiments of the people; for if they do not know, or are not disposed to speak the sentiments of the people, the people do not govern, but the sovereignty is in a few. Now, in a large extended country, it is impossible to have a representation, possessing the sentiments, and of integrity, to declare the minds of the people, without having it so numerous and unwieldy, as to be subject in great measure to the inconveniency of a democratic government.

The territory of the United States is of vast extent; it now contains near three millions of souls, and is capable of containing much more than ten times that number. Is it practicable for a country, so large and so numerous as they will soon become, to elect a representation, that will speak their sentiments, without their becoming so numerous as to be incapable of transacting public business? It certainly is not.

THE DIVERSITY OF THE UNITED STATES

In a republic, the manners, sentiments, and interests of the people should be similar. If this be not the case, there will be a constant clashing of opinions; and the representatives of one part will be continually striving against those of the other. This will retard the operations of government and prevent such conclusions as will promote the public good. If we apply this remark to the condition of the United States, we shall be convinced that it forbids that we should be one government. The United States includes a variety of climates. The productions of the different parts of the union are very variant, and their interests, of consequence, diverse. Their manners and habits differ as much as their climates and productions; and their sentiments are by no means coincident. The laws and customs of the several states are, in many respects, very diverse, and in some opposite; each would be in favor of its own interests and customs, and, of consequence, a legislature, formed of representatives from the respective parts, would not only be too numerous to act with any care or decision, but would be composed of such heterogenous and discordant principles, as would constantly be contending with each other.

The laws cannot be executed in a republic, of an extent equal to that of the United States, with promptitude....

A free republic cannot long subsist over a country of the great extent of these states.

In a republic of such vast extent as the United States, the legislature cannot attend to the various concerns and wants of its different parts. It cannot be sufficiently numerous to be acquainted with the local condition and wants of the different districts, and if it could, it is impossible it should have sufficient time to attend to and provide for all the variety of cases of this nature, that would be continually arising.

THE ABUSE OF POWER

In so extensive a republic, the great officers of government would soon become above the controul of the people, and abuse their power to the purpose of aggrandizing themselves, and oppressing them. The trust committed to the executive offices, in a country of the extent of the United States, must be various and of magnitude. The command of all the troops and navy of the republic, the appointment of officers, the power of pardoning offences, the collecting of all the public revenues, and the power of expending them, with a number of other powers, must be lodged and exercised in every state in the hands of a few. When these are attended with great honor and emolument, as they always will be in large states, so as greatly to interest men to pursue them, and to be proper objects for ambitious and designing men, such men will be ever restless in their pursuit after them. They will use the power, when they have acquired it, to the purposes of gratifying their own interest and ambition, and it is scarcely possible, in a very large republic, to call them to account for their misconduct, or to prevent their abuse of power.

These are some of the reasons by which it appears, that a free republic cannot long subsist over a country of the great extent of these states. If then this new constitution is calculated to consolidate the thirteen states into one, as it evidently is, it ought not to be adopted.

Viewpoint 15B

A Viable Republic Can Be Large and Diverse (1787)

James Madison (1751–1836)

INTRODUCTION *Political theorist and future president James Madison played a significant role in both insti- gating and influencing the 1787 Constitutional Con- vention. During the ensuing months of debate he wrote numerous articles and pamphlets urging ratification of the Constitution. These included the famous* Federalist Papers, *a series of newspaper articles he coauthored with Alexander Hamilton and John Jay under the pseud- onym "Publius." The following viewpoint is taken from* The Federalist *No. 10, Madison's first and most famous contribution to the series; the article was origi- nally published on November 22, 1787, in the* New York Daily Advertiser. *Madison was responding in part to arguments made by "Brutus" and other anti-federalists who believed that republican governments were viable only in small communities where the "interests of the people should be similar." Madison argues here that republican governments in such situations are vulnerable to the problems of "factions"—the ability of local majorities motivated by selfish concerns to dominate government, create bad law, and tyrannize the minority. Creating a government over a larger territory, Madison contends, can "extend the sphere" and prevent a single faction from gaining control over the government.*

How does Madison define and describe "factions"? How does he differentiate between a republic and a democracy? Which of the arguments found here can be seen as direct answers to arguments by "Brutus" in the opposing viewpoint?

To the People of the State of New-York.

Among the numerous advantages promised by a well-constructed Union, none deserves to be more accu- rately developed than its tendency to break and control the violence of faction. . . .

THE DANGERS OF FACTIONS

By a faction, I understand a number of citizens, whether amounting to a majority or minority of the whole, who are united and actuated by some common impulse of passion, or of interest, adverse to the rights of other citi- zens, or to the permanent and aggregate interests of the community.

There are two methods of curing the mischiefs of faction: the one, by removing its causes; the other, by controlling its effects.

From an open letter "To the People of the State of New-York" by "Publius" (James Madison) that appeared in the November 22, 1787, *New York Daily Advertiser.*

There are again two methods of removing the causes of faction: the one, by destroying the liberty which is essential to its existence; the other, by giving to every citizen the same opinions, the same passions, and the same interests.

It could never be more truly said than of the first remedy, that it was worse than the disease. Liberty is to faction what air is to fire, an aliment without which it instantly expires. But it could not be less folly to abolish liberty, which is essential to political life, because it nour- ishes faction, than it would be to wish the annihilation of air, which is essential to animal life, because it imparts to fire its destructive agency.

The second expedient is as impracticable as the first would be unwise. As long as the reason of man continues fallible, and he is at liberty to exercise it, different opin- ions will be formed. As long as the connection subsists between his reason and his self-love, his opinions and his passions will have a reciprocal influence on each other: and the former will be objects to which the latter will attach themselves. The diversity in the faculties of men, from which the rights of property originate, is not less an insuperable obstacle to a uniformity of interests. The protection of these faculties is the first object of gov- ernment. From the protection of different and unequal faculties of acquiring property, the possession of different degrees and kinds of property immediately results; and from the influence of these on the sentiments and views of the respective proprietors, ensues a division of the society into different interests and parties.

THE CAUSES OF FACTION

The latent causes of faction are thus sown in the nature of man; and we see them everywhere brought into different degrees of activity, according to the different circumstan- ces of civil society. A zeal for different opinions concern- ing religion, concerning government, and many other points, as well of speculation as of practice; an attachment to different leaders ambitiously contending for pre- eminence and power; or to persons of other descriptions whose fortunes have been interesting to the human pas- sions, have, in turn, divided mankind into parties, inflamed them with mutual animosity, and rendered them much more disposed to vex and oppress each other than to co-operate for their common good. So strong is this propensity of mankind to fall into mutual animosities, that where no substantial occasion presents itself, the most frivolous and fanciful distinctions have been sufficient to kindle their unfriendly passions and excite their most violent conflicts. But the most common and durable source of factions has been the various and unequal distribution of property. Those who hold and those who are without property have ever formed distinct interests in society. Those who are creditors, and those who are debtors, fall under a like discrimination. A landed interest, a manufacturing interest, a mercantile interest, a moneyed interest, with many lesser interests, grow up of necessity in civilized nations, and divide them into different classes, actuated by different sentiments and views. The regulation of these various and interfering interests forms the principal task of modern legislation, and involves the spirit of party and faction in the necessary and ordinary operations of the government. . . .

It is in vain to say that enlightened statesmen will be able to adjust these clashing interests, and render them all subservient to the public good. Enlightened statesmen will not always be at the helm. Nor, in many cases, can such an adjustment be made at all without taking into view indirect and remote considerations, which will rarely prevail over the immediate interest which one party may find in disregarding the rights of another or the good of the whole.

The inference to which we are brought is, that the *causes* of faction cannot be removed, and that relief is only to be sought in the means of controlling its *effects*.

If a faction consists of less than a majority, relief is supplied by the republican principle, which enables the majority to defeat its sinister views by regular vote. It may clog the administration, it may convulse the society; but it will be unable to execute and mask its violence under the forms of the Constitution. When a majority is included in a faction, the form of popular government, on the other hand, enables it to sacrifice to its ruling passion or interest both the public good and the rights of other citizens. To secure the public good and private rights against the danger of such a faction, and at the same time to preserve the spirit and the form of popular government, is then the great object to which our inquiries are directed. . . .

COMPARING REPUBLICS AND DEMOCRACIES

From this view of the subject it may be concluded that a pure democracy, by which I mean a society consisting of a small number of citizens, who assemble and administer the government in person, can admit of no cure for the mischiefs of faction. A common passion or interest will, in almost every case, be felt by a majority of the whole; a communication and concert result from the form of government itself; and there is nothing to check the inducements to sacrifice the weaker party or an obnoxious individual. Hence it is that such democracies have ever been spectacles of turbulence and contention; have ever been found incompatible with personal security or the rights of property; and have in general been as short in their lives as they have been violent in their deaths. . . .

A republic, by which I mean a government in which the scheme of representation takes place, opens a different

prospect, and promises the cure for which we are seeking. Let us examine the points in which it varies from pure democracy, and we shall comprehend both the nature of the cure and the efficacy which it must derive from the Union.

The two great points of difference between a democracy and a republic are: first, the delegation of the government, in the latter, to a small number of citizens elected by the rest; secondly, the greater number of citizens, and greater sphere of country, over which the latter may be extended.

The effect of the first difference is, on the one hand, to refine and enlarge the public views, by passing them through the medium of a chosen body of citizens, whose wisdom may best discern the true interest of their country, and whose patriotism and love of justice will be least likely to sacrifice it to temporary or partial considerations. Under such a regulation, it may well happen that the public voice, pronounced by the representatives of the people, will be more consonant to the public good than if pronounced by the people themselves, convened for the purpose. On the other hand, the effect may be inverted. Men of factious tempers, of local prejudices, or of sinister designs, may, by intrigue, by corruption, or by other means, first obtain the suffrages, and then betray the interests, of the people. The question resulting is, whether small or extensive republics are more favorable to the election of proper guardians of the public weal; and it is clearly decided in favor of the latter by two obvious considerations:

In the first place, it is to be remarked that, however small the republic may be, the representatives must be raised to a certain number, in order to guard against the cabals of a few; and that, however large it may be, they must be limited to a certain number, in order to guard against the confusion of a multitude. Hence, the number of representatives in the two cases not being in proportion to that of the two constituents, and being proportionally greater in the small republic, it follows that, if the proportion of fit characters be not less in the large than in the small republic, the former will present a greater option, and consequently a greater probability of a fit choice.

In the next place, as each representative will be chosen by a greater number of citizens in the large than in the small republic, it will be more difficult for unworthy candidates to practise with success the vicious arts by which elections are too often carried; and the suffrages of the people being more free, will be more likely to centre in men who possess the most attractive merit and the most diffusive and established characters.

It must be confessed that in this, as in most other cases, there is a mean, on both sides of which inconveniences will be found to lie. By enlarging too much the number of electors, you render the representative too little acquainted with all their local circumstances and lesser interests; as by reducing it too much, you render him unduly attached to these, and too little fit to comprehend and pursue great and national objects. The federal Constitution forms a happy combination in this respect; the great and aggregate interests being referred to the national, the local and particular to the State legislatures.

The extent of the Union gives it the most palpable advantage.

EXTENDING THE SPHERE

The other point of difference is, the greater number of citizens and extent of territory which may be brought within the compass of republican than of democratic government; and it is this circumstance principally which renders factious combinations less to be dreaded in the former than in the latter. The smaller the society, the fewer probably will be the distinct parties and interests composing it; the fewer the distinct parties and interests, the more frequently will a majority be found of the same party; and the smaller the number of individuals composing a majority, and the smaller the compass within which they are placed, the most easily will they concert and execute their plans of oppression. Extend the sphere, and you take in a greater variety of parties and interests; you make it less probable that a majority of the whole will have a common motive to invade the rights of other citizens; or if such a common motive exists, it will be more difficult for all who feel it to discover their own strength, and to act in unison with each other. Besides other impediments, it may be remarked that, where there is a consciousness of unjust or dishonorable purposes, communication is always checked by distrust in proportion to the number whose concurrence is necessary.

Hence, it clearly appears, that the same advantage which a republic has over a democracy, in controlling the effects of faction, is enjoyed by a large over a small republic,—is enjoyed by the Union over the States composing it. Does the advantage consist in the substitution of representatives whose enlightened views and virtuous sentiments render them superior to local prejudices and to schemes of injustice? It will not be denied that the representation of the Union will be most likely to possess these requisite endowments. Does it consist in the greater security afforded by a greater variety of parties, against the event of any one party being able to outnumber and oppress the rest? In an equal degree does the increased variety of parties comprised within the Union, increase

this security. Does it, in fine, consist in the greater obstacles opposed to the concert and accomplishment of the secret wishes of an unjust and interested majority? Here, again, the extent of the Union gives it the most palpable advantage.

The influence of factious leaders may kindle a flame within their particular States, but will be unable to spread a general conflagration through the other States. A religious sect may degenerate into a political faction in a part of the Confederacy; but the variety of sects dispersed over the entire face of it must secure the national councils against any danger from that source. A rage for paper money, for an abolition of debts, for an equal division of property, or for any other improper or wicked project, will be less apt to pervade the whole body of the Union than a particular member of it; in the same proportion as such a malady is more likely to taint a particular county or district, than an entire State.

In the extent and proper structure of the Union, therefore, we behold a republican remedy for the diseases most incident to republican government. And according to the degree of pleasure and pride we feel in being republicans, ought to be our zeal in cherishing the spirit and supporting the character of Federalists.

FOR FURTHER READING

Bernard Bailyn, ed., *The Debate on the Constitution.* New York: Library of America, 1993.

Max M. Edling, *A Revolution in Favor of Government: Origins of the U.S. Constitution and the Making of the American State.* New York: Oxford University Press, 2003.

John P. Kaminski and Richard Leffler, eds., *Creating the Constitution: A History with Documents.* Madison, WI: The Center for the Study of the American Constitution, 1991.

Marvin Meyer, *The Mind of the Founder: Sources of the Political Thought of James Madison.* Hanover, NH: University Press of New England, 1981.

Herbert Storing, *What the Antifederalists Were For.* Chicago: University of Chicago Press, 1981.

Viewpoint 16A
The Constitution Needs a Bill of Rights (1788)
Patrick Henry (1736–1799)

INTRODUCTION *A recurring criticism of the Constitution created in Philadelphia in 1787 was that it lacked a bill of rights—a list of fundamental freedoms retained by the people that the government could not infringe upon. Beginning in Virginia in 1776, many of the new states had included a bill of rights in the constitutions they wrote during the American Revolution. However, the new federal constitution did not include such a list. Those opposed to creating a more powerful national government argued that this omission was evidence that such a government could threaten people's liberties. One influential advocate of this view was Patrick Henry, a longtime Virginia political leader whose oratorical skills had helped to inspire the American Revolution. He dominated Virginia state politics during the 1770s and 1780s, serving both as governor and leading member of Virginia's House of Delegates. The following viewpoint is taken from a speech made in June 1788 before a special convention meeting to decide whether to ratify the new Constitution. Henry argues that the Constitution—lacking a bill of rights—will supersede Virginia's constitution and its state bill of rights, thus endangering the people's freedoms.*

What examples of government abuses of rights does Henry suggest might happen? Some historians have argued that Henry and other anti-federalists were more concerned about retaining the powers of the state governments than about individual liberties; do the excerpts presented here support or refute that theory?

Mr. Chairman.—The necessity of a Bill of Rights appear to me to be greater in this Government, than ever it was in any Government before. . . .

VIRGINIA'S EXAMPLE

Let us consider the sentiments which have been entertained by the people of America on this subject. At the revolution, it must be admitted, that it was their sense to put down those great rights which ought in all countries to be held inviolable and sacred. Virginia did so we all remember. She made a compact to reserve, expressly, certain rights. When fortified with full, adequate, and abundant representation, was she satisfied with that representation? No.—She most cautiously and guardedly reserved and secured those invaluable, inestimable rights and privileges, which no people, inspired with the least glow of the patriotic love of liberty, ever did, or ever can, abandon. She is called upon now to abandon them, and dissolve that compact which secured them to her. She is called upon to accede to another compact which most infallibly supercedes and annihilates her present one. Will she do it?—That is the question. If you intend to reserve your unalienable rights, you must have the most express stipulation. For if implication be allowed, you are ousted of those rights. If the people do not think it necessary to reserve them, they will be supposed to be given up. How were the Congressional rights defined when the people of America united by a confederacy to defend their liberties and rights against the tyrannical attempts of Great-Britain? The States were not then contented with implied reservation. No, Mr. Chairman. It was expressly declared in our Confederation that every right was retained by the States respectively,

From Patrick Henry's speech before the Virginia ratifying convention, June 16, 1788.

which was not given up to the Government of the United States. But there is no such thing here. You therefore by a natural and unavoidable implication, give up your rights to the General Government. Your own example furnishes an argument against it. If you give up these powers, without a Bill of Rights, you will exhibit the most, absurd thing to mankind that ever the world saw—A Government that has abandoned all its powers—The powers of direct taxation, the sword, and the purse. You have disposed of them to Congress, without a Bill of Rights—without check, limitation, or controul. And still you have checks and guards—still you keep barriers—pointed where? Pointed against your weakened, prostrated, enervated State Government! You have a Bill of Rights to defend you against the State Government, which is bereaved of all power; and yet you have none against Congress, though in full and exclusive possession of all power! You arm yourselves against the weak and defenceless, and expose yourselves naked to the armed and powerful. Is not this a conduct of unexampled absurdity? . . .

THE PEOPLE WANT A BILL OF RIGHTS

In this business of legislation, your Members of Congress will lose the restriction of not imposing excessive fines, demanding excessive bail, and inflicting cruel and unusual punishments.—These are prohibited by your Declaration of Rights. What has distinguished our ancestors?—That they would not admit of tortures, or cruel and barbarous punishments. But Congress may introduce the practice of the civil law, in preference to that of the common law.—They may introduce the practice of France, Spain, and Germany—Of torturing to extort a confession of the crime. They will say that they might as well draw examples from those countries as from Great-Britain; and they will tell you, that there is such a necessity of strengthening the arm of Government that they must have a criminal equity, and extort confession by torture, in order to punish with still more relentless severity. We are then lost and undone.—And can any man think it troublesome, when we can by a small interference prevent our rights from being lost?—If yon will, like the Virginian Government, give them knowledge of the extent of the rights retained by the people, and the powers themselves, they will, if they be honest men, thank you for it.—Will they not wish to go on sure grounds?—But if you leave them otherwise, they will not know how to proceed; and being in a state of uncertainty, they will assume rather than give up powers by implication. A Bill of Rights may be summed up in a few words. What do they tell us?—That our rights are reserved.—Why not say so? Is it because it will consume too much paper? Gentlemen's reasonings against a Bill of Rights, do not satisfy me. Without saying which has the right side, it remains doubtful. A Bill of Rights is a favourite thing with the Virginians, and the people of the other States likewise. It may be their prejudice, but the Government ought to suit their geniuses, otherwise its operation will be unhappy. A Bill of Rights, even if its necessity be doubtful, will exclude the possibly of dispute, and with great submission, I think the best way is to have no dispute. In the present Constitution, they are restrained from issuing general warrants to search suspected places, or seize persons not named, without evidence of the commission of the fact, &c. There was certainly some celestial influence governing those who deliberated on that Constitution:—For they have with the most cautious and enlightened circumspection, guarded those indefeasible rights, which ought ever to be held sacred. The officers of Congress may come upon you, fortified with all the terrors of paramount federal authority.—Excisemen may come in multitudes:— For the limitation of their numbers no man knows.— They may, unless the General Government be restrained by a Bill of Rights, or some similar restriction, go into your cellars and rooms, and search, ransack and measure, every thing you eat, drink and wear. They ought to be restrained within proper bounds. With respect to the freedom of the press, I need say nothing; for it is hoped that the Gentlemen who shall compose Congress, will take care as little as possible, to infringe the rights of human nature.—This will result from their integrity. They should from prudence, abstain from violating the rights of their constituents. They are not however expressly restrained.—But whether they will intermeddle with that palladium of our liberties or not. I leave you to determine.

Viewpoint 16B

The Constitution Does Not Need a Bill of Rights (1788)

Alexander Hamilton (1755–1804)

INTRODUCTION *Alexander Hamilton, a military aide to General George Washington during the Revolutionary War, and later secretary of the treasury during Washington's presidency, was one of the leading pro-Constitution participants in the debate over whether the states should ratify the document. He collaborated with James Madison and John Jay in writing a series of letters to newspapers under the pseudonym "Publius." The essays, which defended the Constitution against various criticisms, were published in 1788 in book form as* The Federalist.

Hamilton wrote the bulk of the essays, including No. 84, from which the following viewpoint is taken. In this essay he takes up the criticism that the new Constitution lacked a bill of rights. Hamilton asserts that the rights of Americans are protected by state constitutions, and that the new federal government is

not being given express power to infringe upon individual liberties. The structure of the new government, he argues, with its separation of powers between its branches and the guaranteed right of people to elect their representatives, among other features, is enough to ensure the people's liberties. Hamilton goes on to conclude that a listing of rights might be dangerous, because it could be construed to mean that any rights not explicitly listed would lack protection.

Hamilton was partially successful in convincing others of his arguments. The states ultimately voted to ratify the new Constitution. However, enough people raised concerns about the lack of a bill of rights to convince the new Congress to immediately amend the document. These amendments—the federal Bill of Rights—were completed in 1791.

What are the true sources of liberty, according to Hamilton? In his view, in what ways is the whole Constitution a bill of rights?

To the People of the State of New-York.

In the course of the foregoing review of the constitution I have taken notice of, and endeavoured to answer, most of the objections which have appeared against it. There however remain a few which either did not fall naturally under any particular head, or were forgotten in their proper places. These shall now be discussed: but as the subject has been drawn into great length, I shall so far consult brevity as to comprise all my observations on these miscellaneous points in a single paper.

———————◼———————

Bills of rights . . . are not only unnecessary in the proposed constitution, but would even be dangerous.

———————◼———————

The most considerable of these remaining objections is, that the plan of the convention contains no bill of rights. . . .

It has been several times truly remarked, that bills of rights are in their origin, stipulations between kings and their subjects, abridgments of prerogative in favor of privilege, reservations of rights not surrendered to the prince. Such was Magna Charta, obtained by the Barons, sword in hand, from king John. . . . Such also was the declaration of right presented by the lords and commons to the prince of Orange in 1688, and afterwards thrown into the form of an act of parliament, called the bill of rights. It is evident, therefore, that according to their primitive signification, they have no application to constitutions

From *The Federalist No. 84* by Alexander Hamilton, under the pseudonym Publius (New York, 1788).

professedly founded upon the power of the people, and executed by their immediate representatives and servants. Here, in strictness, the people surrender nothing, and as they retain every thing, they have no need of particular reservations. "We the people of the United States, to secure the blessings of liberty to ourselves and our posterity, do ordain and establish this constitution for the United States of America." Here is a better recognition of popular rights than volumes of those aphorisms which make the principal figure in several of our state bills of rights, and which would sound much better in a treatise of ethics than in a constitution of government....

A BILL OF RIGHTS WOULD BE DANGEROUS

I go further, and affirm that bills of rights, in the sense and in the extent in which they are contended for, are not only unnecessary in the proposed constitution, but would even be dangerous. They would contain various exceptions to powers which are not granted; and on this very account, would afford a colourable pretext to claim more than were granted. For why declare that things shall not be done which there is no power to do? Why for instance, should it be said, that the liberty of the press shall not be restrained, when no power is given by which restrictions may be imposed? I will not contend that such a provision would confer a regulating power; but it is evident that it would furnish, to men disposed to usurp, a plausible pretence for claiming that power. They might urge with a semblance of reason, that the constitution ought not to be charged with the absurdity of providing against the abuse of an authority, which was not given, and that the provision against restraining the liberty of the press afforded a clear implication, that a power to prescribe proper regulations concerning it, was intended to be vested in the national government. This may serve as a specimen of the numerous handles which would be given to the doctrine of constructive powers, by the indulgence of an injudicious zeal for bills of rights.

On the subject of the liberty of the press, as much has been said, I cannot forbear adding a remark or two: In the first place, I observe that there is not a syllable concerning it in the constitution of this state, and in the next, I contend that whatever has been said about it in that of any other state, amounts to nothing. What signifies a declaration that "the liberty of the press shall be inviolably preserved"? What is the liberty of the press? Who can give it any definition which would not leave the utmost latitude for evasion? I hold it to be impracticable; and from this, I infer, that its security, whatever fine declarations may be inserted in any constitution respecting it, must altogether depend on public opinion, and on the general spirit of the people and of the government. And here, after all, as intimated upon another occasion, must we seek for the only solid basis of all our rights.

THE CONSTITUTION IS A BILL OF RIGHTS

There remains but one other view of this matter to conclude the point. The truth is, after all the declamation we have heard, that the constitution is itself in every rational sense, and to every useful purpose, a Bill of Rights. The several bills of rights, in Great-Britain, form its constitution, and conversely the constitution of each state is its bill of rights. And the proposed constitution, if adopted, will be the bill of rights of the union. Is it one object of a bill of rights to declare and specify the political privileges of the citizens in the structure and administration of the government? This is done in the most ample and precise manner in the plan of the convention, comprehending various precautions for the public security, which are not to be found in any of the state constitutions. Is another object of a bill of rights to define certain immunities and modes of proceeding, which are relative to personal and private concerns? This we have seen has also been attended to, in a variety of cases, in the same plan. Adverting therefore to the substantial meaning of a bill of rights, it is absurd to allege that it is not to be found in the work of the convention. It may be said that it does not go far enough, though it will not be easy to make this appear; but it can with no propriety be contended that there is no such thing. It certainly must be immaterial what mode is observed as to the order of declaring the rights of the citizens, if they are to be found in any part of the instrument which establishes the government. And hence it must be apparent that much of what has been said on this subject rests merely on verbal and nominal distinctions, which are entirely foreign from the substance of the thing.

FOR FURTHER READING

James MacGregor Burns and Stewart Burns, *A People's Charter: The Pursuit of Rights in America.* New York: Knopf, 1991.

Ronald Hoffman and Peter J. Albert, eds. *The Bill of Rights: Government Proscribed.* Charlottesville: University Press of Virginia, 1997.

Henry Mayer, *A Son of Thunder.* New York: Franklin Watts, 1986.

Bernard Schwartz, *The Bill of Rights: A Documentary History*, New York: Chelsea House, 1971.

Garry Wills, *Explaining America: The Federalist.* New York: Doubleday, 1982.

Viewpoint 17A
Jay's Treaty Should Be Rejected (1795)
Robert R. Livingston (1746–1813)

INTRODUCTION *A major diplomatic challenge facing the United States following independence was managing its relations with the leading world powers of the time— Great Britain and France. Disagreements over U.S. foreign policy also reflected growing political divisions, which erupted during the national controversy over Jay's Treaty in 1795.*

President George Washington sent lawyer and diplomat John Jay to Great Britain in 1794 to negotiate a treaty at a time when the two nations appeared to be heading toward a military showdown. Great Britain—then at war with France—was upset with American trade with France and with losing British sailors who were deserting to serve on American ships. The United States was upset about British naval actions against U.S. trade, which included the confiscation of American trade goods and the "impressments" of American sailors suspected of being British deserters. Great Britain had also been slow to relinquish its military forts in America's western territories (as promised in the 1783 Treaty of Paris). Many Americans accused the British of assisting Indian attacks on American settlers.

The treaty Jay was able to negotiate caused a nationwide uproar when it was revealed to the public in 1795, with critics arguing that it was too favorable to Great Britain. While Britain made new promises to withdraw its western forts, it made few concessions elsewhere, and it reserved the rights to impress American sailors and to seize (with compensation) American trade cargo headed for France. The following viewpoint is taken from a pamphlet by "Cato," a pseudonym for Robert R. Livingston. A New York lawyer and member of the Continental Congress committee that drafted America's Declaration of Independence in 1776, Livingston was later appointed minister to France.

How does Livingston describe the balance of power in Europe? Why should the United States be especially concerned about Great Britain's presence in the western territories, according to Livingston?

Britain, on the day of the signature of the treaty, was involved in a war with the bravest people in Europe [France]: in the whole course of this war, she had experienced continued defeats and disgraces; her treasures were wasted upon allies that either deserted or were too feeble to afford her effectual aid; her debt had grown to the enormous sum of three hundred millions; her navy could only be manned by the most destructive burthens upon her commerce; her manufactures were languishing; her fleets were unable to protect her trade, which had suffered unexampled losses. And while she was sinking under her burdens, her antagonist was consolidating her government, and growing so rapidly in strength, reputation, and vigour, as to threaten her existence as a nation. The United States were, on the other hand, in the highest prosperity; their numbers had doubled since they had successfully

From *Examination of the Treaty of Amity, Commerce, and Navigation, Between the United States and Great-Britain, in Several Numbers* by Cato (Robert R. Livingston), 1795.

measured swords with Britain; they possessed men, arms, military stores, and an ally, who was alone too powerful for her enemies. Sweden and Denmark who had received insults from Britain, were ready to make a common cause with her; as the marine of England and France were nearly balanced, the weight of America, had she been forced into the war, would have turned the scale, and compleated the ruin of the British commerce.... We could have forced her into any measure that it was just or proper for us to ask. And, indeed, so fully satisfied were the Americans, of every party, of the superiority of our situation, that no doubt was entertained of a favorable issue to Mr. Jay's negociation....

THE WESTERN TERRITORIES

By the 2d article of the treaty, the British promise to evacuate the western posts by the 1st of June, 1796. By the treaty of Paris, in 1783, they promised to evacuate with all convenient speed; which, if we may judge by the speed with which they have found it convenient to evacuate all their posts in France, Flanders, Germany, Holland, and Brabant, one would have supposed must have meant a much shorter time than eighteen months, so that all that the treaty acquires with respect to the posts, is less than we were entitled to by the treaty of Paris. Surely we might expect better security than a mere promise, from a nation which has already shewn, in their violation of the past, the little reliance that can be placed on their future engagements. By June, 1796, it is not improbable that our situation, or that of Britain, may be changed; what security shall we then have for the performance of the treaty? It is said (by those shameless apologists who are determined to find every ministerial measure right) that every treaty is a promise, and that if we are not to rely upon a promise, there can be no treaties, I answer, that it is the practice of negociators, where the character of the nation, or other circumstances, give reason to suspect a violation of their engagements, *not to rely* upon a naked promise, but to expect some guarantee or surety for the performance; that in the present case, as the promise was evidently extorted by the pressure of existing circumstances, we should see to the performance while those circumstances continue to exist. It is evident, before Mr. Jay left this country, that the British were so far from intending to evacuate the posts, that they had determined to extend their limits; this may not only be inferred from the encouragement they gave to the depredations of the Indians, but undeniably proved by [governor-general of Canada] Lord Dorchester's speech, which, though disavowed by [British secretary of war Henry] Dundas, is now admitted to have been made in consequence of express instructions. The promise, then to evacuate, has been extorted by French victories, by the humiliation of the British nation, and by their apprehension that we might at last be provoked to do ourselves justice while they were embarrassed with France. Surely then the evacuation should have been insisted upon, while these circumstances operated with full force. . . . Are we not at this moment at war with the savages? Is not this war attended with much expence to the nation, and much private distress? Is not the blood of our citizens daily shed? These evils must continue as long as the posts are in the hands of the British, or a peace, if practicable, must be purchased by the United States at very considerable expence. Were we to estimate the difference on this point of view, between an immediate evacuation, and one that is to take place in June 1796, it would certainly not fall short of one million of dollars, independent of the price. If to this we add the annual profits of the Indian trade, amounting to 800,000, it will appear, that the United States lose above a million of dollars by retention of the posts, supposing (which is at least problematical) that they will be surrendered at the period proposed. Those who think with me, that decision of the part of our government, and firmness in our minister, could not have failed to effect an immediate restitution of our territory, will know to what account to charge this heavy loss of blood and treasure. . . .

------------■------------

The treaty has obtained no adequate compensation for the injuries we have suffered.

------------■------------

Even the coward advocates for peace, feel their spirits rise on the unexampled indignities which this treaty imposes. And for what? Are we nearer peace (if by peace is meant the security of our persons and property, from foreign depredations) than when Mr. Jay left this country? Is there a single outrage which we suffered before which is not continued to this moment? And yet the advocates for the treaty are continually ringing in our ears, the blessings of peace, the horrors of war; and they have the effrontery to assure us, that we enjoy the first and have escaped the last, merely (to borrow a ministerial term) through the instrumentality of the treaty. Does any body believe, that if we had continued to suffer the British to plunder our trade, to man their ships with our seamen, to possess our frontiers in quiet, that they would have declared war upon us, at least till they had conquered France? . . . In a political view, the treaty is bad, as it detaches us from engagements which our interest and honour equally invite us to maintain; as it sacrifices our friends to our enemies, and holds forth to the world, that those nations who treat us worst, will share the greatest portion of our attachment, and that,

like fawning spaniels, we can be beaten into love and submission. . . .

I trust, however, that enough has been said to shew, that the treaty has obtained no adequate compensation for the injuries we have suffered; that it has relinquished important claims that we had upon British government, that it has given no protection to our seamen, that it is injurious to our commerce, and ruinous to our navigation, that it takes from us the means we possessed of retaliating injuries without the hazard of a war, that it pledged the country for immense sums of money, which it does not owe, while it curtails our demands upon Britain; that it gives the British subjects a variety of privileges in our country, which are but partially returned to us, that it counteracts the existing laws, and violates the federal constitution, and that it infringes the rights of individual states.

Viewpoint 17B
Jay's Treaty Should Be Accepted (1796)
Fisher Ames (1758–1808)

INTRODUCTION *The national debate that erupted over Jay's Treaty between Great Britain and America reflected the development of opposing political powers that were then being formed around two key members of President George Washington's cabinet: the Federalists, led by Secretary of the Treasury Alexander Hamilton, and the Democratic-Republicans, led by Secretary of State Thomas Jefferson. Federalists (not to be confused with the federalists that supported the ratification of the Constitution in 1789) generally supported closer diplomatic ties with Great Britain and favored Jay's Treaty. Jefferson's Democratic-Republicans, on the other hand, supported France and were harshly critical of Jay's Treaty as being too favorable to Great Britain.*

The Senate, controlled by the Federalists, narrowly voted to ratify Jay's Treaty in 1795. In 1796, however, the House of Representatives debated whether to withhold funding to implement the agreement. The following viewpoint is taken from a speech in support of Jay's Treaty by Fisher Ames, a leading Federalist and member of Congress from 1789 to 1797. He argues that the treaty helps the United States by enabling it to remain neutral in the ongoing wars between Great Britain and France. The House ultimately decided to appropriate funding.

What argument does Ames make about opponents of the treaty? Why would rejecting it be on the grounds that it damaged U.S. prestige, according to Ames? How do his views on Indian hostilities differ from those of Robert R. Livingston, author of the opposing viewpoint?

The Treaty is bad, fatally bad, is the cry. It sacrifices the interest, the honor, the independence of the United States, and the faith of our engagements to France.... The language of passion and exaggeration may silence that of sober reason in other places, it has not done it here. The question here is, whether the treaty be really so very fatal as to oblige the nation to break its faith....

HONOR OF THE UNITED STATES

Justice, the laws and practice of nations, a just regard for peace as a duty to mankind, and the known wish of our citizens, as well as that self-respect which required it of the nation to act with dignity and moderation, all these forbid an appeal to arms before we had tried the effect of negotiation. The honor of the United States was saved, not forfeited by treaty. The Treaty itself by its stipulations for the posts, for indemnity and for a due observation of our neutral rights, has justly raised the character of the nation. Never did the name of America appear in Europe with more lustre than upon the event of ratifying this instrument. The fact is of a nature to overcome all contradiction.

But *the independence of the country—we are colonists again*. This is the cry of the very men who tell us that France will resent our exercise of the rights of an independent nation to adjust our wrongs with an aggressor, without giving her the opportunity to say those wrongs shall subsist and shall not be adjusted. This is an admirable specimen of independence. The Treaty with Great Britain, it cannot be denied is unfavorable to this strange sort of independence....

Why do they pretend that if they reject this, and insist upon more, more will be accomplished? Let us be explicit—more would not satisfy. If all was granted, would not a Treaty of amity with Britain still be obnoxious? Have we not this instant heard it urged against our Envoy, that he was not ardent enough in his hatred of Great-Britain? A Treaty of Amity is condemned because it was not made by a foe, and in the spirit of one. The same gentleman at the same instant repeats a very prevailing objection, that no Treaty should be made with the enemy of France. No Treaty, exclaim others, should be made with a monarch or a despot. There will be no naval security while those sea robbers domineer on the ocean. Their den must be destroyed. That nation must be extirpated....

THE WESTERN FORTS

The refusal of [Great Britain to withdraw from] the posts (inevitable if we reject the treaty) is a measure too decisive in its nature to be neutral in its consequences. From great causes we are to look for great effects. A plain and obvious

From *Speech in Support of the Motion: Resolved, That It Is Expedient to Pass the Laws Necessary to Carry into Effect the Treaty Between the United States and Great-Britain* by Fisher Ames (Boston, 1796), reprinted in *American History Told by Contemporaries*, Albert B. Hart, ed., New York: Macmillan, 1901.

one will be, the price of the western lands will fall. Settlers will not chuse to fix their habitation on a field of battle. Those who talk so much of the interest of the United States should calculate how deeply it will be affected by rejecting the treaty—how vast a tract of wild land will almost cease to be property. This loss, let it be observed, will fall upon a fund expressly devoted to sink the national debt....

Will the tendency to Indian hostilities be contested by any one? Experience gives the answer. The frontiers were scourged with war until the negociation with Great-Britain was far advanced, and then the state of hostility ceased. Perhaps the public agents of both nations are innocent of fomenting the Indian war, and perhaps they are not. We ought not however to expect that neighbouring nations, highly irritated against each other, will neglect the friendship of the savages, the traders will gain an influence and will abuse it—and who is ignorant that their passions are easily raised and hardly restrained from violence? Their situation will oblige them to chuse between this country and Great-Britain, in case the Treaty should be rejected. They will not be our friends and at the same time the friends of our enemies....

It is not the part of prudence to be inattentive to the tendencies of measures. Where there is any ground to fear that these will be pernicious, wisdom and duty forbid that we should underate them.—If we reject the treaty, will our peace be as safe as if we execute it with good faith?...

Are the Posts to remain forever in the possession of Great-Britain? Let those who reject them, when the Treaty offers them to our hands, say, if they chuse, they are of no importance. If they are, will they take them by force? The argument I am urging would then come to a point. To use force is war. To talk of Treaty again is too absurd. Posts and redress must come from voluntary good will, Treaty or war.

The conclusion is plain, if the state of peace shall continue, so will the British possession of the posts....

AMERICAN NEUTRALITY

Let me cheer the mind, weary no doubt and ready to despond on this prospect, by presenting another which it is yet in our power to realise. Is it possible for a real American to look at the prosperity of this country without some desire for its continuance, without some respect for the measures which, any will say, produced, and all will confess have preserved it?... The great interest and the general desire of our people was to enjoy the advantages of neutrality. This instrument, however misrepresented, affords America that inestimable security. The causes of our disputes are either cut up by the roots, or referred to a new negociation, after the end of the European war. This was gaining every thing, because it confirmed our neutrality, by which our citizens are gaining every thing. This alone would justify the engagements of the government. For, when the fiery vapors of the war lowered in the skirts of our horizon, all our wishes were concentered in this one, that we might escape the desolation of the storm. This treaty, like a rainbow on the edge of the cloud, marked to our eyes the space where it was raging, and afforded at the same time the sure prognostic of fair weather. If we reject it, the vivid colours will grow pale, it will be a baleful meteor portending tempest and war.

FOR FURTHER READING

Jerald A. Combs, *The Jay Treaty: Political Battleground of the Founding Fathers.* Berkeley: University of California Press, 1970.

Joseph J. Ellis, *Founding Brothers: The Revolutionary Generation.* New York: Vintage, 2000.

Todd Estes, *The Jay Treaty Debate, Public Opinion, And the Evolution of Early American Political Culture.* Amherst: University of Massachusetts Press, 2006.

Daniel G. Lang, *Foreign Policy in the Early Republic: The Law of Nations and the Balance of Power.* Baton Rouge: University of Louisiana Press, 1985.

Viewpoint 18A

The Sedition Act Violates the Bill of Rights (1799)

George Hay (1765–1830)

INTRODUCTION *In 1798 the United States again stood on the brink of war with a major European power, only this time with France rather than Great Britain. In preparation for this anticipated war, Congress passed the Alien and Sedition Acts. The Sedition Act proscribed "any false, scandalous and malicious" speech and writing against the government and its officials. Anyone speaking, writing, or publishing "with intent to defame . . . or bring into contempt or disrepute" the president or other government official was subject to fines and jail. The fears of some that the law would be used to stifle political criticism of the pro-British Federalist Party appeared to be realized after several prominent opposition party newspaper editors and leaders were jailed.*

Sedition Act critics argued that the law violated the first amendment of the Bill of Rights, which stated that "Congress shall make no law . . . abridging the freedom of speech, or of the press." Those who defended the law argued that as long as Congress did not create a "prior restraint" on what newspapers could publish, it could still punish and hold accountable newspaper publishers for seditious or otherwise harmful discourse after publication. A less narrow interpretation of the First Amendment is found in the following viewpoint, taken from a 1799 pamphlet by George Hay (using the pseudonym "Horensius"). Hay, a member of the

Virginia House of Delegates and a political opponent of the Federalist Party, contends that the Sedition Act does indeed violate the First Amendment, which he argues should be defined broadly.

How does Hay define freedom? What did the authors of the First Amendment intend, according to Hay? How does he respond to the argument that the First Amendment prohibits only the "prior restraint" of newspapers?

It is the object of the succeeding letters, to demonstrate, that so much of the Sedition Bill, as relates to *printed* libels, is expressly forbidden by the constitution of the United States. . . .

The words of the constitution, which contain the express prohibition here relied on, are, "Congress shall make no law abridging the freedom of speech or of the press." . . .

The words, "freedom of the press," like most other words, have a meaning, a clear, precise, and definite meaning, which the times require, should be unequivocally ascertained. That this has not been done before, is a wonderful and melancholy evidence of the imbecility of the human mind, and of the slow progress which it makes, in acquiring knowledge even on subjects the most useful and interesting.

It will, I presume, be admitted, that the words in question have a meaning, and that the framers of the amendment containing these words, meant something when they declared, that the freedom of the press should not be abridged.

To ascertain what the "freedom of the press" is, we have only to ascertain what freedom itself is. For, surely, it will be conceded, that freedom applied to one subject, means the same, as freedom applied to another subject.

TWO KINDS OF FREEDOM

Now freedom is of two kinds, and of two kinds only: one is, that absolute freedom which belongs to man, previous to any social institution; and the other, that qualified or abridged freedom, which he is content to enjoy, for the sake of government and society. I believe there is no other sort of freedom in which man is concerned.

The absolute freedom then, or what is the same thing, the freedom, belonging to man before any social compact, is the power uncontrouled by law, of doing what he pleases, *provided he does no injury to any other individual.* If this definition of freedom be applied to the press, as surely it ought to be, the press, if I may personify it, may do whatever it pleases to do, uncontrouled by any law, *taking care however to do no injury to any individual.* This injury can only be by slander or defamation,

From *An Essay on the Liberty of the Press* by George Hay (Philadelphia, 1799).

and reparation should be made for it in a state of nature as well as in society.

But freedom in society, or what is called civil liberty, is defined to be, natural liberty, so far, restrained by law as the public good requires, and no farther. This is the definition given by a writer, particularly distinguished for the accuracy of his definitions, and which, perhaps, cannot be mended. Now let freedom, under this definition, be applied to the press, and what will the freedom of the press amount to? It will amount precisely to the privilege of publishing, as far as the legislative power shall say, the public good requires: that is to say, the freedom of the press will be regulated by law. If the word freedom was used in this sense, by the framers of the amendment, they meant to say, Congress shall make no law abridging the freedom of the press, which freedom, however, is to be regulated by law. Folly itself does not speak such language.

It has been admitted by the reader, who has advanced thus far, that the framers of the amendment meant something. They knew, no doubt, that the power granted to Congress, did not authorise any controul over the press, but they knew that its freedom could not be too cautiously guarded from invasion. The amendment in question was therefore introduced. Now if they used the word "freedom" under the first definition, they did mean something, and something of infinite importance in all free countries, the total exemption of the press from any kind of legislative controul. But if they used the word freedom under the second definition they meant nothing; for if they supposed that the freedom of the press, was absolute freedom, so far restrained by law as the public good required, and no farther, the amendment left the legislative power of the government on this subject, precisely where it was before. But it has been already admired that the amendment had a meaning: the construction therefore which allows it no meaning is absurd and must be rejected.

THE MEANING OF FREEDOM

This argument may be summed up in a few words. The word "freedom" has meaning. It is either absolute, that is exempt from all law, or it is qualified, that is, regulated by law. If it be exempt from the controul of law, the Sedition Bill which controuls the "freedom of the press" is unconstitutional. But if it is to be regulated by law, the amendment which declares that Congress shall make no law to abridge the freedom of the press, which freedom however may be regulated by law, is the grossest absurdity that ever was conceived by the human mind.

That by the words "freedom of the press," is meant a total exemption of the press from legislative controul, will further appear from the following cases, in which it is manifest, that the word freedom is used with this signification and no other.

It is obvious in itself and it is admitted by all men, that freedom of speech means the power uncontroued by law, of speaking either truth or falsehood at the discretion of each individual, *provided no other individual be injured.* This power is, *as yet,* in its full extent in the United States. A man may say every thing which his passion can suggest; he may employ all his time, and all his talents, if he is wicked enough to do so, in *speaking* against the government matters that are false, scandalous, and malicious; but he is admired by the majority of Congress to be sheltered by the article in question, which forbids a law abridging the freedom of speech. If then freedom of speech means, in the construction of the Constitution, the privilege of speaking *any thing* without controul, the words freedom of the press, which form a part of the same sentence, mean the privilege of printing *any thing* without controul.

FREEDOM OF SPEECH AND RELIGION

Happily for mankind, the word "freedom" begins now to be applied to religion also. In the United States it is applied in its fullest force, and religious freedom is completely understood to mean the power uncontroued by law of professing and publishing any opinion on religious topics, which any individual may choose to profess or publish, and of supporting these opinions by any statements he may think proper to make. The fool may not only say in his heart, there is no God, but he may announce if he pleases his atheism to the world. He may endeavor to corrupt mankind, not only by opinions that are erroneous, but by facts which are false. Still however he will be safe, because he lives in a country where religious freedom is established. If then freedom of religion, will not permit a man to be punished, for publishing any opinions on religious topics and supporting those opinions by false facts, surely freedom of the press, which is the medium of all publications, will not permit a man to be punished, for publishing any opinion on any subject, and supporting it by any statement whatever....

I contend therefore, that if the words freedom of the press, have any meaning at all they mean a total exemption from any law making any publication whatever criminal. Whether the unequivocal avowal of this doctrine in the United States would produce mischief or not, is a question which perhaps I may have leisure to discuss. I must be content here to observe, that the mischief if any, which might arise from this doctrine could not be remedied or prevented, but by means of a power fatal to the liberty of the people....

PRIOR RESTRAINT

But, it has been said, that the freedom of the press, consists not in the privilege of printing truth; but in an exemption from previous restraint, and as the Sedition Bill imposes no previous restraint, it does not abridge the freedom of the press. This *profound* remark is borrowed from [William] Blackstone and [Jean Louis] De Lolme, and is gravely repeated, by those who are weak enough to take opinions upon trust.

If these writers meant to state what the law was understood to be in England, they are correct. But this definition does not deserve to be transplanted into America. In Britain, a legislative controul over the press, is, perhaps essential to the preservation of the "present order of things;" but it does not follow, that such controul is essential here. In Britain, a vast standing army is necessary to keep the people in peace, and the monarch on his throne; but it does not follow that the tranquillity of America, or the personal safety of the President, would be promoted by a similar institution.

---◼︎---

The freedom of the press . . . means the total exemption of the press from any kind of legislative control.

---◼︎---

A single remark will be sufficient to expose the extreme fallacy of the idea, when applied to the Constitution of the United States. If the freedom of the press consists in an exemption from previous restraint, Congress may, without injury to the freedom of the press, punish with death, any thing *actually* published, which a political inquisition may choose to condemn.

But on what ground is this British doctrine respecting the freedom of the press introduced here? In Britain, the parliament is acknowledged to be omnipotent. . . . In Britain there is no constitution, no limitation of legislative power; but in America, there is a constitution, the power of the legislature is limited, and the object of one limitation is to secure the freedom of the press. . . .

The freedom of the press, therefore, means the total exemption of the press from any kind of legislative controul, and consequently the Sedition Bill, which is an act of legislative controul, is an abridgment of its liberty, and expressly forbidden by the constitution. Which was to be demonstrated.

The Sedition Act Does Not Violate the Bill of Rights (1799)

5th Congress Majority Report

INTRODUCTION *The Sedition Act of 1798 made it a crime to "print, utter, or publish . . . any false, scandalous, and malicious writing" against the government.*

Enforcement of the law seemed to indicate that political criticism of the ruling Federalist Party and its support of war with France constituted "malicious writing." Under the law several prominent newspaper editors who had questioned Federalist policies were jailed, as was Congressman Matthew Lyon, who spent four months in prison for publishing a sharp attack on President John Adams. Critics of the law argued that it violated free speech and press rights found in the First Amendment of the Bill of Rights.

In 1799 the House of Representatives, with Federalist members still in the majority, debated the constitutionality of the Sedition Act. Members of the opposing Federalist Party and Democratic-Republican Party did not agree, resulting in two reports; the following viewpoint is excerpted from the Majority Report. The report defends the Sedition Act, arguing that while the Constitution forbids Congress from censoring speeches and newspaper writings, it has the power to pass laws punishing false and seditious writing. The primary author of the majority report was Chauncey Goodrich, a Federalist congressman from Connecticut.

Why was it necessary for Congress to pass the Sedition Act, according to the report? Do the authors of the report have similar or different conceptions of freedom than George Hay, author of the opposing viewpoint?

The "Act in addition to an act entitled an act for the punishment of certain crimes against the United States," commonly called the sedition act, contains provisions of a twofold nature: first, against seditious acts, and, second, against libellous and seditious writings. The first have never been complained of, nor has any objection been made to its validity. The objection applies solely to the second; and on the ground, in the first place, that Congress have no power by the Constitution to pass any act for punishing libels, no such power being expressly given, and all powers not given to Congress, being reserved to the States respectively, or the people thereof.

To this objection it is answered, that a law to punish false, scandalous, and malicious writings against the Government, with intent to stir up sedition, is a law necessary for carrying into effect the power vested by the Constitution in the Government of the United States, and in the departments and officers thereof, and, consequently, such a law as Congress may pass; because the direct tendency of such writings is to obstruct the acts of the Government by exciting opposition to them, to endanger its existence by rendering it odious and contemptible in the eyes of the people, and to produce seditious combinations against the laws, the power to punish which has never been questioned; because it would be manifestly absurd to suppose

From the Majority and Minority Reports on the Repeal of the Sedition Act, *Annals of Congress*, 5th Cong., 3rd sess. (February 25, 1799).

that a Government might punish sedition, and yet be void of power to prevent it by punishing those acts which plainly and necessarily lead to it; and, because, under the general power to make all laws proper and necessary for carrying into effect the powers vested by the Constitution in the Government of the United States, Congress has passed many laws for which no express provision can be found in the Constitution, and the constitutionality of which has never been questioned. . . .

The liberty of the press consists not in a license for every man to publish what he pleases without being liable to punishment.

It is objected to this act, in the second place, that it is expressly contrary to that part of the Constitution which declares, that "Congress shall make no law respecting an establishment of religion, or prohibiting the free exercise thereof, or abridging the liberty of the press." The act in question is said to be an "abridgment of the liberty of the press," and therefore unconstitutional.

WHAT TRUE LIBERTY CONSISTS OF

To this it is answered, in the first place, that the liberty of the press consists not in a license for every man to publish what he pleases without being liable to punishment, if he should abuse this license to the injury of others, but in a permission to publish, without previous restraint, whatever he may think proper, being answerable to the public and individuals, for any abuse of this permission to their prejudice. In like manner, as the liberty of speech does not authorize a man to speak malicious slanders against his neighbor, nor the liberty of action justify him in going, by violence, into another man's house, or in assaulting any person whom he may meet in the streets. In the several States the liberty of the press has always been understood in this manner, and no other; and the Constitution of every State which has been framed and adopted since the Declaration of Independence, asserts "the liberty of the press;" while in several, if not all, their laws provide for the punishment of libellous publications, which would be a manifest absurdity and contradiction, if the liberty of the press meant to publish any and everything, without being amenable to the laws for the abuse of this license. According to this just, legal, and universally admitted definition of "the liberty of the press," a law to restrain its licentiousness, in publishing false, scandalous, and malicious libels against the Government, cannot be considered as "an abridgment" of its "liberty."

It is answered, in the second place, that the liberty of the press did never extend, according to the laws of any State, or of the United States, or of England, from whence our laws are derived, to the publication of false, scandalous, and malicious writings against the Government, written or published with intent to do mischief; such publications being unlawful, and punishable in every State; from whence it follows, undeniably, that a law to punish seditious and malicious publications, is not an abridgment of the liberty of the press, for it would be a manifest absurdity to say, that a man's liberty was abridged by punishing him for doing that which he never had a liberty to do. . . .

And, lastly, it is answered, that had the Constitution intended to prohibit Congress from legislating at all on the subject of the press, which is the construction whereon the objections to this law are founded, it would have used the same expressions as in that part of the clause which relates to religion and religious texts; whereas, the words are wholly different: "Congress," says the Constitution, (amendment 3d.) "shall make no law respecting an establishment of religion, or prohibiting the free exercise thereof, or abridging the freedom of speech of the press." Here it is manifest that the Constitution intended to prohibit Congress from legislating at all on the subject of religious establishments, and the prohibition is made in the most express terms. Had the same intention prevailed respecting the press, the same expressions would have been used, and Congress would have been "prohibited from passing any law respecting the press." They are not, however, "prohibited" from legislating at all on the subject, but merely from abridging the liberty of the press. It is evident they may legislate respecting the press, may pass laws for its regulation, and to punish those who pervert it into an engine of mischief, provided those laws do not abridge its liberty. Its liberty, according to the well known and universally admitted definition, consists in permission to publish, without previous restraint upon the press, but subject to punishment afterwards for improper publications. A law, therefore, to impose previous restraint upon the press, and not one to inflict punishment on wicked and malicious publications, would be a law to abridge the liberty of the press, and, as such, unconstitutional.

FOR FURTHER READING

James E. Leehy, *The First Amendment, 1791–1991*. Jefferson, NC: McFarland and Company, 1991.

Leonard Levy, *Legacy of Supression: Freedom of Speech and Press in Early American History*. Cambridge, MA: Belknap Press of Harvard University Press, 1960.

Geoffrey R. Stone, *Perilous Times: Free Speech in Wartime from The Sedition Act of 1798 to The War on Terrorism*. New York: W.W. Norton, 2004

Part 3
ANTEBELLUM AMERICA (1800–1850)

CHRONOLOGY

1800

November John Adams becomes first president to occupy the White House.

1801

January 20 Adams appoints John Marshall chief justice of Supreme Court.

March 4 Thomas Jefferson inaugurated as president.

1802

October Spain suspends right of Americans to deposit goods at New Orleans; two weeks later, transfers control of city and all Louisiana to France.

1803

February 24 Supreme Court declares a federal law unconstitutional for the first time in *Marbury v. Madison.*

March 1 Ohio enters Union.

April U.S. buys Louisiana Territory from France for $15 million.

May War resumes between England and France.

May 14 Lewis and Clark expedition begins.

1804

July Aaron Burr kills Alexander Hamilton in duel.

December 5 Jefferson reelected president.

1807

August 17 Successful debut of Robert Fulton's steamboat.

December Congress passes Embargo Act, suspending all American trade.

1808

December 7 James Madison elected president.

1811

November Battle of Tippecanoe breaks military strength of Tecumseh-led Indian alliance.

1812

June Congress votes for war with England.

December 2 Madison reelected president.

1814

August 24 British troops occupy Washington, D.C.

September 13 Francis Scott Key writes "Star-Spangled Banner."

December Hartford Convention of New England states meets to discuss opposition to war.

December 24 Treaty of Ghent signed between Great Britain and U.S.

1815

January 8 Battle of New Orleans makes hero of General Andrew Jackson.

1816

April 10 Second National Bank incorporated by act of Congress.

December 4 James Monroe elected president.

December 11 Indiana enters Union.

1817

April U.S. and England negotiate Rush-Bagot Agreement calling for mutual naval disarmament on the Great Lakes.

April 30 Louisiana enters Union.

July 4 Construction of Erie Canal begins.

1818

December 3 Illinois enters Union.

1819

February 22 U.S. acquires Florida from Spain.

March 6 Supreme Court upholds constitutionality of a national bank.

December 14 Alabama enters Union.

1820

March 15 Missouri Compromise: Missouri enters Union as slave state, Maine as free state, and line is drawn dividing remaining Louisiana territory into free and slave regions.

December 6 Monroe reelected president.

1823

December 2 The Monroe Doctrine declares the Western Hemisphere off-limits to European colonization.

1825

March 4 John Quincy Adams is inaugurated president after an electoral vote throws the decision to the House of Representatives; opponents decry "corrupt bargain" with Henry Clay.

October 26 Erie Canal opens.

1828

December 3 Andrew Jackson elected president.

1830

April 6 Mormon Church organized by Joseph Smith.

May 28 Indian Removal Act signed by President Jackson.

December *Moral Physiology*, first American book on birth control, published.

1831

January 1 First issue of abolitionist newspaper *The Liberator* published.

August 22 Nat Turner slave rebellion occurs.

December Choctaw Indians begin forced migration from Mississippi.

1832

April 6 Black Hawk War begins in Illinois.

July 10 President Jackson vetoes bill to recharter Second National Bank.

November South Carolina convention declares federal tariffs of 1828 and 1832 "null, void, and no law."

December 5 Jackson reelected president.

December 10 Jackson issues proclamation against state nullification of federal laws.

1834

Winter Whig Party is formed.

1836

March 2 Texas declares itself an independent republic.

June 15 Arkansas enters Union.

December 7 Martin Van Buren elected president.

1837

May Financial panic leads to economic depression.

January 26 Michigan enters Union.

November Abolitionist printer Elijah Lovejoy murdered in Alton, Illinois.

1838

December Remaining Cherokee Indians in Georgia forcibly removed and herded to Oklahoma by U.S. troops.

1840

December 2 William Henry Harrison elected president.

1841

Spring First university degrees granted to women in U.S.

April 4 Harrison becomes first president to die in office: Vice President John Tyler becomes president.

1844

May 24 First telegraph message sent.

June 27 Mob kills Mormon leader Joseph Smith in Carthage, Illinois.

December 4 James K. Polk elected president.

1845

March 1 Texas annexed to U.S. by joint resolution of Congress.

March 3 Florida enters Union.

December 29 Texas enters Union.

1846

May 13 Congress declares war on Mexico.

August 8 Wilmot Proviso introduced in Congress.

September 10 Elias Howe patents sewing machine.

December 28 Iowa enters Union.

1847

September 14 American forces seize Mexico City.

1848

January 24 Gold found in California.

February 2 Treaty ends Mexican War; U.S. gains California and New Mexico territories from Mexico.

May 29 Wisconsin enters Union.

July 19 First women's rights conference held at Seneca Falls, New York.

August 9 Free-Soil Party born.

November 7 Zachary Taylor elected president.

1849

December California seeks admission to Union as free state.

PREFACE

The first half of the nineteenth century was a time of tremendous growth and ferment for the United States of America. Through purchase, diplomacy, annexation, and war, the United States attained most of its present territorial dimensions. Fifteen states entered the Union between 1800 and 1850. During that time the nation's population grew from about 5 million to 23 million: Both agricultural and manufacturing production soared to unprecedented levels. The telegraph, newspaper, and railroad all helped knit the country together. The era was marked by national debates over expansion, democracy, and social reform as Americans reacted to the transformation of their country into a nation far different from the one that existed when the Constitution was written in 1787.

THE JEFFERSONIAN ERA

Thomas Jefferson, Andrew Jackson, and James K. Polk were arguably the three most influential presidents in the years 1800–1850. All three were committed, with different degrees of emphasis, to democratic values and the expansion of the United States.

The first years of the nineteenth century are commonly known as the Jeffersonian era after the author of the Declaration of Independence, who defeated John Adams in the 1800 presidential election. Never again would the Federalists win the presidency. As if to symbolize the party's declining fortunes, the architect of the Federalist economic program, Alexander Hamilton, was killed in a duel in 1804.

However, the Federalists' loss of power did not necessarily result in the reversal of their policies. In part this was because Jefferson the president and politician proved to be more flexible and open to Federalist policies than Jefferson the political theorist. Jefferson's vision for the future of America was focused on a nation of small independent farmers who would be largely self-sufficient and in little need of government. In that context, Jefferson had attacked Hamilton's call for the federal government to fully fund the national debt and establish a national bank. As president, however, he kept much of the broad outline of Hamilton's economic programs in place. Prior to assuming the presidency Jefferson had advocated the doctrine of states' rights and a "strict" reading of the Constitution in which the federal government had only the powers expressly given to it. However, in 1803, as president, Jefferson approved purchasing the Louisiana Territory from France even though the Constitution did not specifically give the federal government the power to buy territory—a decision that helped expand the powers of the national government at the expense of the doctrine of states' rights. (The Louisiana Purchase, by doubling the nation's size and setting the nation on the course of westward expansion, was momentous in several respects.) Jefferson's successors as president also adopted as their own some key Federalist programs, including tariff protection for beginning industries, federal support for internal improvements such as roads, and the reestablishment of a national bank.

Another important reason for the continuing influence of the Federalist Party, despite its failure to elect presidents and congressional majorities, was its hold on America's judicial branch of government through the lifetime judicial appointments made by Presidents George Washington and John Adams. Of special significance was Adams appointee John Marshall, chief justice of the Supreme Court from 1801 to 1835. The Supreme Court under Marshall's leadership issued several significant opinions that established the right of the Supreme Court to disallow federal or state laws as unconstitutional. In several other opinions, notably in *McCulloch v. Maryland*, the Supreme Court under Marshall supported the supremacy of the federal government over the states as well as other important Federalist Party principles, raising charges of "judicial tyranny" from Jefferson and others who argued, to no avail, that Marshall was changing the Constitution without following the amending process.

THE WAR OF 1812

Jefferson's administration, like those that preceded and followed it, was buffeted by European wars. In 1803 war broke out between Great Britain and France. Both nations began seizing American merchant ships destined for their opponents, and Great Britain renewed its practice of impressment—seizing American seamen and forcing them to join the British navy. Presidents Thomas Jefferson and James Madison attempted to assert neutral trading rights without resorting to war by imposing economic embargoes that restricted trade between the United States and the warring nations, but these policies seemed to hurt American traders, shipbuilders, and farmers more than the intended targets of Great Britain and France. U.S.-British relations were also marred by the belief of many Americans that the British in Canada were conspiring with American Indians in the Ohio Valley and elsewhere.

In 1812 Congress declared war on Great Britain. Supporters of the war envisioned an easy invasion and conquest of Canada, but such notions were quickly dispelled as early defeats revealed serious weaknesses in American army and naval forces. The British in turn invaded the American capital of Washington, D.C., and burned much of the city, including the president's mansion. In response, the Americans mustered popular support and gained military victories more in defending their homeland than in invading Canada. The country also found a new hero in General Andrew Jackson, who led American forces to a spectacular victory over a British invading force in New Orleans in 1815.

The Treaty of Ghent agreed to by the two nations late in 1814 (shortly before Jackson's New Orleans triumph) resolved none of the trade and impressment issues that were the ostensible reason for the war. However, the War of 1812 had several important effects on the United States. It brought about the final demise of the Federalist Party, many of whose members, consistent with Federalist pro-British leanings, had opposed the war. It signaled the end of significant Native American resistance to white settlement in lands east of the Mississippi River. It laid foundations for an enduring peaceful relationship with Canada. Finally, it created a new feeling of nationalism among Americans, who emerged from the war more united than when they entered it.

AMERICAN SOCIETY IS TRANSFORMED

In the decades following the War of 1812 the United States was the site of numerous important economic developments and social controversies. Agricultural production grew significantly. In the South, Eli Whitney's invention of the cotton gin enabled cotton to replace tobacco and rice as the region's leading cash crop—and further entrench the plantation/slavery system of agriculture. Cotton became America's leading export, accounting for about half of America's exports to Great Britain between 1820 and 1860. In the Midwest, Cyrus McCormick's invention of the mechanical reaper helped establish wheat as an important cash crop, with farmers expanding their holdings to sell surplus wheat both to the eastern United States and abroad.

The change in American farms from self-sufficiency to growing cash crops for export was facilitated by a "transportation revolution"—the improvement of roads, the development of steamboats, and the building of canals and railroads. The steamboat, successfully demonstrated by American inventor Robert Fulton in 1807, made two-way river transportation feasible. The Erie Canal, opened in 1825, connected the Hudson River to Lake Erie. Its successful operation greatly reduced shipping costs and sparked a frenzy of canal construction; by 1840 three thousand miles of canals were built. The canal was then supplemented, and in some cases superseded, by the railroad. From a few experimental developments in the 1820s, railroads spread rapidly; by 1850 more than nine thousand miles of track had been laid. The new transportation infrastructure made the movement of people and freight within the nation's interior relatively efficient and helped bind the frontier to the rest of the nation. Railroads made it possible for westward migration to be an individual or family affair, rather than a community wagon-train endeavor.

CITIES AND MANUFACTURING

The transportation revolution not only helped people move west but also contributed to the growth of cities in America. Established cities grew in population: New York City, for instance, grew from 124,000 in 1820 to 800,000 in 1860. The number of incorporated towns with populations between 2,500 and 10,000 grew from 56 in 1820 to more than 350 in 1850. The population of America living in towns of 2,500 or more rose from 6.1 percent in 1820 to nearly 20 percent in 1860.

Many of the city residents were immigrants. In the 1840s 1.5 million Europeans moved to America, and 2.5 million did so the following decade. The majority of immigrants came from Ireland and Germany and settled in the North and West. Some Americans reacted to this new wave of immigrants by organizing a large nativist movement to combat the "alien menace" that they believed created slums, stole jobs, and corrupted politics.

Urbanization was also boosted by the rise of manufacturing, which evolved from the household or "cottage" industries of colonial times to larger factories using unskilled workers and power-driven machinery. Manufacturing, like agriculture, was helped by key technological advances, such as Charles Goodyear's invention of vulcanized rubber and Isaac Singer's improvements on the sewing machine. Manufacturing was concentrated in the Northeast, which had more than half of America's manufacturing establishments and more than two-thirds of America's mill and factory workers. The emergence of industrial workers as a new class was another important social development of the period, as was the fact that many of the workers were women. During the 1830s many workers took steps toward organizing in unions and even striking for better working conditions, but the nascent labor movement was set back by the economic depression of 1837 (despite a favorable 1841 ruling by the Massachusetts Supreme Court in *Commonwealth v. Hunt* that labor unions were not illegal conspiracies).

JACKSONIAN ERA

Andrew Jackson was the leading political figure for much of the 1820s and 1830s, when much of this economic and social transformation was taking place. Jackson lost a controversial presidential election in 1824, despite receiving the most votes of the four candidates; won the next two presidential elections; and handpicked his successor.

Jackson set several important precedents just by being elected. All previous U.S. presidents were from either Massachusetts or Virginia. Jackson was from Tennessee, a frontier state. Past presidents also had significant records of government service. Jackson's main achievements to this time were from military exploits in the War of 1812 and against American Indians. Previous presidents had been born into and were elected by America's social and economic elite. Jackson, although wealthy when he became president, was born and had grown up in poverty and portrayed himself as a self-made man of the people and opponent of elitism. Jackson attained and cultivated an unprecedented popularity with the "common man" at a time when states were revising or repealing property qualification laws to make universal suffrage for white males (but not blacks, women, or Native Americans) the rule.

President Jackson replaced many government employees with his own political supporters (on the theory that just about anyone could do the government's business). He responded to South Carolina's efforts to nullify federal tariff laws within state borders by proclaiming nullification treason and threatening to use the federal military to enforce federal law. He increased efforts to relocate American Indians across the Mississippi River. Perhaps most famously, he vetoed the charter for and effectively closed the Second Bank of the United States. These actions, coupled with Jackson's contentious personality, helped revive the two-party system that had been dormant since the demise of the Federalists. Jackson's supporters created what became known as the Democratic Party (heirs to Jefferson's Democratic Republicans, but recreated in Jackson's image). The Democrats generally espoused a minimal role for the federal government and were especially against government-granted monopolies, charters, and tariffs that they believed favored the rich at the expense of the poor. Opponents to "King Andrew" created the Whig Party in the 1830s, a diverse organization united mainly by opposition to Jackson. Henry Clay and Daniel Webster, two leading Whigs, maintained that the national government could help the economy through a national banking system, a protective tariff, and expenditures for internal improvements.

REFORM FERMENT

Many Americans in the 1830s and 1840s devoted their energies to various social reforms, both within and outside party politics. Some reformers were inspired by the wave of evangelical revival that swept much of the nation in the 1820s and 1830s. Among the various goals of those seeking reform were free public schools, temperance with alcohol, better treatment of the mentally ill, the preaching of Christianity in foreign lands, and prison reform. Some idealists withdrew from American society to create utopian communities.

Women were very active in many of the reform efforts and often took a leading role in moral reform societies and other public movements. The position of women in the American republic was itself debated. Early feminists, including Frances Wright and Margaret Fuller, wrote and lectured to public audiences on women's need for marriage and divorce rights, legal equality, and equal education. In 1848 the first women's rights meeting was held in Seneca Falls, New York, passing, among other resolutions, the demand for the right to vote.

Women and men were both involved in perhaps the most controversial social reform issue of the period: the abolition of slavery. By the 1820s most Northern states had abolished the institution, and antislavery activists sought its gradual repeal in the remaining states by appealing to the consciences of slaveholders. In the 1830s a new militant abolitionist movement harshly criticized slavery in speeches and articles, calling for its immediate abolition. Leaders of the abolitionist movement were often threatened and attacked by mobs in the North, but the movement still attracted thousands of supporters, including free blacks and escaped slaves. In the South, many whites blamed Nat Turner's 1831 slave rebellion in Virginia on William Garrison's antislavery writings. They successfully persuaded the federal post office to destroy and/or refuse to deliver any abolitionist literature within the South. Slavery remained firmly entrenched. Although Congress had outlawed the importation of slaves in 1808, the slave population in the United States grew from 1.2 million in 1810 to around 4 million in 1860.

POLK AND THE EXPANSIONISTS

The issue of slavery was firmly intertwined with another important American development—expansion. Politicians from Thomas Jefferson onward had envisioned the expansion of the United States of America to include most of the North American continent. Expansion became a national controversy after 1835 when American settlers in the Mexican province of Texas successfully fought for independence and later sought admission to the Union. After intensive congressional debate, in which Whig/Democratic divisions were overshadowed by North/South ones, America annexed Texas in 1845, worsening relations with Mexico. James K. Polk, who won the 1844 presidential election over Henry Clay in a contest in which expansion was the leading issue, coveted more Mexican territories. Mindful of trade opportunities in Asia, he especially wanted California, with its harbors on the Pacific Ocean.

Polk's aggressive diplomacy with Mexico in quest of the territories, combined with long-standing tensions between the two nations dating almost from Mexico's independence from Spain in 1821, resulted in war with Mexico in 1846. The United States won spectacular military victories, and in 1848 Mexico agreed to cede the territories Polk had sought. Shortly thereafter news of gold discoveries in California inspired thousands of Americans to journey to that territory—a circumstance that to many Americans confirmed their self-image as a nation of special destiny.

The acquisition of new territories, however, intensified the slavery controversy within the United States. In August 1846 Pennsylvania congressman David Wilmot introduced a provision prohibiting slavery in any newly acquired territory. The Wilmot Proviso was passed in the House but defeated in the Senate and was later unsuccessfully attached to many subsequent bills. It gained the support of many Northerners, including some who did not support the abolitionist movement. The debate over whether the new territories should be slave or free divided the nation in the 1850s and ultimately led to Southern secession and the Civil War.

EXPANDING NATION, EXPANDING GOVERNMENT

Viewpoint 19A

The Louisiana Purchase Should Be Approved (1803)

Thomas Jefferson (1743–1826)

INTRODUCTION *Thomas Jefferson was elected president in 1800 while pledging to trim government expenses and to adhere strictly to limits of power expressed in the Constitution. However, his arguably most significant decision as president was the Louisiana Purchase, in which America doubled its size by acquiring millions of acres of territory from France. The $15 million price tag wiped out all the progress Jefferson had made in reducing the national debt, and the Constitution did not explicitly give the federal government authority to purchase new territory or incorporate it within the Union.*

Jefferson had originally sent diplomats to France with congressional approval to purchase the city of New Orleans or otherwise secure a southern port for the goods of America's western farmers—a long-sought goal of the nation that was threatened, Jefferson and others believed, by France's acquisition of the Louisiana Territory from Spain in 1800. However, French ruler Napoleon Bonaparte unexpectedly offered to sell the entire Louisiana Territory. Afraid that the deal might fall through before a new constitutional amendment authorizing such an acquisition could be ratified, Jefferson agreed to the purchase in 1803.

The following viewpoint consists of two parts. The first is an excerpt from an August 12, 1803, letter Jefferson wrote to John Breckinridge, a close friend and political associate. (Jefferson later asked Breckinridge to keep the letter's contents secret.) Jefferson writes about the purchase and the objections raised by Federalist opponents, as well as his own constitutional concerns. The second part is excerpted from Jefferson's Third Annual Message to Congress, delivered in October 1803, in which he urges the approval and ratification of the Louisiana Purchase.

What differences in opinion over the constitutional legality exist, if any, between the private letter and public message of Jefferson? What arguments against the Louisiana Purchase does Jefferson recite? How does he answer them?

I

The enclosed letter . . . gives me occasion to write a word to you on the subject of Louisiana, which, being a new one, an interchange of sentiments may produce correct ideas before we are to act on them.

Our information as to the country is very incomplete. We have taken measures to obtain it in full as to the settled part, which I hope to receive in time for Congress. The boundaries, which I deem not admitting question, are the highlands on the western side of the Mississippi enclosing all its waters, the Missouri, of course, and terminating in the line drawn from the northwestern point of the Lake of the Woods to the nearest source of the Mississippi, as lately settled between Great Britain and the United States. We have some claims to extend on the seacoast westwardly to the Rio Norte or Bravo [Rio Grande], and, better, to go eastwardly to the Rio Perdido, between Mobile and Pensacola, the ancient boundary of Louisiana. These claims will be a subject of negotiation with Spain and if, as soon as she is at war, we push them strongly with one hand, holding out a price in the other, we shall certainly obtain the Floridas, and all in good time. . . .

FEDERALIST OBJECTIONS

Objections are raising to the eastward [in New England] against the vast extent of our boundaries, and propositions are made to exchange Louisiana, or a part of it, for the Floridas. But, as I have said, we shall get the Floridas without, and I would not give one inch of the waters of the Mississippi to any nation because I see, in a light very important to our peace, the exclusive right to its navigation, and the admission of no nation into it, but as into the Potomac or Delaware, with our consent and under our police.

These Federalists see in this acquisition the formation of a new confederacy, embracing all the waters of the Mississippi on both sides of it, and a separation of its eastern waters from us. These combinations depend on so many circumstances which we cannot foresee that I place little reliance on them. We have seldom seen neighborhood produce affection among nations. The reverse is almost the universal truth. Besides, if it should become the great interest of those nations to separate from this, if their happiness should depend on it so strongly as to induce them to go through that convulsion, why should the Atlantic states dread it? But, especially, why should we, their present inhabitants, take side in such a question? . . .

From *Memoirs, Correspondence, and Private Papers of Thomas Jefferson*, edited by Thomas Jefferson Randolph (Charlottesville, VA, 1829) and *The Writings of Thomas Jefferson*, vol. 3, edited by Albert Bergh (Washington, DC: Thomas Jefferson Memorial Society, 1905).

The inhabited part of Louisiana, from Point Coupée to the sea, will of course be immediately a territorial government and soon a state. But, above that, the best use we can make of the country for some time will be to give establishments in it to the Indians on the east side of the Mississippi in exchange for their present country, and open land offices in the last, and thus make this acquisition the means of filling up the eastern side instead of drawing off its population. When we shall be full on this side, we may lay off a range of states on the western bank from the head to the mouth, and so, range after range, advancing compactly as we multiply.

CONGRESS AND THE CONSTITUTION

This treaty must, of course, be laid before both houses, because both have important functions to exercise respecting it. They, I presume, will see their duty to their country in ratifying and paying for it so as to secure a good which would otherwise probably be never again in their power. But I suppose they must then appeal to the nation for an additional article to the Constitution, approving and confirming an act which the nation had not previously authorized. The Constitution has made no provision for our holding foreign territory, still less for incorporating foreign nations into our Union. The executive, in seizing the fugitive occurrence which so much advances the good of their country, have done an act beyond the Constitution. The legislature in casting behind them metaphysical subtleties, and risking themselves like faithful servants, must ratify and pay for it and throw themselves on their country for doing for them unauthorized what we know they would have done for themselves had they been in a situation to do it.

It is the case of a guardian investing the money of his ward in purchasing an important adjacent territory, and saying to him when of age, I did this for your good; I pretend to no right to bind you; you may disavow me, and I must get out of the scrape as I can; I thought it my duty to risk myself for you. But we shall not be disavowed by the nation, and their act of indemnity will confirm and not weaken the Constitution by more strongly marking out its lines.

II

To the Senate and House of Representatives of the United States:—

In calling you together, fellow citizens, at an earlier day than was contemplated by the act of the last session of Congress, I have not been insensible to the personal inconveniences necessarily resulting from an unexpected change in your arrangements. But matters of great public concernment have rendered this call necessary, and the interest you feel in these will supersede in your minds all private considerations.

----■----

The fertility of the country, its climate and extent, promise in due season important aids to our treasury, an ample provision for our posterity, and a widespread field for the blessing of freedom and equal laws.

----■----

THE IMPORTANCE OF NEW ORLEANS

Congress witnessed, at their last session, the extraordinary agitation produced in the public mind by the suspension of our right of deposit [of agricultural goods for export] at the port of New Orleans, no assignment of another place having been made according to treaty. They were sensible that the continuance of that privation would be more injurious to our nation than any consequences which could flow from any mode of redress, but reposing just confidence in the good faith of the government whose officer had committed the wrong, friendly and reasonable representations were resorted to, and the right of deposit was restored.

Previous, however, to this period, we had not been unaware of the danger to which our peace would be perpetually exposed while so important a key to the commerce of the western country remained under foreign power. Difficulties, too, were presenting themselves as to the navigation of other streams, which, arising within our territories, pass through those adjacent. Propositions had, therefore, been authorized for obtaining, on fair conditions, the sovereignty of New Orleans, and of other possessions in that quarter interesting to our quiet, to such extent as was deemed practicable; and the provisional appropriation of two millions of dollars, to be applied and accounted for by the president of the United States, intended as part of the price, was considered as conveying the sanction of Congress to the acquisition proposed. The enlightened Government of France saw, with just discernment, the importance to both nations of such liberal arrangements as might best and permanently promote the peace, friendship, and interests of both; and the property and sovereignty of all Louisiana, which had been restored to them, have on certain conditions been transferred to the United States by instruments bearing date the 30th of April last. When these shall have received the constitutional sanction of the senate, they will without delay be communicated to the representatives also, for the exercise of their functions, as to those conditions which are within the powers vested by the constitution in Congress. While the property and sovereignty of the Mississippi and its waters secure an independent outlet for the produce of the western States, and an uncontrolled navigation through their whole course, free from collision with other powers and the dangers to our peace from that source, the fertility of the country, its climate and extent, promise in due season important aids to our treasury, an ample provision for our posterity, and a widespread field for the blessings of freedom and equal laws.

With the wisdom of Congress it will rest to take those ulterior measures which may be necessary for the immediate occupation and temporary government of the country; for its incorporation into our Union; for rendering the change of government a blessing to our newly-adopted brethren; for securing to them the rights of conscience and of property; for confirming to the Indian inhabitants their occupancy and self-government, establishing friendly and commercial relations with them, and for ascertaining the geography of the country acquired. Such materials for your information, relative to its affairs in general, as the short space of time has permitted me to collect, will be laid before you when the subject shall be in a state for your consideration.

Viewpoint 19B

The Louisiana Purchase Should Be Opposed (1803)

Samuel White (1770–1809)

INTRODUCTION *The United States doubled its territory with the Louisiana Purchase, acquiring 828,000 square mile from France for a few cents an acre. The agreement with France was ratified by the U.S. Senate in late 1803 by a large margin. However, not all senators or Americans were in favor of the purchase. The following viewpoint excerpted from a Senate speech by Samuel White, a lawyer and senator from Delaware from 1801 to 1809. He argues that he supports the U.S. acquisition of the port city of New Orleans, but wonders whether the United States could readily absorb the immense Louisiana territory and the westward migration it will stimulate. He also questions the price—$15 million—being paid for the territory. Left unspoken was the fear of White and other Federalist politicians that such a large expansion and subsequent westward migration would weaken the political influence of the New England states, their political stronghold.*

How does White believe the addition of territory would harm the United States? Why did France decide to sell its territory at that particular time, according to White?

Possession of it we must have—I mean of New Orleans; and of such other positions on the Mississippi as

may be necessary to secure to us forever the complete and uninterrupted navigation of that river. This I have ever been in favor of; I think it essential to the peace of the United States, and to the prosperity of our Western country. But as to Louisiana, this new, immense, unbounded world, if it should ever be incorporated into this Union, which I have no idea can be done but by altering the Constitution, I believe it will be the greatest curse that could at present befall us; it may be productive of innumerable evils, and especially of one that I fear even to look upon. Gentlemen on all sides, with very few exceptions, agree that the settlement of this country will be highly injurious and dangerous to the United States; but as to what has been suggested of removing the Creeks and other nations of Indians from the eastern to the western banks of the Mississippi, and of making the fertile regions of Louisiana a howling wilderness, never to be trodden by the foot of civilized man, it is impracticable. The gentleman from Tennessee (Mr. Cocke) has shown his usual candor on this subject, and I believe with him, to use his strong language, that you had as well pretend to inhibit the fish from swimming in the sea as to prevent the population of that country after its sovereignty shall become ours. To every man acquainted with the adventurous, roving, and enterprising temper of our people, and with the manner in which our Western country has been settled, such an idea must be chimerical. The inducements will be so strong that it will be impossible to restrain our citizens from crossing the river. Louisiana must and will become settled, if we hold it, and with the very population that would otherwise occupy part of our present territory. Thus our citizens will be removed to the immense distance of two or three thousand miles from the capital of the Union, where they will scarcely ever feel the rays of the General Government; their affections will become alienated; they will gradually begin to view us as strangers; they will form other commercial connexions, and our interests will become distinct.

These, with other causes that human wisdom may not now foresee, will in time effect a separation, and I fear our bounds will be fixed nearer to our houses than the waters of the Mississippi. We have already territory enough, and when I contemplate the evils that may arise to these States, from this intended incorporation of Louisiana into the Union, I would rather see it given to France, to Spain, or to any other nation of the earth, upon the mere condition that no citizen of the United States should ever settle within its limits, than to see the territory sold for an hundred millions of dollars, and we retain the sovereignty. But however dangerous

From Samuel White's Senate speech of November 2, 1803, in *The Debates and Proceedings in the Congress of the United States, First to Eighteenth Congresses, March 3, 1789, to May 27, 1824, Inclusive* (Washington, DC: Gales & Seaton, 1852).

the possession of Louisiana might prove to us, I do not presume to say that the retention of it would not have been very convenient to France, and we know that at the time of the mission of Mr. [James] Monroe, our Administration had never thought of the purchase of Louisiana, and that nothing short of the fullest conviction on the part of the First Consul [Napoléon] that he was on the very eve of a war with England; that this being the most defenceless point of his possessions, if such they could be called, was the one at which the British would first strike, and that it must inevitably fall into their hands, could ever have induced his pride and ambition to make the sale. He judged wisely, that he had better sell it for as much as he could get than lose it entirely. And I do say that under existing circumstances, even supposing that this extent of territory was a desirable acquisition, fifteen millions of dollars was a most enormous sum to give. Our Commissioners were negotiating in Paris—they must have known the relative situation of France and England—they must have known at the moment that a war was unavoidable between the two countries, and they knew the pecuniary necessities of France and the naval power of Great Britain. These imperious circumstances should have been turned to our advantage, and if we were to purchase, should have lessened the consideration. Viewing this subject in any point of light—either as it regards the territory purchased, the high consideration to be given, the contract itself, or any of the circumstances attending it, I see no necessity for precipitating the passage of this bill; and if this motion for postponement should fail, and the question on the final passage of the bill be taken now, I shall certainly vote against it.

FOR FURTHER READING

Charles A. Cerami, *Jefferson's Great Gamble: The Remarkable Story of Jefferson, Napoleon and the Men Behind the Louisiana Purchase.* Naperville, IL: Sourcebooks, 2003.

Thomas Fleming, *The Louisiana Purchase.* Hoboken, NJ: John Wiley & Sons, 2003.

Forrest McDonald, *The Presidency of Thomas Jefferson.* Lawrence: University Press of Kansas, 1987.

Viewpoint 20A

The Federal Government Is Supreme Over the States (1819)

John Marshall (1755–1835)

INTRODUCTION *John Marshall, a Virginia politician and jurist, was appointed by President John Adams to be the nation's fourth chief justice of the Supreme Court in 1801; Marshall led the Court for more than three decades and authored numerous influential rulings that still guide constitutional interpretation today. Marshall, a supporter of the Federalist Party (which became*

extinct during his long term on the Supreme Court), consistently ruled in favor a strong national government at a time when most presidents and many members of Congress favored states' rights. Among the many landmark Supreme Court opinions penned by Marshall were Marbury v. Madison *(1803), which established the power of the judicial system to declare a law by Congress unconstitutional;* Fletcher v. Peck *(1810), which established the Supreme Court's authority to declare a state law unconstitutional, and* McCulloch v. Maryland *(1819), represented in this viewpoint.*

The case of McCulloch v. Maryland *arose when the state of Maryland passed a stiff tax on the operations of the Baltimore branch of the Second Bank of the United States, which had been chartered by Congress in 1816. The bank's cashier in Baltimore, James McCulloch, refused to pay the tax and was sued by the state. In the Supreme Court decision delivered by Marshall on March 7, 1819, and excerpted here, the Court answers two fundamental questions: Did Congress have the constitutional right to charter a national bank, and did states have the right to tax an agency of the national government. Marshall defends the constitutionality of the bank by arguing that the Constitution gives Congress broad implied powers. He then rules that the Constitution establishes a supremacy of federal power over state power that forbids state governments from taxing or otherwise interfering with the lawful operations of the federal government.*

From what source does the Constitution, and the federal government it created, derive its authority, according to Marshall? How does this understanding of federal power affect his ruling?

In the case now to be determined, the defendant, a sovereign State, denies the obligation of a law enacted by the legislature of the Union, and the plaintiff, on his part, contests the validity of an act which has been passed by the legislature of that State. The constitution of our country, in its most interesting and vital parts, is to be considered; the conflicting powers of the government of the Union and of its members, as marked in that constitution, are to be discussed; and an opinion given, which may essentially influence the great operations of the government. No tribunal can approach such a question without a deep sense of its importance, and of the awful responsibility involved in its decision. But it must be decided peacefully, or remain a source of hostile legislation, perhaps of hostility of a still more serious nature; and if it is to be so decided, by this tribunal alone can the decision be made. On the Supreme Court of the United States has the constitution of our country devolved this important duty.

McCulloch v. Maryland, 4 Wheaton 316, 1819.

The first question made in the cause is, has Congress power to incorporate a bank? . . .

In discussing this question, the counsel for the State of Maryland have deemed it of some importance, in the construction of the constitution, to consider that instrument not as emanating from the people, but as the act of sovereign and independent States. The powers of the general government, it has been said, are delegated by the States, who alone are truly sovereign; and must be exercised in subordination to the States, who alone possess supreme dominion.

It would be difficult to sustain this proposition. The Convention which framed the constitution was indeed elected by the State legislatures. But the instrument, when it came from their hands, was a mere proposal, without obligation, or pretensions to it. It was reported to the then existing Congress of the United States, with a request that it might "be submitted to a Convention of Delegates, chosen in each State by the people thereof, under the recommendation of its Legislature, for their assent and ratification." This mode of proceeding was adopted; and by the Convention, by Congress, and by the State Legislatures, the instrument was submitted to the people. They acted upon it in the only manner in which they can act safely, effectively, and wisely, on such a subject by assembling in Convention. It is true, they assembled in their several States—and where else should they have assembled? No political dreamer was ever wild enough to think of breaking down the lines which separate the States, and of compounding the American people into one common mass. Of consequence, when they act, they act in their States. But the measures they adopt do not, on that account, cease to be the measures of the people themselves, or become the measures of the State governments.

From these Conventions the constitution derives its whole authority. The government proceeds directly from the people; is "ordained and established" in the name of the people; and is declared to be ordained, "in order to form a more perfect union, establish justice, ensure domestic tranquillity, and secure the blessings of liberty to themselves and to their posterity." The assent of the States, in their sovereign capacity, is implied in calling a Convention, and thus submitting that instrument to the people. But the people were at perfect liberty to accept or reject it; and their act was final. It required not the affirmance, and could not be negatived, by the State governments. The constitution, when thus adopted, was of complete obligation, and bound the State sovereignties. . . .

The government of the Union, then, (whatever may be the influence of this fact on the case,) is, emphatically, and truly, a government of the people. In form and in substance it emanates from them. Its powers are granted by them, and are to be exercised directly on them, and for their benefit.

This government is acknowledged by all to be one of enumerated powers. The principle, that it can exercise only the powers granted to it, would seem too apparent to have required to be enforced by all those arguments which its enlightened friends, while it was depending before the people, found it necessary to urge. That principle is now universally admitted. But the question respecting the extent of the powers actually granted, is perpetually arising, and will probably continue to arise, as long as our system shall exist.

In discussing these questions, the conflicting powers of the general and State governments must be brought into view, and the supremacy of their respective laws, when they are in opposition, must be settled.

NATIONAL GOVERNMENT IS SUPREME

If any one proposition could command the universal assent of mankind, we might expect it would he this— that the government of the Union, though limited in its powers, is supreme within its sphere of action. This would seem to result necessarily from its nature. It is the government of all; its powers are delegated by all; it represents all, and acts for all. Though any one State may be willing to control its operations, no State is willing to allow others to control them. The nation, on those subjects on which it can act, must necessarily bind its component parts. But this question is not left to mere reason: the people have, in express terms, decided it, by saying, "this constitution, and the laws of the United States, which shall be made in pursuance thereof," "shall be the supreme law of the land," and by requiring that the members of the State legislatures, and the officers of the executive and judicial departments of the States, shall take the oath of fidelity to it.

The government of the United States, then, though limited in its powers, is supreme; and its laws, when made in pursuance of the constitution, form the supreme law of the land, "any thing in the constitution or laws of any State to the contrary notwithstanding."

Among the enumerated powers, we do not find that of establishing a bank or creating a corporation. But there is no phrase in the instrument which, like the articles of confederation, excludes incidental or implied powers; and which requires that every thing granted shall be expressly and minutely described. . . .

A constitution, to contain an accurate detail of all the subdivisions of which its great powers will admit, and of all the means by which they may be carried into execution, would partake of the prolixity of a legal code, and could scarcely be embraced by the human mind. It would probably never be understood by the public. Its nature, therefore, requires, that only its great outlines should be marked, its important objects designated, and the minor ingredients which compose those objects be deduced from the nature of the objects themselves. That this idea was entertained by the framers of the American constitution, is not only to be inferred from the nature of the instrument, but from the language. Why else were some of the limitations, found in the ninth section of the 1st article, introduced? It is also, in some degree, warranted by their having omitted to use any restrictive term which might prevent its receiving a fair and just interpretation. In considering this question, then, we must never forget, that it is *a constitution* we are expounding.

MEANS OF EXECUTION

Although, among the enumerated powers of government, we do not find the word "bank" or "incorporation," we find the great powers to lay and collect taxes; to borrow money; to regulate commerce; to declare and conduct a war; and to raise and support armies and navies. The sword and the purse, all the external relations, and no inconsiderable portion of the industry of the nation, are entrusted to its government. It can never be pretended that these vast powers draw after them others of inferior importance, merely because they are inferior. Such an idea can never be advanced. But it may with great reason be contended, that a government, entrusted with such ample powers, on the due execution of which the happiness and prosperity of the nation so vitally depends, must also be entrusted with ample means for their execution. The power being given, it is the interest of the nation to facilitate its execution. It can never be their interest, and cannot be presumed to have been their intention, to clog and embarrass its execution by withholding the most appropriate means. Throughout this vast republic, from the St. Croix to the Gulph of Mexico, from the Atlantic to the Pacific, revenue is to be collected and expended, armies are to be marched and supported. The exigencies of the nation may require that the treasure raised in the north should be transported to the south, *that* raised in the east conveyed to the west, or that this order should be reversed. Is that construction of the constitution to be preferred which would render these operations difficult, hazardous, and expensive? Can we adopt that construction, (unless the words imperiously require it,) which would impute to the framers of that instrument, when granting these powers for the public good, the intention of impeding their exercise by withholding a choice of means? If, indeed, such be the mandate of the constitution, we have only to obey; but that instrument does not profess to enumerate the means by which the powers it confers may be executed; nor does

it prohibit the creation of a corporation, if the existence of such a being be essential to the beneficial exercise of those powers....

But the constitution of the United States has not left the right of Congress to employ the necessary means, for the execution of the powers conferred on the government, to general reasoning. To its enumeration of powers is added that of making "all laws which shall be necessary and proper, for carrying into execution the foregoing powers, and all other powers vested by this constitution, in the government of the United States, or in any department thereof." ...

We admit, as all must admit, that the powers of the government are limited, and that its limits are not to be transcended. But we think the sound construction of the constitution must allow to the national legislature that discretion, with respect to the means by which the powers it confers are to be carried into execution, which will enable that body to perform the high duties assigned to it, in the manner most beneficial to the people. Let the end be legitimate, let it be within the scope of the constitution, and all means which are appropriate, which are plainly adapted to that end, which are not prohibited, but consist with the letter and spirit of the constitution, are constitutional....

Should Congress; in the execution of its powers, adopt measures which are prohibited by the constitution; or should Congress, under the pretext of executing its powers, pass laws for the accomplishment of objects not entrusted to the government; it would become the painful duty of this tribunal, should a case requiring such a decision come before it, to say that such an act was not the law of the land. But where the law is not prohibited, and is really calculated to effect any of the objects entrusted to the government, to undertake here to inquire into the degree of its necessity, would be to pass the line which circumscribes the judicial department, and to tread on legislative ground. This court disclaims all pretensions to such a power....

MARYLAND'S TAX

It being the opinion of the Court, that the act incorporating the bank is constitutional; and that the power of establishing a branch in the State of Maryland might be properly exercised by the bank itself, we proceed to inquire—

2. Whether the State of Maryland may, without violating the constitution, tax that branch?

That the power of taxation is one of vital importance; that it is retained by the States; that it is not abridged by the grant of a similar power to the government of the Union; that it is to be concurrently exercised by the two governments: are truths which have never been denied. But, such is the paramount character of the constitution, that its capacity to withdraw any subject from the action of even this power, is admitted. The States are expressly forbidden to lay any duties on imports or exports, except what may be absolutely necessary for executing their inspection laws. If the obligation of this prohibition must be conceded—if it may restrain a State from the exercise of its taxing power on imports and exports; the same paramount character would seem to restrain, as it certainly may restrain, a State from such other exercise of this power, as is in its nature incompatible with, and repugnant to, the constitutional laws of the Union. A law, absolutely repugnant to another, as entirely repeals that other as if express terms of repeal were used.

On this ground the counsel for the bank place its claim to be exempted from the power of a State to tax its operations. There is no express provision for the case, but the claim has been sustained on a principle which so entirely pervades the constitution, is so intermixed with the materials which compose it, so interwoven with its web, so blended with its texture, as to be incapable of being separated from it, without rending it into shreds.

This great principle is, that the constitution and the laws made in pursuance thereof are supreme; that they control the constitution and laws of the respective States, and cannot be controlled by them. From this, which may be almost termed an axiom, other propositions are deduced as corollaries, on the truth or error of which, and on their application to this case, the cause has been supposed to depend. These are, 1st. that a power to create implies a power to preserve. 2nd. That a power to destroy, if wielded by a different hand, is hostile to, and incompatible with these powers to create and to preserve. 3d. That where this repugnancy exists, that authority which is supreme must control, not yield to that over which it is supreme. . . .

The sovereignty of a State extends to every thing which exists by its own authority, or is introduced by its permission; but does it extend to those means which are employed by Congress to carry into execution powers conferred on that body by the people of the United States? We think it demonstrable that it does not. Those powers are not given by the people of a single State. They are given by the people of the United States, to a government whose laws, made in pursuance of the constitution, are declared to be supreme. Consequently, the people of a single State cannot confer a sovereignty which will extend over them.

If we apply the principle for which the State of Maryland contends, to the constitution generally, we shall find it capable of changing totally the character of that instrument. We shall find it capable of arresting all the measures of the government, and of prostrating it at the foot of the States. The American people have declared their constitution, and the laws made in pursuance thereof, to be supreme; but this principle would transfer the supremacy, in fact, to the States.

States have no power . . . to retard . . . the operations of the constitutional laws enacted by Congress.

If the States may tax one instrument, employed by the government in the execution of its powers, they may tax any and every other instrument. They may tax the mail; they may tax the mint; they may tax patent rights; they may tax the papers of the custom house; they may tax judicial process; they may tax all the means employed by the government, to an excess which would defeat all the ends of government. This was not intended by the American people. They did not design to make their government dependent on the States. . . .

The people of all the States have created the general government, and have conferred upon it the general power of taxation. The people of all the States, and the States themselves, are represented in Congress, and, by their representatives, exercise this power. When they tax the chartered institutions of the States, they tax their constituents; and these taxes must be uniform. But, when a State taxes the operations of the government of the United States, it acts upon institutions created, not by their own constituents, but by people over whom they claim no control. It acts upon the measures of a government created by others as well as themselves, for the benefit of others in common with themselves. The difference is that which always exists, and always must exist, between the action of the whole on a part, and the action of a part on the whole—between the laws of a government declared to be supreme, and those of a government which, when in opposition to those laws, is not supreme. . . .

The Court has bestowed on this subject its most deliberate consideration. The result is a conviction that the States have no power, by taxation or otherwise, to retard, impede, burden, or in any manner control, the operations of the constitutional laws enacted by Congress to carry into execution the powers vested in the general government. This is, we think, the unavoidable consequence of that supremacy which the constitution has declared.

We are unanimously of opinion, that the law passed by the legislature of Maryland, imposing a tax on the Bank of the United States, is unconstitutional and void.

The Federal Government Is Not Supreme Over the States (1819)
Spencer Roane (1762–1822)

INTRODUCTION *In* McCulloch v. Maryland, *the United States Supreme Court led by Chief Justice John Marshall ruled that a Maryland state tax on the federally chartered Bank of the United States was unconstitutional. The decision drew criticism from those who argued that the ruling—and other decisions by Marshall and the Supreme Court—were imperiling the sovereignty of the states and the freedoms of the American people. One critic was Spencer Roane, a judge of the Virginia Supreme Court of Appeals from 1794 to 1821. In the following viewpoint, taken from editorials published in a journal founded by Roane, he disputes the basic findings of* McCulloch v. Maryland, *questioning whether Congress had the constitutional authority to establish a national bank and whether states had no constitutional right to tax such an institution.*

What three basic assumptions about the Constitution does Roane postulate? How do they differ from the assumptions of John Marshall found in the previous viewpoint? What does Roane mean when he asserts that "a new mode of amending the Constitution" has been created?

It has been the happiness of the American people to be connected together in a confederate republic; to be united by a system which extends the sphere of popular government and reconciles the advantages of monarchy with those of a republic; a system which combines all the internal advantages of the latter with all the force of the former. It has been our happiness to believe that, in the partition of powers between the general and state governments, the former possessed only such as were expressly granted, or passed therewith as necessary incidents, while all the residuary powers were reserved by the latter. It was deemed by the enlightened founders of the Constitution as essential to the internal happiness and welfare of their constituents to reserve some powers to the state governments; as to their external safety, to grant others to the government of the Union. This, it is believed, was done by the Constitution, in its original shape; but such were the natural fears and jealousies of our citizens, in relation to this all-important subject, that it was deemed necessary to quiet those fears by the Tenth Amendment to the Constitution. It is not easy to devise stronger terms to effect that object than those used in that amendment.

From Spencer Roane's editorial in the June 11, 1819, *Richmond Enquirer*, as reprinted in *The John P. Branch Historical Papers of Randolph-Macon College* (1905).

[The] Constitution conveyed only a limited grant of powers to the general government, and reserved the residuary powers to the governments of the states and to the people.

Such, however, is the proneness of all men to extend and abuse their power—to "feel power and forget right"—that even this article has afforded us no security. That legislative power, which is everywhere extending the sphere of its activity and drawing all power into its impetuous vortex, has blinked even the strong words of this amendment. That judicial power, which, according to [French political philosopher Charles-Louis de] Montesquieu is "in some measure, next to nothing"; and whose province this great writer limits to "punishing criminals and determining the disputes which arise between individuals"; that judiciary which, in Rome, according to the same author, was not entrusted to decide questions which concerned "the interests of the state, in the relation which it bears to its citizens"; and which, in England, has only invaded the Constitution in the worst of times, and then, always, on the side of arbitrary power, has also deemed its interference necessary in our country. It will readily be perceived that I allude to the decision of the Supreme Court of the United States, in the case of M'Culloch against the State of Maryland....

It was only necessary, in that case, to decide whether or not the bank law was "necessary and proper," within the meaning of the Constitution, for carrying into effect some of the granted powers; but the Court have, in effect, expunged those words from the Constitution.... The power of the Supreme Court is indeed great, but it does not extend to everything; it is not great enough to *change* the Constitution....

THREE PROPOSITIONS

I beg leave to lay down the following propositions as being equally incontestable in themselves, and assented to by the enlightened advocates of the Constitution at the time of its adoption.

1. That that Constitution conveyed only a limited grant of powers to the general government, and reserved the residuary powers to the governments of the states and to the people; and that the Tenth Amendment was merely declaratory of this principle, and inserted only to quiet what the Court is pleased to call "the excessive jealousies of the people."

2. That the limited grant to Congress of certain enumerated powers only carried with it such additional powers as were *fairly incidental* to them, or, in other words, were necessary and proper for their execution.

3. That the insertion of the words "necessary and proper," in the last part of the 8th Section of the 1st Article, did not enlarge the powers previously given, but were inserted only through abundant caution.

On the first point it is to be remarked that the Constitution does not give to Congress *general* legislative powers but the legislative powers "*herein granted*."...So it is said in *The Federalist*, that the jurisdiction of the general government extends to certain enumerated objects only and leaves to the states a residuary and inviolable sovereignty over all other objects; that in the *new* as well as the old government, the general powers are limited, and the states, in all the unenumerated cases, are left in the enjoyment of their sovereign and independent jurisdiction; that the powers given to the general government are few and defined; and that all authorities of which the states are not *explicitly* divested, in favor of the Union, remain with them in full force; as is admitted by the affirmative grants to the general government, and the prohibitions of some powers by negative clauses to the state governments.

It was said by Mr. [James] Madison, in the [Constitution ratifying] convention of Virginia, that the powers of the general government were enumerated and that its legislative powers are on defined objects, beyond which it cannot extend its jurisdiction; that the general government has no power but what is given and delegated, and that the delegation alone warranted the power; and that the powers of the general government are but *few*, and relate to external objects, whereas those of the states relate to those great objects which immediately concern the prosperity of the people. It was said by Mr. [John] Marshall that Congress cannot go beyond the delegated powers, and that a law not warranted by any of the enumerated powers would be void; and that the powers not given to Congress were *retained* by the states, and that without the aid of implication. Mr. [John] Randolph said that every power not given by this system is left with the states. And it was said by Mr. Geo. Nicholas that the people retain the powers not conferred on the general government, and that Congress cannot meddle with a power not enumerated....

POWERS EXPRESSLY GRANTED

I am to show in the second place that by the provisions of the Constitution (taken in exclusion of the words "necessary and proper" in the 8th [Section] of the 1st Article) such powers were only conveyed to the general government as were expressly granted or were (to use the language of the report) fairly incident to them. I shall afterward show that the insertion of those words, in that article, made no difference whatever and created no extension of the powers previously granted.

I take it to be a clear principle of universal law—of the law of nature, of nations, of war, of reason, and of the common law—that the general grant of a thing or power carries with it all those means (and those only) which are necessary to the perfection of the grant or the execution of the power. All those entirely concur in this respect, and are bestowed upon a clear principle. That principle is one which, while it completely effects the object of the grant or power, is a safe one as it relates to the reserved rights of the other party.

This is the true principle, and it is a universal one, applying to *all* pacts and conventions, high or low, or of which nature or kind soever. It cannot be stretched or extended even in relation to the American government; although, for purposes which can easily be conjectured, the Supreme Court has used high-sounding words as to it. They have stated it to be a government extending from St. Croix to the Gulf of Mexico, and from the Atlantic to the Pacific Ocean. This principle depends on a basis which applies to all cases whatsoever, and is inflexible and universal....

We are told in *The Federalist* that all powers *indispensably necessary* are granted by the Constitution, though they be not expressly; and that all the particular powers *requisite* to carry the enumerated ones into effect would have resulted to the government by unavoidable implications *without* the words "necessary and proper"; and that when a power is given, every particular power *necessary* for doing it is included. Again, it is said that a power is nothing but the ability or faculty of doing a thing, and that that ability includes the means *necessary* for its execution.

It is laid down in the report before mentioned that Congress under the terms "necessary and proper" have only all incidental powers necessary and proper, etc., and that the only inquiry is whether the power is properly an *incident* to an express power and *necessary* to its execution, and that, if it is not, Congress cannot exercise it; and that this [understanding of the] Constitution provided [was assumed] during all the discussions and ratifications of the Constitution, and is *absolutely necessary to consist* with the idea of defined or particular powers. Again, it is said, that none but the express powers and those *fairly incident* to them were granted by the Constitution.

The terms "incident" and "incidental powers" are not only the terms used in the early stages and by the *friends* of the Constitution but they are the terms used by the *Court* itself, in more passages than one, in relation to the power in question....Can it be then said that means which are of an independent or paramount character can be implied as incidental ones? Certainly not, unless, to say the least, they be absolutely necessary.

Can it be said, after this, that we are at liberty to invent terms at our pleasure in relation to this all-important question? Are we not tied down to the terms used by the founders of the Constitution; terms, too, of limited, well-defined, and established signification? On the contrary, I see great danger in using the *general* term now introduced; it may cover the latent designs of ambition and change the nature of the general government. It is entirely unimportant, as is before said, by what means this end is effected.

I come in the third place to show that the words "necessary and proper," in the Constitution, add nothing to the powers before given to the general government. They were only added (says *The Federalist*) for greater caution, and are tautologous and redundant, though harmless. It is also said, in the report aforesaid, that these words do not amount to a grant of *new* power, but for the removal of all uncertainty the declaration was made that the means were included in the grant. I might multiply authorities on this point to infinity; but if these do not suffice, neither would one were he to arise from the dead. If this power existed in the government before these words were used, its repetition or reduplication, in the Constitution, does not increase it. The "expression of that which before existed in the grant, has no operation." So these words, "necessary and proper," have no power or other effect than if they had been annexed to and repeated in every specific grant; and in that case they would have been equally unnecessary and harmless. As a friend, however, to the just powers of the general government, I do not object to them, considered as merely declaratory words, and inserted for greater caution. I only deny to them an extension to which they are not entitled, and which may be fatal to the reserved rights by the states and of the people.

FOR FURTHER READING

Margaret E. Horsnell, *Spencer Roane: Judicial Advocate of Jeffersonian Principles.* New York: Garland, 1986.

Herbert A. Johnson, *The Chief Justiceship of John Marshall,* Columbia: University of South Carolina Press, 1997.

Frances N. Stites, *John Marshall, Defender of the Constitution.* Boston: Little, Brown, 1981.

Viewpoint 21A

Indians Should Be Removed to the West (1830)

Andrew Jackson (1767–1845)

INTRODUCTION *Between 1815 and 1860 most of the American Indians residing in the territory between the Appalachian Mountains and the Mississippi River were forced to cede their lands and move from their homes. The United States government actively pursued this end by purchasing or seizing Indian territories and using threatened or actual military force to relocate Native Americans. Some Indian tribes responded with battle; others tried different methods of resistance. Among the latter group were the Cherokee Indians in Georgia,*

Alabama, and Tennessee. After signing treaties with the federal government, they sought to accommodate themselves to change by adopting numerous traits of white American culture, including writing, a governing constitution, and agricultural plantations (complete with black slaves).

In 1827 the Cherokee proclaimed themselves an independent nation, much to the dissatisfaction of local whites who coveted their land. The state of Georgia promptly passed laws nullifying the Cherokee declaration and extending state authority over Cherokee lands, actions that violated existing treaties between the Cherokee and the federal government. Both sides looked to Washington for support in resolving the dispute.

The white settlers were to find an ally in Andrew Jackson, elected president in 1828. Jackson had gained much of his fame as an Indian fighter. He sought for and gained Congressional passage in 1830 of the Indian Removal Act, which authorized funds for the removal of all Indian tribes still east of the Mississippi, including the Cherokee. The following viewpoint is excerpted from Jackson's 1830 message to Congress, in which he praises Congress for passing the law and defends his policy of Indian removal.

What benefits of Indian removal does Jackson describe? What comparison does Jackson make between Indians and immigrants? Why does he say that it is the duty of the federal government to expedite Indian removal?

It gives me pleasure to announce to Congress that the benevolent policy of the Government, steadily pursued for nearly thirty years, in relation to the removal of the Indians beyond the white settlements is approaching to a happy consummation. Two important tribes [the Choctaws and the Chickasaws] have accepted the provision made for their removal at the last session of Congress, and it is believed that their example will induce the remaining tribes also to seek the same obvious advantages.

The consequences of a speedy removal will be important to the United States, to individual States, and to the Indians themselves. The pecuniary advantages which it promises to the Government are the least of its recommendations. It puts an end to all possible danger of collision between the authorities of the General and State Governments on account of the Indians. It will place a dense and civilized population in large tracts of country now occupied by a few savage hunters. By opening the whole territory between Tennessee on the north and Louisiana on the south to the settlement of the whites it will incalculably strengthen the southwestern frontier and render the adjacent States strong enough to repel future invasions without remote aid. It will relieve the

From *A Compilation of the Messages and Papers of the Presidents*, vol. 3, edited by James D. Richardson (New York: Bureau of National Literature), 1897.

whole State of Mississippi and the western part of Alabama of Indian occupancy, and enable those States to advance rapidly in population, wealth, and power. It will separate the Indians from immediate contact with settlements of whites; free them from the power of the States; enable them to pursue happiness in their own way and under their own rude institutions; will retard the progress of decay, which is lessening their numbers, and perhaps cause them gradually, under the protection of the Government and through the influence of good counsels, to cast off their savage habits and become an interesting, civilized, and Christian community. These consequences, some of them so certain and the rest so probable, make the complete execution of the plan sanctioned by Congress at their last session [the 1830 Indian Removal Act] an object of much solicitude. . . .

TRUE PHILANTHROPY

Humanity has often wept over the fate of the aborigines of this country, and Philanthropy has been long busily employed in devising means to avert it, but its progress has never for a moment been arrested, and one by one have many powerful tribes disappeared from the earth. To follow to the tomb the last of his race and to tread on the graves of extinct nations excite melancholy reflections. But true philanthropy reconciles the mind to these vicissitudes as it does to the extinction of one generation to make room for another. In the monuments and fortresses of an unknown people, spread over the extensive regions of the West, we behold the memorials of a once powerful race, which was exterminated or has disappeared to make room for the existing savage tribes. Nor is there anything in this which, upon a comprehensive view of the general interests of the human race, is to be regretted. Philanthropy could not wish to see this continent restored to the condition in which it was found by our forefathers. What good man would prefer a country covered with forests and ranged by a few thousand savages to our extensive Republic, studded with cities, towns, and prosperous farms, embellished with all the improvements which art can devise or industry execute, occupied by more than 12,000,000 happy people, and filled with all the blessings of liberty, civilization, and religion?

The present policy of the Government is but a continuation of the same progressive change by a milder process. The tribes which occupied the countries now constituting the Eastern States were annihilated or have melted away to make room for the whites. The waves of population and civilization are rolling to the westward, and we now propose to acquire the countries occupied by the red men of the South and West by a fair exchange, and, at the expense of the United States, to send them to a land where their existence may be prolonged and perhaps made perpetual. Doubtless it will be painful to leave the graves of their fathers; but what do they more than our ancestors did or than our children are now doing? To better their condition in an unknown land our forefathers left all that was dear in earthly objects. Our children by thousands yearly leave the land of their birth to seek new homes in distant regions. Does Humanity weep at these painful separations from everything, animate and inanimate, with which the young heart has become entwined? Far from it. It is rather a source of joy that our country affords scope where our young population may range unconstrained in body or in mind, developing the power and faculties of man in their highest perfection. These remove hundreds and almost thousands of miles at their own expense, purchase the lands they occupy, and support themselves at their new homes from the moment of their arrival. Can it be cruel in this Government when, by events which it can not control, the Indian is made discontented in his ancient home to purchase his lands, to give him a new and extensive territory, to pay the expense of his removal, and support him a year in his new abode? How many thousands of our own people would gladly embrace the opportunity of removing to the West on such conditions! If the offers made to the Indians were extended to them, they would be hailed with gratitude and joy.

And is it supposed that the wandering savage has a stronger attachment to his home than the settled, civilized Christian? Is it more afflicting to him to leave the graves of his fathers than it is to our brothers and children? Rightly considered, the policy of the General Government toward the red man is not only liberal, but generous. He is unwilling to submit to the laws of the States and mingle with their population. To save him from this alternative, or perhaps utter annihilation, the General Government kindly offers him a new home, and proposes to pay the whole expense of his removal and settlement.

THE DUTIES OF THIS GOVERNMENT

In the consummation of a policy originating at an early period, and steadily pursued by every Administration within the present century—so just to the States and so generous to the Indians—the Executive feels it has a right to expect the cooperation of Congress and of all good and disinterested men. The States, moreover, have a right to demand it. It was substantially a part of the compact which made them members of our Confederacy. With Georgia there is an express contract; with the new States an implied one of equal obligation. Why, in authorizing Ohio, Indiana, Illinois, Missouri, Mississippi, and Alabama to form constitutions and become separate States, did Congress include within their limits extensive tracts of Indian lands, and, in some instances, powerful Indian tribes? Was it not understood by both parties that the power of the States was to be coextensive with their limits, and that with all convenient dispatch the General Government should extinguish the Indian title and remove every obstruction to the complete jurisdiction of the State governments over the soil? Probably not one of those States would have accepted a separate existence—certainly it would never have been granted by Congress—had it been understood that they were to be confined forever to those small portions of their nominal territory the Indian title to which had at the time been extinguished.

It is, therefore, a duty which this Government owes to the new States to extinguish as soon as possible the Indian title to all lands which Congress themselves have included within their limits. When this is done the duties of the General Government in relation to the States and the Indians within their limits are at an end. The Indians may leave the State or not, as they choose. The purchase of their lands does not alter in the least their personal relations with the State government. No act of the General Government has ever been deemed necessary to give the States jurisdiction over the persons of the Indians. That they possess by virtue of their sovereign power within their own limits in as full a manner before as after the purchase of the Indian lands; nor can this Government add to or diminish it.

May we not hope, therefore, that all good citizens, and none more zealously than those who think the Indians oppressed by subjection to the laws of the States, will unite in attempting to open the eyes of those children of the forest to their true condition, and by a speedy removal to relieve them from all the evils, real or imaginary, present or prospective, with which they may be supposed to be threatened.

Viewpoint 21B

Indians Should Be Allowed to Remain in Their Homeland (1830)

The Cherokee Nation

INTRODUCTION *The Cherokee Indians in the early 1800s had successfully adopted and combined traits of Indian and white culture to create a prosperous agricultural society with plantations, gristmills, a newspaper, and a governing constitution. In 1828, however, the state government of Georgia passed laws ordering the seizure of Indian lands and declaring all Cherokee laws void. Faced with the growing threat of forced removal from their homes, the Cherokees sent a delegation to Washington in 1830 to plead their case before Congress and President Andrew Jackson. Finding both the president and Congress unreceptive, they published an appeal to the American people, excerpted below, pleading for the right to stay in their homeland.*

*Despite some success, including an 1832 Supreme Court ruling (*Worcester v. Georgia*) in their favor,*

the Cherokee Nation was ultimately unable to prevent relocation. In 1838 U.S. troops forced the remaining Cherokee in Georgia to leave for lands in Oklahoma. Many perished while on the "trail of tears."

On what legal basis do the Cherokee lose their arguments? What reasons do they give for not wishing to move? How, in their view, has the state of Georgia treated them unfairly?

Permit us to state what we conceive to be our relations with the United States. After the peace of 1783, the Cherokees were an independent people; absolutely so, as much as any people on earth. They had been allies to Great Britain, and as a faithful ally took a part in the colonial war on her side. They had placed themselves under her protection, and had they, without cause, declared hostility against their protector, and had the colonies been subdued, what might not have been their fate? But her power on this continent was broken. She acknowledged the independence of the United States, and made peace. The Cherokees therefore stood alone; and, in these circumstances, continued the war. They were then under no obligations to the United States any more than to Great Britain, France or Spain. The United States never subjugated the Cherokees; on the contrary, our fathers remained in possession of their country, and with arms in their hands.

PEACE TREATIES

The people of the United States sought a peace; and, in 1785, the treaty of Hopewell was formed, by which the Cherokees came under the protection of the United States, and submitted to such limitations of sovereignty as are mentioned in that instrument. None of these limitations, however, affected, in the slightest degree, their rights of self-government and inviolate territory. The citizens of the United States had no right of passage through the Cherokee country till the year 1791, and then only in one direction, and by an express treaty stipulation. When the federal constitution was adopted, the treaty of Hopewell was confirmed, with all other treaties, as the supreme law of the land. In 1791, the treaty of Holston was made, by which the sovereignty of the Cherokees was qualified as follows: The Cherokees acknowledged themselves to be under the protection of the United States, and of no other sovereign.—They engaged that they would not hold any treaty with a foreign power, with any separate state of the union, or with individuals. They agreed that the United States should have the exclusive right of regulating their trade; that the citizens of the United States should have a right of way in one direction through the Cherokee country; and that if an Indian should do

From the "Memorial of the Cherokee Nation" (July 17, 1830), as reprinted in *Nile's Weekly Register*, August 21, 1830.

injury to a citizen of the United States he should be delivered up to be tried and punished. A cession of lands was also made to the United States. On the other hand, the United States paid a sum of money; offered protection; engaged to punish citizens of the United States who should do any injury to the Cherokees; abandoned white settlers on Cherokee lands to the discretion of the Cherokees; stipulated that white men should not hunt on these lands, nor even enter the country without a passport; and gave a solemn guaranty of all Cherokee lands not ceded. This treaty is the basis of all subsequent compacts; and in none of them are the relations of the parties at all changed.

The Cherokees have always fulfilled their engagements. They have never reclaimed those portions of sovereignty which they surrendered by the treaties of Hopewell and Holston. These portions were surrendered for the purpose of obtaining the guaranty which was recommended to them as the great equivalent. Had they refused to comply with their engagements, there is no doubt the United States would have enforced a compliance. Is the duty of fulfilling engagements on the other side less binding than it would be, if the Cherokees had the power of enforcing their just claims?

The people of the United States will have the fairness to reflect, that all the treaties between them and the Cherokees were made, at the solicitation, and for the benefit, of the whites; that valuable considerations were given for every stipulation, on the part of the United States; that it is impossible to reinstate the parties in their former situation, that there are now hundreds of thousands of citizens of the United States residing upon lands ceded by the Cherokees in these very treaties; and that our people have trusted their country to the guaranty of the United States. If this guaranty fails them, in what can they trust, and where can they look for protection?

We wish to remain on the land of our fathers. We have a perfect and original right to remain without interruption or molestation.

WE WISH TO REMAIN

We are aware, that some persons suppose it will be for our advantage to remove beyond the Mississippi. We think otherwise. Our people universally think otherwise. Thinking that it would be fatal to their interests, they have almost to a man sent their memorial to congress, deprecating the necessity of a removal. This question

was distinctly before their minds when they signed their memorial. Not an adult person can be found, who has not an opinion on the subject, and if the people were to understand distinctly, that they could be protected against the laws of the neighboring states, there is probably not an adult person in the nation, who would think it best to remove; though possibly a few might emigrate individually. There are doubtless many, who would flee to an unknown country, however beset with dangers, privations and sufferings, rather than be sentenced to spend six years in a Georgia prison for advising one of their neighbors not to betray his country. And there are others who could not think of living as outlaws in their native land, exposed to numberless vexations, and excluded from being parties or witnesses in a court of justice. It is incredible that Georgia should ever have enacted the oppressive laws to which reference is here made, unless she had supposed that something extremely terrific in its character was necessary in order to make the Cherokees willing to remove. We are not willing to remove; and if we could be brought to this extremity, it would be not by argument, not because our judgment was satisfied, not because our condition will be improved; but only because we cannot endure to be deprived of our national and individual rights and subjected to a process of intolerable oppression.

We wish to remain on the land of our fathers. We have a perfect and original right to remain without interruption or molestation. The treaties with us, and laws of the United States made in pursuance of treaties, guaranty our residence and our privileges, and secure us against intruders. Our only request is, that these treaties may be fulfilled, and these laws executed.

But if we are compelled to leave our country, we see nothing but ruin before us. The country west of the Arkansas territory is unknown to us. From what we can learn of it, we have no prepossessions in its favor. All the inviting parts of it, as we believe, are preoccupied by various Indian nations, to which it has been assigned. They would regard us as intruders, and look upon us with an evil eye. The far greater part of that region is, beyond all controversy, badly supplied with wood and water; and no Indian tribe can live as agriculturists without these articles. All our neighbors, in case of our removal, though crowded into our near vicinity, would speak a language totally different from ours, and practice different customs. The original possessors of that region are now wandering savages lurking for prey in the neighborhood. They have always been at war, and would be easily tempted to turn their arms against peaceful emigrants. Were the country to which we are urged much better than it is represented to be, and were it free from the objections which we have made to it, still it is not the land of our birth, nor of our affections. It contains neither the scenes of our childhood, nor the graves of our fathers.

THE HARMS OF FORCED REMOVAL

The removal of families to a new country, even under the most favorable auspices, and when the spirits are sustained by pleasing visions of the future, is attended with much depression of mind and sinking of heart. This is the case, when the removal is a matter of decided preference, and when the persons concerned are in early youth or vigorous manhood. Judge, then, what must be the circumstances of a removal, when a whole community, embracing persons of all classes and every description, from the infant to the man of extreme old age, the sick, the blind, the lame, the improvident, the reckless, the desperate, as well as the prudent, the considerate, the industrious, are compelled to remove by odious and intolerable vexations and persecutions, brought upon them in the forms of law, when all will agree only in this, that they have been cruelly robbed of their country, in violation of the most solemn compacts, which it is possible for communities to form with each other; and that, if they should make themselves comfortable in their new residence, they have nothing to expect hereafter but to be the victims of a future legalized robbery!

Such we deem, and are absolutely certain, will be the feelings of the whole Cherokee people, if they are forcibly compelled, by the laws of Georgia, to remove; and with these feelings, how is it possible that we should pursue our present course of improvement, or avoid sinking into utter despondency? We have been called a poor, ignorant, and degraded people. We certainly are not rich; nor have we ever boasted of our knowledge, or our moral or intellectual elevation. But there is not a man within our limits so ignorant as not to know that he has a right to live on the land of his fathers, in the possession of his immemorial privileges, and that this right has been acknowledged and guaranteed by the United States; nor is there a man so degraded as not to feel a keen sense of injury, on being deprived of this right and driven into exile.

AN APPEAL TO THE AMERICAN PEOPLE

It is under a sense of the most pungent feelings that we make this, perhaps our last appeal to the good people of the United States. It cannot be that the community we are addressing, remarkable for its intelligence and religious sensibilities, and pre-eminent for its devotion to the rights of man, will lay aside this appeal, without considering that we stand in need of its sympathy and commiseration. We know that to the Christian and to the philanthropist the voice of our multiplied sorrows and fiery trials will not appear as an idle tale. In our own land, on our own soil, and in our own dwellings, which we reared for our wives and for our little ones, when there was peace on our mountains and in our valleys, we are encountering troubles which cannot but try our very souls. But shall we, on account of these troubles, forsake our beloved country? Shall we be compelled by a civilized and Christian people, with whom we have lived in perfect peace for the last forty years, and for whom we have willingly bled in war, to bid a final adieu to our homes, our farms, our streams and our beautiful forests? No. We are still firm. We intend still to cling, with our wonted affection, to the land which gave us birth, and which, every day of our lives, brings to us new and stronger ties of attachment. We appeal to the judge of all the earth, who will finally award us justice, and to the good sense of the American people, whether we are intruders upon the land of others. Our consciences bear us witness that we are the invaders of no man's rights—we have robbed no man of his territory—we have usurped no man's authority, nor have we deprived any one of his unalienable privileges. How then shall we indirectly confess the right of another people to our land by leaving it forever? On the soil which contains the ashes of our beloved men we wish to live—on this soil we wish to die.

LET THEM REMEMBER

We intreat those to whom the foregoing paragraphs are addressed, to remember the great law of love. "Do to others as ye would that others should do to you"—Let them remember that of all nations on the earth, they are under the greatest obligation to obey this law. We pray them to remember that, for the sake of principle, their forefathers were *compelled* to leave, therefore *driven* from the old world, and that the winds of persecution wafted them over the great waters and landed them on the shores of the new world, when the Indian was the sole lord and proprietor of these extensive domains— Let them remember in what way they were received by the savage of America, when power was in his hand, and his ferocity could not be restrained by any human arm. We urge them to bear in mind, that those who would now ask of them a cup of cold water, and a spot of earth, a portion of their own patrimonial possessions, on which to live and die in peace, are the descendants of those, whose origin, as inhabitants of North America, history and tradition are alike insufficient to reveal. Let them bring to remembrance all these facts, and they *cannot*, and we are sure, they *will* not fail to remember, and sympathize with us in these our trials and sufferings.

FOR FURTHER READING

Michael D. Green, *The Policies of Indian Removal.* Lincoln: University of Nebraska Press, 1982.

Theda Persue and Michael P. Green, eds., *The Cherokee Removal: A Brief History with Documents.* New York: Bedford/St. Martin's, 1995.

Michael P. Roggin, *Fathers and Children: Andrew Jackson and the Subjugation of the American Indian.* New York: Knopf, 1975.

Anthony F.C. Wallace, *The Long Bitter Trail: Andrew Jackson and the Indians.* New York: Hill and Wang, 1993.

Viewpoint 22A

The Bank of the United States Should Be Abolished (1832)

Andrew Jackson (1767–1845)

INTRODUCTION *The role of the federal government relative to the people and the states continued to stir national debate during the presidency of Andrew Jackson(1829–1837). One central controversy was the fate of the Second Bank of the United States (BUSA), which had been chartered in 1816 (five years after the charter of the original BUSA had expired). To its supporters, the BUSA was a valuable national institution that served the country by safekeeping and transferring government funds, supplying credit to the western states, and providing through its banknotes a dependable medium of exchange. To its opponents, including Jackson, the bank was a suspect and corrupting institution that exploited its government-chartered monopoly to benefit wealthy stockholders and foreign investors at the expense of farmers and workers. Jackson and others were also suspicious of all banknotes and paper money not fully backed by specie (gold and silver).*

Jackson was given an opportunity to act on his beliefs in 1832 when Congress passed a bill to recharter the bank (even though its existing charter was not due to expire until 1836). The following viewpoint is excerpted from Jackson's veto message to Congress. Drafted primarily by his advisers Amos Kendall and Roger B. Taney, it was sent to Congress on July 10, 1832. Opponents of Jackson, convinced that the public was on their side, printed and distributed thousands of copies of the message during the 1832 presidential election. Their ploy failed, however, and Jackson handily won reelection over Kentucky senator Henry Clay.

Who benefits most from the Bank of the United States, according to Jackson? What, in his view, should the federal government do to promote equality between Americans?

The present corporate body, denominated the president, directors, and company of the Bank of the United States, will have existed at the time this act is intended to take effect twenty years. It enjoys an exclusive privilege of banking under the authority of the General Government, a monopoly of its favor and support, and, as a necessary consequence, almost a monopoly of the foreign and domestic exchange. The powers, privileges, and favors bestowed upon it in the original charter, by increasing the value of the stock far above its par value, operated as a gratuity of many millions to the stockholders....

Every monopoly and all exclusive privileges are granted at the expense of the public, which ought to receive a fair equivalent. The many millions which this act proposes to bestow on the stockholders of the existing bank must come directly or indirectly of the earnings of the American people....

AN UNFAIR MONOPOLY

It is not conceivable how the present stockholders can have any claim to the special favor of the Government. The present corporation has enjoyed its monopoly during the period stipulated in the original contract. If we must have such a corporation, why should not the Government sell out the whole stock and thus secure to the people the full market value of the privileges granted? Why should not Congress create and sell twenty-eight millions of stock, incorporating the purchasers with all the powers and privileges secured in this act and putting the premium upon the sales into the Treasury?

But this act does not permit competition in the purchase of this monopoly. It seems to be predicated on the erroneous idea that the present stockholders have a prescriptive right not only to the favor but to the bounty of Government. It appears that more than a fourth part of the stock is held by foreigners and the residue is held by a few hundred of our own citizens, chiefly of the richest class. For their benefit does this act exclude the whole American people from competition in the purchase of this monopoly and dispose of it for many millions less than it is worth....

FOREIGN CONTROL

In another of its bearings this provision is fraught with danger. Of the twenty-five directors of this bank five are chosen by the Government and twenty by the citizen stockholders. From all voice in these elections the foreign stockholders are excluded by the charter. In proportion, therefore, as the stock is transferred to foreign holders the extent of suffrage in the choice of directors is curtailed. Already is almost a third of the stock in foreign hands and not represented in elections. It is constantly passing out of the country, and this act will accelerate its departure. The entire control of the institution would necessarily fall into the hands of a few citizen stockholders, and the ease with which the object would be accomplished would be a temptation to designing men to secure that control in their own hands by monopolizing the remaining stock. There is danger that a president and directors would then be able to elect themselves from year to year, and without responsibility or control

From Andrew Jackson, "Veto of the Bank Renewal Bill," July 10, 1832, reprinted from *House Miscellaneous Documents*, 53rd Cong., 2nd sess., 1893–1894.

manage the whole concerns of the bank during the existence of its charter. It is easy to conceive that great evils to our country and its institutions might flow from such a concentration of power in the hands of a few men irresponsible to the people.

Is there no danger to our liberty and independence in a bank that in its nature has so little to bind it to our country? The president of the bank has told us that most of the State banks exist by its forbearance. Should its influence become concentered, as it may under the operation of such an act as this, in the hands of a self-elected directory whose interests are identified with those of the foreign stockholders, will there not be cause to tremble for the purity of our elections in peace and for the independence of our country in war? . . .

Should the stock of the bank principally pass into the hands of the subjects of a foreign country, and we should unfortunately become involved in a war with that country, what would be our condition? Of the course which would be pursued by a bank almost wholly owned by the subjects of a foreign power, and managed by those whose interests, if not affections, would run in the same direction there can be no doubt. All its operations within would be in aid of the hostile fleets and armies without. Controlling our currency, receiving our public moneys, and holding thousands of our citizens in dependence, it would be more formidable and dangerous than the naval and military power of the enemy.

If we must have a bank with private stockholders, every consideration of sound policy and every impulse of American feeling admonishes that it should be *purely American*. Its stockholders should be composed exclusively of our own citizens, who at least ought to be friendly to our Government and willing to support it in times of difficulty and danger. . . .

---■---

It is to be regretted that the rich and powerful too often bend the acts of government to their selfish purposes.

---■---

The bank is professedly established as an agent of the executive branch of the Government, and its constitutionality is maintained on that ground. Neither upon the propriety of present action nor upon the provisions of this act was the Executive consulted. It has had no opportunity to say that it neither needs nor wants an agent clothed with such powers and favored by such exemptions. There is nothing in its legitimate functions which makes it necessary or proper. Whatever interest or influence, whether public or private, has given birth to this act, it can not be found either in the wishes or necessities of the

executive department, by which present action is deemed premature, and the powers conferred upon its agent not only unnecessary, but dangerous to the Government and country.

THE RICH AND POWERFUL

It is to be regretted that the rich and powerful too often bend the acts of government to their selfish purposes. Distinctions in society will always exist under every just government. Equality of talents, of education, or of wealth can not be produced by human institutions. In the full enjoyment of the gifts of Heaven and the fruits of superior industry, economy, and virtue, every man is equally entitled to protection by law; but when the laws undertake to add to these natural and just advantages artificial distinctions, to grant titles, gratuities, and exclusive privileges, to make the rich richer and the potent more powerful, the humble members of society—the farmers, mechanics, and laborers—who have neither the time nor the means of securing like favors to themselves, have a right to complain of the injustice of their Government. There are no necessary evils in government. Its evils exist only in its abuses. If it would confine itself to equal protection, and, as Heaven does its rains, shower its favors alike on the high and the low, the rich and the poor, it would be an unqualified blessing. In the act before me there seems to be a wide and unnecessary departure from these just principles.

Nor is our Government to be maintained or our Union preserved by invasions of the rights and powers of the several States. In thus attempting to make our General Government strong we make it weak. Its true strength consists in leaving individuals and States as much as possible to themselves—in making itself felt, not in its power, but in its beneficence; not in its control, but in its protection; not in binding the States more closely to the center, but leaving each to move unobstructed in its proper orbit.

Experience should teach us wisdom. Most of the difficulties our Government now encounters and most of the dangers which impend over our Union have sprung from an abandonment of the legitimate objects of Government by our national legislation, and the adoption of such principles as are embodied in this act. Many of our rich men have not been content with equal protection and equal benefits, but have besought us to make them richer by act of Congress. By attempting to gratify their desires we have in the results of our legislation arrayed section against section, interest against interest, and man against man, in a fearful commotion which threatens to shake the foundations of our Union. It is time to pause in our career to review our principles, and if possible revive that devoted patriotism and spirit of compromise which distinguished the sages of the Revolution and the fathers of our Union. If we can not at once, in justice to interests vested under improvident legislation, make our Government what it ought to be, we can at least take a stand against all new grants of monopolies and exclusive privileges, against any prostitution of our Government to the advancement of the few at the expense of the many, and in favor of compromise and gradual reform in our code of laws and system of political economy.

I have now done my duty to my country. If sustained by my fellow-citizens, I shall be grateful and happy; if not, I shall find in the motives which impel me ample grounds for contentment and peace. In the difficulties which surround us and the dangers which threaten our institutions there is cause for neither dismay nor alarm. For relief and deliverance let us firmly rely on that kind Providence which I am sure watches with peculiar care over the destinies of our Republic, and on the intelligence and wisdom of our countrymen. Through *His* abundant goodness and *their* patriotic devotion our liberty and Union will be preserved.

Viewpoint 22B
The Bank of the United States Should Not Be Abolished (1832)
Daniel Webster (1782–1852)

INTRODUCTION *Daniel Webster was a noted senator, diplomat, lawyer, and perhaps the most famous orator of his time. During the presidency of Andrew Jackson (1829–1837) he represented Massachusetts in the Senate and became the leader of the emerging Whig Party, a political party created in large part to oppose Jackson and his policies.*

The fate of the Second Bank of the United States (BUSA) was perhaps the single most divisive issue between Webster and Jackson. In July 1832 Jackson vetoed a bill that would have renewed the bank's charter. The following viewpoint is excerpted from Webster's July 1832 speech to the U.S. Senate urging Congress to override Jackson's veto. He strongly condemns Jackson for risking the health of the American economy, for abusing his presidential powers, and for his tendency to "inflame the poor against the rich."

What will be the effects of closing the BUSA, according to Webster? Webster's ties to the bank included a personal friendship with its president, Nicholas Biddle, and he received a retainer as attorney for the bank and was the recipient of loans from the institution. How do these considerations affect your assessment of his arguments?

Mr. President [of the Senate], no one will deny the high importance of the subject now before us. Congress, after full deliberation and discussion, has passed a bill, by

From *The Works of Daniel Webster*, vol. 3 (Boston, 1853).

decisive majorities, in both houses, for extending the duration of the Bank of the United States. It has not adopted this measure until its attention had been called to the subject, in three successive annual messages of the President [Andrew Jackson]. The bill having been thus passed by both houses, and having been duly presented to the President, instead of signing and approving it, he has returned it with objections. These objections go against the whole substance of the law originally creating the bank. They deny, in effect, that the bank is constitutional; they deny that it is expedient; they deny that it is necessary for the public service.

It is not to be doubted, that the Constitution gives the President the power which he has now exercised; but while the power is admitted, the grounds upon which it has been exerted become fit subjects of examination. The Constitution makes it the duty of Congress, in cases like this, to reconsider the measure which they have passed, to weigh the force of the President's objections to that measure, and to take a new vote upon the question.

Before the Senate proceeds to this second vote, I propose to make some remarks upon those objections. . . . I will not conceal my opinion that the affairs of the country are approaching an important and dangerous crisis. At the very moment of almost unparalleled general prosperity, there appears an unaccountable disposition to destroy the most useful and most approved institutions of the government. Indeed, it seems to be in the midst of all this national happiness that some are found openly to question the advantages of the Constitution itself; and many more ready to embarrass the exercise of its just power, weaken its authority, and undermine its foundations. How far these notions may be carried, it is impossible yet to say. We have before us the practical result of one of them. The bank has fallen, or is to fall. . . .

> *A great majority of the people are satisfied with the bank as it is, and desirous that it should be continued.*

I hesitate not to say, that, as this *veto* travels to the West, it will depreciate the value of the every man's property from the Atlantic States to the capital of Missouri. Its effects will be felt in the price of lands, the great and leading article of Western property, in the price of crops, in the products of labor, in the repression of enterprise, and in embarrassment to every kind of business and occupation. I state this opinion strongly, because I have no doubt of its truth, and am willing its correctness should be judged by the event. Without personal acquaintance with the Western States, I know enough of their condition to be satisfied that what I have predicted must happen. The people of the West are rich, but their riches consist in their immense quantities of excellent land, in the products of these lands, and in their spirit of enterprise. The actual value of money, or rate of interest, with them is high, because their pecuniary capital bears little proportion to their landed interest. At an average rate, money is not worth less than eight per cent. per annum throughout the whole Western country, notwithstanding that it has now a loan or an advance from the bank of thirty millions, at six per cent. To call in this loan, at the rate of eight millions a year, in addition to the interest on the whole, and to take away, at the same time, that circulation which constitutes so great a portion of the medium of payment throughout that whole region, is an operation, which, however wisely conducted, cannot but inflict a blow on the community of tremendous force and frightful consequences. The thing cannot be done without distress, bankruptcy, and ruin, to many. If the President had seen any practical manner in which this change might be effected without producing these consequences, he would have rendered infinite service to the community by pointing it out. But he has pointed out nothing, he has suggested nothing; he contents himself with saying, without giving any reason, that, if the pressure be heavy, the fault will be the bank's. I hope this is not merely an attempt to forestall opinion, and to throw on the bank the responsibility of those evils which threaten the country, for the sake of removing it from himself.

The responsibility justly lies with him, and there it ought to remain. A great majority of the people are satisfied with the bank as it is, and desirous that it should be continued. They wished no change.

There are some other topics, treated in the message, which ought to be noticed. It commences by an inflamed statement of what it calls the "favor" bestowed upon the original bank by the government, or, indeed, as it is phrased, the "monopoly of its favor and support"; and through the whole message all possible changes are rung on the "gratuity," the "exclusive privileges," and "monopoly," of the bank charter. Now, Sir, the truth is, that the powers conferred on the bank are such, and no others, as are usually conferred on similar institutions. They constitute no monopoly, although some of them are of necessity, and with propriety, exclusive privileges. "The original act," says the message, "operated as a gratuity of many millions to the stockholders." What fair foundation is there for this remark? The stockholders received their charter, not gratuitously, but for a valuable consideration in money, prescribed by Congress, and actually paid. At some times the stock has been above *par*, at other times below *par*, according to prudence in management, or according to commercial occurrences. But if, by

a judicious administration of its affairs, it had kept its stock always above *par*, what pretence would there be, nevertheless, for saying that such augmentation of its value was a "gratuity" from government? The message proceeds to declare, that the present act proposes another donation, another gratuity, to the same men, of at least seven millions more. It seems to me that this is an extraordinary statement, and an extraordinary style of argument, for such a subject and on such an occasion. In the first place, the facts are all assumed; they are taken for true without evidence. There are no proofs that any benefit to that amount will accrue to the stockholders, nor any experience to justify the expectation of it. It rests on random estimates, or mere conjecture. But suppose the continuance of the charter should prove beneficial to the stockholders: do they not pay for it? They give twice as much for a charter of fifteen years, as was given before for one of twenty. And if the proposed *bonus*, or premium, be not, in the President's judgment, large enough, would he, nevertheless, on such a mere matter of opinion as that, negative the whole bill? May not Congress be trusted to decide even on such a subject as the amount of the money premium to be received by government for a charter of this kind?

GREAT PUBLIC INTERESTS

But, Sir, there is a larger and a much more just view of this subject. The bill was not passed for the purpose of benefiting the present stockholders. Their benefit, if any, is incidental and collateral. Nor was it passed on any idea that they had a *right* to a renewed charter, although the message argues against such right, as if it had been somewhere set up and asserted. No such right has been asserted by any body. Congress passed the bill, not as a bounty or a favor to the present stockholders, nor to comply with any demand of right on their part; but to promote great public interests, for great public objects. Every bank must have some stockholders, unless it be such a bank as the President has recommended, and in regard to which he seems not likely to find much concurrence of other men's opinions; and if the stockholders, whoever they may be, conduct the affairs of the bank prudently, the expectation is always, of course, that they will make it profitable to themselves, as well as useful to the public. If a bank charter is not to be granted, because, to some extent, it may be profitable to the stockholders, no charter can be granted. The objection lies against all banks.

Sir, the object aimed at by such institutions is to connect the public safety and convenience with private interests. It has been found by experience, that banks are safest under private management, and that government banks are among the most dangerous of all inventions. Now, Sir, the whole drift of the message is to reverse the settled judgment of all the civilized world, and to set up government banks, independent of private interest or private control. For this purpose the message labors, even beyond the measure of all its other labors, to create jealousies and prejudices, on the ground of the alleged benefit which that individuals will derive from the renewal of this charter. Much less effort is made to show that government, or the public, will be injured by the bill, than that individuals will profit by it. . . .

I will not dwell particularly on this part of the message. Its tone and its arguments are all in the same strain. It speaks of the certain gain of the present stockholders, of the value of the monopoly; it says that all monopolies are granted at the expense of the public; that the many millions which this bill bestows on the stockholders come out of the earnings of the people; that, if government sells monopolies, it ought to sell them in open market; that it is an erroneous idea, that the present stockholders have a prescriptive right either to the favor or the bounty of government; that the stock is in the hands of a few, and that the whole American people are excluded from competition in the purchase of the monopoly. To all this I say, again, that much of it is assumption without proof; much of it is an argument against that which nobody has maintained or asserted; and the rest of it would be equally strong against any charter, at any time. . . .

FOREIGN CAPITAL

From the commencement of the government, it has been thought desirable to invite, rather than to repel, the introduction of foreign capital. Our stocks have all been open to foreign subscriptions; and the State banks, in like manner, are free to foreign ownership. Whatever State has created a debt has been willing that foreigners should become purchasers, and desirous of it. How long is it, Sir, since Congress itself passed a law vesting new powers in the President of the United States over the cities in this District, for the very purpose of increasing their credit abroad, the better to enable them to borrow money to pay their subscriptions to the Chesapeake and Ohio Canal? It is easy to say that there is danger to liberty, danger to independence, in a bank open to foreign stockholders, because it is easy to say any thing. But neither reason nor experience proves any such danger. The foreign stockholder cannot be a director. He has no voice even in the choice of directors. His money is placed entirely in the management of the directors appointed by the President and Senate and by the American stockholders. So far as there is dependence or influence either way, it is to the disadvantage of the foreign stockholder. He has parted with the control over his own property, instead of exercising control over the property or over the actions of others. And, Sir, let it now be added, in further answer to this class of objections, that experience has abundantly confuted them all. This government has existed forty-three years, and has maintained, in full being and operation, a bank, such as is now proposed to be renewed, for thirty-six years out of the forty-three. We have never for a moment had a bank not subject to every one of these objections. Always, foreigners might be stockholders; always, foreign stock has been exempt from State taxation, as much as at present; always the same power and privileges; always, all that which is now called a "monopoly," a "gratuity," a "present," has been possessed by the bank. And yet there has been found no danger to liberty, no introduction of foreign influence, and no accumulation of irresponsible power in a few hands. I cannot but hope, therefore, that the people of the United States will not now yield up their judgment to those notions which would reverse all our best experience, and persuade us to discontinue a useful institution from the influence of vague and unfounded declamation against its danger to the public liberties. Our liberties, indeed, must stand upon very frail foundations, if the government cannot, without endangering them, avail itself of those common facilities, in the collection of its revenues and the management of its finances, which all other governments, in commercial countries, find useful and necessary.

In order to justify its alarm for the security of our independence, the message supposes a case. It supposes that the bank should pass principally into the hands of the subjects of a foreign country, and that we should be involved in war with that country, and then it exclaims, "What would be our condition?" Why, Sir, it is plain that all the advantages would be on our side. The bank would still be our institution, subject to our own laws, and all its directors elected by ourselves; and our means would be enhanced, not by the confiscation and plunder, but by the proper use, of the foreign capital in our hands. And, Sir, it is singular enough, that this very state of war, from which this argument against a bank is drawn, is the very thing which, more than all others, convinced the country and the government of the necessity of a national bank. So much was the want of such an institution felt in the late war [War of 1812], that the subject engaged the attention of Congress, constantly, from the declaration of that war down to the time when the existing bank was actually established; so that in this respect, as well as in others, the argument of the message is directly opposed to the whole experience of the government, and to the general and long-settled convictions of the country. . . .

A NEW EPOCH

Mr. President, we have arrived at a new epoch. We are entering on experiments, with the government and the Constitution of the country, hitherto untried, and of fearful and appalling aspect. This message calls us to the contemplation of a future which little resembles the past. Its principles are at war with all that public opinion has sustained, and all which the experience of the government has sanctioned. It denies first principles; it contradicts truths, heretofore received as indisputable. It denies to the judiciary the interpretation of law, and claims to divide with Congress the power of originating statutes. It extends the grasp of executive pretension over every power of the government. But this is not all. It presents the chief magistrate of the Union in the attitude of arguing away the powers of that government over which he has been chosen to preside; and adopting for this purpose modes of reasoning which, even under the influence of all proper feeling towards high official station, it is difficult to regard as respectable. It appeals to every prejudice which may betray men into a mistaken view of their own interests. and to every passion which may lead them to disobey the impulses of their understanding. It urges all the specious topics of State rights and national encroachment against that which a great majority of the States have affirmed to be rightful, and in which all of them have acquiesced. It sows, in an unsparing manner, the seeds of jealousy and ill-will against that government of which its author is the official head. It raises a cry, that liberty is in danger, at the very moment when it puts forth claims to powers heretofore unknown and unheard of. It effects alarm for the public freedom, when nothing endangers that freedom so much as its own unparalleled pretenses. This, even, is not all. It manifestly seeks to inflame the poor against the rich; it wantonly attacks whole classes of the people, for the purpose of turning against them the prejudices and the resentments of other classes. It is a state paper which finds no topic too exciting for its use, no passion too inflammable for its address and its solicitation.

Such is this message. It remains now for the people of the United States to choose between the principles here avowed and their government. These cannot subsist together. The one or the other must be rejected. If the sentiments of the message shall receive general approbation, the Constitution will have perished even earlier than the moment which its enemies originally allowed for the termination of its existence. It will not have survived to its fiftieth year.

FOR FURTHER READING

Bray Hammond, *Banks and Politics in America from the Revolution to the Civil War.* Princeton, NJ: Princeton University Press, 1991.

Edward S. Kaplan, *The Bank of the United States and the American Economy.* Westport, CT: Greenwood, 1999.

Robert V. Remini, *Andrew Jackson and the Bank War.* New York: Norton, 1967.

Robert V. Remini, *Daniel Webster: The Man and His Time.* New York: Norton, 1997.

SOCIAL REFORM ISSUES OF THE ANTEBELLUM ERA

Viewpoint 23A

Suffrage Should Not Be Based on Property (1821)

Nathan Sanford (1777–1838)

INTRODUCTION *The state constitutions of the original thirteen states made at the time of the American Revolution required property ownership as a qualification for voting. However, beginning in 1815, many of these states rewrote their constitutions to grant suffrage to all (white male) taxpayers—in part because they were losing people to the newer western states that had no such suffrage restrictions. During the 1821 New York convention called to revise the state constitution, Nathan Sanford, a lawyer and public official, chaired a committee that proposed extending the vote to virtually all white male taxpayers and those who served in the state militia. His speech recommending the committee's resolution to the convention is excerpted in the following viewpoint.*

What is the basic principle of the proposed voting reforms, according to Sanford? What importance does he attach to the experiences of other states?

The question before us is the right of suffrage—who shall or who shall not have the right to vote. The committee have presented the scheme they thought best; to abolish all existing distinctions and make the right of voting uniform. Is this not right? Where did these distinctions arise? They arose from British precedents. In England they have their three estates [the nobility, the clergy, and the commons], which must always have their separate interests represented. Here there is but one estate—the people. To me the only qualifications seem to be the virtue and morality of the people; and if they may be safely entrusted to vote for one class of our rulers, why not for all?

THOSE WHO BEAR THE BURDENS

In my opinion, these distinctions are fallacious. We have the experience of almost all the other states against them. The principle of the scheme now proposed is that those who bear the burdens of the state should choose those that rule it. There is no privilege given to property as such; but those who contribute to the public support we consider as entitled to a share in the election of rulers. The burdens are annual, and the elections are annual, and this appears proper. To me, and the majority of the committee, it appeared the only reasonable scheme that those who are to be affected by the acts of the government should be annually entitled to vote for those who administer it.

From *Reports of the Proceedings and Debates of the Convention of 1821, Assembled for the Purpose of Amending the Constitution of the State of New York* (Albany, NY, 1821).

Our taxes are of two sorts, on real and personal property. The payment of a tax on either, we thought, equally entitled a man to a vote, and thus we intended to destroy the odious distinctions of property which now exist. But we have considered personal service, in some cases, equivalent to a tax on personal property, as in work on the high roads. This is a burden and should entitle those subject to it to equivalent privileges. The road duty is equal to a poll tax on every male citizen of twenty-one years, of 62½ cents per annum, which is about the value of each individual's work on the road. This work is a burden imposed by the legislature—a duty required by rulers, and which should entitle those subject to it to a choice of those rulers.

Then, sir, the militia next presents itself; the idea of personal service, as applicable to the road duty, is, in like manner, applicable here; and this criterion has been adopted in other states. In Mississippi mere enrollment gives a vote. In Connecticut, as is proposed here, actual service, and that without the right of commutation, is required. The duty in the militia is obligatory and onerous. The militiaman must find his arms and accouterments and lose his time. But, after admitting all these persons, what restrictions, it will be said, are left on the right of suffrage? (1) The voter must be a citizen. (2) The service required must be performed within the year, on the principle that taxation is annual, and election annual; so that when the person ceases to contribute or serve, he ceases to vote.

A residence is also required. We propose the term of six months, because we find it already in the constitution; but we propose this residence in the state and not in the county or town, so that, wherever a voter may be at the time of election, he may vote there if he has been a resident of the state for six months. The object of this was to enable those who move, as very many do, in the six months preceding an election, out of the town or ward in which they have resided, to retain the right of voting in their new habitations. The term of six months is deemed long enough to qualify those who come into our state from abroad to understand and exercise the privileges of a citizen here.

The course of things in this country is for the extension and not the restriction of popular rights.

THE WHOLE MALE POPULATION

Now, sir, this scheme will embrace almost the whole male population of the state. There is, perhaps, no subject so

purely matter of opinion as the question how far the right of suffrage may be safely carried. We propose to carry it almost as far as the male population of the state. The Convention may perhaps think this too broad. On this subject we have much experience; yet there are respectable citizens who think this extension of suffrage unfavorable to the rights of property. Certainly this would be a fatal objection, if well founded; for any government, however constituted, which does not secure property to its rightful owners is a bad government. But how is the extension of the right of suffrage unfavorable to property? Will not our laws continue the same? Will not the administration of justice continue the same? And, if so, how is private property to suffer? Unless these are changed, and upon them rest the rights and security of property, I am unable to perceive how property is to suffer by the extension of the right of suffrage.

But we have abundant experience on this point in other states. Now, sir, in many of the states the right of suffrage has no restriction; every male inhabitant votes. Yet what harm has been done in those states? What evil has resulted to them from this cause? The course of things in this country is for the extension and not the restriction of popular rights. I do not know that in Ohio or Pennsylvania, where the right of suffrage is universal, there is not the same security for private rights and private happiness as elsewhere.

Viewpoint 23B

Suffrage Should Be Limited to Property Holders (1821)

James Kent (1763–1847)

INTRODUCTION *During the first decades of the American republic, suffrage was considered the right and responsibility of established and self-supporting property holders. By the 1820s, however, such views were in the minority as a new generation of Americans called for increased democracy in voting and other areas of society, and states began to lift voting restrictions. One opponent of such a reform was James Kent, a leading jurist in New York. The following viewpoint is taken from a debate at a New York state convention in 1821; Kent is responding specifically to a committee suggestion that property ownership requirements for voting be removed (see viewpoint 23A). He argues that members of the state senate (one half of the state's legislature) elected by farmers and other property owners. Kent's arguments were unsuccessful; New York joined other states in passing universal suffrage, at least among white adult males.*

What contrasts does Kent draw between farmers and manufacturers? What arguments does he make about the city of New York?

I must beg leave to trespass for a few moments upon the patience of the [Sanford] committee while I state the reasons which have induced me to wish that the Senate should continue, as heretofore, the representative of the landed interest and exempted from the control of universal suffrage. I hope what I may have to say will be kindly received, for it will be well intended. But, if I thought otherwise, I should still prefer to hazard the loss of the little popularity which I might have in this house, or out of it, than to hazard the loss of the approbation of my own conscience. . . .

THE IDOL OF UNIVERSAL SUFFRAGE

The Senate has hitherto been elected by the farmers of the state, by the free and independent lords of the soil, worth at least $250 in freehold estate, over and above all debts charged thereon. The governor has been chosen by the same electors, and we have hitherto elected citizens of elevated rank and character. Our assembly has been chosen by freeholders, possessing a freehold of the value of $50, or by persons renting a tenement of the yearly value of $5, and who have been rated [valued for purposes of taxation] and actually paid taxes to the state. By the report before us, we propose to annihilate, at one stroke, all those property distinctions and to bow before the idol of universal suffrage. That extreme democratic principle, when applied to the Legislative and Executive departments of government, has been regarded with terror by the wise men of every age, because in every European republic, ancient and modern, in which it has been tried, it has terminated disastrously and been productive of corruption, injustice, violence, and tyranny. And dare we flatter ourselves that we are a peculiar people who can run the career of history, exempted from the passions which have disturbed and corrupted the rest of mankind? If we are like other races of men, with similar follies and vices, then I greatly fear that our posterity will have reason to deplore, in sackcloth and ashes, the delusion of the day.

THE AGRICULTURAL INTEREST

It is not my purpose at present to interfere with the report of the committee, so far as respects the qualifications of electors for governor and members of assembly. I shall feel grateful if we may be permitted to retain the stability and security of a Senate, bottomed upon the freehold property of the state. Such a body, so constituted, may prove a sheet anchor amid the future factions and storms of the republic. The great leading and governing interest of this state is, at present, the agricultural; and what madness would it be to commit that interest to the winds. The great body of the people are now the owners and actual cultivators of the soil. With that wholesome population we always expect to find moderation, frugality, order, honesty, and a due sense of independence, liberty, and justice. It is impossible that any people can lose their liberties by internal fraud or violence so long as the country

is parceled out among freeholders of moderate possessions, and those freeholders have a sure and efficient control in the affairs of the government. Their habits, sympathies, and employments necessarily inspire them with a correct spirit of freedom and justice; they are the safest guardians of property and the laws.

We certainly cannot too highly appreciate the value of the agricultural interest. It is the foundation of national wealth and power. According to the opinion of her ablest political economists, it is the surplus produce of the agriculture of England that enables her to support her vast body of manufacturers, her formidable fleets and armies, and the crowds of persons engaged in the liberal professions and the cultivation of the various arts.

Now, sir, I wish to preserve our Senate as the representative of the landed interest. I wish those who have an interest in the soil to retain the exclusive possession of a branch in the legislature as a stronghold in which they may find safety through all the vicissitudes which the state may be destined, in the course of Providence, to experience. I wish them to be always enabled to say that their freeholds cannot be taxed without their consent. The men of no property, together with the crowds of dependents connected with great manufacturing and commercial establishments, and the motley and undefinable population, of crowded ports, may, perhaps, at some future day, under skillful management, predominate in the assembly, and yet we should be perfectly safe if no laws could pass without the free consent of the owners of the soil. That security we at present enjoy; and it is that security which I wish to retain. . . .

A CHANGING NATION

We are no longer to remain plain and simple publics of farmers like the New England colonists or the Dutch settlements on the Hudson. We are fast becoming a great nation, with great commerce, manufactures, population, wealth, luxuries, and with the vices and miseries that they engender. One-seventh of the population of the city of Paris at this day subsists on charity, and one-third of the inhabitants of that city die in the hospitals; what would become of such a city with universal suffrage? France has upward of 4 million, and England upward of 5 million of manufacturing and commercial laborers without property. Could these kingdoms sustain the weight of universal suffrage? The radicals in England, with the force of that mighty, engine, would at once sweep away the property, the laws, and the liberties of that island like a deluge.

The growth of the city of New York is enough to startle and awaken those who are pursuing the *ignis fatuus* [will o' the wisp] of universal suffrage. In 1773 it had 21,000 souls; in 1801 it had 60,000; in 1806 it had 76,000; in 1820 it had 123,000. It is rapidly swelling into the unwieldy population, and with the burdensome pauperism, of a European metropolis. New York is destined to become the future London of America; and in less than a century that city, with the operation of universal suffrage and under skillful direction, will govern this state.

The notion that every man that works a day on the road, or serves an idle hour in the militia, is entitled as of right to an equal participation in the whole power of the government is most unreasonable and has no foundation in justice. We had better at once discard from the report such a nominal test of merit. If such persons have an equal share in one branch of the legislature, it is surely as much as they can in justice or policy demand. Society is an association for the protection of property as well as of life, and the individual who contributes only one cent to the common stock ought not to have the same power and influence in directing the property concerns of the partnership as he who contributes his thousands. He will not have the same inducements to care, and diligence, and fidelity. His inducements and his temptation would be to divide the whole capital upon the principles of an agrarian law. . . .

We are destined to become a great manufacturing as well as commercial state. We have already numerous and prosperous factories of one kind or another, and one master-capitalist, with his 100 apprentices, and jouneymen, and agents, and dependents, will bear down at the polls an equal number of farmers of small estates in his vicinity who cannot safely unite for their common defense. Large manufacturing and mechanical establishments can act in an instant with the unity and efficacy of disciplined troops. It is against such combinations, among others, that I think we ought to give to the freeholders, or those who have interest in land, one branch of the legislature for their asylum and their comfort. Universal suffrage, once granted, is granted forever and never can be recalled. There is no retrograde step in the rear of democracy. However mischievous the precedent may be in its consequences, or however fatal in its effects, universal suffrage never can be recalled or checked but by the strength of the bayonet. We stand, therefore, this moment, on the brink of fate, on the very edge of the precipice. If we let go our present hold on the Senate, we commit our proudest hopes and our most precious interests to the waves.

FOR FURTHER READING

Eric Foner, *The Story of American Freedom.* New York: W.W. Norton, 1999.

Leon F. Litwack, *North of Slavery: The Negro in the Free States, 1790–1860.* Chicago: University of Chicago Press, 1961.

Merill D. Peterson, ed., *Democracy, Liberty, and Property: The State Constitutional Conventions of the 1820s.* Indianapolis: Bobbs-Merill Co., 1966.

Chilton Williamson, *American Suffrage from Property to Democracy, 1760–1860.* Princeton, NJ: Princeton University Press, 1960.

Viewpoint 24A
Immigrants Endanger America (1845)
Native American Party

INTRODUCTION *In the decades preceding the Civil War the United States experienced a large influx of immigrants from Europe. Not all Americans welcomed their arrival. Nativism, a movement devoted to the idea that immigrants threatened the economic and political security of "native" Americans—white, Protestant, established citizens—became an important political force. Some nativists were motivated by anti-Catholic prejudice (many of the new immigrants from Germany and Ireland were Catholic) and were worried that the Roman Catholic Church might gain unwanted influence in American life. Others expressed concern about what they saw as the depraved and ignorant nature of immigrants and were especially worried that such people had the right to vote. In 1844 an anti-immigrant organization, the American Republican Party, managed to elect dozens of officials in the states of New York, Pennsylvania, and Massachusetts. Members of the organization held their first national convention the following year in Philadelphia, where they changed their party's name to the Native American Party and adopted a platform delineating the threats they believed immigrants posed to America. The following viewpoint is excerpted from that platform.*

How does the Native American Party compare new immigrants with those of the previous two centuries? What importance does it attach to recent democratic reforms (see viewpoints 23A and 23B) giving more people the vote? What ominous scenarios does it predict for America?

It is an incontrovertible truth that the civil institutions of the United States of America have been seriously affected, and that they now stand in imminent peril from the rapid and enormous increase of the body of residents of foreign birth, imbued with foreign feelings, and of an ignorant and immoral character, who receive, under the present lax and unreasonable laws of naturalization, the elective franchise and the right of eligibility to political office.

The whole body of foreign citizens, invited to our shores under a constitutional provision adapted to other times and other political conditions of the world, and of our country especially, has been endowed by American hospitality with gratuitous privileges unnecessary to the enjoyment of those inalienable rights of man—life, lib-

From *Address to the Delegates of the Native American National Convention, Assembled at Philadelphia, July 4, 1845, to the Citizens of the United States.*

erty, and the pursuit of happiness—privileges wisely reserved to the Natives of the soil by the governments of all other civilized nations. But, familiarized by habit with the exercise of these indulgences, and emboldened by increasing numbers, a vast majority of those who constitute this foreign body, now claim as an original right that which has been so incautiously granted as a favour—thus attempting to render inevitable the prospective action of laws adopted upon a principle of mere expediency, made variable at the will of Congress by the express terms of the Constitution, and heretofore repeatedly revised to meet the exigencies of the times.

In former years, this body was recruited chiefly from the victims of political oppression, or the active and intelligent mercantile adventurers of other lands; and it then constituted a slender representation of the best classes of the foreign population well fitted to add strength to the state, and capable of being readily educated in the peculiarly American science of political self-government. Moreover, while welcoming the stranger of every condition, laws then wisely demanded of every foreign aspirant for political rights a certificate of practical good citizenship. Such a class of aliens were followed by no foreign demagogues—they were courted by no domestic demagogues; they were purchased by no parties—they were debauched by no emissaries of kings. A wall of fire separated them from such a baneful influence, erected by their intelligence, their knowledge, their virtue and love of freedom. But for the last twenty years the road to civil preferment and participation in the legislative and executive government of the land has been laid broadly open, alike to the ignorant, the vicious and the criminal; and a large proportion of the foreign body of citizens and voters now constitutes a representation of the worst and most degraded of the European population—victims of social oppression or personal vices, utterly divested, by ignorance or crime, of the moral and intellectual requisites for political self-government.

A NEW CLASS OF IMMIGRANTS

Thus tempted by the suicidal policy of these United States, and favoured by the facilities resulting from the modern improvements of navigation, numerous societies and corporate bodies in foreign countries have found it economical to transport to our shores, at public and private expense, the feeble, the imbecile, the idle, and intractable, thus relieving themselves of the burdens resulting from the vices of the European social systems by availing themselves of the generous errors of our own.

The almshouses of Europe are emptied upon our coast, and this by our own invitation—not casually, or to a trivial extent, but systematically, and upon a constantly increasing scale. The Bedlams [insane asylums] of the old world have contributed their share to the torrent of immigration, and the lives of our citizens have been attempted in the streets of our capital cities by mad-men, just liberated from European hospitals upon the express condition that they should be transported to America. By the orders of European governments, the punishment of crimes has been commuted for banishment to the land of the free; and criminals in iron have crossed the ocean to be cast loose upon society on their arrival upon our shores. The United States are rapidly becoming the lazar house [hospital for the poor with contagious diseases] and penal colony of Europe; nor can we reasonably censure such proceedings. They are legitimate consequences of our own unlimited benevolence; and it is of such material that we profess to manufacture free and enlightened citizens, by a process occupying five short years at most, but practically oftentimes embraced in a much shorter period of time.

The mass of foreign voters, formerly lost among the Natives of the soil, has increased from the ratio of 1 in 40 to that of 1 in 7! A like advance in fifteen years will leave the Native citizens a minority in their own land! Thirty years ago these strangers came by units and tens—now they swarm by thousands. Formerly, most of them sought only for an honest livelihood and a provision for their families, and rarely meddled with the institutions, of which it was impossible they could comprehend the nature; now each newcomer seeks political preferment, and struggles to fasten on the public purse with an avidity, in strict proportion to his ignorance and unworthiness of public trust—having been sent for the purpose of obtaining political ascendancy in the government of the nation; having been sent to exalt their allies to power; having been sent to work a revolution from republican freedom to the divine rights of monarchs.

From these unhappy circumstances has arisen an *Impertum in Imperio* [a state within a state]—a body uninformed and vicious—foreign in feeling, prejudice, and manner, yet armed with a vast and often a controlling influence over the policy of a nation, whose benevolence it abuses, and whose kindness it habitually insults; a body as dangerous to the rights of the intelligent foreigner as to the prospect of its own immediate progeny, as it is threatening to the liberties of the country, and the hopes of rational freedom throughout the world; a body ever ready to complicate our foreign relations by embroiling us with the hereditary hates and feuds of other lands, and to disturb our domestic peace by its crude ideas, mistaking license for liberty, and the overthrow of individual rights for republican political equality; a body ever the ready tool of foreign and domestic demagogues, and steadily endeavouring by misrule to establish popular tyranny under a cloak of false democracy. Americans, false to their country, and led on to moral crime, by the desire of dishonest gain; have scattered their agents over Europe, inducing the malcontent and the unthrifty to exchange a life of compulsory labour in foreign lands for relative comfort, to be maintained by the tax-paying industry of our overburdened and deeply indebted community....

FUTURE OF FOREIGN CONTROL

The body of adopted citizens, with foreign interests and prejudices, is annually advancing with rapid strides, in geometrical progression. Already it has acquired a control over our elections which cannot be entirely corrected, even by the wisest legislation, until the present generation shall be numbered with the past. Already it has notoriously swayed the course of national legislation, and invaded the purity of local justice. In a few years its unchecked progress would cause it to outnumber the native defenders of our rights, and would then inevitably dispossess our offspring, and its own, of the inheritance for which our fathers bled, or plunge this land of happiness and peace into the horrors of civil war.

The correction of these evils can never be effected by any combination governed by the tactics of other existing parties. If either of the old parties, as such, were to attempt an extension of the term of naturalization, it would be impossible for it to carry out the measure, because they would immediately be abandoned by the foreign voters. This great measure can be carried out only by an organization like our own, made up of those who have given up their former political preferences.

For these reasons, we recommend the immediate organization of the truly patriotic native citizens throughout the United States, for the purpose of resisting the progress of foreign influence in the conduct of American affairs, and the correction of such political abuses as have resulted from unguarded or partisan legislation on the subject of naturalization, so far as these abuses admit of remedy without encroachment upon the vested rights of foreigners who have been already legally adopted into the bosom of the nation.

Viewpoint 24B

Immigrants Do Not Endanger America (1845)

Thomas L. Nichols (1815–1901)

INTRODUCTION *Thomas L. Nichols was a doctor, social historian, and journalist. In 1845 he delivered a lecture (later published) in support of U.S. immigration. By then the annual number of immigrants to the United States was approaching three hundred thousand (the total U.S. population was then about 20 million). Nichols also criticizes the arguments made by the emerging nativist movement against immigrants.*

On what basis do people have a "right" to emigrate, according to Nichols? How have immigrants benefited America? How are his descriptions of immigrants different from those of the authors of the opposing viewpoint?

The questions connected with emigration from Europe to America are interesting to both the old world and the new—are of importance to the present and future generations. They have more consequence than a charter or a state election; they involve the destinies of millions; they are connected with the progress of civilization, the rights of man, and providence of God!

I have examined this subject the more carefully, and speak upon it the more earnestly, because I have been to some extent, in former years, a partaker of the prejudices I have since learned to pity. A native of New England and a descendant of the puritans, I early imbibed, and to some extent promulgated, opinions of which reflection and experience have made me ashamed....

> *The emigration of foreigners... has been in various ways highly beneficial to this country.*

But while I would speak of the motives of men with charity. I claim the right to combat their opinions with earnestness. Believing that the principles and practices of Native Americanism are wrong in themselves, and are doing wrong to those who are the objects of their persecution, justice and humanity require that their fallacy should be exposed, and their iniquity condemned....

THE RIGHT TO EMIGRATE

The right of man to emigrate from one country to another, is one which belongs to him by his own constitution and by every principle of justice. It is one which no law can alter, and no authority destroy. "Life, liberty, and the pursuit of happiness" are set down, in our Declaration of Independence, as among the self-evident, unalienable rights of man. If I have a right to live, I have also a right to what will support existence—food, clothing, and shelter. If then the country in which I reside, from a super-abundant population, or any other cause, does not afford me these, my right to go from it to some other is self-evident and unquestionable. The *right to live*, then, supposes the right of emigration....

I proceed, therefore, to show that the emigration of foreigners to this country is not only defensible on grounds of abstract justice—what we have no possible right to prevent, but that it has been in various ways highly beneficial to this country.

From *Lecture on Immigration and the Right of Naturalization* by Thomas Nichols (New York, 1845).

Emigration first peopled this hemisphere with civilized men. The first settlers of this continent had the same right to come here that belongs to the emigrant of yesterday—no better and no other. They came to improve their condition, to escape from oppression, to enjoy freedom—for the same, or similar, reasons as now prevail. And so far as they violated no private rights, so long as they obtained their lands by fair purchase, or took possession of those which were unclaimed and uncultivated, the highly respectable natives whom the first settlers found here had no right to make any objections. The peopling of this continent with civilized men, the cultivation of the earth, the various processes of productive labor, for the happiness of man, all tend to "the greatest good of the greatest number," and carry out the evident design of Nature or Providence in the formation of the earth and its inhabitants.

Emigration from various countries in Europe to America, producing a mixture of races, has had, and is still having, the most important influence upon the destinies of the human race. It is a principle, laid down by every physiologist, and proved by abundant observation, that man, like other animals, is improved and brought to its highest perfection by an intermingling of the blood and qualities of various races. That nations and families deteriorate from an opposite course has been observed in all ages. The great physiological reason why Americans are superior to other nations in freedom, intelligence, and enterprize, is because that they are the offspring of the greatest intermingling of races. The mingled blood of England has given her predominance over several nations of Europe in these very qualities, and a newer infusion, with favorable circumstances of climate, position, and institutions, has rendered Americans still superior. The Yankees of New England would never have shown those qualities for which they have been distinguished in war and peace throughout the world had there not been mingling with the puritan English, the calculating Scotch, the warm hearted Irish, the gay and chivalric French, the steady persevering Dutch, and the transcendental Germans, for all these nations contributed to make up the New England character, before the Revolution, and ever since to influence that of the whole American people....

IMMIGRANT WEALTH

This country has been continually benefited by the immense amount of capital brought hither by emigrants. There are very few who arrive upon our shores without some little store of wealth, the hoard of years of industry. Small as these means may be in each case, they amount to millions in the aggregate, and every dollar is so much added to the wealth of the country, to be reckoned at compound interest from the time of its arrival, nor are these sums like our European loans, which we must pay back, both principal and interest. Within a few years, especially, and more or less at all periods, men of great wealth have been among the emigrants driven from Europe, by religions oppression or political revolutions. Vast sums have also fallen to emigrants and their descendants by inheritance, for every few days we read in the papers of some poor foreigner, or descendant of foreigners, as are we all, becoming the heir of a princely fortune, which in most cases, is added to the wealth of his adopted country. Besides this, capital naturally follows labor, and it flows upon this country in a constant current, by the laws of trade.

But it is not money alone that adds to the wealth of a country, but every day's productive labor is to be added to its accumulating capital. Every house built, every canal dug, every railroad graded, has added so much to the actual wealth of society; and who have built more houses, dug more canals, or graded more railroads, than the hardy Irishmen? I hardly know how our great national works could have been carried on without them—then; while every pair of sturdy arms has added to our national wealth, every hungry mouth has been a home market for our agriculture, and every broad shoulder has been clothed with our manufactures.

EUROPE'S MOST VALUABLE MEMBERS

From the very nature of the case, America gets from Europe the most valuable of her population. Generally, those who come here are the very ones whom a sensible man would select. Those who are attached to monarchical and aristocratic institutions stay at home where they can enjoy them. Those who lack energy and enterprize can never make up their minds to leave their native land. It is the strong minded, the brave hearted, the free and self-respecting, the enterprizing and the intelligent, who break away from all the ties of country and of home, and brave the dangers of the ocean, in search of liberty and independence, for themselves and for their children, on a distant continent; and it is from this, among other causes, that the great mass of the people of this country are distinguished for the very qualities we should look for in emigrants. The same spirit which sent our fathers across the ocean impels us over the Alleghanies, to the valley of the Mississippi, and thence over the Rocky mountains into Oregon.

For what are we not indebted to foreign emigration, since we are all Europeans or their descendants? We cannot travel on one of our steamboats without remembering that Robert Fulton was the son of an Irishman.... Who of the thousands who every summer pass up and down our great thoroughfare, the North River, fails to catch at least a passing glimpse of the column erected to the memory of [Polish immigrant and American Revolutionary War officer Thaddeus] Kosciusko? I cannot forget that only last night a portion of our citizens celebrated with joyous festivities the birthday of the son of Irish emigrants, I mean the Hero of New Orleans [Andrew Jackson]!...

So might I go for hours, citing individual examples of benefits derived by this country from foreign immigration....

I have enumerated some of the advantages which such emigration has given to America. Let us now very carefully inquire, whether there is danger of any injury arising from these causes, at all proportionable to the palpable good.

"Our country is in danger," is the cry of Nativism. During my brief existence I have seen this country on the very verge of ruin a considerable number of times. It is always in the most imminent peril every four years; but, hitherto, the efforts of one party or the other have proved sufficient to rescue it, just in the latest gasp of its expiring agonies, and we have breathed more freely, when we have been assured that "the country's safe." Let us look steadily in the face of this new danger.

Are foreigners coming here to overturn our government? Those who came before the Revolution appear to have been generally favorable to Republican institutions. Those who have come here since have left friends, home, country, all that man naturally holds dearest, that they might live under a free government—they and their children. Is there common sense in the supposition that men would voluntarily set about destroying the very liberties they came so far to enjoy?

"But they lack intelligence," it is said. Are the immigrants of today less intelligent than those of fifty or a hundred years ago? Has Europe and the human race stood still all this time?...The facts of men preferring this country to any other, of their desire to live under its institutions, of their migration hither, indicate to my mind anything but a lack of proper intelligence and enterprise....

The truth is, a foreigner who emigrates to this country comes here saying, "Where Liberty dwells, there is my country." He sees our free institutions in the strong light of contrast. The sun seems brighter, because he has come out of darkness. What we know by hearsay only of the superiority of our institutions, he knows by actual observation and experience. Hence it is that America has had no truer patriots—freedom no more enthusiastic admirers—the cause of Liberty no more heroic defenders, than have been found among our adopted citizens....

But if naturalized citizens of foreign birth had the disposition, they have not the power, to endanger our liberties, on account of their comparatively small and decreasing numbers. There appears to be a most extraordinary misapprehension upon this subject. To read one of our "Native" papers one might suppose that our country was becoming overrun by foreigners, and that there was real danger of their having a majority of votes....

There is a point beyond which immigration cannot be carried. It must be limited by the capacity of the vessels employed in bringing passengers, while our entire population goes on increasing in geometrical progression, so that in one century from now, we shall have a population of one hundred and sixty millions, but a few hundred thousands of whom at the utmost can be citizens of foreign birth. Thus it may be seen that foreign immigration is of very little account, beyond a certain period, in the population of a country, and at all times is an insignificant item....

I appeal to the observation of every man in this community, whether the Germans and the Irish here, and throughout the country, are not as orderly, as industrious, as quiet, and in the habit of performing as well the common duties of citizens as the great mass of natives among us.

The worst thing that can be brought against any portion of our foreign population is that in many cases they are poor, and when they sink under labor and privation, they have no resources but the almshouse. Alas! shall the rich, for whom they have labored, the owners of the houses they have helped to build, refuse to treat them as kindly as they would their horses when incapable of further toil? Can they grudge them shelter from the storm, and a place where they may die in peace?

FOR FURTHER READING

Edith Abbott, *Historical Aspects of the Immigration Problem: Select Documents.* New York: Arno Press, 1969.

Tyler G. Anbinder, *Nativism and Slavery: The Northern Know Nothings and the Politics of the 1850s.* New York: Oxford University Press, 1994.

Ray Allen Billington, *The Origins of Nativism in the United States, 1800–1844.* New York: Arno Press, 1974.

Maldwyn A. Jones, *American Immigration.* Chicago: University of Chicago Press, 1992.

Viewpoint 25A

Women Hold an Exalted Status in America (1841)

Catharine E. Beecher (1800–1878)

INTRODUCTION *The issue of women's rights began to gain national prominence in the mid-1800s. During this time many people wrote and spoke of the importance of women in managing the household and instilling character in children. One of the most prominent advocates of this point of view was Catharine E. Beecher, a noted author and education reformer. She was a member of a leading New England family; her father and brother were both famous preachers, and her sister, Harriet Beecher Stowe, was the writer of* Uncle Tom's Cabin. *Beecher believed that homemaking and teaching were the proper roles for women in American society, and sought to improve the status of women by stressing their importance in the "domestic sphere." Although active in the abolitionist movement and other social reforms, Beecher opposed women's suffrage and the other goals of the nascent feminist movement.*

The following viewpoint is excerpted from the opening chapter of A Treatise on Domestic Economy, for the Use of Young Ladies At Home, and at School, *a how-to book on homemaking that was a best seller in the 1840s and 1850s. Beecher argues that women gain respect and equality with men by remaining in the domestic sphere. She compares the United States favorably with Europe regarding the position and treatment of women, by quoting extensively from* Democracy in America, *an influential 1835 book by French social philosopher Alexis de Tocqueville.*

What choices do American women have regarding marriage, according to Beecher. What important responsibilities does she say American women have?

There are some reasons why American women should feel an interest in the support of the democratic institutions of their Country, which it is important that they should consider. The great maxim, which is the basis of all our civil and political institutions, is, that "all men are created equal," and that they are equally entitled to "life, liberty, and the pursuit of happiness." . . .

But, in order that each individual may pursue and secure the highest degree of happiness within his reach, unimpeded by the selfish interests of others, a system of laws must be established, which sustain certain relations and dependencies in social and civil life. What these relations and their attending obligations shall be, are to be determined, not with reference to the wishes and interests of a few, but solely with reference to the general good of all; so that each individual shall have his own interest, as much as the public benefit, secured by them.

THE DUTIES OF SUBORDINATION

For this purpose, it is needful that certain relations be sustained, that involve the duties of subordination. There must be the magistrate and the subject, one of whom is the superior, and the other the inferior. There must be the relations of husband and wife, parent and child, teacher and pupil, employer and employed, each involving the relative duties of subordination. The superior in certain particulars is to direct, and the inferior is to yield obedience. Society could never go forward,

From *A Treatise on Domestic Economy* by Catharine E. Beecher (Boston: March, Capen, Lyon, and Webb, 1841).

harmoniously, nor could any craft or profession be successfully pursued, unless these superior and subordinate relations be instituted and sustained.

But who shall take the higher, and who the subordinate, stations in social and civil life? This matter, in the case of parents and children, is decided by the Creator. He has given children to the control of parents, as their superiors, and to them they remain subordinate, to a certain age, or so long as they are members of their household. And parents can delegate such a portion of their authority to teachers and employers, as the interests of their children require.

In most other cases, in a truly democratic state, each individual is allowed to choose for himself, who shall take the position of his superior. No woman is forced to obey any husband but the one she chooses for herself; nor is she obliged to take a husband, if she prefers to remain single. . . .

The institutions of monarchical and aristocratic nations are based on precisely opposite principles. They secure, to certain small and favored classes, advantages which can be maintained, only by sacrificing the interests of the great mass of the people. Thus, the throne and aristocracy of England are supported by laws and customs, that burden the lower classes with taxes, so enormous, as to deprive them of all the luxuries, and of most of the comforts, of life. Poor dwellings, scanty food, unhealthy employments, excessive labor, and entire destitution of the means and time for education, are appointed for the lower classes, that a few may live in palaces, and riot in every indulgence.

THE INTERESTS OF AMERICAN WOMEN

The tendencies of democratic institutions, in reference to the rights and interests of the female sex, have been fully developed in the United States; and it is in this aspect, that the subject is one of peculiar interest to American women. In this Country, it is established, both by opinion and by practice, that women have an equal interest in all social and civil concerns; and that no domestic, civil, or political, institution, is right, that sacrifices her interest to promote that of the other sex. But in order to secure her the more firmly in all these privileges, it is decided, that, in the domestic relation, she take a subordinate station, and that, in civil and political concerns, her interests be intrusted to the other sex, without her taking any part in voting, or in making and administering laws. The result of this order of things has been fairly tested, and is thus portrayed by M. [Alexis] De Tocqueville, a writer, who, for intelligence, fidelity, and ability, ranks second to none.

The following extracts [from *Democracy in America*] present his views.

There are people in Europe, who, confounding together the different characteristics of the sexes, would make of man and woman, beings not only equal, but alike. They would give to both the same functions, impose on both the same duties, and grant to both the same rights. They would mix them in all things,—their business, their occupations, their pleasures. It may readily be conceived, that, by *thus* attempting to make one sex equal to the other, both are degraded; and from so preposterous a medley of the works of Nature, nothing could ever result, but weak men and disorderly women.

It is not thus that the Americans understand the species of democratic equality, which may be established between the sexes. They admit, that, as Nature has appointed such wide differences between the physical and moral constitutions of man and woman, her manifest design was, to give a distinct employment to their various faculties; and they hold, that improvement does not consist in making beings so dissimilar do pretty nearly the same things, but in getting each of them to fulfil their respective tasks, in the best possible manner. The Americans have applied to the sexes the great principle of political economy, which governs the manufactories of our age by carefully dividing the duties of man from those of woman, in order that the great work of society may be the better carried on.

In no country has such constant care been taken, as in America, to trace two clearly distinct lines of action for the two sexes, and to make them keep pace one with the other, but in two pathways which are always different. American women never manage the outward concerns of the family, or conduct a business, or take a part in political life; nor are they, on the other hand, ever compelled to perform the rough labor of the fields, or to make any of those laborious exertions, which demand the exertion of physical strength. No families are so poor, as to form an exception to this rule....

As for myself, I do not hesitate to avow, that, although the women of the United States are confined within the narrow circle of domestic life, and their situation is, in some respects, one of extreme dependence, I have nowhere seen women occupying a loftier position; and if I were asked, now I am drawing to the close of this work, in which I have spoken of so many important things done by the Americans, to what the singular prosperity and growing strength of that people ought mainly to be attributed, I should reply,—*to the superiority of their women.*

WOMEN'S LOFTY POSITION

This testimony of a foreigner, who has had abundant opportunities of making a comparison, is sanctioned by the assent of all candid and intelligent men, who have enjoyed similar opportunities.

It appears, then, that it is in America, alone, that women are raised to an equality with the other sex; and that, both in theory and practice, their interests are regarded as of equal value. They are made subordinate in station, only where a regard to their best interests demands it, while, as if in compensation for this, by custom and courtesy, they are always treated as superiors. Universally, in this Country, through every class of society, precedence is given to woman, in all the comforts, conveniences, and courtesies, of life.

In civil and political affairs, American women take no interest or concern, except so far as they sympathize with their family and personal friends; but in all cases, in which they do feel a concern, their opinions and feelings have a consideration, equal, or even superior, to that of the other sex.

---■---

The democratic institutions of this Country... have secured to American women a lofty and fortunate position.

---■---

In matters pertaining to the education of their children, in the selection and support of a clergyman, in all benevolent enterprises, and in all questions relating to morals or manners, they have a superior influence. In all such concerns, it would be impossible to carry a point contrary to their judgement and feelings; while an enterprise, sustained by them, will seldom fail of success.

If those who are bewailing themselves over the fancied wrongs and injuries of women in this Nation, could only see things as they are, they would know, that, whatever remnants of a barbarous or aristocratic age may remain in our civil institutions, in reference to the interests of women, it is only because they are ignorant of it, or do not use their influence to have them rectified; for it is very certain that there is nothing reasonable which American women would unite in asking, that would not readily be bestowed.

The preceding remarks, then, illustrate the position that the democratic institutions of this Country... tend to place woman in her true position in society, as having equal rights with the other sex; and that, in fact, they have secured to American women a lofty and fortunate position, which, as yet, has been attained by the women of no other nation....

THE IMPORTANT TASK OF WOMEN

The success of democratic restitutions, as is conceded by all, depends upon the intellectual and moral character of the mass of the people. If they are intelligent and virtuous, democracy is a blessing; but if they are ignorant and wicked, it is only a curse, and as much more dreadful than any other form of civil government, as a thousand tyrants are more to be dreaded than one. It is equally conceded, that the formation of the moral and intellectual character of the young is committed mainly to the female hand. The mother writes the character of the future man; the sister bends the fibres that hereafter are the forest tree; the wife sways the heart, whose energies may turn for good or for evil the destinies of a nation. Let the women of a country be made virtuous and intelligent, and the men will certainly be the same. The proper education of a man decides the welfare of an individual; but educate a woman, and the interests of a whole family are secured.

If this be so, as none will deny, then to American women, more than to any others on earth, is committed the exalted privilege of extending over the world those blessed influences, that are to renovate degraded man, and "clothe all climes with beauty."

No American woman, then, has any occasion for feeling that hers is an humble or insignificant lot.

Viewpoint 25B

Women Hold a Degraded Status in America (1848)

Elizabeth Cady Stanton (1815–1902) and the Seneca Falls Convention

INTRODUCTION *The Seneca Falls Convention, held on July 18–19, 1848, in Seneca Falls, New York, was the first public political meeting on women's rights in the United States. It was organized by Elizabeth Cady Stanton and Lucretia Mott, two abolitionists who had met in 1840 at the World's Anti-Slavery Convention in London. There Stanton and the other female delegates were denied participation because of their gender. Stanton and Mott resolved to start a women's rights movement in the United States; their efforts resulted in the Seneca Falls Convention eight years later. Stanton drafted a Declaration of Sentiments (modeled after America's 1776 Declaration of Independence) and a series of resolutions on women's rights. Both the declaration and the resolutions were debated, reworded slightly, and adopted by the several hundred women and men assembled at Seneca Falls. All resolutions save one were passed unanimously; the resolution for women's suffrage passed by only a narrow margin.*

What examples of female oppression does Stanton provide? Judging from the contents of viewpoints 25A,

which points of the Seneca Falls Declaration might Catharine E. Beecher, author of the opposing viewpoint, agree with? Which would she most oppose?

When, in the course of human events, it becomes necessary for one portion of the family of man to assume among the people of the earth a position different from that which they have hitherto occupied, but one to which the laws of nature and of nature's God entitle them, a decent respect to the opinions of mankind requires that they should declare the causes that impel them to such a course.

We hold these truths to be self-evident: that all men and women are created equal; that they are endowed by their Creator with certain inalienable rights; that among these are life, liberty, and the pursuit of happiness; that to secure these rights governments are instituted, deriving their just powers from the consent of the governed. Whenever any form of government becomes destructive of these ends, it is the right of those who suffer from it to refuse allegiance to it, and to insist upon the institution of a new government, laying its foundation on such principles, and organizing its powers in such form, as to them shall seem most likely to effect their safety and happiness. Prudence, indeed, will dictate that governments long established should not be changed for light and transient causes; and accordingly all experience hath shown that mankind are more disposed to suffer, while evils are sufferable, than to right themselves by abolishing the forms to which they are accustomed. But when a long train of abuses and usurpations, pursuing invariably the same object, evinces a design to reduce them under absolute despotism, it is their duty to throw off such government, and to provide new guards for their future security. Such has been the patient sufferance of the women under this government, and such is now the necessity which constrains them to demand the equal station to which they are entitled.

REPEATED INJURIES

The history of mankind is a history of repeated injuries and usurpations on the part of man toward woman, having in direct object the establishment of an absolute tyranny over her. To prove this, let facts be submitted to a candid world.

He has never permitted her to exercise her inalienable right to the elective franchise.

He has compelled her to submit to laws, in the formation of which she had no voice.

He has withheld from her rights which are given to the most ignorant and degraded men—both natives and foreigners.

From *History of Women Suffrage*, vol. 1, edited by Elizabeth Cady Stanton, Susan B. Anthony, and Matilda Joslyn Gage (New York: Fowler & Wells, 1881).

Having deprived her of this first right of a citizen, the elective franchise, thereby leaving her without representation in the halls of legislation, he has oppressed her on all sides.

He has made her, if married, in the eye of the law, civilly dead.

He has taken from her all right in property, even to the wages she earns.

He has made her, morally, an irresponsible being, as she can commit many crimes with impunity, provided they be done in the presence of her husband. In the covenant of marriage, she is compelled to promise obedience to her husband, he becoming, to all intents and purposes, her master—the law giving him power to deprive her of her liberty, and to administer chastisement.

He has so framed the laws of divorce, as to what shall be the proper causes, and in case of separation, to whom the guardianship of the children shall be given, as to be wholly regardless of the happiness of women—the law in all cases, going upon a false supposition of the supremacy of man, and giving all power into his hands.

After depriving her of all rights as a married woman, if single, and the owner of property, he has taxed her to support a government which recognizes her only when her property can be made profitable to it.

He has monopolized nearly all the profitable employments, and from those she is permitted to follow, she receives but a scanty remuneration. He closes against her all the avenues to wealth and distinction which he considers most honorable to himself. As a teacher of theology, medicine, or law, she is not known.

He has denied her the facilities for obtaining a thorough education, all colleges being closed against her.

He allows her in Church, as well as State, but a subordinate position, claiming Apostolic authority for her exclusion from the ministry, and, with some exceptions, from any public participation in the affairs of the Church.

He has created a false public sentiment by giving to the world a different code of morals for men and women, by which moral delinquencies which exclude women from society, are not only tolerated, but deemed of little account in man.

Women do feel themselves aggrieved, oppressed, and fraudulently deprived of their most sacred rights.

He has usurped the prerogative of Jehovah himself, claiming it as his right to assign for her a sphere of action, when that belongs to her conscience and to her God.

He has endeavored, in every way that he could, to destroy her confidence in her own powers, to lessen her self-respect and to make her willing to lead a dependent and abject life.

Now, in view of this entire disfranchisement of one-half the people of this country, their social and religious degradation—in view of the unjust laws above mentioned, and because women do feel themselves aggrieved, oppressed, and fraudulently deprived of their most sacred rights, we insist that they have immediate admission to all the rights and privileges which belong to them as citizens of the United States.

In entering upon the great work before us, we anticipate no small amount of misconception, misrepresentation, and ridicule; but we shall use every instrumentality within our power to effect our object. We shall employ agents, circulate tracts, petition the State and National legislatures, and endeavor to enlist the pulpit and the press in our behalf. We hope this Convention will be followed by a series of Conventions embracing every part of the country.

RESOLUTIONS

Whereas, The great precept of nature is conceded to be, that "man shall pursue his own true and substantial happiness." [William] Blackstone in his *Commentaries* [*on the Laws of England*] remarks, that this law of Nature being coeval with mankind, and dictated by God himself, is of course superior in obligation to any other. It is binding over all the globe, in all countries and at all times; no human laws are of any validity if contrary to this, and such of them as are valid, derive all their force, and all their validity, and all their authority, mediately and immediately, from this original; therefore,

Resolved, That such laws as conflict, in any way with the true and substantial happiness of woman, are contrary to the great precept of nature and of no validity, for this is "superior in obligation to any other."

Resolved, That all laws which prevent woman from occupying such a station in society as her conscience shall dictate, or which place her in a position inferior to that of man, are contrary to the great precept of nature, and therefore of no force or authority.

Resolved, That woman is man's equal—was intended to be so by the Creator, and the highest good of the race demands that she should be recognized as such.

Resolved, That the women of this country ought to be enlightened in regard to the laws under which they live, that they may no longer publish their degradation by declaring themselves satisfied with their present position, nor their ignorance, by asserting that they have all the rights they want.

Resolved, That inasmuch as man, while claiming for himself intellectual superiority, does accord to woman moral superiority, it is pre-eminently his duty to encourage her to speak and teach, as she has an opportunity, in all religious assemblies.

Resolved, That the same amount of virtue, delicacy, and refinement of behavior that is required of woman in the social state, should also be required of man, and the same transgressions should be visited with equal severity on both man and woman.

Resolved, That the objection of indelicacy and impropriety, which is so often brought against woman when she addresses a public audience, comes with a very ill-grace from those who encourage, by their attendance, her appearance on the stage, in the concert, or in feats of the circus.

Resolved, That woman has too long rested satisfied in the circumscribed limits which corrupt customs and a perverted application of the Scriptures have marked out for her, and that it is time she should move in the enlarged sphere which her great Creator has assigned her.

Resolved, That it is the duty of the women of this country to secure to themselves their sacred right to the elective franchise.

Resolved, That the equality of human rights results necessarily from the fact of the identity of the race in capabilities and responsibilities.

Resolved, therefore, That, being invested by the Creator with the same capabilities, and the same consciousness of responsibility for their exercise, it is demonstrably the right and duty of woman, equally with man, to promote every righteous cause by every righteous means; and especially in regard to the great subjects of morals and religion, it is self-evidently her right to participate with her brother in teaching them, both in private and in public, by writing and by speaking, by any instrumentalities proper to be used, and in any assemblies proper to be held; and this being a self-evident truth growing out of the divinely implanted principles of human nature, any custom or authority adverse to it, whether modern or wearing the hoary sanction of antiquity, is to be regarded as a self-evident falsehood, and at war with mankind.

Resolved, That the speedy success of our cause depends upon the zealous and untiring efforts of both men and women, for the overthrow of the monopoly of the pulpit, and for the securing to women an equal participation with men in the various trades, professions, and commerce.

FOR FURTHER READING

Virginia Bernhard and Elizabeth Fox-Genovese, eds., *The Birth of American Feminism: The Seneca Falls Woman's Convention of 1848*. St. James, NY: Brandywine Press, 1995.

Jeanne Boydston et al., *The Limits of Sisterhood: the Beecher Sisters and Women's Rights and the Women's Sphere*. Chapel Hill: University of North Carolina Press, 1988.

Jeff Hill, *Women's Suffrage*. Detroit, MI: Omnigraphics, 2006.

Judith Wellman, The Road to Seneca Falls: Elizabeth Cady Stanton and the First Woman's Rights Convention. Urbana: University of Illinois Press, 2004.

Barbara Anne White, *The Beecher Sisters*. New Haven, CT: Yale University Press, 2003.

MANIFEST DESTINY AND WAR WITH MEXICO

Viewpoint 26A

America Should Not Annex Texas (1844)

Henry Clay (1777–1852)

INTRODUCTION *Henry Clay served a long and distinguished career as Speaker of the House of Representatives, secretary of state under President John Quincy Adams, and U.S. senator from Kentucky. He was known as the "Great Compromiser" because of his work in Congress in settling disputes such as those between Northern and Southern states over the issues of territorial expansion and slavery. Clay was nominated for president by the Whig Party three times, including in 1844, when his opponent was James K. Polk and the central issue facing the nation was Texas.*

Texas, a former Mexican province with a large population of settlers from the United States, had declared independence from Mexico in 1836, and had almost immediately inquired about admission into the Union. For several years the United States, under Presidents Andrew Jackson and Martin Van Buren, decided only to recognize Texas as an independent nation, mindful that annexation of Texas might lead to war with Mexico. Slavery was also an issue, as some antislavery leaders expressed strong opposition to adding another potential slave state to the Union. These two basic concerns—war with Mexico and slavery—are prominent in the following viewpoint, excerpted from Henry Clay's "Raleigh Letter." (He wrote it while in Raleigh, North Carolina.) Responding to President John Tyler's 1844 annexation of Texas (just submitted to the Senate for ratification), Clay argues against incorporating Texas into the Union. The letter was published in various newspapers in April 1844 when Clay was all but assured of the Whig Party's nomination for president. Clay later pulled back somewhat from his opposition to Texas annexation, but that was not enough to prevent Polk, a former Tennessee senator and committed expansionist, from defeating Clay in the 1844 general election.

Does Clay express unconditional opposition to Texas annexation? Why might admission of Texas into the Union lead to possible U.S. expansion into Canada, according to Clay?

Gentlemen: Subsequent to my departure from Ashland [Clay's Kentucky home], in December last, I received various communications from popular assemblages and private individuals, requesting an expression of my opinion upon the question of the annexation of Texas to the United States.... The rejection of the overture of Texas, some years ago, to become annexed to the United States, had met with general acquiescence. Nothing had since occurred materially to vary the question. I had seen no evidence of a desire being entertained, on the part of any considerable portion of the American people, that Texas should become an integral part of the United States.... To the astonishment of the whole nation, we are now informed that a treaty of annexation has been actually concluded, and is to be submitted to the senate for its consideration....

DESIRE TO PREVENT WAR

Annexation and war with Mexico are identical. Now, for one, I certainly am not willing to involve this country in a foreign war for the object of acquiring Texas. I know there are those who regard such a war with indifference and as a trifling affair, on account of the weakness of Mexico, and her inability to inflict serious injury upon this country. But I do not look upon it thus lightly. I regard all wars as great calamities, to be avoided, if possible, and honorable peace as the wisest and truest policy of this country. What the United States most need are union, peace, and patience. Nor do I think that the weakness of a power should form a motive, in any case, for inducing us to engage in or to depreciate the evils of war.—Honor and good faith and justice are equally due from this country towards the weak as towards the strong. And, if an act of injustice were to be perpetrated towards any power, it would be more compatible with the dignity of the nation, and, in my judgment, less dishonorable, to inflict it upon a powerful instead of a weak foreign nation. But are we perfectly sure that we should be free from injury in a state of war with Mexico? Have we any security that countless numbers of foreign vessels, under the authority and flag of Mexico, would not prey upon our defenceless commerce in the Mexican gulf, on the Pacific ocean, and on every other sea and ocean? What commerce, on the other hand, does Mexico offer, as an indemnity for our losses, to the gallantry and enterprise of our countrymen? This view of the subject supposes that the war would be confined to the United States and Mexico as the only belligerents. But have we any certain guaranty that Mexico would obtain no allies among the great European powers? ...

Assuming that the annexation of Texas is war with Mexico, is it competent to the treaty-making power to plunge this country into war, not only without the concurrence of, but without deigning to consult congress, to which, by the constitution, belongs exclusively the power of declaring war?

DOMESTIC CONSIDERATIONS

I have hitherto considered the question upon the supposition that the annexation is attempted without the assent of Mexico. If she yields her consent, that would materially affect the foreign aspect of the question, if it did not remove all foreign difficulties. On the assumption of that assent, the question would be confined to the domestic considerations which belong to it, embracing the terms and conditions upon which annexation is proposed. I do not think that Texas ought to be received into the Union, as an integral part of it, in decided opposition to the wishes of a considerable and respectable portion of the confederacy. I think it far more wise and important to compose and harmonize the present confederacy, as it now exists, than to introduce a new element of discord and distraction into it.... Mr. [Thomas] Jefferson expressed the opinion, and others believed, that it never was in the contemplation of the framers of the constitution to add foreign territory to the confederacy, out of which new states were to be formed. The acquisitions of Louisiana and Florida may be defended upon the peculiar ground of the relation in which they stood to the states of the Union. After they were admitted, we might well pause a while, people our vast wastes, develop our resources, prepare the means of defending what we possess, and augment our strength, power, and greatness. If hereafter further territory should be wanted for an increased population, we need entertain no apprehensions but that it will be acquired by means, it is to be hoped, fair, honorable, and constitutional.

It is useless to disguise that there are those who espouse and those who oppose the annexation of Texas upon the ground of the influence which it would exert, in the balance of political power, between two great sections of the Union. I conceive that no motive for the acquisition of foreign territory would be more unfortunate, or pregnant with more fatal consequences, than that of obtaining it for the purpose of strengthening one part against another part of the common confederacy. Such a principle, put into practical operation, would menace the existence, if it did not certainly sow the seeds of a dissolution of the Union. It would be to proclaim to the world an insatiable and unquenchable thirst for foreign conquest or acquisition of territory. For if today Texas be acquired to strengthen one part of the confederacy, tomorrow Canada may be required to add strength to another. And, after that might have been obtained, still other and further acquisitions would become necessary to equalize and adjust the balance of

From Henry Clay's letter to the editor of the *Daily National Intelligencer*, April 27, 1844.

political power. Finally, in the progress of this spirit of universal dominion, the part of the confederacy which is now weakest, would find itself still weaker from the impossibility of securing new theatres for those peculiar institutions which it is charged with being desirous to extend. . . .

In the future progress of events, it is probable that there will be a voluntary or forcible separation of the British North American possessions from the parent country. I am strongly inclined to think that it will be best for the happiness of all parties that, in that event, they should be erected into a separate and independent republic. With the Canadian republic on one side, that of Texas on the other, and the United States, the friend of both, between them, each could advance its own happiness by such constitutions, laws, and measures, as were best adapted to its peculiar condition. They would be natural allies, ready, by co-operation, to repel any European or foreign attack upon either. Each would afford a secure refuge to the persecuted and oppressed driven into exile by either of the others. They would emulate each other in improvements, in free institutions, and in the science of self-government. Whilst Texas has adopted our constitution as the model of hers, she has, in several important particulars, greatly improved upon it. . . .

AGAINST ANNEXATION

In conclusion, they may be stated in a few words to be, that I consider the annexation of Texas, at this time, without the assent of Mexico, as a measure compromising the national character, involving us certainly in war with Mexico, probably with other foreign powers, dangerous to the integrity of the Union, inexpedient in the present financial condition of the country, and not called for by any general expression of public opinion.

Viewpoint 26B
America Should Annex Texas (1845)
John L. O'Sullivan (1813–1895)

INTRODUCTION *The Senate rejected the Texas annexation treaty submitted by President John Tyler in 1844. In 1845 Tyler proposed that Congress pass a joint resolution that Texas be annexed. Such a resolution required only a majority vote from both houses of Congress, thus avoiding the necessity for a two-thirds Senate majority required for treaty ratification. The stratagem worked; in March 1845 the lame-duck president signed a joint resolution inviting Texas to join the Union. However, the issue remained divisive, with opponents of slavery condemning the admission of Texas as a territorial grab intended to create a new slave state or states.*

In the following viewpoint, newspaper editor John L. O'Sullivan criticizes the opponents of Texas

annexation. He goes beyond the immediate issue of Texas to advocate the expansion of the United States to encompass much, if not all, of the North American continent. O'Sullivan, founder and editor of the United States Magazine and Democratic Review *and editor of the* New York Morning News, *is credited with inventing the term "manifest destiny" to describe his vision of an expanding America—a vision shared by many.*

How does O'Sullivan answer Mexican claims to Texas and California? What future vision of America does he describe? What future does O'Sullivan predict for the "Negro race" in America?

It is time now for opposition to the Annexation of Texas to cease, all further agitation of the waters of bitterness and strife, at least in connection with this question, even though it may perhaps be required of us as a necessary condition of the freedom of our institutions, that we must live on forever in a state of unpausing struggle and excitement upon some subject of party division or other. But, in regard to Texas, enough has now been given to party. It is time for the common duty of patriotism to the country to succeed; or if this claim will not be recognized, it is at least time for common sense to acquiesce with decent grace in the inevitable and the irrevocable.

Texas is now ours. Already, before these words are written, her convention has undoubtedly ratified the acceptance, by her congress, of our proffered invitation into the Union; and made the requisite changes in her already republican form of constitution to adapt it to its future federal relations. Her star and her stripe may already be said to have taken their place in the glorious blazon of our common nationality; and the sweep of our eagle's wing already includes within its circuit the wide extent of her fair and fertile land. She is no longer to us a mere geographical space—a certain combination of coast, plain, mountain, valley, forest, and stream. She is no longer to us a mere country on the map. She comes within the dear and sacred designation of our country; no longer a *pays* [country], she is a part of *la patrie* [homeland]; and that which is at once a sentiment and a virtue, patriotism, already begins to thrill for her too within the national heart. . . .

FOREIGN INTERFERENCE

Why, were other reasoning wanting, in favor of now elevating this question of the reception of Texas into the Union, out of the lower region of our past party dissensions, up to its proper level of a high and broad nationality, it surely is to be found, found abundantly, in the manner in which other nations have undertaken to intrude themselves into it, between us and the proper parties to the case, in a spirit of hostile interference against us, for

John L. O'Sullivan, "Annexation," *United States and Democratic Review,* July 1845.

the avowed object of thwarting our policy and hampering our power, limiting our greatness and checking the fulfillment of our manifest destiny to overspread the continent allotted by Providence for the free development of our yearly multiplying millions. This we have seen done by England, our old rival and enemy; and by France, strangely coupled with her against us, under the influence of the Anglicism strongly tinging the policy of her present prime minister, [Francois-Pierre-Guillaume] Guizot.

The zealous activity with which this effort to defeat us was pushed by the representatives of those governments, together with the character of intrigue accompanying it, fully constituted that case of foreign interference, which Mr. [Henry] Clay himself declared should, and would unite us all in maintaining the common cause of our country against the foreigner and the foe. We are only astonished that this effect has not been more fully and strongly produced, and that the burst of indignation against this unauthorized, insolent, and hostile interference against us, has not been more general even among the party before opposed to annexation, and has not rallied the national spirit and national pride unanimously upon that policy. We are very sure that if Mr. Clay himself were now to add another letter to his former Texas correspondence, he would express this sentiment....

It is wholly untrue, and unjust to ourselves, the pretense that the Annexation has been a measure of spoliation, unrightful and unrighteous—of military conquest under forms of peace and law—of territorial aggrandizement at the expense of justice, and justice due by a double sanctity to the weak. This view of the question is wholly unfounded, and has been before so amply refuted in these pages, as well as in a thousand other modes, that we shall not again dwell upon it....

TEXAS AND SLAVERY

Nor is there any just foundation for the charge that Annexation is a great pro-slavery measure—calculated to increase and perpetuate that institution. Slavery had nothing to do with it. Opinions were and are greatly divided, both at the North and South, as to the influence to be exerted by it on slavery and the slave states. That it will tend to facilitate and hasten the disappearance of slavery from all the northern tier of the present slave states, cannot surely admit of serious question. The greater value in Texas of the slave labor now employed in those states, must soon produce the effect of draining off that labor southwardly, by the same unvarying law that bids water descend the slope that invites it.

———————■———————

Texas has been absorbed into the Union in the inevitable fulfillment of the general law which is rolling our population westward.

———————■———————

Every new slave state in Texas will make at least one free state from among those in which that institution now exists—to say nothing of those portions of Texas on which slavery cannot spring and grow—to say nothing of the far more rapid growth of new states in the free West and Northwest, as these fine regions are overspread by the emigration fast flowing over them from Europe, as well as from the Northern and Eastern states of the Union as it exists. On the other hand, it is undeniably much gained for the cause of the eventual voluntary abolition of slavery, that it should have been thus drained off toward the only outlet which appeared to furnish much probability of the ultimate disappearance of the Negro race from our borders.

The Spanish-Indian-American populations of Mexico, Central America, and South America, afford the only receptacle capable of absorbing that race whenever we shall be prepared to slough it off—to emancipate it from slavery, and (simultaneously necessary) to remove it from the midst of our own. Themselves already of mixed and confused blood, and free from the "prejudices" which among us so insuperably forbid the social amalgamation which can alone elevate the Negro race out of a virtually servile degradation; even though legally free the regions occupied by those populations must strongly attract the black race in that direction; and as soon as the destined hour of emancipation shall arrive, will relieve the question of one of its worst difficulties, if not absolutely the greatest....

Texas has been absorbed into the Union in the inevitable fulfilment of the general law which is rolling our population westward; the connexion of which with that ratio of growth in population which is destined within a hundred years to swell our numbers to the enormous population of *two hundred and fifty millions* (if not more), is too evident to leave us in doubt of the manifest design of Providence in regard to the occupation of this continent. It was disintegrated from Mexico in the natural course of events, by a process perfectly legitimate on its own part, blameless on ours; and in which all the censures due to wrong, perfidy and folly, rest on Mexico alone. And possessed as it was by a population which was in truth but a colonial detachment from our own, and which was still bound by myriad ties of the very heartstrings to its old relations, domestic and political, their incorporation into the Union was not only inevitable, but the most natural, right and proper thing in the world—and it is only astonishing that there should be any among ourselves to say it nay....

CALIFORNIA IS NEXT

California will, probably, next fall away from the loose adhesion which, in such a country as Mexico, holds a remote province in a slight equivocal kind of dependence on the metropolis. Imbecile and distracted, Mexico never can exert any real government authority over such a country. The impotence of the one and the distance of the other, must make the relation one of virtual independence; unless, by stunting the province of all natural growth, and forbidding that immigration which can alone develop its capabilities and fulfill the purposes of its creation, tyranny may retain a military dominion, which is no government in the legitimate sense of the term. In the case of California this is now impossible. The Anglo-Saxon foot is already on its borders. Already the advance guard of the irresistible army of Anglo-Saxon emigration has begun to pour down upon it, armed with the plough and the rifle, and marking its trail with schools and colleges, courts and representative halls, mills and meetinghouses. A population will soon be in actual occupation of California, over which it will be idle for Mexico to dream of dominion. They will necessarily become independent. All this without agency of our government, without responsibility of our people—in the natural flow of events, the spontaneous working of principles; and the adaptation of the tendencies and wants of the human race to the elemental circumstances in the midst of which they find themselves placed....

Whether they will then attach themselves to our Union or not, is not to be predicted with any certainty. Unless the projected railroad across the continent to the Pacific be carried into effect, perhaps they may not; though even in that case, the day is not distant when the empires of the Atlantic and Pacific would again flow together into one, as soon as their inland borders should approach each other. But that great work, colossal as appears the plan on its first suggestion, cannot remain long unbuilt. Its necessity for this very purpose of binding and holding together in its iron clasp our fast-settling Pacific region with that of the Mississippi Valley—the natural facility of the route—the ease with which any amount of labor for the construction can be drawn in from the overcrowded populations of Europe, to be paid in the lands made valuable by the progress of the work itself—and its immense utility to the commerce of the world with the whole eastern coast of Asia, alone almost sufficient for the support of such a road—these considerations give assurance that the day cannot be distant which shall witness the conveyance of the representatives from Oregon and California to Washington within less time than a few years ago was devoted to a similar journey by those from Ohio; while the magnetic telegraph will enable the editors of the *San Francisco Union*, the *Astoria Evening Post*, or the *Nootka Morning News*, to set up in type the first half of the President's inaugural before the echoes of the latter half shall have died away beneath the lofty porch of the Capitol, as spoken from his lips.

A LOOK TO THE FUTURE

Away, then, with all idle French talk of balances of power on the American Continent. There is no growth in Spanish America! Whatever progress of population there may be in the British Canadas, is only for their own early severance of their present colonial relation to the little island 3,000 miles across the Atlantic; soon to be followed by annexation, and destined to swell the still accumulating momentum of our progress.

And whosoever may hold the balance, though they should cast into the opposite scale all the bayonets and cannon, not only of France and England, but of Europe entire, how would it kick the beam against the simple, solid weight of the 250, or 300 millions—and American millions—destined to gather beneath the flutter of the stripes and stars, in the fast hastening year of the Lord 1945!

FOR FURTHER READING

David S. Heidler, *Manifest Destiny*. Westport, CT: Greenwood Press, 2003.

Reginald Horsman, *Race and Manifest Destiny: The Origins of American Racial Anglo-Saxonism*. Cambridge, MA: Harvard University Press, 1981.

Mark S. Joy, *American Expansionism, 1783–1860: A Manifest Destiny?*. New York: Longman, 2003.

Robert V. Remini, *Henry Clay: Statesman for the Union*. New York: W.W. Norton, 1991.

Joel H. Silbey, *Storm Over Texas: The Annexation Controversy and the Road to Civil War*. New York: Oxford University Pres, 2005.

Viewpoint 27A
The United States Must Wage War on Mexico (1846)
James K. Polk (1795–1849)

INTRODUCTION *With Texas recently annexed, James K. Polk began his presidency in 1845 determined to add the Oregon and California territories to the United States. Negotiations with Great Britain were successful in resolving competing claims over Oregon and attaining Polk's goal of a U.S. boundary at the 49th parallel. Negotiations with Mexico were hamstrung by Mexico's decision to break off diplomatic relations with the United States after America's annexation of Texas. An attempt to purchase California failed when the Mexican government refused to receive American diplomat John Slidell.*

In January 1846 Polk responded to Slidell's failed initiative by stationing American troops in Texas on the north bank of the Rio Grande, in territory south of the Nueces River that was claimed by both Mexico and the United States. On April 25, Mexican troops crossed the Rio Grande and attacked two companies of American soldiers. News of the attack reached Washington on May 9, just after Polk and his cabinet had discussed and agreed on sending a war message to Congress. The attack was quickly incorporated into the message Polk sent to Congress on May 11, 1846. Congress responded to the message, excerpted here, by overwhelmingly voting for war with Mexico.

What steps has the United States taken to avoid war, according to Polk? What reasons for war besides the April 25 attack does he cite? What ultimate goals of war with Mexico does Polk mention?

To the Senate and House of Representatives:

The existing state of the relations between the United States and Mexico renders it proper that I should bring the subject to the consideration of Congress. In my message at the commencement of your present session the state of these relations, the causes which led to the suspension of diplomatic intercourse between the two countries in March, 1845, and the long-continued and unredressed wrongs and injuries committed by the Mexican Government on citizens of the United States in their persons and property were briefly set forth....

A DESIRE FOR PEACE

The strong desire to establish peace with Mexico on liberal and honorable terms, and the readiness of this Government to regulate and adjust our boundary and other causes of difference with that power on such fair and equitable principles as would lead to permanent relations of the most friendly nature, induced me in September last [1845] to seek the reopening of diplomatic relations between the two countries. Every measure adopted on our part had for its object the furtherance of these desired results. In communicating to Congress a succinct statement of the injuries which we had suffered from Mexico, and which have been accumulating during a period of more than twenty years, every expression that could tend to inflame the people of Mexico or defeat or delay a pacific result was carefully avoided. An envoy of the United States [John Slidell] repaired to Mexico with full powers to adjust every existing difference. But though present on the Mexican soil by agreement between the two Governments, invested with full powers, and bearing evidence of the most friendly dispositions, his mission has been unavailing. The Mexican Government not only refused to receive him or listen to his propositions, but after a long-continued series of menaces have at last invaded our territory and shed the blood of our fellow-citizens on our own soil....

From James K. Polk's message to Congress on May 11, 1846, as reprinted in *A Compilation of Messages and Papers of the Presidents, 1798–1897*, edited by James D. Richardson (New York: 1896–1899).

DEFENDING TEXAS

In my message at the commencement of the present session I informed you that upon the earnest appeal both of the Congress and convention of Texas I had ordered an efficient military force to take a position "between the Nueces and the Del Norte [Rio Grande]." This had become necessary to meet a threatened invasion of Texas by the Mexican forces, for which extensive military preparations had been made. The invasion was threatened solely because Texas had determined, in accordance with a solemn resolution of the Congress of the United States, to annex herself to our Union, and under these circumstances it was plainly our duty to extend our protection over her citizens and soil.

This force was concentrated at Corpus Christi, and remained there until after I had received such information from Mexico as rendered it probable, if not certain, that the Mexican Government would refuse to receive our envoy.

Meantime Texas, by the final action of our Congress, had become an integral part of our Union. The Congress of Texas, by its act of December 19, 1836, had declared the Rio del Norte to be the boundary of that Republic. Its jurisdiction had been extended and exercised beyond the Nueces. The country between that river and the Del Norte had been represented in the Congress and in the convention of Texas, had thus taken part in the act of annexation itself, and is now included within one of our Congressional districts. Our own Congress had, moreover, with great unanimity, by the act approved December 31, 1845, recognized the country beyond the Nueces as a part of our territory by including it within our own revenue system, and a revenue officer to reside within that district has been appointed by and with the advice and consent of the Senate. It became, therefore, of urgent necessity to provide for the defense of that portion of our country. Accordingly, on the 13th of January last [1846] instructions were issued to the general in command of these troops to occupy the left [northeast] bank of the Del Norte. This river, which is the southwestern boundary of the State of Texas, is an exposed frontier. From this quarter invasion was threatened; upon it and in its immediate vicinity, in the judgment of high military experience, are the proper stations for the protecting forces of the Government....

MEXICAN ATTACK

The Army moved from Corpus Christi on the 11th of March, and on the 28th of that month arrived on the left bank of the Del Norte opposite to Matamoras, where it encamped on a commanding position, which has since been strengthened by the erection of fieldworks. A depot has also been established at Point Isabel, near the

Brazos Santiago, 30 miles in rear of the encampment. The selection of his position was necessarily confided to the judgment of the general in command.

The Mexican forces at Matamoras assumed a belligerent attitude, and on the 12th of April General [Pedro de] Ampudia, then in command, notified General [Zachary] Taylor to break up his camp within twenty-four hours and to retire beyond the Nueces River, and in the event of his failure to comply with these demands announced that arms, and arms alone, must decide the question. But no open act of hostility was committed until the 24th of April. On that day General [Mariano] Arista, who had succeeded to the command of the Mexican forces, communicated to General Taylor that "he considered hostilities commenced and should prosecute them." A party of dragoons of 63 men and officers were on the same day dispatched from the American camp up the Rio del Norte, on its left bank, to ascertain whether the Mexican troops had crossed or were preparing to cross the river, "became engaged with a large body of these troops, and after a short affair, in which some 16 were killed and wounded, appear to have been surrounded and compelled to surrender."

Mexico has . . . invaded our territory and shed American blood upon the American soil.

The grievous wrongs perpetrated by Mexico upon our citizens throughout a long period of years remain unredressed, and solemn treaties pledging her public faith for this redress have been disregarded. A government either unable or unwilling to enforce the execution of such treaties fails to perform one of its plainest duties.

Our commerce with Mexico has been almost annihilated. It was formerly highly beneficial to both nations, but our merchants have been deterred from prosecuting it by the system of outrage and extortion which the Mexican authorities have pursued against them, whilst their appeals through their own Government for indemnity have been made in vain. Our forebearance has gone to such an extreme as to be mistaken in its character. Had we acted with vigor in repelling the insults and redressing the injuries inflicted by Mexico at the commencement, we should doubtless have escaped all the difficulties in which we are now involved.

Instead of this, however, we have been exerting our best efforts to propitiate her good will. Upon the pretext that Texas, a nation as independent as herself, thought proper to unite its destinies with our own she has affected

to believe that we have severed her rightful territory, and in official proclamations and manifestoes has repeatedly threatened to make war upon us for the purpose of reconquering Texas. In the meantime we have tried every effort at reconciliation. The cup of forbearance had been exhausted even before the recent information from the frontier of the Del Norte. But now, after reiterated menaces, Mexico has passed the boundary of the United States, has invaded our territory and shed American blood upon the American soil. She has proclaimed that hostilities have commenced, and that the two nations are now at war.

VINDICATING OUR RIGHTS

As war exists, and, notwithstanding all our efforts to avoid it, exists by the act of Mexico herself, we are called upon by every consideration of duty and patriotism to vindicate with decision the honor, the rights, and the interests of our country. . . .

I deem it proper to declare that it is my anxious desire not only to terminate hostilities speedily, but to bring all matters in dispute between this Government and Mexico to an early and amicable adjustment; and in this view I shall be prepared to renew negotiations whenever Mexico shall be ready to receive propositions or to make propositions of her own.

Viewpoint 27B

The United States Fought Mexico to Gain Territory (1850)

Ramón Alcaraz (1823–1886) et al.

INTRODUCTION *The Mexican War began in May 1846 when Congress passed a declaration of war following President James K. Polk's call to defend America from Mexican attack in Texas. It ended, after a string of U.S. military successes, in February 1848 with the signing of the Treaty of Guadalupe Hidalgo. The Rio Grande was established as the Texas/Mexico boundary, and the United States acquired the Upper California, Utah, and New Mexico territories for a payment of $13 million. Counting Texas (which declared independence from Mexico in 1836 and was annexed by the United States in 1845), Mexico had lost half its territory to the United States since becoming independent from Spain in 1821.*

A Mexican perspective on the war is found in the following viewpoint, excerpted from a pamphlet written by a group of Mexican writers including Mexican Army officer Ramón Alcaraz. The work, with its strong accusations of American greed and duplicity, was translated and published in the United States in 1850, where it received a sympathetic audience from many Americans critical of "Mr. Polk's war."

What main disputes do the writers have with the claims of James K. Polk in the opposing viewpoint? Is their description of the United States similar to the views expressed by John L. O'Sullivan (see viewpoint 26B)?

To explain then in a few words the true origin of the war, it is sufficient to say that the insatiable ambition of the United States, favored by our weakness, caused it. But this assertion, however veracious and well founded, requires the confirmation which we will present, along with some former transactions, to the whole world. This evidence will leave no doubt of the correctness of our impressions.

In throwing off the yoke of the mother country [Great Britain], the United States of the North appeared at once as a powerful nation. This was the result of their excellent elementary principles of government established while in colonial subjection. The Republic announced at its birth, that it was called upon to represent an important part in the world of Columbus. Its rapid advancement, its progressive increase, its wonderful territory, the uninterrupted augmentation of its inhabitants, and the formidable power it had gradually acquired, were many proofs of its becoming a colossus, not only for the feeble nations of Spanish America, but even for the old populations of the ancient continent.

The United States did not hope for the assistance of time in their schemes of aggrandizement. From the days of their independence they adopted the project of extending their dominions, and since then, that line of policy has not deviated in the slightest degree. This conduct, nevertheless, was not perceptible to the most enlightened: but reflecting men, who examined events, were not slow in recognising it. Conde de Aranda [Pedro de Aranda, a participant in Mexico's revolution against Spain], from whose perception the ends which the United States had resolved upon were not concealed, made use of some celebrated words. These we shall now produce as a prophecy verified by events. "This nation has been born a pigmy: in the time to come, it will be a giant, and even a colossus, very formidable in these vast regions. Its first step will be an appropriation of the Floridas to be master of the Gulf of Mexico."

THE AMBITION OF NORTH AMERICANS

The ambition of the North Americans has not been in conformity with this. They desired from the beginning to extend their dominion in such manner as to become the absolute owners of almost all this continent. In two

From *The Other Side, or Notes from the History of the War Between Mexico and the United States*, edited by Ramón Alcaraz et al., translated by Albert C. Ramsey (New York, 1850).

ways they could accomplish their ruling passion: in one by bringing under their laws and authority all America to the Isthmus of Panama; in another, in opening an overland passage to the Pacific Ocean, and making good harbors to facilitate its navigation. By this plan, establishing in some way an easy communication of a few days between both oceans, no nation could compete with them. England herself might show her strength before yielding the field to her fortunate rival, and the mistress of the commercial world might for a while be delayed in touching the point of greatness to which she aspires.

In the short space of some three quarters of a century events have verified the existence of these schemes and their rapid development. The North American Republic has already absorbed territories pertaining to Great Britain, France, Spain, and Mexico. It has employed every means to accomplish this—purchase as well as usurpation, skill as well as force, and nothing has restrained it when treating of territorial acquisition. Louisiana, the Floridas, Oregon, and Texas, have successively fallen into its power....

While the United States seemed to be animated by a sincere desire not to break the peace, their acts of hostility manifested very evidently what were their true intentions. Their ships infested our coasts; their troops continued advancing upon our territory, situated at places which under no aspect could be disputed. Thus violence and insult were united: thus at the very time they usurped part of our territory, they offered to us the hand of treachery, to have soon the audacity to say that our obstinacy and arrogance were the real causes of the war.

———— ◼ ————

Is there one impartial man who would not consider the forcible occupation of our territory by the North American arms a shameful usurpation?

———— ◼ ————

THE TEXAS BORDER QUESTION

To explain the occupation of the Mexican territory by the troops of General [Zachary] Taylor, the strange idea occurred to the United States that the limits of Texas extended to the Rio Bravo del Norte [Rio Grande]. This opinion was predicated upon two distinct principles: one, that the Congress of Texas had so declared it in December, in 1836; and another, that the river mentioned had been the natural line of Louisiana. To state these reasons is equivalent at once to deciding the matter; for no one could defend such palpable absurdities. The first, which this government prizing its intelligence and civilization, supported with refined malice, would have been ridiculous in the mouth of a child. Whom could it convince that the declaration of the Texas Congress bore a legal title for the acquisition of the lands which it appropriated to itself with so little hesitation? If such a principle were recognised, we ought to be very grateful to these gentlemen senators who had the kindness to be satisfied with so little. Why not declare the limits of the rebel state extended to San Luis, to the capital, to our frontier with Guatemala?

The question is so clear in itself that it would only obscure by delaying to examine it further. We pass then to the other less nonsensical than the former. In the first place to pretend that the limits of Louisiana came to the Rio Bravo, it was essential to confound this province with Texas, which never can be tolerated. We have . . . shown the ancient and peaceable possession of Spain over the lands of the latter. Again, this same province, and afterwards State of Texas, never had extended its territory to the Rio Bravo, being only to the Nueces [River], in which always had been established the boundary. Lastly, a large part of the territory situated on the other side of the Bravo, belonged, without dispute or doubt, to other states of the [Mexican] Republic—to New Mexico, Tamaulipas, Coahuila, and Chihuahua.

Then, after so many and such plain proceedings, is there one impartial man who would not consider the forcible occupation of our territory by the North American arms a shameful usurpation? Then further, this power desired to carry to the extreme the sneer and the jest. When the question had resolved itself into one of force

which is the *ultima ratio* [final argument] of nations as well as of kings, when it had spread desolation and despair in our populations, when many of our citizens had perished in the contest, the bloody hand of our treacherous neighbors was turned to present the olive of peace. . . .

THE CAUSE OF THIS WAR

Such are the events that abandoned us to a calamitous war; and, in the relation of which, we have endeavored not to distort even a line of the private data consulted, to prove, on every occasion, all and each of our assertions.

From the acts referred to, it has been demonstrated to the very senses, that the real and effective cause of this war that afflicted us was the spirit of aggrandizement of the United States of the North, availing itself of its power to conquer us.

FOR FURTHER READING

Paul H. Bergeron, *The Presidency of James K. Polk*. Lawrence: University Press of Kansas, 1987.

Gene M. Brack, *Mexico vs. Manifest Destiny*. Albuquerque, University of New Mexico Press, 1975.

Bernard De Voto, *Year of Decision 1846*. New York: St. Martin's Press, 2000.

Richard V. Francaviglia and Douglas W. Richmond, eds., *Dueling Eagles: Reinterpreting the U.S.-Mexican War, 1846–1848*. Fort Worth: Texas Christian University Press, 2000.

John H. Schroeder, *Mr. Polk's War: American Opposition and Dissent, 1846–1848*. Madison: University of Wisconsin Press, 1973.

Part 4
CIVIL WAR AND RECONSTRUCTION
(1850–1877)

CHRONOLOGY

1850

July 9 President Zachary Taylor dies in office: Vice President Millard Fillmore becomes president.

September Compromise of 1850 passed by Congress.

1851

November 14 *Moby Dick* by Herman Melville published.

1852

March 20 *Uncle Tom's Cabin* by Harriet Beecher Stowe published.

November 2 Franklin Pierce elected president.

1853

December 30 Gadsden Purchase of territory from Mexico occurs.

1854

March Formation of Know-Nothing and Republican Parties occurs.

May 30 Pierce signs Kansas-Nebraska Act, voiding 1820 Missouri Compromise.

October American diplomats propose seizing Cuba from Spain in the Ostend Manifesto.

1855

March Violent clashes in "Bleeding Kansas" occur between pro-slavery and anti-slavery settlers.

1856

May 23 Abolitionist John Brown and followers kill five pro-slavery settlers in Kansas in Pottawatomie massacre.

November 4 James Buchanan elected president.

1857

June *The Impending Crisis of the South*, an anti-slavery book written by southern resident Hinton R. Helper, published.

March 6 Supreme Court rules blacks are not citizens and that slaves can be taken anywhere in U.S. in *Dred Scott* decision.

August Panic of 1857 brings economic downturn to northern states.

1858

May 11 Minnesota enters Union.

August 2 Admission of Kansas to Union derailed when residents vote to reject proslavery Lecompton constitution.

August 21–October 15 Lincoln-Douglas debates.

1859

February 14 Oregon enters Union.

August First oil well drilled in U.S.

December 2 John Brown executed after conviction for leading slave insurrection at Harpers Ferry.

1860

June Democratic Party splits into northern and southern factions.

November 4 Abraham Lincoln elected president.

December 20 South Carolina secedes from Union.

1861

January–March Mississippi, Florida, Alabama, Georgia, Louisiana, and Texas secede from Union: Tennessee, North Carolina, Missouri, and Arkansas reject secession.

January 29 Kansas enters Union as free state.

February 7 The Confederate States of America established.

February 27 The Crittenden Compromise (restoring the Missouri Compromise line) rejected by House of Representatives.

March 4 Lincoln inaugurated.

March 29 Lincoln orders resupply of Fort Sumter, South Carolina.

April 12 Fort Sumter attacked by Confederate troops, beginning Civil War.

April–May Virginia, Arkansas, North Carolina, and Tennessee secede from Union and join Confederacy.

July 21 First Battle of Bull Run fought at Manassas, Virginia.

1862

April 12 First official regiment of black troops organized for Union army.

May 20 Homestead Act, signed by Lincoln, grants free public land to settlers.

September 22 Lincoln announces Emancipation Proclamation, to take effect January 1, 1863.

1863

March 3 Congress passes conscription law.

June 20 West Virginia enters Union.

July 1–3 Battle of Gettysburg occurs.

July 11 Draft riots hit New York City.

December 8 Lincoln issues his Proclamation of Amnesty and Reconstruction.

1864

March 12 Ulysses S. Grant placed in charge of all Union armies.

July 2 Congress passes Wade-Davis Bill giving Congress control over Reconstruction; Lincoln pocket-vetoes measure.

October 31 Nevada enters Union.

November 8 Lincoln reelected.

1865

March 3 Freedman's Bureau established.

April 9 Robert E. Lee surrenders to Grant at Appomattox Courthouse.

April 14 Lincoln assassinated by John Wilkes Booth: Vice President Andrew Johnson becomes president.

November 24 Mississippi first state to enact Black Code.

December 18 Thirteenth Amendment, abolishing slavery, ratified.

December 24 Ku Klux Klan founded in Tennessee.

1866

April 9 Congress passes Civil Rights Act of 1866 over Johnson's veto.

July 24 Congress readmits Tennessee to Union.

July 30 Race riot in New Orleans results in 200 casualties.

1867

March 1 Nebraska enters Union.

March 2 Over Johnson's veto, Congress passes First Reconstruction Act dividing Confederacy into five military districts.

March 30 U.S. purchases Alaska from Russia.

1868

May President Johnson avoids impeachment by one vote.

June 22–25 Arkansas, Alabama, Florida, Louisiana, South Carolina, and North Carolina are readmitted to Union.

July 21 Fourteenth Amendment, guaranteeing blacks civil rights, ratified by the states.

November 3 Ulysses S. Grant elected president.

December 25 President Johnson grants amnesty to all Confederate leaders.

1869

March 15 Woman suffrage amendment to the Constitution proposed in Congress.

May 10 Nation's first transcontinental railroad completed.

November 6 First intercollegiate football game played.

December 10 Wyoming Territory grants women right to vote.

1870

January 26 Virginia readmitted to Union.

February 23 Mississippi readmitted to Union.

February 25 Hiram R. Revels of Mississippi becomes nation's first black senator.

March 30 Fifteenth Amendment, forbidding racial restrictions on suffrage, ratified.

1871

March 3 Congress nullifies past treaties and makes Indians wards of federal government.

March 4 First black members of House of Representatives seated.

April 20 Ku Klux Klan Act passed by Congress.

October 8–11 Great Chicago Fire destroys much of the city of Chicago.

1872

March 1 Yellowstone National Park established by Congress.

June 10 Freedman's Bureau abolished.

November 5 Grant reelected president.

1873

March 3 Comstock Law bars obscenity (including birth control information) from federal mails.

April 14 Supreme Court rules that Fourteenth Amendment protects only rights derived from federal, not state, citizenship.

September Major banking failures begin five years of economic depression.

1875

January 5 Grant dispatches federal troops to Vicksburg, Mississippi, to restore order following the killing of 300 blacks by armed whites.

March 1 Civil Rights Act of 1875 forbids racial segregation in public places.

1876

March Alexander Graham Bell invents telephone.

August 1 Colorado enters Union.

1877

March 2 Rutherford B. Hayes declared winner of close and controversial presidential election.

April Remaining federal troops withdrawn from South, ending Reconstruction era.

PREFACE

The United States of America has survived intact many difficulties: foreign invasions, wars with both neighboring and distant countries, economic depressions, massive influxes of new peoples and new ideas, and sharp disagreements over its economic and political policies. Only once has the Union been broken—the result was the Civil War. The causes and consequences of that war, and the Reconstruction Era that followed, have been the subject of great dispute, both among those who lived through that period of American history, and among later historians who have written about it.

SLAVERY AND THE WESTERN TERRITORIES

In 1849 California, its population enlarged by gold seekers, applied for statehood as a free state. This request triggered a national debate over whether this territory newly won in the Mexican War should become a free or slave state. Many Southerners in Congress began to speak of secession if slavery was forbidden in California. In fact, Southern leaders called for a convention in June 1850 to discuss the possibility of secession.

The United States had faced a similar quandary in 1819, when Missouri (part of the Louisiana Territory) applied for statehood as a slave state. At issue, both in 1819 and 1849, was sectional balance between free and slave states. Also at issue was whether Congress had the power to prevent slavery in a new state (it had, under the Constitution, no power to ban slavery in states where it already existed). In 1820 Congress, led by Henry Clay and other members, passed what became known as the Missouri Compromise. Congress admitted Missouri as a slave state (and Maine concurrently as a free state) and drew a line roughly parallel with Missouri's southern border through the rest of the Louisiana Territory, dividing it into slave and free regions.

In 1849 some people proposed that the Missouri compromise line be extended to the Pacific Ocean. This suggestion was opposed by two groups: Northerners who wanted slavery banned altogether in the new territories and slavery partisans of the South who argued that they had a right to bring their "property" into the land they had helped to acquire. The development of a militant abolitionist movement in the North, growing Southern

fears of slave rebellions, and the rise of more assertive pro-slavery defenders in the South after 1820 all helped prevent an extension of the Missouri Compromise.

Slavery was believed by many to be indispensable to the economy and society of the Old South. By 1860 the population of the states that formed the Confederacy consisted of less than 6 million whites and around 4 million blacks, most of them slaves. Although only a minority of white families actually owned slaves, and a few white Southerners suggested abolishing the institution, most white Southerners were determined not just to preserve the institution of slavery, but to guarantee its expansion into new territories.

THE COMPROMISE OF 1850

Congress was able to head off a secession crisis caused by California's statehood application by passing a series of laws known collectively as the Compromise of 1850. This compromise was fashioned by Henry Clay and other members of Congress who had helped pass the Missouri Compromise thirty years before, as well as a new generation of congressional leaders including Illinois Democratic senator Stephen A. Douglas. Concessions made by the South included the admission of California to the Union as a free state and the abolition of the slave trade in Washington, D.C. To satisfy the South, Congress agreed to a strengthened Fugitive Slave Act to assist slaveholders in reclaiming slaves who had escaped to the North. As for the other territories won in the Mexican War, their slave status would be decided on the basis of popular sovereignty (the territorial residents would themselves decide whether to allow or ban slavery). The legislative compromise successfully staved off threats of secession by the South for the time being.

THE KANSAS-NEBRASKA ACT AND POPULAR SOVEREIGNTY

Many Americans were optimistic that the Compromise of 1850 could provide lasting peace on the slavery question. Fundamental disputes remained unresolved, however. In 1852 Harriet Beecher Stowe's best-selling novel *Uncle Tom's Cabin* aroused strong sympathy for slaves among many Northern readers and inspired many communities and local courts in the North to resist enforcing the Fugitive Slave Act. Their defiance of the federal law was bitterly decried by Southern leaders.

Even more damaging to national unity was the passage of the Kansas-Nebraska Act in 1854. The law, supported by Douglas and by Southern members of Congress, explicitly repealed the 1820 Missouri Compromise line and organized the Kansas and Nebraska territories on the basis of popular sovereignty. The act and the widespread Northern dismay at the dismantling of the

Missouri Compromise line divided the Democratic Party into Northern and Southern factions, broke apart the Whig Party, and led to the formation of the Republican Party. The new party was a sectional Northern organization dedicated to the principle of free soil, or no slavery in all U.S. territories (it was in some respects the successor to the smaller Free-Soil Party that had fielded presidential candidates in 1848 and 1852). The Kansas-Nebraska Act also led to violence in Kansas, where proslavery and antislavery settlers fought to determine whether that territory would become a slave or free state.

Sectional divisions continued to grow during the remainder of the 1850s. Most major Protestant churches split into Northern and Southern wings. The Supreme Court in 1857 further inflamed sectional tension by handing down the *Dred Scott* decision, which ruled that blacks were not citizens, that laws against slavery were unconstitutional, and that slave owners had the constitutional right to take their slaves anywhere in the nation. This ruling pleased Southerners but angered Northern abolitionists and free-soil advocates alike.

JOHN BROWN AND ABRAHAM LINCOLN

The actions of two very different people finally led South Carolina and other states to take the fateful step of secession. In 1859 radical abolitionist John Brown attempted to lead a slave insurrection in Virginia. A little more than one year later free-soil partisan and Republican Abraham Lincoln was elected to the presidency.

With secret financial support from prominent Northern abolitionists, Brown and eighteen of his followers (including two of his sons and five black men) raided the federal arsenal at Harpers Ferry in Virginia. Brown and his small army were quickly surrounded and captured by local militia and a detachment of U.S. Army troops commanded by Colonel Robert E. Lee. Tried, convicted, and executed by a Virginia state court on charges of treason, Brown proved to be far more effective as a martyr than as a revolutionary. Northern praise of Brown's goals, along with evidence of abolitionist support for his insurrection, disturbed Southerners even more than the original raid and created an even wider chasm between the two sections.

The sectional divisions magnified by John Brown's rebellion were evident during the second major event leading up to secession—the presidential election of 1860. The Democratic Party, which had controlled the White House for twenty-four of the previous thirty-two years and which was one of the few genuinely national organizations remaining, finally split along sectional lines. Southern delegates, insisting on a platform calling for federal protection of slavery in all western territories

and refusing to support the leading candidate, Stephen A. Douglas, left the party and nominated their own candidate, John Breckinridge. The two Democrats were opposed by John Bell of the newly formed Constitutional Union Party, which sought to avoid the slavery issue, and Republican Party candidate Abraham Lincoln.

The nomination of Lincoln, an Illinois lawyer who had gained national fame during his debates with Stephen A. Douglas in an 1858 senatorial election, was a victory for the moderate wing of the Republican Party. Seeking to deflect criticisms that they were "Black Republicans" determined to abolish slavery and promote social equality between blacks and whites, Lincoln and the Republicans ran on a platform that, while advocating the restriction of slavery in the territories, also endorsed the right of each state to maintain slavery and condemned John Brown's raid as "the gravest of crimes." However, Lincoln was resolute in opposing slavery in the territories and won almost no votes in the South. He won the election by capturing most of the Northern states; within a few months the entire Lower South seceded from the Union to form the Confederate States of America.

In his Inaugural address on March 4, 1861, Lincoln offered to support a constitutional amendment preventing the federal government from interfering with slavery in the states (but not the territories). He went on to argue that no state could leave the Union of its own volition and that he meant to enforce the Constitution and to "hold, occupy, and possess the property and places belonging to the government." Among these properties was Fort Sumter in South Carolina, where a small garrison of soldiers under Major Robert Anderson was attacked by Confederate troops on April 12, 1861. The assault ushered in four years of brutal war.

THE CIVIL WAR

The Civil War was the most destructive conflict in American history. At least 620,000 soldiers perished, a sum almost equal to all other U.S. wars combined. Property damage was enormous, especially in the South, where many cities, plantations, factories, and railroads lay in ruins after the war. The North began the war with large material advantages over the South in terms of population and industrial production. Despite many early Confederate victories, the North was ultimately able to exploit these advantages and turn the tide. A key to its success was the use of 180,000 black soldiers, many of them escaped or former slaves. On April 9, 1865, General Robert E. Lee, the commander of the Confederate army, surrendered to Union commander General Ulysses S. Grant.

President Lincoln faced many wartime challenges, not the least of which was dissent within the North. Some elements within his party, known as Radical

Republicans, fervently called for the abolition of slavery and the use of black troops (steps initially opposed by Lincoln) and in general pushed for a more aggressive war against the South. Lincoln's critics at the other end of the political spectrum consisted of those people (mostly Democrats) who questioned his decision to go to war, who opposed the abolition of slavery and who argued that Lincoln was becoming dictatorial in directing the war effort. Although not as powerful in Congress as the Radical Republicans, the Peace Democrats (also called Copperheads) were well represented in state and local governments. Worry over espionage and sabotage by the Copperheads was a constant concern for the Lincoln administration. During the war thousands of suspected Confederate sympathizers were jailed, one of the most prominent being Ohio Democratic leader Clement L. Vallandigham.

Confederate president Jefferson Davis faced comparable challenges, including criticism of his leadership. Ironically, the ideal of states' rights—the stated reason for the Southern states' secession and the subsequent creation of the Confederacy—became itself a source of division as some state governors resisted orders from Davis. Another important source of division within the Confederacy was the defiance and resistance of its slaves.

THE EMANCIPATION PROCLAMATION

Abolitionists believed that the Civil War presented an opportunity for the United States to extinguish the institution of slavery. Many argued that emancipating the slaves would deprive the South of its labor force, weaken the rebelling states, and hasten the end of war—an argument that gained increasing support even from people who had not been abolitionists before the war. Lincoln at first sought to placate slave owners from the four slave states that did not secede (as the president put it, he liked having God on his side, but he needed Kentucky). He therefore resisted entreaties by abolitionists to use his presidential powers to free the slaves. But later, stating that "we . . . must change our tactics, or risk losing the game," Lincoln finally decided to issue the Emancipation Proclamation, which took effect on January 1, 1863. The proclamation declared freedom for slaves in all areas of the Confederacy still in rebellion against the Union. Although it did not immediately abolish slavery in all the states, it dramatically changed the nature and aims of the war and helped ensure the death of slavery, after the war was over.

Overall, Lincoln was able to bridge serious divisions within the North as he led it to victory, ended slavery,

and restored the Union. Whether he would have been as successful in leading the nation following the war will never be known; one week after Lee's surrender, Lincoln was assassinated.

RECONSTRUCTION

The Civil War may have settled the questions of secession and slavery, but the aftermath of the war presented many puzzling problems to the new president, Andrew Johnson, and the congressional leadership. Two questions were primary: How should the rebellious states be reintegrated into the Union, and how should the four million ex-slaves be integrated into American society?

Northerners divided into two groups in answering these questions. One sought to restore the states to the Union with a minimum of federal interference, thus giving them a free hand in dealing with former slaves. Those in this group included Lincoln and his successor, Johnson, conservative Republicans and Democrats in Congress, and white Southerners. In the summer of 1865 Johnson oversaw the restoration of state governments in most of the former Confederate states after they met the conditions of abolishing slavery, repudiating secession, and abrogating Confederates debts. Southern whites were given a relatively free hand in establishing their restored state governments. Blacks, who had been offered no role in Johnson's reconstruction plans, found themselves bound under state-passed "Black Codes" that punished blacks for "insulting" whites, kept them bound to year-long labor contracts on plantations, and otherwise severely restricted their economic and political freedoms.

Radical Republicans in Congress proposed a much different approach to reconstruction. They considered the South a conquered territory that was under the jurisdiction of Congress and sought to use their authority to re-create Southern society with equality between blacks and whites. In 1866 and 1867 they were able to turn their ideas into law by passing many bills over Johnson's opposition. They abolished the state governments established in 1865 and, under federal military control, established new governments in which blacks and whites shared political power. Among other achievements of the Radical Republicans in Congress were the Fourteenth and Fifteenth Amendments, which granted citizenship to blacks and suffrage to black men, respectively. However, by the 1870s Radical Republicans were in the minority in Congress. Remaining state governments in which blacks had significant political clout fell after federal troops were withdrawn from the South in 1877. Questions of social, political and economic equality for blacks remained a controversial issue throughout the nation.

SLAVERY AND THE ROAD TO SECESSION

Viewpoint 28A

Southern States May Be Forced to Leave the Union (1850)

John C. Calhoun (1782–1850)

INTRODUCTION *In 1850 secession was openly discussed by many leaders in the South in response to President Zachary Taylor's proposed admission of California to the Union as a free state. Granting statehood to the newly acquired territory would give free states a 16–15 majority over slave states. On January 29, 1850, Senator Henry Clay introduced a series of laws that sought to ease sectional tensions over slavery. His legislative package included admitting California as a free state, organizing the New Mexico and Utah territories without mention of slavery, and, to placate the South, a stricter federal law for the return of runaway slaves and the removal of Congress from any role in regulating the slave trade between Southern states. Clay warned in a February 6, 1850, speech that his proposals were necessary to save the Union and that "the dissolution of the Union and war are identical and inseparable."*

The following viewpoint is excerpted from a Senate speech written by John C. Calhoun in response to Clay's proposals. Calhoun, who at various times in his long political career was secretary of war, vice president, secretary of state, and U.S. senator, was recognized as the preeminent defender of the South and its institutions, including slavery. He argues that the "equilibrium" between Northern and Southern interests that existed at the time of the nation's birth had been lost, and asserts that nothing less than a permanent end to antislavery "agitation," the opening of all western territories to slavery, more stringent enforcement of fugitive slave laws, and amending the Constitution to ensure that Southern states could veto any national attempt to abolish slavery, will preserve the "cords" that bind the Union.

What are the causes of Northern dominance over the South, according to Calhoun? Why, in his view, are slavery abolitionists in part responsible for national discord?

I have, Senators, believed from the first that the agitation of the subject of slavery would, if not prevented by some timely and effective measure, end in disunion. Entertaining this opinion, I have, on all proper occasions, endeavored to call the attention of both the two great parties which divide the country to adopt some measure to prevent so great a disaster, but without success. The agitation has been permitted to proceed, with almost no attempt to resist it, until it has reached a point when it can no longer be disguised or denied that the Union is in danger. You have thus had forced upon you the greatest and gravest question that can ever come under your consideration—How can the Union be preserved?

To give a satisfactory answer to this mighty question, it is indispensable to have an accurate and thorough knowledge of the nature and the character of the cause by which the Union is endangered. Without such knowledge it is impossible to pronounce, with any certainty, by what measure it can be saved; just as it would be impossible for a physician to pronounce, in the case of some dangerous disease, with any certainty, by what remedy the patient could be saved, without similar knowledge of the nature and character of the cause which produced it. The first question, then, presented for consideration, in the investigation I propose to make, in order to obtain such knowledge, is—What is it that has endangered the Union?

SOUTHERN DISCONTENT

To this question there can be but one answer,—that the immediate cause is the almost universal discontent which pervades all the States composing the Southern section of the Union. . . .

What is the cause of this discontent? It will be found in the belief of the people of the Southern States, as prevalent as the discontent itself, that they cannot remain, as things now are, consistently with honor and safety, in the Union. The next question to be considered is—What has caused this belief?

One of the causes is, undoubtedly, to be traced to the long-continued agitation of the slave question on the part of the North, and the many aggressions which they have made on the rights of the South during the time. I will not enumerate them at present, as it will be done hereafter in its proper place.

There is another lying back of it—with which this is intimately connected—that may be regarded as the great and primary cause. This is to be found in the fact that the equilibrium between the two sections, in the Government as it stood when the constitution was ratified and the Government put in action, has been destroyed. At that time there was nearly a perfect equilibrium between the

From John C. Calhoun's speech before the U.S. Senate on March 4, 1850.

141

two, which afforded ample means to each to protect itself against the aggression of the other; but, as it now stands, one section has the exclusive power of controlling the Government, which leaves the other without any adequate means of protecting itself against its encroachment and oppression. To place this subject distinctly before you, I have, Senators, prepared a brief statistical statement, showing the relative weight of the two sections in the Government under the first census of 1790 and the last census of 1840.

CHANGING POPULATIONS

According to the former, the population of the United States, including Vermont, Kentucky, and Tennessee, which then were in their incipient condition of becoming States, but were not actually admitted, amounted to 3,929.827. Of this number the Northern States had 1,997,899, and the Southern 1,952,072, making a difference of only 45,827 in favor of the former States. The number of States, including Vermont, Kentucky, and Tennessee, were sixteen; of which eight, including Vermont, belonged to the Northern section, and eight, including Kentucky and Tennessee, to the Southern—making an equal division of the States between the two sections under the first census. There was a small preponderance in the House of Representatives, and in the electoral college, in favor of the Northern, owing to the fact that, according to the provisions of the constitution, in estimating federal numbers five slaves count but three; but it was too small to affect sensibly the perfect equilibrium which, with that exception, existed at the time. Such was the equality of the two sections when the States composing them agreed to enter into a Federal Union. Since then the equilibrium between them has been greatly disturbed.

According to the last census the aggregate population of the United States amounted to 17,063,357, of which the Northern section contained 9,728,920, and the Southern 7,334,437, making a difference, in round numbers, of 2,400,000. The number of States had increased from sixteen to twenty-six, making an addition of ten States. In the mean time the position of Delaware had become doubtful as to which section she properly belonged. Considering her as neutral, the Northern States will have thirteen and the Southern States twelve, making a difference in the Senate of two Senators in favor of the former. According to the apportionment under the census of 1840, there were two hundred and twenty-three members of the House of Representatives, of which the Northern States had one hundred and thirty-five, and the Southern States (considering Delaware as neutral) eighty-seven, making a difference in favor of the former in the House of Representatives of forty-eight. The difference in the Senate of two members, added to this, gives to the

North, in the electoral college, a majority of fifty. Since the census of 1840, four States have been added to the Union—Iowa, Wisconsin, Florida, and Texas. They leave the difference in the Senate as it stood when the census was taken; but add two to the side of the North in the House, making the present majority in the House in its favor fifty, and in the electoral college fifty-two.

The result of the whole is to give the Northern section a pre-dominance in every department of the Government, and thereby concentrate in it the two elements which constitute the Federal Government,—majority of States, and a majority of their population, estimated in federal numbers. Whatever section concentrates the two in itself possesses the control of the entire Government.

But we are just at the close of the sixth decade, and the commencement of the seventh. The census is to be taken this year, which must add greatly to the decided preponderance of the North in the House of Representatives and in the electoral college. The prospect is, also, that a great increase will be added to its present preponderance in the Senate, during the period of the decade, by the addition of new States. This great increase of Senators, added to the great increase of members of the House of Representatives and the electoral college on the part of the North, which must take place under the next decade, will effectually and irretrievably destroy the equilibrium which existed when the Government commenced.

The result of the whole of these causes combined is—that the North has acquired a decided ascendancy over every department of this Government, and through it a control over all the powers of the system. A single section governed by the will of the numerical majority, has now, in fact, the control of the Government and the entire powers of the system. What was once a constitutional federal republic, is now converted, in reality, into one as absolute as that of the Autocrat of Russia, and as despotic in its tendency as any absolute government that ever existed.

As, then, the North has the absolute control over the Government, it is manifest, that on all questions between it and the South, where there is a diversity of interests, the interest of the latter will be sacrificed to the former, however oppressive the effects may be; as the South possesses no means by which it can resist, through the action of the Government. But if there was no question of vital importance to the South, in reference to which there was a diversity of views between the two sections, this state of things might be endured, without the hazard of destruction to the South. But such is not the fact. There is a question of vital importance to the Southern section, in reference to which the views and feelings of the two sections are as opposite and hostile as they can possibly be.

THE TWO RACES

I refer to the relation between the two races in the Southern section, which constitutes a vital portion of her social organization. Every portion of the North entertains views and feelings more or less hostile to it. Those most opposed and hostile, regard it as a sin, and consider themselves under the most sacred obligation to use every effort to destroy it. Indeed, to the extent that they conceive they have power, they regard themselves as implicated in the sin, and responsible for not suppressing it by the use of all and every means. Those less opposed and hostile, regard it as a crime—an offence against humanity, as they call it; and, although not so fanatical, feel themselves bound to use all efforts to effect the same object; while those who are least opposed and hostile, regard it as a blot and a stain on the character of what they call the Nation, and feel themselves accordingly bound to give it no countenance or support. On the contrary, the Southern section regards the relation as one which cannot be destroyed without subjecting the two races to the greatest calamity, and the section to poverty, desolation, and wretchedness; and accordingly they feel bound, by every consideration of interest and safety, to defend it.

This hostile feeling on the part of the North towards the social organization of the South long lay dormant, but it only required some cause to act on those who felt most intensely that they were responsible for its continuance, to call it into action. The increasing power of this Government, and of the control of the Northern section over all its departments, furnished the cause. It was this which made an impression on the minds of many, that there was little or no restraint to prevent the Government from doing whatever it might choose to do. This was sufficient of itself to put the most fanatical portion of the North in action, for the purpose of destroying the existing relation between the two races in the South.

The first organized movement towards it commenced in 1835. Then, for the first time, societies were organized, presses established, lecturers sent forth to excite the people of the North, and incendiary publications scattered over the whole South, through the mail. The South was thoroughly aroused. Meetings were held every where, and resolutions adopted, calling upon the North to apply a remedy to arrest the threatened evil, and pledging themselves to adopt measures for their own protection, if it was not arrested. At the meeting of Congress, petitions poured in from the North, calling upon Congress to abolish slavery in the District of Columbia, and to prohibit, what they called, the internal slave trade between the States—announcing at the same time, that their ultimate object was to abolish slavery, not only in the District, but in the States and throughout the Union. At this period, the number engaged in the agitation was small, and possessed little or no personal influence....

[Yet] the [abolitionist] party succeeded in their first movements, in gaining what they proposed—a position in Congress, from which agitation could be extended over the whole Union. This was the commencement of the agitation, which has ever since continued, and which, as is now acknowledged, has endangered the Union itself....

Unless something decisive is done, I again ask, what is to stop this agitation, before the great and final object at which it aims—the abolition of slavery in the States—is consummated? Is it, then, not certain, that if something is not done to arrest it, the South will be forced to choose between abolition and secession?...

HOW CAN THE UNION BE SAVED?

Having now Senators, explained what it is that endangers the Union, and traced it to its cause, and explained its nature and character, the question again recurs—How can the Union be saved? To this I answer, there is but one way by which it can be—and that is—by adopting such measures as will satisfy the States belonging to the Southern section, that they can remain in the Union consistently with their honor and their safety. There is, again, only one way by which this can be effected, and that is—by removing the causes by which this belief has been produced. Do *this*, and discontent will cease—harmony and kind feelings between the sections be restored—and every apprehension of danger to the Union removed. The question, then, is—How can this be done? But, before I undertake to answer this question, I propose to show by what the Union cannot be saved.

It cannot, then, be saved by eulogies on the Union, however splendid or numerous. The cry of "Union, Union—the glorious Union!" can no more prevent disunion than the cry of "Health, health—glorious health!" on the part of the physician, can save a patient lying dangerously ill. So long as the Union, instead of being regarded as a protector, is regarded in the opposite character, by not much less than a majority of the States, it will be in vain to attempt to conciliate them by pronouncing eulogies on it....

Nor can the Union be saved by invoking the name of the illustrious Southerner [George Washington] whose mortal remains repose on the western bank of the Potomac. He was one of us—a slaveholder and a planter. We have studied his history, and find nothing in it to justify submission to wrong. On the contrary, his great fame rests on the solid foundation, that, while he was careful to avoid doing wrong to others, he was prompt and decided in repelling wrong. I trust that, in this respect, we profited by his example.

———— ■ ————

*The South asks for justice, simple justice,
and less she ought not to take.*

———— ■ ————

Nor can we find any thing in his history to deter us from seceding from the Union, should it fail to fulfill the objects for which it was instituted, by being permanently and hopelessly converted into the means of oppressing instead of protecting us. On the contrary, we find much in his example to encourage us, should we be forced to the extremity of deciding between submission and disunion....

Nor can the plan proposed by the distinguished Senator from Kentucky [Henry Clay], nor that of the administration save the Union....

SIMPLE JUSTICE

Having now shown what cannot save the Union, I return to the question with which I commenced. How can the Union be saved? There is but one way by which it can with any certainty; and that is, by a full and final settlement, on the principle of justice, of all the questions at issue between the two sections. The South asks for justice, simple justice, and less she ought not to take. She has no compromise to offer, but the constitution; and no concession or surrender to make. She has already surrendered so much that she has little left to surrender. Such a settlement would go to the root of the evil, and remove all cause of discontent, by satisfying the South, she could remain honorably and safely in the Union, and thereby restore the harmony and fraternal feelings between the sections, which existed anterior to the Missouri agitation. Nothing else can, with any certainty, finally and for ever settle the questions at issue, terminate agitation, and save the Union.

But can this be done? Yes, easily; not by the weaker party, for it can of itself do nothing—not even protect itself—but by the stronger. The North has only to will it to accomplish it—to do justice by conceding to the South an equal right in the acquired territory, and to do her duty by causing the stipulations relative to fugitive slaves to be faithfully fulfilled—to cease the agitation of the slave question, and to provide for the insertion of a provision in the constitution, by an amendment, which will restore to the South, in substance, the power she possessed of protecting herself, before the equilibrium between the sections was destroyed by the action of this Government. There will be no difficulty in devising such a provision—one that will protect the South, and which, at the same time, will improve and strengthen the Government, instead of impairing and weakening it.

But will the North agree to this? It is for her to answer the question. But, I will say, she cannot refuse, if she has half the love of the Union which she professes to have, or without justly exposing herself to the charge that her love of power and aggrandizement is far greater than her love of the Union. At all events, the responsibility of saving the Union rests on the North, and not on the South. The South cannot save it by any act of hers, and the North may save it without any sacrifice whatever, unless to do justice, and to perform her duties under the constitution, should be regarded by her as a sacrifice.

Viewpoint 28B
The Union Must Be Preserved (1850)
Daniel Webster (1782–1852)

INTRODUCTION *Daniel Webster of Massachusetts, Henry Clay of Kentucky, and John C. Calhoun of South Carolina were the "great triumvirate" of U.S. senators whose oratorical skills and achievements dominated American political life from 1815 to 1850. Like Clay and Calhoun, Webster capped his long political career by playing a major role in the debate about the Compromise of 1850, a package of laws aimed at incorporating the territories won in the Mexican War while preventing the nation's rupturing over slavery.*

Webster, a strong Unionist, supported the compromise legislation proposed by Clay in January 1850. Clay's proposals included admitting California as a free state (one that banned slavery), organizing New Mexico and Utah as territories without determining their status on slavery (allowing residents there to choose), compensating Texas for relinquishing its claims on New Mexican territory, and strengthening national laws to make it easier for slave owners to recover slaves who had escaped to free states. The proposed compromise was opposed by Northern antislavery leaders who wanted slavery banned for all new territories, and by Southern proslavery leaders (notably Calhoun) who wanted their property rights to slaves protected in the new territories, and who insisted on measures guaranteeing slavery's continuing existence in the South.

The following viewpoint consists of excerpts from Daniel Webster's famous Senate speech of March 7, 1850, given partially in response to Calhoun's speech presented three days earlier (see viewpoint 28A), and partially in response to Northern opponents of slavery. Webster attacks both sides for extremism and refusal to compromise.

How does Webster identify himself at the start of the speech? How do his views on U.S. history (especially the relative strength of the Southern and Northern sections) differ from those expressed by John C. Calhoun in the opposing viewpoint? What are Webster's views on slavery?

Mr. President [of the Senate],—I wish to speak to-day, not as a Massachusetts man, nor as a Northern man, but as an American....

I speak to-day for the preservation of the Union. "Hear me for my cause." I speak to-day, out of a solicitous and anxious heart, for the restoration to the country of that quiet and that harmony which make the blessings of this Union so rich, and so dear to us all. These are the topics that I propose to myself to discuss; these are the motives, and the sole motives, that influence me in the wish to communicate my opinions to the Senate and the country; and if I can do any thing, however little, for the promotion of these ends, I shall have accomplished all that I expect....

THE QUESTION OF SLAVERY

It is obvious that the question which has so long harassed the country, and at some times very seriously alarmed the minds of wise and good men, has come upon us for a fresh discussion; the question of slavery in these United States....

Now, sir, upon the general nature and influence of slavery there exists a wide difference of opinion between the northern portion of this country and the southern. It is said on the one side, that, although not the subject of any injunction or direct prohibition in the New Testament, slavery is a wrong; that it is founded merely in the right of the strongest; and that it is an oppression, like unjust wars, like all those conflicts by which a powerful nation subjects a weaker to its will. These are sentiments that are cherished, and of late with greatly augmented force, among the people of the Northern States. They have taken hold of the religious sentiment of that part of the country, as they have, more or less, taken hold of the religious feelings of a considerable portion of mankind. The South, upon the other side, having been accustomed to this relation between the two races all their lives, from their birth, having been taught, in general, to treat the subjects of this bondage with care and kindness, and I believe, in general, feeling great kindness for them, have not taken the view of the subject which I have mentioned. There are thousands of religious men, with consciences as tender as any of their brethren at the North, who do not see the unlawfulness of slavery; and there are more thousands, perhaps, that, whatsoever they may think of it in its origin, and as a matter depending upon natural right, yet take things as they are, and, finding slavery to be an established relation of the society in which they live, can see no way in which, let their opinions on the abstract question be what they may, it is in the power of the present generation to relieve themselves from this relation. And candor obliges me to say, that I

believe they are just as conscientious, many of them, and the religious people, all of them, as they are at the North who hold different opinions....

But we must view things as they are. Slavery does exist in the United States. It did exist in the States before the adoption of this Constitution, and at that time. Let us, therefore, consider for a moment what was the state of sentiment, North and South, in regard to slavery, at the time this Constitution was adopted. A remarkable change has taken place since; but what did the wise and great men of all parts of the country think of slavery then? In what estimation did they hold it at the time when this Constitution was adopted? It will be found, sir, if we will carry ourselves by historical research back to that day, and ascertain men's opinions by authentic records still existing among us, that there was then no diversity of opinion between the North and South upon the subject of slavery. It will be found that both parts of the country held it equally an evil, a moral and political evil. It will not be found that, either at the North or at the South, there was much, though there was some, invective against slavery as inhuman and cruel. The great ground of objection to it was political; that it weakened the social fabric; that, taking the place of free labor, society became less strong and labor less productive; and therefore we find from all the eminent men of the time the clearest expression of their opinion that slavery is an evil....

HISTORICAL TRUTHS

Mr. President, three things are quite clear as historical truths. One is, that there was an expectation that, on the ceasing of the importation of slaves from Africa, slavery would begin to run out here. That was hoped and expected. Another is, that, as far as there was any power in Congress to prevent the spread of slavery in the United States, that power was executed in the most absolute manner, and to the fullest extent....

The other and third clear historical truth is, that the Convention meant to leave slavery in the States as they found it, entirely under the authority and control of the States themselves....

SLAVERY AND COTTON

What, then, have been the causes which have created so new a feeling in favor of slavery in the South, which have changed the whole nomenclature of the South on that subject, so that, from being thought and described in the terms I have mentioned and will not repeat, it has now become an institution, a cherished institution, in that quarter; no evil, no scourge, but a great religious, social, and moral blessing, as I think I have heard it latterly spoken of? I suppose this, sir, is owing to the rapid growth and sudden extension of the *cotton* plantations of the South. So far as any motive consistent with honor, justice, and general judgment could act, it was

From Daniel Webster's speech before the U.S. Senate on March 7, 1850.

the *cotton* interest that gave a new desire to promote slavery, to spread it, and to use its labor. I again say that this change was produced by causes which must always produce like effects. The whole interest of the South became connected, more or less, with the extension of slavery. . . .

The age of cotton became the golden age of our Southern brethren. It gratified their desire for improvement and accumulation, at the same time that it excited it. The desire grew by what it fed upon, and there soon came to be an eagerness for other territory, a new area or new areas for the cultivation of the cotton crop; and measures leading to this result were brought about rapidly, one after another, under the lead of Southern men at the head of the government, they having a majority in both branches of Congress to accomplish their ends. . . . No man acquainted with the history of the Union can deny that the general lead in the politics of the country, for three fourths of the period that has elapsed since the adoption of the Constitution, has been a Southern lead.

In 1802, in pursuit of the idea of opening a new cotton region, the United States obtained a cession from Georgia of the whole of her western territory, now embracing the rich and growing States of Alabama and Mississippi. In 1803 Louisiana was purchased from France, out of which the States of Louisiana, Arkansas, and Missouri have been framed, as slave-holding States. In 1819 the cession of Florida was made, bringing in another region adapted to cultivation by slaves. Sir, the honorable member from South Carolina [John C. Calhoun] thought he saw in certain operations of the government, such as the manner of collecting the revenue, and the tendency of measures calculated to promote emigration into the country; what accounts for the more rapid growth of the North than the South. He ascribes that more rapid growth, not to the operation of time, but to the system of government and administration established under this Constitution. That is a matter of opinion. To a certain extent it may be true; but it does seem to me that, if any operation of the government can be shown in any degree to have promoted the population, and growth, and wealth of the North, it is much more sure that there are sundry important and distinct operations of the government, about which no man can doubt, tending to promote, and which absolutely have promoted, the increase of the slave interest and the slave territory of the South. It was not time that brought in Louisiana; it was the act of men. It was not time that brought in Florida; it was the act of men. And lastly, sir, to complete those acts of legislation which have contributed so much to enlarge the area of the institution of slavery, Texas, great and vast and illimitable Texas, was added to the Union as a slave State in 1845. . . .

CALIFORNIA AND NEW MEXICO

Now, as to California and New Mexico, I hold slavery to be excluded from those territories by a law even superior to that which admits and sanctions it in Texas. I mean the law of nature, of physical geography, the law of the formation of the earth. That law settles for ever, with a strength beyond all terms of human enactment, that slavery cannot exist in California or New Mexico. Understand me, sir; I mean slavery as we regard it; the slavery of the colored race as it exists in the Southern States. . . . It is as impossible that African slavery, as we see it among us, should find its way, or be introduced, into California and New Mexico, as any other natural impossibility. California and New Mexico are Asiatic in their formation and scenery. They are composed of vast ridges of mountains, of great height, with broken ridges and deep valleys. The sides of these mountains are entirely barren; their tops capped by perennial snow. There may be in California, now made free by its constitution, and no doubt there are, some tracts of valuable land. But it is not so in New Mexico. Pray, what is the evidence which every gentleman must have obtained on this subject, from information sought by himself or communicated by others? I have inquired and read all I could find, in order to acquire information on this important subject. What is there in New Mexico that could, by any possibility, induce any body to go there with slaves? There are some narrow strips of tillable land on the borders of the rivers; but the rivers themselves dry up before midsummer is gone. All that the people can do in that region is to raise some little articles, some little wheat for their *tortillas*, and that by irrigation. And who expects to see a hundred black men cultivating tobacco, corn, cotton, rice, or any thing else, on lands in New Mexico, made fertile only by irrigation? . . .

Now, Mr. President, I have established, so far as I proposed to do so, the proposition with which I set out, and upon which I intend to stand or fall; and that is, that the whole territory within the former United States, or in the newly acquired Mexican provinces, has a fixed and settled character, now fixed and settled by law which cannot be repealed; in the case of Texas without a violation of public faith, and by no human power in regard to California or New Mexico; that, therefore, under one or other of these laws, every foot of land in the States or in the Territories has already received a fixed and decided character.

FUGITIVE SLAVES

Mr. President, in the excited times in which we live, there is found to exist a state of crimination and recrimination between the North and South. There are lists of grievances produced by each; and those grievances, real or supposed, alienate the minds of one portion of the country from the other, exasperate the feelings, and subdue the sense of fraternal affection, patriotic love, and mutual regard. I shall bestow a little attention, sir, upon these various grievances existing on the one side and on the other. I begin with complaints of the South. I will not answer, further than I have, the general statements of the honorable Senator from South Carolina [Calhoun], that the North has prospered at the expense of the South in consequence of the manner of administering this government, in the collecting of its revenues, and so forth. These are disputed topics, and I have no inclination to enter into them. But I will allude to other complaints of the South, and especially to one which has in my opinion just foundation; and that is, that there has been found at the North, among individuals and among legislators, a disinclination to perform fully their constitutional duties in regard to the return of persons bound to service who have escaped into the free States. In that respect, the South, in my judgment, is right, and the North is wrong. Every member of every Northern legislature is bound by oath, like every other officer in the country, to support the Constitution of the United States; and the article of the Constitution which says to these States that they shall deliver up fugitives from service is as binding in honor and conscience as any other article. . . . What right have they, in their legislative capacity or any other capacity, to endeavor to get round this Constitution, or to embarrass the free exercise of the rights secured by the Constitution to the persons whose slaves escape from them? None at all; none at all. Neither in the forum of conscience, nor before the face of the Constitution, are they, in my opinion, justified in such an attempt. . . .

Peaceable secession is an utter impossibility.

Then, sir, there are the Abolition societies, of which I am unwilling to speak, but in regard to which I have very clear notions and opinions. I do not think them useful. I think their operations for the last twenty years have produced nothing good or valuable. At the same time, I believe thousands of their members to be honest and good men, perfectly well-meaning men. They have excited feelings; they think they must do something for the cause of liberty; and, in their sphere of action, they do not see what else they can do than to contribute to an Abolition press, or an Abolition society, or to pay an Abolition lecturer. I do not mean to impute gross motives even to the leaders of these societies, but I am not blind to the consequences of their proceedings. I cannot but see what

mischiefs their interference with the South has produced. And is it not plain to every man? . . .

SECESSION WITHOUT WAR IS IMPOSSIBLE

Mr. President, I should much prefer to have heard from every member on this floor declarations of opinion that this Union could never be dissolved, than the declaration of opinion by any body, that, in any case, under the pressure of any circumstances, such a dissolution was possible. I hear with distress and anguish the word "secession," especially when it falls from the lips of those who are patriotic, and known to the country, and known all over the world, for their political services. Secession! Peaceable secession! Sir, your eyes and mine are never destined to see that miracle. The dismemberment of this vast country without convulsion! The breaking up of the fountains of the great deep without ruffling the surface! Who is so foolish, I beg every body's pardon, as to expect to see any such thing? Sir, he who sees these States, now revolving in harmony around a common centre, and expects to see them quit their places and fly off without convulsion, may look the next hour to see the heavenly bodies rush from their spheres, and jostle against each other in the realms of space, without causing the wreck of the universe. There can be no such thing as a peaceable secession. Peaceable secession is an utter impossibility. Is the great Constitution under which we live, covering this whole country, is it to be thawed and melted away by secession, as the snows on the mountain melt under the influence of a vernal sun, disappear almost unobserved, and run off? No, sir! No, sir! I will not state what might produce the disruption of the Union; but, sir, I see as plainly as I see the sun in heaven what that disruption itself must produce; I see that it must produce war. . . .

And now, Mr. President, instead of speaking of the possibility or utility of secession, instead of dwelling in those caverns of darkness, instead of groping with those ideas so full of all that is horrid and horrible, let us come out into the light of day; let us enjoy the fresh air of Liberty and Union; let us cherish those hopes which belong to us; let us devote ourselves to those great objects that are fit for our consideration and our action; let us raise our conceptions to the magnitude and the importance of the duties that devolve upon us; let our comprehension be as broad as the country for which we act, our aspirations as high as its certain destiny; let us not be pigmies in a case that calls for men. Never did there devolve on any generation of men higher trusts than now devolve upon us, for the preservation of this Constitution and the harmony and peace of all who are destined to live under it. Let us make our generation one of the strongest and brightest links in that golden chain which is destined,

I fondly believe, to grapple the people of all the States to this Constitution for ages to come.

FOR FURTHER READING

William W. Freehling, *The Road to Disunion: Secessionists at Bay, 1776–1854.* New York: Oxford University Press, 1990.

Michael F. Holt, *The Fate of Their Country: Politicians, Slavery Extension, and the Coming of the Civil War.* New York: Hill and Wang, 2004.

Merrill D. Peterson, *The Great Triumvirate: Webster, Clay, and Calhoun.* New York: Oxford University Press, 1988.

John C. Waugh, *On the Brink of Civil War: The Compromise of 1850 and How It Changed the Course of American History.* Wilmington, DE: Scholarly Resources, 2003.

Viewpoint 29A

Constitutional Rights Do Not Extend to Blacks (1857)

Roger Taney (1777–1864)

INTRODUCTION *Roger Taney was the chief justice of the U.S. Supreme Court from 1836 until his death in 1864. He is best remembered for a single case: Dred Scott v. John F.A. Sandford, in which Taney attempted to interject the Supreme Court into the national debate over slavery and the power of Congress to regulate it.*

Congress and the nation were enmeshed in controversy over the extension of slavery to the western territories, and whether new states, as they were admitted, would allow slavery. In the 1787 Northwest Ordinance and the 1820 Missouri Compromise, Congress forbade the introduction of slavery into western territories north of certain latitudes, thus dividing the country into slave and free regions. Dred Scott was a slave who had accompanied his master from Missouri, where slavery was legal, to the state of Illinois and the Wisconsin Territory, where slavery was forbidden. Scott's master died shortly after the two returned to Missouri. Scott, backed by abolitionists, sued the widow for his freedom in 1846 on the grounds that his residence in a free state and free territory had ended his bondage. The case ultimately reached the U.S. Supreme Court, which ruled against Scott in 1857. Each of the nine justices in the 7 to 2 decision wrote a separate opinion on the case; the following viewpoint is excerpted from Taney's ruling.

The Dred Scott case involved three important issues. One was whether Scott's residence in a free state effectively freed him from slavery. A second was the constitutionality of the 1820 Missouri Compromise. Taney ruled against Scott on both these matters, concluding that Congress had no power to regulate slavery in the

territories and that the Missouri Compromise was unconstitutional. The excerpts reprinted here concentrate on a third issue: whether Scott was a citizen of Missouri and thus able to sue in a federal court. Taney argues that slaves and their black descendants were never meant to be part of the political community of citizens envisioned by the writers of the U.S. Constitution, and that Scott had no legal standing as a U.S. citizen.

Rather than settling the nation's controversy over slavery, as Taney had hoped, the Dred Scott decision instead intensified it. Dred Scott was freed in 1857 (he had been purchased by abolitionists who had planned to emancipate Scott in any case); he died in 1858. The decision itself was nullified after the Civil War by the Thirteenth and Fourteenth Amendments to the U.S. Constitution.

What reasoning and historical evidence does Taney use in arguing the language in the Declaration of Independence stating that "all men are created equal" does not refer to blacks? Which clauses in the Constitution does he cite to argue that the document treats blacks as noncitizens?

The question is simply this: Can a negro, whose ancestors were imported into this country, and sold as slaves, become a member of the political community formed and brought into existence by the Constitution of the United States, and as such become entitled to all the rights, and privileges, and immunities, guarantied by that instrument to the citizen? One of which rights is the privilege of suing in a court of the United States in the cases specified in the Constitution.

CAN BLACKS BE CITIZENS?

It will be observed, that the plea applies to that class of persons only whose ancestors were negroes of the African race, and imported into this country, and sold and held as slaves. The only matter in issue before the court, therefore, is, whether the descendants of such slaves, when they shall be emancipated, or who are born of parents who had become free before their birth, are citizens of a State, in the sense in which the word citizen is used in the Constitution of the United States. And this being the only matter in dispute on the pleadings, the court must be understood as speaking in this opinion of that class only, that is, of those persons who are the descendants of Africans who were imported into this country, and sold as slaves....

The Constitution has conferred on Congress the right to establish a uniform rule of naturalization, and

From Roger Taney's majority opinion in the *Dred Scott* case, as recorded in the *Report of the Decision of the Supreme Court of the United States and the Opinions of the Judges Thereof, in the Case of Dred Scott v. John F.A. Sandford* (Washington, D.C., 1857).

this right is evidently exclusive, and has always been held by this court to be so. Consequently, no State, since the adoption of the Constitution, can by naturalizing an alien invest him with the rights and privileges secured to a citizen of a State under the Federal Government. . . .

The question then arises, whether the provisions of the Constitution, in relation to the personal rights and privileges to which the citizen of a State should be entitled, embraced the negro African race, at that time in this country, or who might afterwards be imported, who had then or should afterwards be made free in any State; and to put it in the power of a single State to make him a citizen of the United States, and endue him with the full rights of citizenship in every other State without their consent? Does the Constitution of the United States act upon him whenever he shall be made free under the laws of a State, and raised there to the rank of a citizen, and immediately clothe him with all the privileges of a citizen in every other State, and in its own courts?

The court thinks the affirmative of these propositions cannot be maintained. And if it cannot, the plaintiff in error [Dred Scott] could not be a citizen of the State of Missouri, within the meaning of the Constitution of the United States, and, consequently, was not entitled to sue in its courts.

MEMBERS OF THE POLITICAL BODY

It is true, every person, and every class and description of persons, who were at the time of the adoption of the Constitution recognised as citizens in the several States, became also citizens of this new political body; but none other; it was formed by them, and for them and their posterity, but for no one else. And the personal rights and privileges guarantied to citizens of this new sovereignty were intended to embrace those only who were then members of the several State communities, or who should afterwards by birthright or otherwise become members, according to the provisions of the Constitution and the principles on which it was founded. It was the union of those who were at that time members of distinct and separate political communities into one political family, whose power, for certain specified purposes, was to extend over the whole territory of the United States. And it gave to each citizen rights and privileges outside of his State which he did not before possess, and placed him in every other State upon a perfect equality with its own citizens as to rights of person and rights of property; it made him a citizen of the United States.

It becomes necessary, therefore, to determine who were citizens of the several States when the Constitution was adopted. And in order to do this, we must recur to the Governments and institutions of the thirteen colonies, when they separated from Great Britain and formed new sovereignties, and took their places in the family of independent nations. We must inquire who, at that time, were recognised as the people or citizens of a State, whose rights and liberties had been outraged by the English Government; and who declared their independence, and assumed the powers of Government to defend their rights by force of arms.

In the opinion of the court, the legislation and histories of the times, and the language used in the Declaration of Independence, show, that neither the class of persons who had been imported as slaves, nor their descendants, whether they had become free or not, were then acknowledged as a part of the people, nor intended to be included in the general words used in that memorable instrument.

It is difficult at this day to realize the state of public opinion in relation to that unfortunate race, which prevailed in the civilized and enlightened portions of the world at the time of the Declaration of Independence, and when the Constitution of the United States was framed and adopted. But the public history of every European nation displays it in a manner too plain to be mistaken.

AN INFERIOR RACE

They had for more than a century before been regarded as beings of an inferior order, and altogether unfit to associate with the white race, either in social or political relations; and so far inferior, that they had no rights which the white man was bound to respect; and that the negro might justly and lawfully be reduced to slavery for his benefit. He was bought and sold, and treated as an ordinary article of merchandise and traffic, whenever a profit could be made by it. This opinion was at that time fixed and universal in the civilized portion of the white race. . . .

And in no nation was this opinion more firmly fixed or more uniformly acted upon than by the English Government and English people. They not only seized them on the coast of Africa, and sold them or held them in slavery for their own use; but they took them as ordinary articles of merchandise to every country where they could make a profit on them, and were far more extensively engaged in this commerce than any other nation in the world.

The opinion thus entertained and acted upon in England was naturally impressed upon the colonies they founded on this side of the Atlantic. And, accordingly, a negro of the African race was regarded by them as an article of property, and held, and bought and sold as such, in every one of the thirteen colonies which united in the Declaration of Independence, and afterwards formed the Constitution of the United States. The slaves were more or less numerous in the different colonies, as slave labor was found more or less profitable. But no one seems to have doubted the correctness of the prevailing opinion of the time.

The legislation of the different colonies furnishes positive and indisputable proof of this fact. . . .

They show that a perpetual and impassable barrier was intended to be erected between the white race and the one which they had reduced to slavery, and governed as subjects with absolute and despotic power, and which they then looked upon as so far below them in the scale of created beings, that intermarriages between white persons and negroes or mulattoes were regarded as unnatural and immoral, and punished as crimes, not only in the parties, but in the person who joined them in marriage. And no distinction in this respect was made between the free negro or mulatto and the slave, but this stigma, of the deepest degradation, was fixed upon the whole race.

We refer to these historical facts for the purpose of showing the fixed opinions concerning that race, upon which the statesmen of that day spoke and acted. It is necessary to do this, in order to determine whether the general terms used in the Constitution of the United States, as to the rights of man and the rights of the people, was intended to include them, or to give to them or their posterity the benefit of any of its provisions.

DECLARATION OF INDEPENDENCE

The language of the Declaration of Independence is equally conclusive:

It begins by declaring that, "when in the course of human events it becomes necessary for one people to dissolve the political bands which have connected them with another, and to assume among the powers of the earth the separate and equal station to which the laws of nature and nature's God entitle them, a decent respect for the opinions of mankind requires that they should declare the causes which impel them to the separation."

It then proceeds to say: "We hold these truths to be serf-evident: that all men are created equal: that they are endowed by their Creator with certain unalienable rights; that among them is life, liberty, and the pursuit of happiness; that to secure these rights, Governments are instituted, deriving their just powers from the consent of the governed."

The general words above quoted would seem to embrace the whole human family, and if they were used in a similar instrument at this day would be so understood. But it is too clear for dispute, that the enslaved African race were not intended to be included, and formed no part of the people who framed and adopted this declaration; for if the language, as understood in

that day, would embrace them, the conduct of the distinguished men who framed the Declaration of Independence would have been utterly and flagrantly inconsistent with the principles they asserted; and instead of the sympathy of mankind, to which they so confidently appealed, they would have deserved and received universal rebuke and reprobation.

Yet the men who framed this declaration were great men—high in literary acquirements—high in their sense of honor, and incapable of asserting principles inconsistent with those on which they were acting. They perfectly understood the meaning of the language they used, and how it would be understood by others; and they knew that it would not in any part of the civilized world be supposed to embrace the negro race, which, by common consent, had been excluded from civilized Governments and the family of nations, and doomed to slavery. They spoke and acted according to the then established doctrines and principles, and in the ordinary language of the day, and no one misunderstood them. The unhappy black race were separated from the white by indelible marks, and laws long before established, and were never thought of or spoken of except as property, and when the claims of the owner or the profit of the trader were supposed to need protection.

There are two clauses in the Constitution which point directly . . . to the negro race as a separate class of persons, and show clearly that they were not regarded as . . . citizens.

This state of public opinion had undergone no change when the Constitution was adopted, as is equally evident from its provisions and language.

THE U.S. CONSTITUTION

The brief preamble sets forth by whom it was formed, for what purposes, and for whose benefit and protection. It declares that it is formed by the *people* of the United States; that is to say by those who were members of the different political communities in the several States; and its great object is declared to be to secure the blessings of liberty to themselves and their posterity. It speaks in general terms of the *people* of the United States, and of *citizens* of the several States, when it is providing for the exercise of the powers granted or the privileges secured to the citizen. It does not define what description of persons are intended to be included under these terms, or who shall be regarded as a citizen and one of the people. It uses them as terms so well understood, that no further description or definition was necessary.

But there are two clauses in the Constitution which point directly and specifically to the negro race as a separate class of persons, and show clearly that they were not regarded as a portion of the people or citizens of the Government they formed.

One of these clauses reserves to each of the thirteen States the right to import slaves until the year 1808, if it thinks proper. And the importation which it thus sanctions was unquestionably of persons of the race of which we are speaking, as the traffic in slaves in the United States had always been confined to them. And by the other provision the States pledge themselves to each other to maintain the right of property of the master, by delivering up to him any slave who may have escaped from his service, and be found within their respective territories. By the first above-mentioned clause, therefore, the right to purchase and hold this property is directly sanctioned and authorized for twenty years by the people who framed the Constitution. And by the second, they pledge themselves to maintain and uphold the right of the master in the manner specified, as long as the Government they then formed should endure. And these two provisions show, conclusively, that neither the description of persons therein referred to, nor their descendants, were embraced in any of the other provisions of the Constitution; for certainly these two clauses were not intended to confer on them or their posterity the blessings of liberty, or any of the personal rights so carefully provided for the citizen.

No one of that race had ever migrated to the United States voluntarily; all of them had been brought here as articles of merchandise. The number that had been emancipated at that time were but few in comparison with those held in slavery; and they were identified in the public mind with the race to which they belonged, and regarded as a part of the slave population rather than the free. It is obvious that they were not even in the minds of the framers of the Constitution when they were conferring special rights and privileges upon the citizens of a State in every other part of the Union.

Indeed, when we look to the condition of this race in the several States at the time, it is impossible to believe that these rights and privileges were intended to be extended to them.

It is very true, that in that portion of the Union where the labor of the negro race was found to be unsuited to the climate and unprofitable to the master, but few slaves were held at the time of the Declaration of Independence; and when the Constitution was adopted, it had entirely worn out in one of them, and measures had been taken for its gradual abolition in several others. But this change had not been produced by any change of opinion in relation to this race; but because it was discovered, from experience, that slave labor was unsuited to the climate and productions of these States: for some of the States, where it had ceased or nearly ceased to exist, were actively engaged in the slave trade, procuring cargoes on the coast of Africa, and transporting them for sale to those parts of the Union where their labor was found to be profitable, and suited to the climate and productions. And this traffic was openly carried on, and fortunes accumulated by it, without reproach from the people of the States where they resided. And it can hardly be supposed that, in the States where it was then countenanced in its worst form—that is, in the seizure and transportation—the people could have regarded those who were emancipated as entitled to equal rights with themselves.

STATE LAWS

And we may here again refer, in support of this proposition to the plain and unequivocal language of the laws of the several States, some passed after the Declaration of Independence and before the Constitution was adopted, and some since the Government went into operation. . . .

It would be impossible to enumerate and compress in the space usually allotted to an opinion of a court, the various laws, marking the condition of this race, which were passed from time to time after the Revolution, and before and since the adoption of the Constitution of the United States. In addition to those already referred to, it is sufficient to say, that Chancellor [James] Kent, whose accuracy and research no one will question, states in the sixth edition of his *Commentaries*, (published in 1848, 2 vol., 258, note b,) that in no part of the country except Maine, did the African race, in point of fact, participate equally with the whites in the exercise of civil and political rights.

The legislation of the States therefore shows, in a manner not to be mistaken, the inferior and subject condition of that race at the time the Constitution was adopted. . . . It cannot be believed that the large slaveholding States regarded them as included in the word citizens, or would have consented to a Constitution, which might compel them to receive them in that character from another State. . . .

What the construction was at that time, we think can hardly admit of doubt. We have the language of the Declaration of Independence and of the Articles of Confederation, in addition to the plain words of the Constitution itself; we have the legislation of the different States, before, about the time, and since, the Constitution was adopted; we have the legislation of Congress, from the time of its adoption to a recent period; and we have the constant and uniform action of the Executive Department, all concurring together, and leading to the same result. And if anything in relation to the construction of the Constitution can be regarded as settled, it is that which we now give to the word "citizen" and the word "people."

And upon a full and careful consideration of the subject, the court is of opinion, that, upon the facts stated in the plea in abatement, Dred Scott was not a citizen of Missouri within the meaning of the Constitution of the United States, and not entitled as such to sue in its courts.

Constitutional Rights Do Extend to Blacks (1857)

Benjamin Robbins Curtis (1809–1874)

INTRODUCTION *Massachusetts-born Benjamin Robbins Curtis was a Supreme Court justice from 1851 to 1857. He is most famous for being one of two dissenters in the* Dred Scott *case of 1857. Curtis resigned from the court shortly afterwards in protest of that decision.*

Dred Scott was a slave who had sued for his freedom on the grounds that he had resided with his master for a time in a state where slavery was outlawed. The Supreme Court ruled against him, in part on the basis that slaves and their descendants had no legal standing as citizens under the U.S. Constitution. In the following excerpts from his dissenting opinion, Curtis challenges this argument. He contends that the Constitution contains no provisions excluding blacks from U.S. citizenship, that the states themselves have the power to determine citizenship, and that all citizens of individual states are also citizens of the United States.

What are the major differences between the analysis of Curtis and that of Roger Taney, author of the opposing viewpoint? How does Curtis respond to the argument that the Constitution was meant for whites only?

The question is, whether any person of African descent, whose ancestors were sold as slaves in the United States, can be a citizen of the United States. If any such person can be a citizen, this plaintiff has the right to the judgment of the court that he is so; for no cause is shown by the plea why he is not so, except his descent and the slavery of his ancestors.

The first section of the second article of the Constitution uses the language, "a citizen of the United States at the time of the adoption of the Constitution." One mode of approaching this question is, to inquire who were citizens of the United States at the time of the adoption of the Constitution.

From Benjamin Robbins Curtis's dissenting opinion in the *Dred Scott* case, as recorded in the *Report of the Decision of the Supreme Court of the United States and the Opinions of the Judges Thereof, in the Case of Dred Scott v. John F.A. Sandford* (Washington, D.C., 1857).

Citizens of the United States at the time of the adoption of the Constitution can have been no other than citizens of the United States under the Confederation. By the Articles of Confederation, a Government was organized, the style whereof was, "The United States of America." This Government was in existence when the Constitution was framed and proposed for adoption, and was to be superseded by the new Government of the United States of America, organized under the Constitution. When, therefore, the Constitution speaks of citizenship of the United States, existing at the time of the adoption of the Constitution, it must necessarily refer to citizenship under the Government which existed prior to and at the time of such adoption. . . .

CITIZENS OF THE STATES

That Government was simply a confederacy of the several States, possessing a few defined powers over subjects of general concern, each State retaining every power, jurisdiction, and right, not expressly delegated to the United States in Congress assembled. And no power was thus delegated to the Government of the Confederation, to act on any question of citizenship, or to make any rules in respect thereto. The whole matter was left to stand upon the action of the several States, and to the natural consequence of such action, that the citizens of each State should be citizens of that Confederacy into which that State had entered, the style whereof was, "The United States of America."

To determine whether any free persons, descended from Africans held in slavery, were citizens of the United States under the Confederation, and consequently at the time of the adoption of the Constitution of the United States, it is only necessary to know whether any such persons were citizens of either of the States under the Confederation, at the time of the adoption of the Constitution.

Of this there can be no doubt. At the time of the ratification of the Articles of Confederation, all free native-born inhabitants of the States of New Hampshire, Massachusetts, New York, New Jersey, and North Carolina, though descended from African slaves, were not only citizens of those States, but such of them as had the other necessary qualifications possessed the franchise of electors, on equal terms with other citizens. . . .

Did the Constitution of the United States deprive them or their descendants of citizenship?

THE CONSTITUTION AND BLACK CITIZENSHIP

That Constitution was ordained and established by the people of the United States, through the action, in each State, of those persons who were qualified by its laws to act thereon, in behalf of themselves and all other citizens of that State. In some of the States, as we have seen, colored persons were among those qualified by law to act on this subject. These colored persons were not only included in the body of "the people of the United States," by whom the Constitution was ordained and established, but in at least five of the States they had the power to act, and doubtless did act, by their suffrages, upon the question of its adoption. It would be strange, if we were to find in that instrument anything which deprived of their citizenship any part of the people of the United States who were among those by whom it was established.

I can find nothing in the Constitution which, *proprio vigore* [by its own force], deprives of their citizenship any class of persons who were citizens of the United States at the time of its adoption, or who should be native-born citizens of any State after its adoption; nor any power enabling Congress to disfranchise persons born on the soil of any State, and entitled to citizenship of such State by its Constitution and laws. And my opinion is, that, under the Constitution of the United States, every free person born on the soil of a State, who is a citizen of that State by force of its Constitution or laws, is also a citizen of the United States. . . .

It may be proper here to notice some supposed objections to this view of the subject.

It has been often asserted that the Constitution was made exclusively by and for the white race. It has already been shown that in five of the thirteen original States, colored persons then possessed the elective franchise, and were among those by whom the Constitution was ordained and established. If so, it is not true, in point or fact, that the Constitution was made exclusively by the white race. And that it was made exclusively for the white race is, in my opinion, not only an assumption not warranted by anything in the Constitution, but contradicted by its opening declaration, that it was ordained and established by the people of the United States, for themselves and their posterity. And as free colored persons were then citizens of at least five States, and so in every sense part of the people of the United States, they were among those for whom and whose posterity the Constitution was ordained and established.

Again, it has been objected, that if the Constitution has left to the several States the rightful power to determine who of their inhabitants shall be citizens of the United States, the States may make aliens citizens.

The answer is obvious. The Constitution has left to the States the determination what persons, born within their respective limits, shall acquire by birth citizenship of the United States; it has not left to them any power to prescribe any rule for the removal of the disabilities of alienage. This power is exclusively in Congress.

It has been further objected, that if free colored persons, born within a particular State, and made citizens of that State by its Constitution and laws, are thereby made citizens of the United States, then, under the second section of the fourth article of the Constitution, such persons would be entitled to all the privileges and immunities of citizens in the several States; and if so, then colored persons could vote, and be eligible to not only Federal offices, but offices even in those States whose Constitutions and laws disqualify colored persons from voting or being elected to office.

But this position rests upon an assumption which I deem untenable. Its basis is, that no one can be deemed a citizen of the United States who is not entitled to enjoy all the privileges and franchises which are conferred on any citizen. That this is not true, under the Constitution of the United States, seems to me clear.

CITIZENS AND THEIR RIGHTS

A naturalized citizen cannot be President of the United States, nor a Senator till after the lapse of nine years, nor a Representative till after the lapse of seven years, from his naturalization. Yet, as soon as naturalized, he is certainly a citizen of the United States. Nor is any inhabitant of the District of Columbia, or of either of the Territories, eligible to the office of Senator or Representative in Congress, though they may be citizens of the United States. So, in all the States, numerous persons, though citizens, cannot vote, or cannot hold office, either on account of their age, or sex, or the want of the necessary legal qualifications. The truth is, that citizenship, under the Constitution of the United States, is not dependent on the possession of any particular political or even of all civil rights; and any attempt so to define it must lead to error. To what citizens the elective franchise shall be confided, is a question to be determined by each State, in accordance with its own views of the necessities or expediencies of its condition. What civil rights shall be enjoyed by its citizens, and whether all shall enjoy the same, or how they may be gained or lost, are to be determined in the same way. . . .

It has sometimes been urged that colored persons are shown not to be citizens of the United States by the fact that the naturalization laws apply only to white persons. But whether a person born in the United States be or be not a citizen, cannot depend on laws which refer only to aliens, and do not affect the *status* of persons born in the United States. The utmost effect which can be attributed to them is, to show that Congress has not deemed it expedient generally to apply the role to colored aliens. That they might do so, if thought fit, is clear. The Constitution has not excluded them. And since that has conferred the power on Congress to naturalize colored aliens, it certainly shows color is not a necessary qualification for citizenship under the Constitution of the United States. It may be added, that the power to make colored persons citizens of the United States, under the Constitution, has been actually exercised in repeated and important instances. (See the Treaties with the Choctaws, of September 27, 1830, art. 14: with the Cherokees, of May 23, 1836, art. 12; Treaty of Guadalupe Hidalgo [with Mexico following the Mexican War], February 2, 1848, art. 8.)

I do not deem it necessary to review at length the legislation of Congress having more or less bearing on the citizenship of colored persons. It does not seem to me to have any considerable tendency to prove that it has been considered by the legislative department of the Government, that no such persons are citizens of the United States. Undoubtedly they have been debarred from the exercise of particular rights or privileges extended to white persons, but, I believe, always in terms which, by implication, admit they may be citizens. Thus the act of May 17, 1792, for the organization of the militia, directs the enrollment of "every free, able-bodied, white male citizen." An assumption that none but white persons are citizens, would be as inconsistent with the just import of this language, as that all citizens are able-bodied, or males....

CONCLUSIONS

The conclusions at which I have arrived on this part of the case are:

First. That the free native-born citizens of each State are citizens of the United States.

Second. That as free colored persons born within some of the States are citizens of those States, such persons are also citizens of the United States.

———————■———————

I dissent...from...the Opinion...that a person of African descent cannot be a citizen of the United States.

———————■———————

Third. That every such citizen, residing in any State, has the right to sue and is liable it be sued in the Federal courts, as a citizen of that State in which he resides.

Fourth. That as the plea to the jurisdiction in this case shows no facts, except that the plaintiff was of African descent, and his ancestors were sold as slaves, and as these facts are not inconsistent with his citizenship of the United States, and his residence in the State of Missouri, the plea to the jurisdiction was bad, and the judgment of the Circuit Court overruling it was correct.

I dissent, therefore, from that part of the opinion of the majority of the court, in which it is held that a person of African descent cannot be a citizen of the United States.

FOR FURTHER READING

Walter Ehrlich, *They Have No Rights: Dred Scott's Struggle for Freedom.* Westport, CT: Greenwood Press, 1979.

Don. E. Fehrenbacher, *The Dred Scott Case: Its Significance in American Law and Politics.* New York: Oxford University Press, 2001.

Paul Finkelman, *Dred Scott v. Sandford: A Brief History with Documents.* Boston: Bedford/St. Martins, 1997.

The complete Supreme Court opinions by Roger Taney and Benjamin Robbins Curtis can be found at the Oyez Project's U.S. Supreme Court Center Web site at http://www.justia.us/us/60/393/case.html.

Viewpoint 30A
Popular Sovereignty Should Settle the Slavery Question (1858)
Stephen A. Douglas (1813–1861)

INTRODUCTION *Stephen A. Douglas, U.S. senator from Illinois, was one of America's leading political figures in the 1850s. Elected to the U.S. Senate in 1846, Douglas was instrumental in passing the Compromise of 1850 and the Kansas-Nebraska Act of 1854—both attempts by Congress to resolve the issue of legalizing slavery in America's western territories. Douglas's sponsorship of these laws positioned him as the champion of "popular sovereignty"—the idea that resident settlers should decide whether to legalize slavery in their territory or state.*

By 1858 the doctrine of popular sovereignty was under attack from several quarters. For four years the Kansas territory had been beset by violent confrontations between proslavery and abolitionist settlers. Meanwhile the Supreme Court in the Dred Scott *case ruled that Congress lacked the authority to exclude slavery from the western territories—a decision that many people argued made slavery legal in all territories regardless of the wishes of their inhabitants. The Republican Party was formed to oppose the spread of slavery; the new political party fielded as its candidate for Douglas's senate seat a relatively unknown lawyer named Abraham Lincoln.*

Lincoln and Douglas held a series of seven debates on the future of slavery and of America. The following viewpoint is excerpted from Douglas's opening speech at the last debate, which was held in Alton, Illinois, on October 15, 1858. Douglas reviews what he regards as the basic issues of the debate, and makes his case for popular sovereignty as the true democratic and constitutional alternative to civil war. Douglas won the 1858 race, but two years later was defeated by Lincoln in the 1860 election for president.

What does Douglas argue to be Lincoln's three main errors? What attitudes does Douglas reveal about blacks? In 1860 Douglas was unable to garner Southern support for his presidential bid; what clues do the excerpts here provide as to why Southerners would not support him?

It is now nearly four months since the canvass between Mr. Lincoln and myself commenced. On the sixteenth of June the Republican Convention assembled at Springfield and nominated Mr. Lincoln as their candidate for the United States Senate, and he, on that occasion, delivered a speech in which he laid down what he understood to be the Republican creed and the platform on which he proposed to stand during the contest.

The principal points in that speech of Mr. Lincoln's were: First, that this government could not endure permanently divided into free and slave states, as our fathers made it; that they must all become free or all become slave; all become one thing or all become the other, otherwise this Union could not continue to exist. I give you his opinions almost in the identical language he used. His second proposition was a crusade against the Supreme Court of the United States because of the Dred Scott decision; urging as an especial reason for his opposition to that decision that it deprived the Negroes of the rights and benefits of that clause in the Constitution of the United States which guarantees to the citizens of each state all the rights, privileges, and immunities of the citizens of the several states.

On the tenth of July I returned home and delivered a speech to the people of Chicago. . . . In that speech I joined issue with Mr. Lincoln on the points which he had presented. Thus there was an issue clear and distinct made up between us on these two propositions laid down in the speech of Mr. Lincoln at Springfield and controverted by me in my reply to him at Chicago.

---■---

This Union was established on the right of each state to do as it pleased on the question of slavery.

---■---

On the next day, the eleventh of July, Mr. Lincoln replied to me at Chicago, explaining at some length, and reaffirming the positions which he had taken in his Springfield speech. In that Chicago speech he even

From *Political Debates Between Hon. Abraham Lincoln and Hon. Stephen A. Douglas, in the Celebrated Campaign of 1858*, published by Follet, Foster & Co., 1860, for the Ohio Republican State Central Committee.

went further than he had before and uttered sentiments in regard to the Negro being on an equality with the white man. . . . He insisted, in that speech, that the Declaration of Independence included the Negro in the clause, asserting that all men were created equal, and went so far as to say that if one man was allowed to take the position that it did not include the Negro, others might take the position that it did not include other men. He said that all these distinctions between this man and that man, this race and the other race, must be discarded, and we must all stand by the Declaration of Independence, declaring that all men were created equal.

LINCOLN'S THREE ERRORS

The issue thus being made up between Mr. Lincoln and myself on three points, we went before the people of the state. . . . In my speeches I confined myself closely to those three positions which he had taken, controverting his proposition that this Union could not exist as our fathers made it, divided into free and slave states, controverting his proposition of a crusade against the Supreme Court because of the Dred Scott decision, and controverting his proposition that the Declaration of Independence included and meant the Negroes as well as the white men when it declared all men to be created equal. . . . I took up Mr. Lincoln's three propositions in my several speeches, analyzed them, and pointed out what I believed to be the radical errors contained in them. First, in regard to his doctrine that this government was in violation of the law of God, which says that a house divided against itself cannot stand, I repudiated it as a slander upon the immortal framers of our Constitution. I then said, I have often repeated, and now again assert, that in my opinion our government can endure forever, divided into free and slave states as our fathers made it—each state having the right to prohibit, abolish, or sustain slavery, just as it pleases. This government was made upon the great basis of the sovereignty of the states, the right of each state to regulate its own domestic institutions to suit itself, and that right was conferred with the understanding and expectation that, inasmuch as each locality had separate interests, each locality must have different and distinct local and domestic institutions, corresponding to its wants and interests. Our fathers knew when they made the government that the laws and institutions which were well adapted to the Green Mountains of Vermont were unsuited to the rice plantations of South Carolina. They knew then, as well as we know now, that the laws and institutions which would be well adapted to the beautiful prairies of Illinois would not be suited to the mining regions of California. They knew that in a republic as broad as this, having such a variety of soil, climate, and interest, there must necessarily be a corresponding variety of local laws—the policy and institutions of each state adapted to its condition and wants. For this reason this Union was established on the right of each state to do as it pleased on the question of slavery and every other question; and the various states were not allowed to complain of, much less interfere with, the policy of their neighbors....

It was under that principle that slavery was abolished in New Hampshire, Rhode Island, Connecticut, New York, New Jersey and Pennsylvania; it was under that principle that one-half of the slaveholding states became free; it was under that principle that the number of free states increased until, from being one out of twelve states, we have grown to be the majority of states of the whole Union, with the power to control the House of Representatives and Senate, and the power, consequently, to elect a President by northern votes without the aid of a southern state. Having obtained this power under the operation of that great principle, are you now prepared to abandon the principle and declare that merely because we have the power you will wage a war against the southern states and their institutions until you force them to abolish slavery everywhere...?

I say to you that there is but one hope, one safety, for this country, and that is to stand immovably by that principle which declares the right of each state and each territory to decide these questions for themselves. This government was founded on that principle and must be administered in the same sense in which it was founded.

DECLARATION OF INDEPENDENCE FOR WHITES

But the Abolition party really think that under the Declaration of Independence the Negro is equal to the white man and that Negro equality is an inalienable right conferred by the Almighty, and hence that all human laws in violation of it are null and void. With such men it is no use for me to argue. I hold that the signers of the Declaration of Independence had no reference to Negroes at all when they declared all men to be created equal. They did not mean Negro, nor the savage Indians, nor the Fiji Islanders, nor any other barbarous race. They were speaking of white men. They alluded to men of European birth and European descent—to white men and to none others—when they declared that doctrine. I hold that this government was established on the white basis. It was established by white men for the benefit of white men and their posterity forever and should be administered by white men and none others. But it does not follow, by any means, that merely because the Negro is not a citizen, and merely because he is not our equal, that, therefore, he should be a slave. On the contrary, it does follow that we ought to extend to the Negro race, and

to all other dependent races all the rights, all the privileges, and all the immunities which they can exercise consistently with the safety of society. Humanity requires that we should give them all these privileges; Christianity commands that we should extend those privileges to them. The question then arises: What are those privileges and what is the nature and extent of them. My answer is that that is a question which each state must answer for itself. We in Illinois have decided it for ourselves. We tried slavery, kept it up for twelve years, and, finding that it was not profitable, we abolished it for that reason, and became a free state. We adopted in its stead the policy that a Negro in this state shall not be a slave and shall not be a citizen. We have a right to adopt that policy. For my part I think it is a wise and sound policy for us. You in Missouri must judge for yourselves whether it is a wise policy for you. If you choose to follow our example, very good; if you reject it, still well, it is your business, not ours. So with Kentucky. Let Kentucky adopt a policy to suit herself. If we do not like it, we will keep away from it, and if she does not like ours let her stay at home, mind her own business and let us alone. If the people of all the states will act on that great principle, and each state mind its own business, attend to its own affairs, take care of its own Negroes, and not meddle with its neighbors, then there will be peace between the North and the South, the East and the West, throughout the whole Union. Why can we not thus have peace? Why should we thus allow a sectional party to agitate this country, to array the North against the South, and convert us into enemies instead of friends, merely that a few ambitious men may ride into power on a sectional hobby?

Viewpoint 30B

Slavery Should Not Be Allowed to Spread (1858)

Abraham Lincoln (1809–1865)

INTRODUCTION *Abraham Lincoln's election to the presidency in 1860 was due in part to the national prominence he gained while campaigning unsuccessfully for the U.S. Senate in 1858. During that contest, Lincoln and his opponent, incumbent Illinois senator Stephen A. Douglas, held a series of seven public debates in which the main issues discussed were slavery and the future of the American nation.*

Lincoln, a self-taught lawyer who had served a term in Congress and had established a successful legal practice, opened his senatorial campaign with a famous speech in Springfield, Illinois. Quoting a passage from the Bible, Lincoln stated: "A house divided against itself cannot stand." I believe this government cannot endure, permanently, half slave and half free.... It will become all one thing, or all the other. This statement and others like it were attacked by Douglas, who accused Lincoln of being a radical "Black Republican" who wished to abolish slavery in all the states, promote racial equality, and whose policies would lead the nation into war. In his debates with Douglas, Lincoln denied all of these charges. The following viewpoint is excerpted from Lincoln's last speech in the debates, given in Alton, Illinois, on October 15, 1858.

On what issues does Lincoln express agreement with Stephen A. Douglas, his opponent? What does he say is their fundamental difference? What position does Lincoln take on the abolition of slavery?

The Judge [Stephen Douglas] alludes very often in the course of his remarks to the exclusive right which the states have to decide the whole thing [slavery] for themselves. I agree with him very readily that the different states have that right. He is but fighting a man of straw when he assumes that I am contending against the right of the states to do as they please about it. Our controversy with him is in regard to the new territories. We agree that when the states come in as states they have the right and the power to do as they please. We have no power as citizens of the free states, or in our federal capacity as members of the federal Union through the general government, to disturb slavery in the states where it exists.

We profess constantly that we have no more inclination than belief in the power of the government to disturb it; yet we are driven constantly to defend ourselves from the assumption that we are warring upon the rights of the *states*. What I insist upon is that the new territories shall be kept free from it while in the territorial condition. Judge Douglas assumes that we have no interest in them, that we have no right whatever to interfere. I think we have some interest. I think that as white men we have.

Do we not wish for an outlet for our surplus population, if I may so express myself? Do we not feel an interest in getting to that outlet with such institutions as we would like to have prevail there? If you go to the territory opposed to slavery, and another man comes upon the same ground with his slaves, upon the assumption that the things are equal, it turns out that he has the equal right all his way, and you have no part of it your way. If he goes in and makes it a slave territory and, by consequence, a slave state, is it not time that those who desire to have it a free state were on equal ground?

Let me suggest it in a different way. How many Democrats are there about here who have left slave states and come into the free state of Illinois to get rid of the institution of slavery? I reckon there are a thousand and one. I will ask you, if the policy you are now advocating had prevailed when this country was in a territorial

condition, where would you have gone to get rid of it? Where would you have found your free state or territory to go to? And when, hereafter, for any cause, the people in this place shall desire to find new homes, if they wish to be rid of the institution, where will they find the place to go to? ...

[Slavery] should ... be treated as a wrong, and one of the methods ... is to *make provision that it shall grow no larger.*

Now irrespective of the moral aspect of this question as to whether there is a right or wrong in enslaving a Negro, I am still in favor of our new territories being in such a condition that white men may find a home— may find some spot where they can better their condition— where they can settle upon new soil and better their condition in life. I am in favor of this not merely (I must say it here as I have elsewhere) for our own people who are born amongst us, but as an outlet for *free white people everywhere*, the world over—in which Hans and Baptiste and Patrick, and all other men from all the world, may find new homes and better their conditions in life.

THE REAL ISSUE

I have stated upon former occasions, and I may as well state again, what I understand to be the real issue in this controversy between Judge Douglas and myself. On the point of my wanting to make war between the free and the slave states, there has been no issue between us. So, too, when he assumes that I am in favor of introducing a perfect social and political equality between the white and black races. These are false issues, upon which Judge Douglas has tried to force the controversy. There is no foundation in truth for the charge that I maintain either of these propositions. The real issue in this controversy—the one pressing upon every mind— is the sentiment on the part of one class that looks upon the institution of slavery *as a wrong* and of another class that *does not* look upon it as a wrong. The sentiment that contemplates the institution of slavery in this country as a wrong is the sentiment of the Republican party. It is the sentiment around which all their actions—all their arguments circle—from which all their propositions radiate. They look upon it as being a moral, social, and political wrong; and, while they contemplate it as such, they nevertheless have due regard for its actual existence among us, and the difficulties of getting rid of it in any satisfactory way and to all the constitutional obligations

From *Political Debates Between Hon. Abraham Lincoln and Hon. Stephen A. Douglas, in the Celebrated Campaign of 1858*, published by Follet, Foster & Co., 1860, for the Ohio Republican State Central Committee.

thrown about it. Yet having a due regard for these, they desire a policy in regard to it that looks to its not creating any more danger. They insist that it should, as far as may be, *be treated* as a wrong, and one of the methods of treating it as a wrong is to *make provision that it shall grow no larger.* They also desire a policy that looks to a peaceful end of slavery at some time as being wrong. These are the views they entertain in regard to it as I understand them; and all their sentiments—all their arguments and propositions—are brought within this range. I have said, and I repeat it here, that if there be a man amongst us who does not think that the institution of slavery is wrong in any one of the aspects of which I have spoken, he is misplaced and ought not to be with us. And if there be a man amongst us who is so impatient of it as a wrong as to disregard its actual presence among us and the difficulty of getting rid of it suddenly in a satisfactory way, and to disregard the constitutional obligations thrown about it, that man is misplaced if he is on our platform. We disclaim sympathy with him in practical action. He is not placed properly with us.

On this subject of treating it as a wrong, and limiting its spread, let me say a word. Has anything ever threatened the existence of this Union save and except this very institution of slavery? What is it that we hold most dear amongst us? Our own liberty and prosperity. What has ever threatened our liberty and prosperity save and except this institution of slavery? If this is true, how do you propose to improve the condition of things by enlarging slavery—by spreading it out and making it bigger? You may have a wen or cancer upon your person and not be able to cut it out lest you bleed to death; but surely it is no way to cure it, to engraft it and spread it over your whole body. That is no proper way of treating what you regard a wrong. You see this peaceful way of dealing with it as a wrong—restricting the spread of it, and not allowing it to go into new countries where it has not already existed. That is the peaceful way, the old-fashioned way, the way in which the fathers themselves set us the example.

IS SLAVERY WRONG?

On the other hand, I have said there is a sentiment which treats it as *not* being wrong. That is the Democratic sentiment of this day. I do not mean to say that every man who stands within that range positively asserts that it is right. That class will include all who positively assert that it is right, and all who like Judge Douglas treat it as indifferent and do not say it is either right or wrong. These two classes of men fall within the general class of those who do not look upon it as a wrong. . . .

The Democratic policy in regard to that institution will not tolerate the merest breath, the slightest hint, of

the least degree of wrong about it. Try it by some of Judge Douglas' arguments. He says he "don't care whether it is voted up or voted down" in the territories. I do not care myself in dealing with that expression, whether it is intended to be expressive of his individual sentiments on the subject or only of the national policy he desires to have established. It is alike valuable for my purpose. Any man can say that who does not see anything wrong in slavery, but no man can logically say it who does see a wrong in it; because no man can logically say he does not care whether a wrong is voted up or voted down. He may say he does not care whether an indifferent thing is voted up or down, but he must logically have a choice between a right thing and a wrong thing. He contends that whatever community wants slaves has a right to have them. So they have if it is not a wrong. But if it is a wrong, he cannot say people have a right to do wrong. He says that, upon the score of equality, slaves should be allowed to go in a new territory, like other property. This is strictly logical if there is no difference between it and other property. If it and other property are equal, his argument is entirely logical. But if you insist that one is wrong and the other right, there is no use to institute a comparison between right and wrong. You may turn over everything in the Democratic policy from beginning to end, whether in the shape it takes on the statute book, in the shape it takes in the Dred Scott decision, in the shape it takes in conversation, or the shape it takes in short maxim-like arguments—it everywhere carefully excludes the idea that there is anything wrong in it.

That is the real issue. That is the issue that will continue in this country when these poor tongues of Judge Douglas and myself shall be silent. It is the eternal struggle between these two principles—right and wrong—throughout the world. They are the two principles that have stood face to face from the beginning of time and will ever continue to struggle. The one is the common right of humanity and the other the divine right of kings. It is the same principle in whatever shape it develops itself. It is the same spirit that says, "You work and toil and earn bread, and I'll eat it." No matter in what shape it comes, whether from the mouth of a king who seeks to bestride the people of his own nation and live by the fruit of their labor, or from one race of men as an apology for enslaving another race, it is the same tyrannical principle.

FOR FURTHER READING

Eric Foner, *Free Soil, Free Labor, Free Men: The Ideology of the Republican Party Before the Civil War.* New York: Oxford University Press, 1970.

Harold Holzer, ed., *The Lincoln-Douglas Debates.* New York: HarperCollins, 1993.

Robert W. Johannsen, *Stephen A. Douglas.* Champaign: University of Illinois Press, 1997.

The complete texts of all the Lincoln-Douglas debates can be found on the Lincoln/Net Web site, a project of Northern Illinois University, at http://lincoln.lib.niu.edu/debates.html.

Viewpoint 31A

Secession Is Justified (1861)

South Carolina Declaration

INTRODUCTION *Many leaders of the Southern states threatened to secede from the Union if Abraham Lincoln, the Republican presidential candidate in 1860, was elected president. South Carolina's state legislature was in session when news arrived of Lincoln's election, and legislators immediately called for a special secession convention. On December 20, 1860, the state became the first to declare separation from the United States. The convention presented reasons for seceding in the form of a declaration—excerpted here—analogous to America's 1776 Declaration of Independence from Great Britain. A few weeks later, representatives from South Carolina and six other states established the Confederate States of America.*

What legal arguments does the secession convention make concerning the United States? What grievances against the Northern states does this document describe? What similarities do you find between this viewpoint and the views of John Calhoun as expressed in viewpoint 28A?

The people of the state of South Carolina, in convention assembled, on the 2nd day of April, A.D. 1852, declared that the frequent violations of the Constitution of the United States by the federal government, and its encroachments upon the reserved rights of the states, fully justified this state in their withdrawal from the federal Union; but in deference to the opinions and wishes of the other slaveholding states, she forbore at that time to exercise this right. Since that time, these encroachments have continued to increase, and further forbearance ceases to be a virtue.

And, now, the state of South Carolina, having resumed her separate and equal place among nations, deems it due to herself, to the remaining United States of America, and to the nations of the world, that she should declare the immediate causes which have led to this act.

THE RIGHT OF SELF-GOVERNMENT

In the year 1765, that portion of the British empire embracing Great Britain undertook to make laws for

From *The Rebellion Record: A Diary of American Events, with Documents, Narratives, Illustrative Incidents, Poetry, etc. etc.* vol. 1, edited by Frank Moore (New York: Putnam, 1861).

the government of that portion composed of the thirteen American colonies. A struggle for the right of self-government ensued, which resulted, on the 4th of July, 1776, in a Declaration, by the colonies, "that they are, and of right ought to be, FREE AND INDEPENDENT STATES; and that, as free and independent states, they have full power to levy war, conclude peace, contract alliances, establish commerce, and to do all other acts and things which independent states may of right do." . . .

In pursuance of this Declaration of Independence, each of the thirteen states proceeded to exercise its separate sovereignty; adopted for itself a constitution, and appointed officers for the administration of government in all its departments—Legislative, Executive, and Judicial. For purposes of defense, they united their arms and their counsels, and, in 1778, they entered into a league known as the Articles of Confederation. . . .

Under this Confederation, the War of the Revolution was carried on; and on the 3rd of September, 1783, the contest ended, and a definite treaty was signed by Great Britain, in which she acknowledged the independence of the colonies in the following terms:

> Article I. His Britannic Majesty acknowledges the said United States, viz.: New Hampshire, Massachusetts Bay, Rhode Island and Providence Plantations, Connecticut, New York, New Jersey, Pennsylvania, Delaware, Maryland, Virginia, North Carolina, South Carolina, and Georgia, to be FREE, SOVEREIGN, AND INDEPENDENT STATES; that he treats with them as such; and, for himself, his heirs, and successors, relinquishes all claims to the government, propriety, and territorial rights of the same and every part thereof.

Thus were established the two great principles asserted by the colonies, namely, the right of a state to govern itself; and the right of a people to abolish a government when it becomes destructive of the ends for which it was instituted. And concurrent with the establishment of these principles was the fact that each colony became and was recognized by the mother country as a FREE, SOVEREIGN, AND INDEPENDENT STATE.

THE CONSTITUTION

In 1787, deputies were appointed by the states to revise the Articles of Confederation; and on Sept. 17, 1787, these deputies recommended, for the adoption of the states, the Articles of Union, known as the Constitution of the United States. . . .

By this Constitution, certain duties were imposed upon the several states, and the exercise of certain of their powers was restrained, which necessarily impelled their continued existence as sovereign states. But, to remove all doubt, an amendment was added which declared that the powers not delegated to the United States by the Constitution, nor prohibited by it to the states, are reserved to the states respectively, or to the people. On the 23rd of May, 1788, South Carolina, by a convention of her people, passed an ordinance assenting to this Constitution, and afterward altered her own constitution to conform herself to the obligations she had undertaken.

Thus was established, by compact between the states, a government with defined objects and powers, limited to the express words of the grant. This limitation left the whole remaining mass of power subject to the clause reserving it to the states or the people, and rendered unnecessary any specification of reserved rights. We hold that the government thus established is subject to the two great principles asserted in the Declaration of Independence; and we hold further that the mode of its formation subjects it to a third fundamental principle, namely, the law of compact. We maintain that in every compact between two or more parties, the obligation is mutual; that the failure of one of the contracting parties to perform a material part of the agreement entirely releases the obligation of the other; and that, where no arbiter is provided, each party is remitted to his own judgment to determine the fact of failure, with all its consequences.

In the present case, the fact is established with certainty. We assert that fourteen of the states have deliberately refused for years past to fulfill their constitutional obligations, and we refer to their own statutes for the proof.

The constitutional compact has been deliberately broken and disregarded by the nonslaveholding states; and the consequence follows that South Carolina is released from her obligation.

THE FUGITIVE SLAVE PROVISION

The Constitution of the United States, in its 4th Article, provides as follows: "No person held to service or labor in one state, under the laws thereof, escaping into another shall, in consequence of any law or regulation therein, be discharged from such service or labor, but shall be delivered up, on claim of the party to whom such service or labor may be due."

This stipulation was so material to the compact that without it that compact would not have been made. The greater number of the contracting parties held slaves, and they had previously evinced their estimate of the value of such a stipulation by making it a condition in the ordinance for the government of the territory ceded by Virginia, which obligations, and the laws of the general government, have ceased to effect the objects of the Constitution. The states of Maine, New Hampshire, Vermont, Massachusetts, Connecticut, Rhode Island, New York, Pennsylvania, Illinois, Indiana, Michigan, Wisconsin, and Iowa have enacted laws which either nullify the acts of Congress or render useless any attempt to execute them. In many of these states the fugitive is discharged from the service of labor claimed; and in none of them has the state government complied with the stipulation made in the Constitution.

The state of New Jersey, at an early day, passed a law in conformity with her constitutional obligation; but the current of antislavery feeling has led her more recently to enact laws which render inoperative the remedies provided by her own laws and by the laws of Congress. In the state of New York even the right of transit for a slave has been denied by her tribunals; and the states of Ohio and Iowa have refused to surrender to justice fugitives charged with murder and with inciting servile insurrection in the state of Virginia. Thus the constitutional compact has been deliberately broken and disregarded by the nonslaveholding states; and the consequence follows that South Carolina is released from her obligation.

The ends for which this Constitution was framed are declared by itself to be "to form a more perfect union, to establish justice, insure domestic tranquillity, provide for the common defense, promote the general welfare, and secure the blessings of liberty to ourselves and our posterity." These ends it endeavored to accomplish by a federal government in which each state was recognized as an equal and had separate control over its own institutions. The right of property in slaves was recognized by giving to free persons distinct political rights; by giving them the right to represent, and burdening them with direct taxes for, three-fifths of their slaves; by authorizing the importation of slaves for twenty years; and by stipulating for the rendition of fugitives from labor.

ANTISLAVERY AGITATION

We affirm that these ends for which this government was instituted have been defeated, and the government itself has been destructive of them by the action of the nonslaveholding states. Those states have assumed the right of deciding upon the propriety of our domestic institutions; and have denied the rights of property established in fifteen of the states and recognized by the Constitution. They have denounced as sinful the institution of slavery; they have permitted the open establishment among them of societies, whose avowed object is to disturb the peace of and eloign [take away] the property of the citizens of other states. They have encouraged and assisted thousands of our slaves to leave their homes; and, those who remain, have been incited by emissaries, books, and pictures to servile insurrection.

For twenty-five years this agitation has been steadily increasing, until it has now secured to its aid the power of the common government. Observing the *forms* of the Constitution, a sectional party has found, within that article establishing the Executive Department, the means of subverting the Constitution itself. A geographical line has been drawn across the Union, and all the states north of that line have united in the election of a man [Abraham Lincoln] to the high office of President of the United States whose opinions and purposes are hostile to slavery. He is to be entrusted with the administration of the common government, because he has declared that "Government cannot endure permanently half slave, half free," and that the public mind must rest in the belief that slavery is in the course of ultimate extinction. . . .

On the 4th of March next (1861) this party will take possession of the government. It has announced that the South shall be excluded from the common territory, that the judicial tribunal shall be made sectional, and that a war must be waged against slavery until it shall cease throughout the United States.

The guarantees of the Constitution will then no longer exist; the equal rights of the states will be lost. The slaveholding states will no longer have the power of self-government or self-protection, and the federal government will have become their enemy.

Sectional interest and animosity will deepen the irritation; and all hope of remedy is rendered vain by the fact that the public opinion at the North has invested a great political error with the sanctions of a more erroneous religious belief.

We, therefore, the people of South Carolina, by our delegates in convention assembled, appealing to the Supreme Judge of the world for the rectitude of our intentions, have solemnly declared that the Union heretofore existing between this state and the other states of North America is dissolved; and that the state of South Carolina has resumed her position among the nations of the world, as [a] separate and independent state, with full power to levy war, conclude peace, contract alliances, establish commerce, and to do all other acts and things which independent states may of right do.

Viewpoint 31B

Secession Is Not Justified (1861)

Abraham Lincoln (1809–1865)

INTRODUCTION *Abraham Lincoln was elected president of the United States on November 6, 1860. In the four months between the election and Lincoln's inauguration, seven Southern states—South Carolina, Mississippi, Florida, Alabama, Georgia, Louisiana, and*

Texas—seceded from the Union and formed the Confederate States of America. Southern politicians resigned from Congress and Southern states seized federal property. Lame-duck U.S. president James Buchanan hesitated to act, arguing that the Constitution did not give states the legal right to secede, but that Congress and the president had no power under the Constitution to prevent them. Slave states in the upper South and further west were deeply divided over whether to join the Confederacy. Various settlement proposals were discussed in Congress and elsewhere, only to founder on the issue of federal protection of slavery in the western territories.

It was against this backdrop that Lincoln on March 4, 1861, took the presidential oath "to preserve, protect, and defend the Constitution of the United States." In his inaugural address, excerpted here, Lincoln seeks to placate the South by pledging not to interfere with slavery in the Southern states and to enforce fugitive slave laws nationwide. But he also refutes the legal arguments found in the secession declarations of South Carolina and other states, arguing that "the union of these states is perpetual." Six weeks later, the Civil War began when Confederate guns fired on Fort Sumter.

What is the basic difference between Lincoln's views on the founding of the United States and the views expressed by South Carolina in the opposing viewpoint? What does Lincoln take to be the only substantial issue dividing the North and the South?

Fellow Citizens of the United States:

In compliance with a custom as old as the government itself, I appear before you to address you briefly and to take, in your presence, the oath prescribed by the Constitution of the United States to be taken by the President "before he enters on the execution of his office."

I do not consider it necessary, at present, for me to discuss those matters of administration about which there is no special anxiety or excitement. Apprehension seems to exist among the people of the Southern states that, by the accession of a Republican administration, their property and their peace and personal security are to be endangered. There has never been any reasonable cause for such apprehension. Indeed, the most ample evidence to the contrary has all the while existed and been open to their inspection. It is found in nearly all the published speeches of him who now addresses you.

NO INTENT TO ABOLISH SLAVERY

I do but quote from one of those speeches when I declare that "I have no purpose, directly or indirectly,

From Abraham Lincoln's first inaugural address, March 4, 1861, as reprinted in *A Compilation of Messages and Papers of the Presidents, 1798–1897*, edited by James D. Richardson (New York: 1896–1899).

to interfere with the institution of slavery in the states where it exists. I believe I have no lawful right to do so, and I have no inclination to do so." Those who nominated and elected me did so with full knowledge that I had made this and many similar declarations, and had never recanted them.

And, more than this, they placed in the platform, for my acceptance, and as a law to themselves and to me, the clear and emphatic resolution which I now read:

> *Resolved*, that the maintenance inviolate of the rights of the states, and especially the right of each state, to order and control its own domestic institutions according to its own judgment exclusively is essential to that balance of power on which the perfection and endurance of our political fabric depend; and we denounce the lawless invasion by armed force of the soil of any state or territory, no matter under what pretext, as among the gravest of crimes.

I now reiterate these sentiments; and in doing so, I only press upon the public attention the most conclusive evidence, of which the case is susceptible, that the property, peace, and security of no section are to be in any way endangered by the now incoming administration. I add, too, that all the protection which, consistently with the Constitution and the laws, can be given will be cheerfully given to all the states when lawfully demanded, for whatever cause—as cheerfully to one section as to another....

It is seventy-two years since the first inauguration of a President under our national Constitution. During that period fifteen different and greatly distinguished citizens have, in succession, administered the executive branch of the government. They have conducted it through many perils, and generally with great success. Yet, with all this scope of precedent, I now enter upon the same task for the brief constitutional term of four years under great and peculiar difficulties.

A disruption of the federal Union, heretofore only menaced, is now formidably attempted.

THE UNION IS PERPETUAL

I hold that, in contemplation of universal law and of the Constitution, the Union of these states is perpetual. Perpetuity is implied, if not expressed, in the fundamental law of all national governments. It is safe to assert that no government proper ever had a provision in its organic law for its own termination. Continue to execute all the express provisions of our national Constitution, and the Union will endure forever—it being impossible to destroy it except by some action not provided for in the instrument itself.

Again, if the United States be not a government proper, but an association of states in the nature of a contract merely, can it, as a contract, be peaceably unmade by less than all the parties who made it? One party to a contract may violate it—break it, so to speak—but does it not require all to lawfully rescind it? Descending from these general principles, we find the proposition that in legal contemplation, the Union is perpetual, confirmed by the history of the Union itself.

The Union is much older than the Constitution. It was formed, in fact, by the Articles of Association in 1774. It was matured and continued by the Declaration of Independence in 1776. It was further matured, and the faith of all the then thirteen states expressedly plighted and engaged, that it should be perpetual by the Articles of Confederation of 1778. And finally, in 1787, one of the declared objects for ordaining and establishing the Constitution, was *"to form a more perfect Union."*

But if destruction of the Union by one or by a part only of the states be lawfully possible, the Union is *less* perfect than before the Constitution, having lost the vital element of perpetuity.

It follows from these views that no state, upon its own mere motion, can lawfully get out of the Union—that *resolves* and *ordinances* to that effect are legally void; and that acts of violence within any state or states against the authority of the United States are insurrectionary or revolutionary, according to circumstances.

I therefore consider that, in view of the Constitution and the laws, the Union is unbroken; and to the extent of my ability, I shall take care, as the Constitution itself expressly enjoins upon me, that the laws of the Union be faithfully executed in all the states. Doing this I deem to be only a simple duty on my part; and I shall perform it, so far as practicable, unless my rightful masters, the American people, shall withhold the requisite means or in some authoritative manner direct the contrary....

All profess to be content in the Union if all constitutional rights can be maintained. Is it true, then, that any right plainly written in the Constitution has been denied? I think not. Happily, the human mind is so constituted that no party can reach to the audacity of doing this. Think, if you can, of a single instance in which a plainly written provision of the Constitution has ever been denied. If, by the mere force of numbers, a majority should deprive a minority of any clearly written constitutional right, it might, in a moral point of view, justify revolution—certainly would, if such right were a vital one. But such is not our case.

All the vital rights of minorities and of individuals are so plainly assured to them by affirmations and negations, guarantees and prohibitions, in the Constitution that controversies never arise concerning them. But no organic law can ever be framed with a provision specifically applicable to every question which may occur in practical administration. No foresight can anticipate nor any document of reasonable length contain express provisions for all possible questions. Shall fugitives from labor be surrendered by national or by state authority? The Constitution does not expressly say. *May* Congress prohibit slavery in the territories? The Constitution does not expressly say. *Must* Congress protect slavery in the territories? The Constitution does not expressly say.

Plainly, the central idea of secession is the essence of anarchy.

SECESSION IS ANARCHY

From questions of this class spring all our constitutional controversies, and we divide upon them into majorities and minorities. If the minority will not acquiesce, the majority must, or the government must cease. There is no other alternative; for continuing the government is acquiescence on one side or the other. If a minority, in such case, will secede rather than acquiesce, they make a precedent which in turn will divide and ruin them; for a minority of their own will secede from them whenever a majority refuses to be controlled by such minority.

For instance, why may not any portion of a new confederacy, a year or two hence, arbitrarily secede again, precisely as portions of the present Union now claim to secede from it? All who cherish disunion sentiments are now being educated to the exact temper of doing this. Is there such perfect identity of interests among the states to compose a new Union as to produce harmony only and prevent renewed secession?

Plainly, the central idea of secession is the essence of anarchy. A majority, held in restraint by constitutional checks and limitations, and always changing easily with deliberate changes of popular opinions and sentiments, is the only true sovereign of a free people. Whoever rejects it does of necessity fly to anarchy or to despotism. Unanimity is impossible. The rule of a minority, as a permanent arrangement, is wholly inadmissible; so that, rejecting the majority principle, anarchy or despotism in some form is all that is left. . . .

One section of our country believes slavery is *right* and ought to be extended, while the other believes it is *wrong* and ought not to be extended. This is the only substantial dispute. The fugitive slave clause of the Constitution and the law for the suppression of the foreign slave trade are each as well enforced, perhaps, as any law can ever be in a community where the moral sense of the people imperfectly supports the law itself. The great body of the people abide by the dry legal obligation in both cases, and a few break over in each. This, I think, cannot be perfectly cured; and it would be worse in both cases *after* the separation of the sections than before. The foreign slave trade, now imperfectly suppressed, would be ultimately revived without restriction in one section; while fugitive slaves, now only partially surrendered, would not be surrendered at all by the other.

WE CANNOT SEPARATE

Physically speaking, we cannot separate. We cannot remove our respective sections from each other, nor build an impassable wall between them. A husband and wife may be divorced, and go out of the presence and beyond the reach of each other, but the different parts of our country cannot do this. They cannot but remain face to face; and intercourse, either amicable or hostile, must continue between them. Is it possible, then, to make that intercourse more advantageous or more satisfactory *after* separation than *before*? Can aliens make treaties easier than friends can make laws? Can treaties be more faithfully enforced between aliens than laws can among friends? Suppose you go to war, you cannot fight always; and when, after much loss on both sides and no gain on either, you cease fighting, the identical old questions as to terms of intercourse are again upon you.

This country, with its institutions, belongs to the people who inhabit it. Whenever they shall grow weary of the existing government, they can exercise their *constitutional* right of amending it or their *revolutionary* right to dismember or overthrow it. I cannot be ignorant of the fact that many worthy and patriotic citizens are desirous of having the national Constitution amended. While I make no recommendation of amendments, I fully recognize the rightful authority of the people over the whole subject, to be exercised in either of the modes prescribed in the instrument itself; and I should, under existing circumstances, favor rather than oppose a fair opportunity being afforded the people to act upon it. . . .

Such of you as are now dissatisfied still have the old Constitution unimpaired, and, on the sensitive point, the laws of your own framing under it; while the new administration will have no immediate power, if it would, to change either.

If it were admitted that you who are dissatisfied hold the right side in the dispute, there still is no single good reason for precipitate action. Intelligence, patriotism, Christianity, and a firm reliance on Him, who has never yet forsaken this favored land, are still competent to adjust, in the best way, all our present difficulty.

PLEADING AGAINST WAR

In *your* hands, my dissatisfied fellow countrymen, and not in *mine* is the momentous issue of civil war. The government will not assail *you*. You can have no conflict without being yourselves the aggressors. *You* have no oath registered in heaven to destroy the government, while *I* shall have the most solemn one to "preserve, protect, and defend" it.

I am loath to close. We are not enemies but friends. We must not be enemies. Though passion may have strained, it must not break our bonds of affection.

The mystic chords of memory, stretching from every battlefield and patriot grave to every living heart and hearthstone all over this broad land, will yet swell the chorus of the Union, when again touched, as surely they will be, by the better angels of our nature.

FOR FURTHER READING

Charles B. Dew, *Apostles of Disunion: Southern Secession Commissioners and the Causes of the Civil War.* Charlottesville: University Press of Virginia, 2001.

Eric Foner and Olivia Mahoney, *A House Divided: America in the Age of Lincoln.* New York: W.W. Norton, 1990.

John Hope Franklin, *The Militant South, 1860–1861.* Urbana: University of Illinois Press, 2002.

David M. Potter, *The Impending Crisis.* New York: Harper & Row, 1976.

Kenneth M. Stampp, *And the War Came: The North and the Secession Crisis, 1860–1861.* Baton Rouge: Louisiana State University Press, 1970.

The complete text of the South Carolina Declaration can be found at the Web site of the Avalon Project at Yale Law School at http://www.yale.edu/lawweb/avalon/csa/scarsec.htm.

The complete text of Lincoln's 1861 inaugural address can be found at the same Web site at http://www.yale.edu/lawweb/avalon/presiden/inaug/lincoln1.htm.

THE CIVIL WAR

Viewpoint 32A
Freeing the Slaves Should Be the Primary War Aim (1862)

Horace Greeley (1811–1872)

INTRODUCTION *During the first half of the Civil War the issue of slave emancipation divided the North. Abolitionists called for President Abraham Lincoln to use his powers as commander in chief to issue a legal edict freeing the slaves. Lincoln—mindful of the importance of keeping Kentucky and other border slave states out of the Confederacy—resisted such a step. Lincoln also rescinded orders some Union generals had made freeing slaves within their military jurisdiction. Among the antislavery leaders angered by Lincoln's actions was*

Horace Greeley, founder of the New York Tribune *in 1841 and editor of the influential newspaper for more than thirty years.*

On August 19, 1862, the newspaper carried an open letter from Greeley to Lincoln. In the letter, excerpted here, Greeley excoriates Lincoln for timidity and inaction on the slavery issue. He urges Lincoln to actively enforce the Confiscation Act, a law passed by Congress in August 1861 and revised in July 1862, which authorized the confiscation of Confederate property—including slaves—and their use in the war effort.

How have some slaves who have escaped behind Union lines been treated, according to Greeley? What connection does Greeley make emancipation and prospects for Northern victory?

Dear Sir:

I do not intrude to tell you—for you must know already—that a great proportion of those who triumphed in your election, and of all who desire the unqualified suppression of the rebellion now desolating our country, are sorely disappointed and deeply pained by the policy you seem to be pursuing with regard to the slaves of Rebels. I write only to set succinctly and unmistakably before you what we require, what we think we have a right to expect, and of what we complain.

I. We require of you, as the first servant of the republic, charged especially and pre-eminently with this duty, that you EXECUTE THE LAWS. Most emphatically do we demand that such laws as have been recently enacted, which therefore may fairly be presumed to embody the public will and to be dictated by the *present* needs of the republic, and which, after due consideration, have received your personal sanction, shall by you be carried into full effect and that you publicly and decisively instruct your subordinates that such laws exist, that they are binding on all functionaries and citizens, and that they are to be obeyed to the letter.

The Union cause has suffered and is not suffering immensely from mistaken deference to Rebel slavery.

II. We think you are strangely and disastrously remiss in the discharge of your official and imperative duty with regard to the emancipating provisions of the new Confiscation Act. Those provisions were designed to fight slavery

"The Prayer of Twenty Millions" by Horace Greeley, *New York Tribune*, August 19, 1862. Reprinted in *The Rebellion Record*, Supplement, vol. 1, edited by Frank Moore (New York: Putnam, 1866).

with liberty. They prescribe that men loyal to the Union, and willing to shed their blood in her behalf, shall no longer be held, with the nation's consent, in bondage to persistent, malignant traitors, who for twenty years have been plotting and for sixteen months have been fighting to divide and destroy our country. Why these traitors should be treated with tenderness by you, to the prejudice of the dearest rights of loyal men, we cannot conceive.

SLAVERY THE CAUSE OF TREASON

III. We think you rare unduly influenced by the councils, the representations, the menaces, of certain fossil politicians hailing from the border Slave states. Knowing well that the heartily, unconditionally loyal portion of the white citizens of those states do not expect nor desire that slavery shall be upheld to the prejudice of the Union-we ask you to consider that slavery is everywhere the inciting cause and sustaining base of treason: the most slaveholding sections of Maryland and Delaware being this day, though under the Union flag, in full sympathy with the rebellion, while the free labor portions of Tennessee and of Texas, though writhing under the bloody heel of treason, are unconquerably loyal to the Union....

DEFERENCE TO SLAVERY

V. We complain that the Union cause has suffered and is now suffering immensely from mistaken deference to Rebel slavery. Had you, sir, in your inaugural address, unmistakably given notice that in case the rebellion already commenced were persisted in and your efforts to preserve the Union and enforce the laws should be resisted by armed force, *you would recognize no loyal person as rightfully held in slavery by a traitor*, we believe the rebellion would therein have received a staggering if not fatal blow. At that moment, according to the returns of the most recent elections, the Unionists were a large majority of the voters of the Slave states. But they were composed in good part of the aged, the feeble, the wealthy, the timid—the young, the reckless, the aspiring, the adventurous had already been largely lured by the gamblers and Negro traders, the politicians by trade and the conspirators by instinct, into the toils of treason. Had you then proclaimed that rebellion would strike the shackles from the slaves of every traitor, the wealthy and the cautious would have been supplied with a powerful inducement to remain loyal....

VI. We complain that the Confiscation Act which you approved is habitually disregarded by your generals, and that no word of rebuke for them from you has yet reached the public ear....

We complain that the officers of your armies have habitually repelled rather than invited the approach of slaves who would have gladly taken the risks of escaping from their Rebel masters to our camps, bringing intelligence often of inestimable value to the Union cause. We complain that those who *have* thus escaped to us, avowing a willingness to do for us whatever might be required, have been brutally and madly repulsed, and often surrendered to be scourged, maimed, and tortured by the ruffian traitors who pretend to own them. We complain that a large proportion of our regular Army officers, with many of the volunteers, evince far more solicitude to uphold slavery than to put down the rebellion.

And, finally, we complain that you, Mr. President, elected as a Republican, knowing well what an abomination slavery is and how emphatically it is the core and essence of this atrocious rebellion, seem never to interfere with these atrocities and never give a direction to your military subordinates, which does not appear to have been conceived in the interest of slavery rather than of freedom....

EXECUTE THE LAWS

IX. I close as I began with the statement that what an immense majority of the loyal millions of your countrymen require of you is a frank, declared unqualified, ungrudging execution of the laws of the land, more especially of the Confiscation Act. That act gives freedom to the slaves of Rebels coming within our lines, or whom those lines may at any time enclose—we ask you to render it due obedience by publicly requiring all your subordinates to recognize and obey it. The Rebels are everywhere using the late anti-Negro riots in the North, as they have long used your officers' treatment of Negroes in the South, to convince the slaves that they have nothing to hope from a Union success, that we mean in that case to sell them into a bitter bondage to defray the cost of the war.

Let them impress this as a truth on the great mass of their ignorant and credulous bondmen, and the Union will never be restored—never. We cannot conquer 10 million people united in solid phalanx against us, powerfully aided by Northern sympathizers and European allies. We must have scouts, guides, spies, cooks, teamsters, diggers, and choppers from the blacks of the South, whether we allow them to fight for us or not, or we shall be baffled and repelled.

As one of the millions who would gladly have avoided this struggle at any sacrifice but that of principle and honor, but who now feel that the triumph of the Union is indispensable, not only to the existence of our country but to the well-being of mankind, I entreat you to render a hearty and unequivocal obedience to the law of the land.

*Preserving the Union Should Be
the Primary War Aim (1862)*

Abraham Lincoln (1809–1865)

INTRODUCTION *Abraham Lincoln, president of the
United States from 1861 to 1865, was noted for his
single-minded devotion to preserving the Union. During
the Civil War Lincoln was continually challenged, both
by abolitionists who attacked his unwillingness to end
slavery and by those who advocated an end to the Civil
War by negotiating a settlement with the Confederacy.
During the first part of his term Lincoln tried to persuade the leaders of the Southern states that did not
secede to plan for the gradual and compensated emancipation of slaves. But he hesitated to issue a general
proclamation abolishing slavery, believing that preserving the Union should take highest priority. Lincoln
succinctly expressed his views in the following viewpoint,
a letter he wrote in response to* New York Tribune
*editor Horace Greeley's criticism of his policies (see the
previous viewpoint). Lincoln's reply, dated August 22,
1862, was published in the* Tribune *and elsewhere.*

*How does Lincoln respond to Greeley's criticisms? Is his
message solely aimed at abolitionists? Lincoln had in
July 1862 discussed with his cabinet his intention of
issuing an emancipation proclamation, had prepared a
draft of such a proclamation, and was waiting for the
right moment to announce his decision. How does this
affect your understanding of this letter written and
published in August of that year?*

Dear Sir:

My paramount object in this struggle is *to
save the Union, and is* not *either to save or
destroy slavery.*

I have just read yours of the 19th, addressed to
myself through the *New York Tribune.* If there be in
it any statements or assumptions of fact which I may
know to be erroneous, I do not now and here contro-
vert them. If there be in it any inferences which I may
believe to be falsely drawn, I do not now and here
argue against them. If there be perceptible in it an
impatient and dictatorial tone, I waive it in deference
to an old friend, whose heart I have always supposed
to be right.

As to the policy I "seem to be pursuing," as you say,
I have not meant to leave any one in doubt.

From *The Rebellion Record,* Supplement, vol. 1, edited by Frank Moore (New York:
Putnam, 1866).

THE UNION MUST BE SAVED

I would save the Union. I would save it the shortest way
under the Constitution. The sooner the national authority can be restored, the nearer the Union will be "the
Union as it was." If there be those who would not save
the Union unless they could at the same time *save* slavery,
I do not agree with them. If there be those who would not
save the Union unless they could at the same time *destroy*
slavery, I do not agree with them. My paramount object
in this struggle *is* to save the Union, and is *not* either to
save or to destroy slavery. If I could save the Union without freeing *any* slave, I would do it, and if I could save it
by freeing *all* the slaves, I would do it; and if I could do it
by freeing some and leaving others alone, I would also
do that.

What I do about slavery and the colored race I do
because I believe it helps to save this Union; and what I
forbear I forbear because I do *not* believe it would help
to save the Union. I shall do *less* whenever I shall believe
what I am doing hurts the cause, and I shall do *more*
whenever I shall believe doing more will help the cause.
I shall try to correct errors when shown to be errors;
and I shall adopt new views so fast as they shall appear
to be true views.

I have here stated my purpose according to my view
of *official* duty, and I intend no modification of my oft-
expressed *personal* wish that all men, everywhere, could
be free.

FOR FURTHER READING

Ira Berlin et al., eds., *Free at Last: A Documentary History of
Slavery, Freedom, and the Civil War.* New York: New Press,
1992.

Louis S. Gerteis, *From Contraband to Freedmen: Federal Policy
Toward Southern Blacks, 1861–1865.* Westport, CT: Greenwood Press, 1973.

Harlan H. Horner, *Lincoln and Greeley,* Urbana: University of
Illinois Press, 1953.

Michael P. Johnson, ed., *Abraham Lincoln, Slavery, and the Civil
War: Selected Writings and Speeches.* Boston: Bedford/St.
Martin's, 2000.

William K. Klingaman, *Abraham Lincoln and the Road to
Emancipation, 1861–1865.* New York: Viking, 2001.

*The Emancipation Proclamation
Is a Significant Achievement (1862)*

Frederick Douglass (1817–1895)

INTRODUCTION *Abraham Lincoln issued a preliminary
Emancipation Proclamation on September 22, 1863,
shortly after Union forces scored a partial victory in the
Battle of Antietam. The proclamation stated that on
January 1, 1863, all slaves residing in every part of the*

South still in rebellion would be declared "then, thenceforward, and forever free." The following viewpoint features the reaction of Frederick Douglass, an escaped slave who had gained national and international fame as an abolitionist, lecturer, and writer. Douglass was a strong and early advocate of both emancipation of slaves and the enlistment of black soldiers for the Union. In the October 1862 issue of Douglass' Monthly, *a newspaper he edited and published, Douglass criticizes Lincoln for not acting sooner to free the slaves, but praises Lincoln for finally issuing the proclamation. He predicts freeing the slaves will help defeat the Confederacy.*

What comments does Douglass make about the character of Abraham Lincoln? What reasons does he give for his confidence that the Confederacy will be defeated?

Common sense, the necessities of the war, to say nothing of the dictation of justice and humanity have at last prevailed. We shout for joy that we live to record this righteous decree. *Abraham Lincoln*, President of the United States, Commander-in-Chief of the army and navy, in his own peculiar, cautious, forbearing and hesitating way, slow, but we hope sure, has, while the loyal heart was near breaking with despair, proclaimed and declared: *"That on the First of January, in the Year of Our Lord One Thousand, Eight Hundred and Sixty-three, All Persons Held as Slaves Within Any State or Any Designated Part of a State, The People Whereof Shall Then be in Rebellion Against the United States, Shall be Thenceforward and Forever Free."* "Free forever" oh! long enslaved millions, whose cries have so vexed the air and sky, suffer on a few more days in sorrow, the hour of your deliverance draws nigh! Oh! Ye millions of free and loyal men who have earnestly sought to free your bleeding country from the dreadful ravages of revolution and anarchy, lift up now your voices with joy and thanksgiving for with freedom to the slave will come peace and safety to your country....

REACTIONS

Opinions will widely differ as to the practical effect of this measure upon the war. All that class at the North who have not lost their affection for slavery will regard the measure as the very worst that could be devised, and as likely to lead to endless mischief. All their plans for the future have been projected with a view to a reconstruction of the American Government upon the basis of compromise between slaveholding and non-slaveholding States. The thought of a country unified in sentiments, objects and ideas, has not entered into their political calculations, and hence this newly declared policy of the Government, which contemplates one glorious homogeneous people, doing away at a blow with the whole

From an editorial of Frederick Douglass, *Douglass' Monthly*, October 1862.

class of compromisers and corrupters, will meet their stern opposition. Will that opposition prevail? Will it lead the President to reconsider and retract? Not a word of it. Abraham Lincoln may be slow, Abraham Lincoln may desire peace even at the price of leaving our terrible national sore untouched, to fester on for generations, but Abraham Lincoln is not the man to reconsider, retract and contradict words and purposes solemnly proclaimed over his official signature....

The effect of this paper upon the disposition of Europe will be great and increasing. It changes the character of the war in European eyes and gives it an important principle as an object, instead of national pride and interest. It recognizes and declares the real nature of the contest, and places the North on the side of justice and civilization, and the rebels on the side of robbery and barbarism. It will disarm all purpose on the part of European Government to intervene in favor of the rebels and thus cast off at a blow one source of rebel power. All through the war thus far, the rebel ambassadors in foreign countries have been able to silence all expression of sympathy with the North as to slavery. With much more than a show of truth, they said that the Federal Government, no more than the Confederate Government, contemplated the abolition of slavery.

---■---

The Star Spangled Banner is now the harbinger of Liberty and the millions in bondage . . . will rally under that banner.

---■---

But will not this measure be frowned upon by our officers and men in the field? We have heard of many thousands who have resolved that they will throw up their commissions and lay down their arms, just so soon as they are required to carry on a war against slavery. Making all allowances for exaggeration there are doubtless far too many of this sort in the loyal army. Putting this kind of loyalty and patriotism to the test, will be one of the best collateral effects of the measure. Any man who leaves the field on such a ground will be an argument in favor of the proclamation, and will prove that his heart has been more with slavery than with his country. Let the army be cleansed from all such pro-slavery vermin, and its health and strength will be greatly improved. But there can be no reason to fear the loss of many officers or men by resignation or desertion. We have no doubt that the measure was brought to the attention of most of our leading Generals, and blind as some of them have seemed to be in the earlier part of the war, most of them have seen enough to convince them that there can be no end to this war that does not end slavery. At any rate, we may hope that for every pro-slavery man that shall start from the ranks of our loyal army, there will be two anti-slavery men to fill up the vacancy, and in this war one truly devoted to the cause of Emancipation is worth two of the opposite sort.

TWO NECESSARY CONDITIONS

Whether slavery will be abolished in the manner now proposed by President Lincoln, depends of course upon two conditions, the first specified and the second implied. The first is that the slave States shall be in rebellion on and after the first day of January 1863 and the second is we must have the ability to put down that rebellion. About the first there can be very little doubt. The South is thoroughly in earnest and confident. It has staked everything upon the rebellion. Its experience thus far in the field has rather increased its hopes of final success than diminished them. Its armies now hold us at bay at all points, and the war is confined to the border States slave and free. If Richmond were in our hands and Virginia at our mercy, the vast regions beyond would still remain to be subdued. But the rebels confront us on the Potomac, the Ohio, and the Mississippi. Kentucky, Maryland, Missouri, and Virginia are in debate on the battlefields and their people are divided by the line which separates treason from loyalty. In short we are yet, after eighteen months of war, confined to the outer margin of the rebellion. We have scarcely more than touched the surface of the terrible evil. It has been raising large quantities of food during the past summer. While the masters have been fighting abroad, the slaves have been busy working at home to supply them with the means of continuing the straggle. They will not [back] down at the bidding of this Proclamation, but may be safely relied upon till January and long after January. A month or two will put an end to general fighting for the winter. When the leaves fall we shall hear again of bad roads, winter quarters and spring campaigns. The South which has thus far withstood our arms will not fall at once before our pens. All fears for the abolition of slavery arising from this apprehension may be dismissed. Whoever, therefore, lives to see the first day of next January, should Abraham Lincoln be then alive and President of the United States, may confidently look in the morning papers for the final proclamation, granting freedom, and freedom forever, to all slaves within the rebel States. On the next point nothing need be said. We have full power to put down the rebellion. Unless one man is more than a match for four, unless the South breeds braver and better men than the North, unless slavery is more precious than liberty, unless a just cause kindles a feebler enthusiasm than a wicked and villainous one, the men of the loyal States will put down this rebellion and slavery, and all the sooner will they put down that rebellion by coupling slavery with that object. Tenderness towards slavery has been the loyal weakness during the war. Fighting the slaveholders with one hand and holding the slaves with the other, has been fairly tried and has failed. We have now inaugurated a wiser and better policy, a policy which is better for the loyal cause than an hundred thousand armed men. The Star Spangled Banner is now the harbinger of Liberty and the millions in bondage, inured to hardships, accustomed to toil, ready to suffer, ready to fight, to dare and to die, will rally under that banner wherever they see it gloriously unfolded to the breeze. Now let the Government go forward in its mission of Liberty as the only condition of peace and union, by weeding out the army and navy of all such officers as the late Col. [Dixon] Miles, whose sympathies are now known to have been with the rebels. Let only the men who assent heartily to the wisdom and the justice of the anti-slavery policy of the Government be lifted into command; let the black man have an arm as well as a heart in this war, and the tide of battle which has thus far only waved backward and forward, will steadily set in our favor. The rebellion suppressed, slavery abolished, and America will, higher than ever, sit as a queen among the nations of the earth.

Viewpoint 33B

The Emancipation Proclamation Is a Worthless Act (1863)

Clement L. Vallandigham (1820–1871)

INTRODUCTION *Abraham Lincoln's Emancipation Proclamation on January 1, 1863, (following a preliminary proclamation on September 22, 1862) declared all the slaves in areas of rebelling states to be free. The proclamation provoked criticism, not only from Confederate leaders, but also from political opponents in the North. One of the most prominent of the Northern dissenters was Clement L. Vallandigham, a Democratic representative from Ohio. Vallandigham was a leader of the "Peace Democrats" or "Copperheads" who opposed many of Lincoln's policies and who denounced the Civil War as an unjust and unnecessary conflict.*

The following viewpoint is taken from a speech delivered on January 14, 1863, in the House of Representatives. Vallandigham argues that Lincoln's September 1862 proclamation, which warned of pending emancipation in January 1863 for the slaves in any state "in rebellion" had failed to persuade any Confederate state to return to the Union. The Emancipation Proclamation will not end slavery, he predicts, but instead will scuttle any effort to end the Civil War by peaceful compromise with the South—something Vallandigham had long advocated.

Why does Vallandigham consider the Emancipation Proclamation an admission of defeat for the North? What opinions does he express about the morality of slavery?

Now, sir, on the 14th of April [1861], I believed that coercion would bring on war, and war disunion. More than that, I believed, what you all in your hearts believe to-day, that the South could never be conquered—never. And not that only, but I was satisfied—and you of the abolition party have now proved it to the world—that the secret but real purpose of the war was to abolish slavery in the States. In any event, I did not doubt that whatever might be the momentary impulses of those in power, and whatever pledges they might make in the midst of the fury for the Constitution, the Union, and the flag, yet the natural and inexorable logic of revolutions would, sooner or later, drive them into that policy, and with it to its final but inevitable result, the change of our present democratical form of government into an imperial despotism....

You cannot abolish slavery by the sword; still less by proclamations.

And now, sir, I recur to the state of the Union to-day....

You have not conquered the South. You never will. It is not in the nature of things possible; much less under your auspices. But money you have expended without limit, and blood poured out like water. Defeat, debt, taxation, sepulchers, these are your trophies. In vain the people gave you treasure and the soldier yielded up his life. "Fight, tax, emancipate, let these," said the gentleman from Maine, (Mr. Pike,) at the last session, "be the trinity of our salvation." Sir, they have become the trinity of your deep damnation. The war for the Union is, in your hands, a most bloody and costly failure. The President confessed it on the 22d of September [1862], solemnly, officially, and under the broad seal of the United States. And he has now repeated the confession. The priests and rabbis of abolition taught him that God would not prosper such a cause. War for the Union was abandoned; war for the negro openly begun, and with stronger battalions than before. With what success? Let the dead at Fredericksburg and Vicksburg [sites of Civil War battles] answer....

THE GREAT QUESTION

And now, sir, I come to the great and controlling question within which the whole issue of union or disunion

From Clement L. Vallandigham's speech before Congress, January 14, 1863, in *Appendix to the Congressional Globe*, 1863.

is bound up: is there "an irrepressible conflict" between the slaveholding and non-slaveholding States? ... If so, then there is an end of all union and forever. You cannot abolish slavery by the sword; still less by proclamations, though the President were to "proclaim" every month. Of what possible avail was his proclamation of September? Did the South submit? Was she even alarmed? And yet he has now fulmined another "bull against the comet"—*brutum fulmen* [irrational threat]—and, threatening servile insurrection with all its horrors, has yet coolly appealed to the judgment of mankind, and invoked the blessing of the God of peace and love! But declaring it a military necessity, an essential measure of war to subdue the rebels, yet, with admirable wisdom, he expressly exempts from its operation the only States and parts of States in the South where he has the military power to execute it.

Neither, sir, can you abolish slavery by argument. As well attempt to abolish marriage or the relation of paternity. The South is resolved to maintain it at every hazard and by every sacrifice; and if "this Union cannot endure part slave and part free," then it is already and finally dissolved....

AGAINST DISUNION

But I deny the doctrine. It is full of disunion and civil war. It is disunion itself. Whoever first taught it ought to be dealt with as not only hostile to the Union, but an enemy of the human race. Sir, the fundamental idea of the Constitution is the perfect and eternal compatibility of a union of States "part slave and part free;" else the Constitution never would have been framed, nor the Union founded; and seventy years of successful experiment have approved the wisdom of the plan. In my deliberate judgment, a confederacy made up of slaveholding and nonslaveholding States is, in the nature of things, the strongest of all popular governments. African slavery has been, and is, eminently conservative. It makes the absolute political equality of the white race everywhere practicable. It dispenses with the English Order of nobility, and leaves every white man, North and South, owning slaves or owning none, the equal of every other white man. It has reconciled universal suffrage throughout the free States with the stability of government. I speak not now of its material benefits to the North and West, which are many and more obvious. But the South, too, has profited many ways by a union with the nonslaveholding States. Enterprise, industry, self-reliance, perseverance, and the other hardy virtues of a people living in a higher latitude and without hereditary servants, she has learned or received from the North. Sir, it is easy, I know, to denounce all this, and to revile him who utters it. Be it so. The English is, of all languages, the most copious in words of bitterness and reproach. "Pour on: I will endure."...

Whoever hates negro slavery more than he loves the Union, must demand separation at last. I think that you can never abolish slavery by fighting. Certainly you never can till you have first destroyed the South, and then...converted this Government into an imperial despotism. And, sir, whenever I am forced to a choice between the loss to my own country and race, of personal and political liberty with all its blessings, and the involuntary domestic servitude of the negro, I shall not hesitate one moment to choose the latter alternative. The sole question to-day is between the Union with slavery, or final disunion, and, I think, anarchy and despotism. I am for the Union. It was good enough for my fathers. It is good enough for us and our children after us.

FOR FURTHER READING

David W. Blight, *Frederick Douglass' Civil War: Keeping Faith in Jubilee.* Baton Rouge: Louisiana State University Press, 1989.

Allen C. Guelzo, *Lincoln's Emancipation Proclamation: The End of Slavery in America.* New York: Simon & Schuster, 2004.

Maria L. Howell, ed., *The Emancipation Proclamation.* Farmington Hills, MI: Greenhaven Press/Thomson Gale, 2006.

Forrest Wood, *Black Scare: The Racist Response to Emancipation and Reconstruction.* Berkeley: University of California Press, 1968.

Viewpoint 34A

War Justifies the Restriction of Civil Liberties (1863)

Abraham Lincoln (1809–1865)

INTRODUCTION *The question of whether and how to maintain civil liberties while conducting a war faced leaders of both sides of the Civil War. Abraham Lincoln, the sixteenth president of the United States, and Jefferson Davis, the first and only president of the Confederacy, took contrasting approaches. Davis maintained civil liberties for most Southerners (excluding slaves). Lincoln, however, issued several proclamations suspending the writ of habeas corpus, a constitutional right forbidding unlawful detention. Union military forces arrested and detained thousands of suspected Confederate sympathizers.*

In 1863 a group of Democrats from Albany, New York, wrote to Lincoln complaining of what they saw as serious violations of the Constitution and the Bill of Rights. High among their concerns was the fate of Clement L. Vallandigham, a Democratic congressman from Ohio who had actively opposed conscription and denounced Lincoln and other leaders (see viewpoint

33B). In May 1863 he was arrested and tried by the army for treason. After being found guilty of "weakening the power of the Government" in putting down "an unlawful rebellion," he was sentenced to imprisonment—a sentence commuted by Lincoln to banishment to the Confederacy.

Lincoln replied to the group's plea with a June 12, 1863, letter that was widely reprinted in pamphlet form and is excerpted here. Defending his war policies, he argues that the "inherent power" of the executive justifies using whatever measures are necessary to protect the American people, and cites the dangers of spies and traitors to the Union cause.

Why are civil liberties not accorded as much protection during a rebellion as during peaceful times, according to Lincoln? How does he justify the detention of Clement L. Vallandigham?

Gentlemen:

Your letter of May 19, inclosing the resolutions of a public meeting held at Albany, New York, on the 16th of the same month, was received several days ago....

CRITICAL RESOLUTIONS

The resolutions promise to support me in every constitutional and lawful measure to suppress the rebellion; and I have not knowingly employed, nor shall knowingly employ, any other. But the meeting, by their resolutions, assert and argue that certain military arrests and proceedings following them, for which I am ultimately responsible, are unconstitutional. I think they are not. The resolutions quote from the Constitution the definition of treason, and also the limiting safeguards and guarantees therein provided for the citizen on trials for treason, and on his being held to answer for capital or otherwise infamous crimes, and in criminal prosecutions his right to a speedy and public trial by an impartial jury. They proceed to resolve "that these safeguards of the rights of the citizen against the pretensions of arbitrary power were intended more especially for his protection in times of civil commotion." And, apparently to demonstrate the proposition, the resolutions proceed: "They were secured substantially to the English people after years of protracted civil war, and were adopted into our Constitution at the close of the revolution." Would not the demonstration have been better if it could have been truly said that these safeguards had been adopted and applied during the civil wars and during our revolution, instead of after the one and at the close of the other? I, too, am devotedly for them after civil war and before civil war, and at all times, "except when, in cases of rebellion or invasion, the public safety may require" their suspension....

Reprinted from *The Complete Works of Lincoln*, edited by J. Nicolay and J. Hay (New York: F.D. Tandy, 1905).

[The rebel] sympathizers pervaded all departments of the government and nearly all communities of the people. From this material, under cover of "liberty of speech," "liberty of the press," and "*habeas corpus*," they hoped to keep on foot amongst us a most efficient corps of spies, informers, suppliers and aiders and abettors of their cause in a thousand ways. They knew that in times such as they were inaugurating, by the Constitution itself the "*habeas corpus*" might be suspended; but they also knew they had friends who would make a question as to who was to suspend it; meanwhile their spies and others might remain at large to help on their cause. Or if, as has happened, the Executive should suspend the writ without ruinous waste of time, instances of arresting innocent persons might occur, as are always likely to occur in such cases; and then a clamor could be raised in regard to this. . . . Yet . . . I was slow to adopt the strong measures which [are] . . . indispensable to the public safety. Nothing is better known to history than that courts of justice are utterly incompetent to such cases. Civil courts are organized chiefly for trials of individuals, or, at most, a few individuals acting in concert—and this in quiet times, and on charges of crimes well defined in the law. Even in times of peace hands of horse-thieves and robbers frequently grow too numerous and powerful for the ordinary courts of justice. But what comparison, in numbers, have such bands ever borne to the insurgent sympathizers even in many of the loyal States? Again, a jury too frequently has at least one member more ready to hang the panel than to hang the traitor. And yet again, he who dissuades one man from volunteering, or induces one soldier to desert, weakens the Union cause as much as he who kills a Union soldier in battle. Yet this dissuasion or inducement may be so conducted as to be no defined crime of which any civil court would take cognizance.

A CASE OF REBELLION

Ours is a case of rebellion. . . . [The Suspension Clause from Section 9 of Article I of the Constitution] plainly attests the understanding of those who made the Constitution that ordinary courts of justice are inadequate to "cases of rebellion"—attests their purpose that, in such cases, men may be held in custody whom the courts, acting on ordinary rules, would discharge. *Habeas corpus* does not discharge men who are proved to be guilty of defined crime; and its suspension is allowed by the Constitution on purpose that men may be arrested and held who can not be proved to be guilty of defined crime, "when, in cases of rebellion or invasion, the public safety may require it."

This is precisely our present case—a case of rebellion wherein the public safety does require the suspension. . . .

Arrests in cases of rebellion do not proceed altogether upon the same basis. In the latter case arrests are made not so much for what has been done, as for what probably would be done. The latter is more for the preventive and less for the vindictive than the former. In such cases the purposes of men are much more easily understood than in cases of ordinary crime. The man who stands by and says nothing when the peril of his government is discussed, cannot be misunderstood. If not hindered, he is sure to help the enemy; much more if he talks ambiguously—talks for his country with "buts," and "ifs" and "ands." [Several Confederate leaders] were all within the power of the government since the rebellion began, and were nearly as well known to be traitors then as now. Unquestionably if we had seized and held them, the insurgent cause would be much weaker. But no one of them had then committed any crime defined in the law. Every one of them, if arrested, would have been discharged on *habeas corpus* were the writ allowed to operate. In view of these and similar cases, I think the time not unlikely to come when I shall be blamed for having made too few arrests rather than too many. . . .

——————■——————

The Constitution is not in its Application . . . the same in cases of rebellion . . . as it is in times of profound peace.

——————■——————

CLEMENT L. VALLANDIGHAM

Take the particular case mentioned by the meeting. It is asserted in substance, that Mr. Vallandigham was, by a military commander, seized and tried "for no other reason than words addressed to a public meeting in criticism of the course of the administration, and in condemnation of the military orders of the general." Now, if there be no mistake about this, if this assertion is the truth and the whole truth, if there was no other reason for the arrest, then I concede that the arrest was wrong. But the arrest, as I understand, was made for a very different reason. Mr. Vallandigham avows his hostility to the war on the part of the Union; and his arrest was made because he was laboring, with some effect, to prevent the raising of troops, to encourage desertions from the army, and to leave the rebellion without an adequate military force to suppress it. He was not arrested because he was damaging the political prospects of the administration or the personal interests of the commanding general but because he was damaging the army, upon the existence and vigor of which the life of the nation depends. He was warring upon the military, and this gave the military constitutional jurisdiction to lay hands upon him. . . . Long experience has shown that armies cannot be maintained unless desertion shall be punished by the severe penalty of death. . . . Must I shoot a simple-minded soldier boy who deserts, while I must not touch a hair of a wily agitator who induces him to desert? This is none the less injurious when effected by getting a father, or brother, or friend into a public meeting, and there working upon his feelings till he is persuaded to write the soldier boy that he is fighting in a bad cause, for a wicked administration of a contemptible government, too weak to arrest and punish him if he shall desert. I think that, in such a case, to silence the agitator and save the boy is not only constitutional, but withal a great mercy.

If I be wrong . . . my error lies in believing . . . that the Constitution is not in its application in all respects the same in cases of rebellion or invasion involving the public safety, as it is in times of profound peace and public security. The Constitution itself makes the distinction, and I can no more be persuaded that the government can constitutionally take no strong measures in times of rebellion, because it can be shown that the same could not be lawfully taken in time of peace, than I can be persuaded that a particular drug is not good medicine for a sick man because it can be shown to not be good food for a well one. Nor am I able to appreciate the danger apprehended by the meeting, that the American people will by means of military arrests during the rebellion lose the right of public discussion, the liberty of speech and the press, the law of evidence, trial by jury, and *habeas corpus* throughout the indefinite peaceful future which I trust lies before them, any more than I am able to believe that a man could contract so strong an appetite for emetics during temporary illness as to persist in feeding upon them during the remainder of his healthful life. . . .

I am specifically called on to discharge Mr. Vallandigham. . . . In response to such appeal I have to say . . . it will afford me great pleasure to discharge him so soon as I can by any means believe the public safety will not suffer by it.

Viewpoint 34B
War Does Not Justify the Violation of Civil Liberties (1863)
Ohio Democratic Convention

INTRODUCTION *During the Civil War President Abraham Lincoln was accused by some political opponents of violating the U.S. Constitution. One action that attracted such criticism was the arrest of Clement L. Vallandigham, a Democratic member of Congress from Ohio who was perhaps the most prominent of Northern political dissenters (known as "Copperheads") during the Civil War. His case provoked much political controversy and at least two petitions to the president.*

Lincoln responded to the first petition, sent by a group of New York Democrats, by issuing a June 12, 1863, letter defending his actions given the national crisis America was facing (see viewpoint 34A).

Many people remained unconvinced—including the group of Ohio Democrats who sent Lincoln a second petition and letter excerpted in this viewpoint. In their June 26, 1863, letter, the Ohio politicians argue that the arrest of Vallandigham, whom they had just nominated for governor, was unjustifiable. They contend that freedom of speech and of the press are just as important during war as during peacetime. The petitioners also criticize Lincoln for his suspension of the writ of habeas corpus (which outlaws government detention without showing just cause to the courts), arguing that under the Constitution only Congress, not the President, has the power to make such a decision.

What constitutional liberties are being threatened by Lincoln, according to the Ohio petitioners? How do they characterize Vallandigham?

The arrest, unusual trial, and banishment of Mr. Vallandigham, have created wide-spread and alarming disaffection among the people of the State, not only endangering the harmony of the friends of the Constitution and the Union, and tending to disturb the peace and tranquillity of the State, but also impairing that confidence in the fidelity of your Administration to the great landmarks of free government essential to a peaceful and successful enforcement of the laws of Ohio.

You are reported to have used, in a public communication on this subject, the following language:

> It gave me pain when I learned that Mr. Vallandigham had been arrested—that is, I was pained that there should have seemed to be a necessity for arresting him; and that it will afford me great pleasure to discharge him so soon as I can by any means believe the public safety will not suffer by it.

The undersigned assure your Excellency, from our personal knowledge of the feelings of the people of Ohio, that the public safety will be far more endangered by continuing Mr. Vallandigham in exile than by releasing him. It may be true that persons differing from him in political views may be found in Ohio; and elsewhere, who will express a different opinion; but they are certainly mistaken.

Mr. Vallandigham may differ with the President, and even with some of his own political party, as to the true and most effectual means of maintaining the Constitution and restoring the Union; but this difference of

Reprinted from *A Life of Clement L. Vallandigham* by James L. Vallandigham (Baltimore: Turnbull Bros., 1872).

opinion does not prove him to be unfaithful to his duties as an American citizen. If a man, devotedly attached to the Constitution and the Union, conscientiously believes that, from the inherent nature of the Federal compact, the war, in the present condition of things in this country, can not be used as a means of restoring the Union; or that a war to subjugate a part of the States, or a war to revolutionise the social system in a part of the States, could not restore, but would inevitably result in the final destruction of both the Constitution and the Union—is he not to be allowed the right of an American citizen to appeal to the judgment of the people for a change of policy by the constitutional remedy of the ballot-box?

The undersigned are unable to agree . . . that the Constitution is different in time of insurrection or invasion from what it is in time of peace.

FREEDOM OF SPEECH INDISPENSABLE

During the war with Mexico many of the political opponents of the Administration then in power thought it their duty to oppose and denounce the war, and to urge before the people of the country that it was unjust and prosecuted for unholy purposes. With equal reason it might have been said of them that their discussions before the people were calculated to "discourage enlistments," "to prevent the raising of troops," and to "induce desertions from the army," and "leave the Government without an adequate military force to carry on the war."

If the freedom of speech and of the press are to be suspended in time of war, then the essential element of popular government to effect a change of policy in the constitutional mode is at an end. The freedom of speech and of the press is indispensable, and necessarily, incident to the nature of popular government itself. If any inconvenience or evils arise from its exercise, they are unavoidable. . . .

EXAMINING THE CONSTITUTION

The undersigned are unable to agree with you in the opinion you have expressed, that the Constitution is different in time of insurrection or invasion from what it is in time of peace and public security. The Constitution provides for no limitation upon, or exceptions to, the guarantees of personal liberty, except as to the writ of *habeas corpus*. Has the President, at the time of invasion or

insurrection, the right to engraft limitations or exceptions upon these constitutional guarantees whenever, in his judgement, the public safety requires it?

True it is, the article of the Constitution which defines the various powers delegated to Congress, declares that the "privilege of the writ of *habeas corpus* shall not be suspended unless where, in case of rebellion or invasion, the public safety may require it." But this qualification or limitation upon this restriction upon the powers of Congress has no reference to, or connection with, the other constitutional guarantees of personal liberty. Expunge from the Constitution this limitation upon the power of Congress to suspend the writ of *habeas corpus*, and yet the other guarantees of personal liberty would remain unchanged.

Although a man might not have a constitutional right to have an immediate investigation made as to the legality of his arrest upon *habeas corpus*, yet his "right to a speedy and public trial by an impartial jury of the State and District wherein the crime shall have been committed," will not be altered; neither will his right to the exemption from "cruel and unusual punishments;" nor his right to be secure in his person, houses, papers and effects against any unreasonable seizures and searches; nor his right [not] to be deprived of life, liberty or property, without due process of law; nor his right not to be held to answer for a capital or otherwise infamous offence unless on presentment or indictment of a grand jury, be in anywise changed.

And certainly the restriction upon the power of Congress to suspend the writ of *habeas corpus* in time of insurrection or invasion, could not affect the guarantee that the freedom of speech and of the press shall not be abridged. It is sometimes urged that the proceedings in the civil tribunals are too tardy and ineffective for cases arising in times of insurrection or invasion. It is a full reply to this to say, that arrests by civil process may be equally as expeditious and effective as arrests by military orders.

True, a summary trial and punishment are not allowed in the civil courts. But if the offender be under arrest and imprisoned, and not entitled to a discharge under a writ of *habeas corpus*, before trial, what more can be required for the purposes of the Government? The idea that all the constitutional guarantees of personal liberty are suspended throughout the country at a time of insurrection or invasion in any part of it, places us upon a sea of uncertainty, and subjects the life, liberty and property of every citizen to the mere will of a military commander, or what he may say he considers the public safety requires. Does your Excellency wish to have it understood that you hold that the rights of every man throughout this vast country are subject to be annulled whenever you may say that you consider the public safety requires it, in time of invasion or insurrection?...

IMPORTANT QUESTIONS

Did the Constitution intend to throw the shield of its securities around the man liable to be charged with treason as defined by it, and yet leave the man not liable to any such charge unprotected by the safeguard of personal liberty and personal security? Can a man not in the military or naval service, nor within the field of the operations of the army; be arrested and imprisoned without any law of the land to authorise it? Can a man thus in civil life be punished without any law defining the offence and prescribing the punishment? If the President or a court-martial may prescribe one kind of punishment unauthorised by law, why not any other kind? Banishment is an unusual punishment, and unknown to our laws. If the President has the right to prescribe the punishment of banishment, why not that of death and confiscation of property? If the President has the right to change the punishment prescribed by the court-martial from imprisonment to banishment, why not from imprisonment to torture upon the rack, or execution upon the gibbet?

If an indefinable kind of constructive treason is to be introduced and engrafted upon the Constitution, unknown to the laws of the land, and subject to the will of the President whenever an insurrection or invasion shall occur in any part of this vast country, what safety or security will be left for the liberties of the people?

The "constructive treason" that gave the friends of freedom so many years of toil and trouble in England, was inconsiderable compared to this. The precedents which you make will become a part of the Constitution for your successors, if sanctioned and acquiesced in by the people now.

The people of Ohio are willing to co-operate zealously with you in every effort warranted by the Constitution to restore the Union of the States, but they cannot consent to abandon those fundamental principles of civil liberty which are essential to their existence as a free people.

In their name we ask that, by a revocation of the order of his Banishment, Mr. Vallandigham may be restored to the enjoyment of those rights of which they believe he has been unconstitutionally deprived.

FOR FURTHER READING

Frank L. Klement, *Dark Lanterns: Secret Political Societies, Conspiracies, and Treason Trials in the Civil War.* Baton Rouge: Louisiana State University Press, 1984.

Michael Linfield, *Freedom Under Fire: U.S. Civil Liberties in Times of War.* Boston: South End Press, 1990.

Mark E. Neely, *The Fate of Liberty.* New York: Oxford University Press, 1991.

RECONSTRUCTION
Viewpoint 35A
The South Is a Separate, Conquered Nation (1866)
Joint Committee on Reconstruction

INTRODUCTION *Following the Civil War the nation faced the dilemma of how to reintegrate the Southern states that had rebelled. The years 1865–1868 were marked by struggle between Republicans in Congress and President Andrew Johnson over the proper way to do this. In the summer of 1865 former vice president Johnson, a Tennessean and former Democrat who became president following Abraham Lincoln's assassination, officially pardoned many Confederate officials and attempted to quickly reinstate former Confederate states with a minimum of federal involvement. But the new state governments organized under Johnson's reconstruction program were criticized by some for electing former rebels to positions of leadership (including Congress) and for passing laws designed to restrict the political and economic activities of newly freed black slaves.*

Johnson's harshest critics in Congress, dubbed Radical Republicans, advocated a thorough restructuring of Southern society, including the providing of civil rights protection and educational opportunities for former slaves. An able summary of Radical Republican views is found in the following viewpoint, excerpted from the June 20, 1866, report to Congress of the Joint Committee on Reconstruction. Congress had established the special committee in December 1865, instructing its fifteen members to investigate the conditions of the South and to make recommendations for all reconstruction bills. Thaddeus Stevens, a Radical Republican congressman, set the agenda for the Republican-dominated committee (only three members were Democrats). In the report, the majority members argue that the states of the former Confederacy had forfeited all rights previously held as states of the Union. The South, in this view, was in effect a conquered nation and could not claim any constitutional guarantees or congressional representation. The implications of this argument were important: Without rights as states, the South could be remolded as Congress saw fit; without representation, the Southern Democrats would be barred from the U.S. Congress.

How does the Committee describe the attitude of former Confederates? Why, in the committee's view, is it important that Confederate states not be immediately brought back into the Union?

A claim for the immediate admission of Senators and Representatives from the so-called Confederate States has

From Part 3 of the *Report of the Joint Committee on Reconstruction*, 39th Cong., 1st sess., 1866.

been urged, which seems to your committee not to be founded either in reason or in law, and which cannot be passed without comment. Stated in a few words, it amounts to this: That inasmuch as the lately insurgent States had no legal right to separate themselves from the Union, they still retain their positions as States, and consequently the people thereof have a right to immediate representation in Congress without the imposition of any conditions whatever; and further, that until such admission Congress has no right to tax them for the support of the Government. It has even been contended that until such admission all legislation affecting their interests is, if not unconstitutional, at least unjustifiable and oppressive.

It is believed by your committee that all these propositions are not only wholly untenable, but, if admitted, would tend to the destruction of the Government.

WHAT THE REBELS DID

It must not be forgotten that the people of these States, without justification or excuse, rose in insurrection against the United States. They deliberately abolished their State governments so far as the same connected them politically with the Union as members thereof under the Constitution. They deliberately renounced their allegiance to the Federal Government, and proceeded to establish an independent government for themselves. In the prosecution of this enterprise they seized the national forts, arsenals, dockyards, and other public property within their borders, drove out from among them those who remained true to the Union, and heaped every imaginable insult and injury upon the United States and its citizens. Finally they opened hostilities, and levied war against the Government.

They continued this war for four years with the most determined and malignant spirit, killing in battle and otherwise large numbers of loyal people, destroying the property of loyal citizens on the sea and on the land, and entailing on the Government an enormous debt, incurred to sustain its rightful authority. Whether legally and constitutionally or not, they did, in fact, withdraw from the Union and made themselves subjects of another government of their own creation. And they only yielded when, after a long, bloody, and wasting war, they were compelled by utter exhaustion to lay down their arms; and this they did not willingly, but declaring that they yielded because they could no longer resist, affording no evidence whatever of repentance for their crime, and expressing no regret, except that they had no longer the power to continue the desperate struggle.

It cannot, we think, be denied by any one, having a tolerable acquaintance with public law, that the war thus waged was a civil war of the greatest magnitude. The people waging it were necessarily subject to all the rules which, by

the law of nations, control a contest of that character, and to all the legitimate consequences following it. One of those consequences was that, within the limits prescribed by humanity, the conquered rebels were at the mercy of the conquerors. That a government thus outraged had a most perfect right to exact indemnity for the injuries done and security against the recurrence of such outrages in the future would seem too clear for dispute. What the nature of that security should be, what proof should be required of a return to allegiance, what time should elapse before a people thus demoralized should be restored in full to the enjoyment of political rights and privileges, are questions for the law-making power to decide, and that decision must depend on grave considerations of the public safety and the general welfare.

It is moreover contended, and with apparent gravity, that, from the peculiar nature and character of our Government, no such right on the part of the conqueror can exist; that from the moment when rebellion lays down its arms and actual hostilities cease, all political rights of rebellious communities are at once restored; that, because the people of a State of the Union were once an organized community within the Union, they necessarily so remain, and their right to be represented in Congress at any and all times, and to participate in the government of the country under all circumstances, admits of neither question or dispute. If this is indeed true, then is the Government of the United States powerless for its own protection, and flagrant rebellion, carried to the extreme of civil war, is a pastime which any State may play at, not only certain that it can lose nothing in any event, but may even be the gainer by defeat. If rebellion succeeds, it accomplishes its purpose and destroys the government. If it fails, the war has been barren of results, and the battle may be still fought out in the legislative halls of the country. Treason, defeated in the field, has only to take possession of Congress and the cabinet.

Your committee does not deem it either necessary or proper to discuss the question whether the late Confederate States are still States of this Union, or can even be otherwise. Granting this profitless abstraction, about which so many words have been wasted, it by no means follows that the people of those States may not place themselves in a condition to abrogate the powers and privileges incident to a State of the Union, and deprive themselves of all pretence of right to exercise those powers and enjoy those privileges. A State within the Union has obligations to discharge as a member of the Union. It must submit to federal laws and uphold federal authority. It must have a government republican in form, under and by which it is connected with the General Government, and through which it can discharge its obligations. It is more than idle, it is a mockery, to contend that a people who have thrown off their allegiance, destroyed the local government which bound their States to the Union as members thereof, defied its authority, refused to execute its laws, and abrogated every provision which gave them political rights within the Union, still retain, through all, the perfect and entire right to resume, at their own will and pleasure, all their privileges within the Union, and especially to participate in its government, and to control the conduct of its affairs. To admit such a principle for one moment would be to declare that treason is always master and loyalty a blunder. Such a principle is void by its very nature and essence, because inconsistent with the theory of government, and fatal to its very existence. . . .

THE ATTITUDE OF FORMER REBELS

Hardly is the war closed before the people of these insurrectionary States come forward and haughtily claim, as a right, the privilege of participating at once in that Government which they had for four years been fighting to overthrow. Allowed and encouraged by the Executive to organize State governments, they at once placed in power leading rebels, unrepentant and unpardoned, excluding with contempt those who had manifested an attachment to the Union and preferring, in many instances, those who had rendered themselves the most obnoxious. In the face of the law requiring an oath which would necessarily exclude all such men from federal offices, they elect, with very few exceptions, as Senators and Representatives in Congress men who had actively participated in the rebellion, insultingly denouncing the law as unconstitutional. It is only necessary to instance the election to the Senate of the late vice president of the Confederacy [Alexander H. Stephens of Georgia], a man who, against his own declared convictions, had lent all the weight of his acknowledged ability and of his influence as a most prominent public man to the cause of the rebellion, and who, unpardoned rebel as he is, with that oath staring him in the face, had the assurance to lay his credentials on the table of the Senate. Other rebels of scarcely less note or notoriety were selected from other quarters. Professing no repentance, glorying apparently in the crime they had committed, avowing still, as the uncontradicted testimony of Mr. Stephens and many others proves, an adherence to the pernicious doctrine of secession, and declaring that they yielded only to necessity, they insist, with unanimous voice, upon their rights as States, and proclaim that they will submit to no conditions whatever as preliminary to their resumption of power under that Constitution which they still claim the right to repudiate. . . .

THE RIGHTS OF CONQUERED ENEMIES

The question before Congress is, then, whether conquered enemies have the right, and shall be permitted at their own pleasure and on their own terms, to participate in making laws for their conquerors; whether conquered rebels may change their theater of operations from the battle-field, where they were defeated and overthrown, to the halls of Congress, and, through their representatives, seize upon the Government which they fought to destroy; whether the national treasury, the army of the nation, its navy, its forts and arsenals, its whole civil administration, its credit, its pensioners, the widows and orphans of those who perished in the war, the public honor, peace and safety, shall all be turned over to the keeping of its recent enemies without delay, and without imposing such conditions as, in the opinion of Congress, the security of the country and its institutions may demand. . . .

The history of mankind exhibits no example of such madness and folly. The instinct of self-preservation protests against it. . . .

The conclusion of your committee therefore is, that the so-called Confederate States are not at present entitled to representation in the Congress of the United States; that, before allowing such representation, adequate security for future peace and safety should be required; that this can only be found in such changes of the organic law as shall determine the civil rights and privileges of all citizens in all parts of the Republic, shall place representation on an equitable basis, shall fix a stigma upon treason, and protect the loyal people against future claims for the expenses incurred in support of rebellion and for manumitted slaves, together with an express grant of power in Congress to enforce those provisions.

Viewpoint 35B
The South Is Not a Separate, Conquered Nation (1867)
Andrew Johnson (1808–1875)

INTRODUCTION *Andrew Johnson was the only Southern senator not to resign from the Senate during the Civil War. The Tennessean was selected to be President Abraham Lincoln's running mate for the 1864 presidential election; he became president after Lincoln was shot and killed in April 1865. As president he attempted to administer a reconstruction program that emphasized the rapid readmission of former Confederate states into the Union and deemphasized federal enforcement of black suffrage and civil rights. However, for most of his presidency Johnson found his program opposed by Republican members of Congress who passed numerous reconstruction bills over his veto.*

One of the debated points between the president and Congress was the status of former Confederate states. In 1867 Congress, acting over Johnson's veto, dismantled the provisional state governments Johnson had helped to establish and divided the South into military districts under Union army rule. In his State of the Union Address of December 3, 1867, excerpted here, Johnson asserts that the Southern states have never been separated from the Union, and thus cannot be denied representation in Congress.

What does Johnson mean when he says that "there is no Union as our fathers understood the term"? What threats to the Constitution does Johnson perceive in the Radical Republicans' programs?

When a civil war has been brought to a close, it is manifestly the first interest and duty of the state to repair the injuries which the war has inflicted, and to secure the benefit of the lessons it teaches as fully and as speedily as possible. This duty was, upon the termination of the rebellion, promptly accepted, not only by the executive department, but by the insurrectionary States themselves, and restoration in the first moment of peace was believed to be as easy and certain as it was indispensable. The expectations, however, then so reasonably and confidently entertained were disappointed by legislation from which I felt constrained by my obligations to the Constitution to withhold my assent.

———————■———————

It is clear to my apprehension that the States lately in rebellion are still members of the National Union.

———————■———————

It is therefore a source of profound regret that in complying with the obligation imposed upon the President by the Constitution to give to Congress from time to time information of the state of the Union I am unable to communicate any definitive adjustment, satisfactory to the American people, of the questions which since the close of the rebellion have agitated the public mind. On the contrary, candor compels me to declare that at this time there is no Union as our fathers understood the term, and as they meant it to be understood by us. The Union which they established can exist only where all the States are represented in both Houses of Congress; where one State is as free as another to regulate its internal concerns according to its own will, and where the laws of the central Government, strictly confined to matters of national jurisdiction, apply with equal force to all the people of every section. That such is not the present "state of the Union" is a melancholy fact, and we must all acknowledge that the restoration of the States to their proper legal relations with the Federal Government and with one another, according to the terms of the original

compact, would be the greatest temporal blessing which God, in His kindest providence, could bestow upon this nation. It becomes our imperative duty to consider whether or not it is impossible to effect this most desirable consummation. . . .

To me the process of restoration seems perfectly plain and simple. It consists merely in a faithful application of the Constitution and laws. The execution of the laws is not now obstructed or opposed by physical force. There is no military or other necessity, real or pretended, which can prevent obedience to the Constitution, either North or South. All the rights and all the obligations of States and individuals can be protected and enforced by means perfectly consistent with the fundamental law. The courts may be everywhere open, and if open their process would be unimpeded. Crimes against the United States can be prevented or punished by the proper judicial authorities in a manner entirely practicable and legal. There is therefore no reason why the Constitution should not be obeyed, unless those who exercise its powers have determined that it shall be disregarded and violated. The mere naked will of this Government, or of some one or more of its branches, is the only obstacle that can exist to a perfect union of all the States. . . .

It is clear to my apprehension that the States lately in rebellion are still members of the National Union. When did they cease to be so? The "ordinances of secession" adopted by a portion (in most of them a very small portion) of their citizens were mere nullities. If we admit now that they were valid and effectual for the purpose intended by their authors, we sweep from under our feet the whole ground upon which we justified the war. Were those States afterwards expelled from the Union by the war? The direct contrary was averred by this Government to be its purpose, and was so understood by all those who gave their blood and treasure to aid in its prosecution. It can not be that a successful war, waged for the preservation of the Union, had the legal effect of dissolving it. The victory of the nation's arms was not the disgrace of her policy; the defeat of secession on the battlefield was not the triumph of its lawless principle. Nor could Congress, with or without the consent of the Executive, do anything which would have the effect, directly or indirectly, of separating the States from each other. To dissolve the Union is to repeal the Constitution which holds it together, and that is a power which does not belong to any department of this Government, or to all of them united.

TREATED AS STATES

This is so plain that it has been acknowledged by all branches of the Federal Government. The Executive (my predecessor as well as myself) and the heads of all the Departments have uniformly acted upon the principle

Andrew Johnson, State of the Union address, December 3, 1867.

that the Union is not only undissolved, but indissoluble. Congress submitted an amendment of the Constitution to be ratified by the Southern States, and accepted their acts of ratification as a necessary and lawful exercise of their highest function. If they were not States, or were States out of the Union, their consent to a change in the fundamental law of the Union would have been nugatory, and Congress in asking it committed a political absurdity. The judiciary has also given the solemn sanction of its authority to the same view of the case. The judges of the Supreme Court have included the Southern States in their circuits, and they are constantly, *in banc* and elsewhere, exercising jurisdiction which does not belong to them unless those States are States of the Union.

If the Southern States are component parts of the Union, the Constitution is the supreme law for them, as it is for all the other States. They are bound to obey it, and so are we. The right of the Federal Government, which is clear and unquestionable, to enforce the Constitution upon them implies the correlative obligation on our part to observe its limitations and execute its guaranties. Without the Constitution we are nothing; by, through, and under the Constitution we are what it makes us. We may doubt the wisdom of the law, we may not approve of its provisions, but we can not violate it merely because it seems to confine our powers within limits narrower than we could wish. It is not a question of individual or class or sectional interest, much less of party predominance, but of duty—of high and sacred duty—which we are all sworn to perform....

UNJUST PUNISHMENT

I have no desire to save from the proper and just consequences of their great crime those who engaged in rebellion against the Government, but as a mode of punishment the measures under consideration are the most unreasonable that could be invented. Many of those people are perfectly innocent; many kept their fidelity to the Union untainted to the last; many were incapable of any legal offense; a large proportion even of the persons able to bear arms were forced into rebellion against their will, and of those who are guilty with their own consent the degrees of guilt are as various as the shades of their character and temper. But these acts of Congress confound them all together in one common doom. Indiscriminate vengeance upon classes, sects, and parties, or upon whole communities, for offenses committed by a portion of them against the governments to which they owed obedience was common in the barbarous ages of the world; but Christianity and civilization have made such progress that recourse to a punishment so cruel and unjust would meet with the condemnation of all unprejudiced and right-minded men. The punitive justice of this age, and especially of this country, does not

consist in stripping whole States of their liberties and reducing all their people, without distinction, to the condition of slavery. It deals separately with each individual, confines itself to the forms of law, and vindicates its own purity by an impartial examination of every case before a competent judicial tribunal. If this does not satisfy all our desires with regard to Southern rebels, let us console ourselves by reflecting that a free Constitution, triumphant in war and unbroken in peace, is worth far more to us and our children than the gratification of any present feeling.

I am aware it is assumed that this system of government for the Southern States is not to be perpetual. It is true this military government is to be only provisional, but it is through this temporary evil that a greater evil is to be made perpetual. If the guaranties of the Constitution can be broken provisionally to serve a temporary purpose, and in a part only of the country, we can destroy them everywhere and for all time. Arbitrary measures often change, but they generally change for the worse. It is the curse of despotism that it has no halting place. The intermitted exercise of its power brings no sense of security to its subjects, for they can never know what more they will be called to endure when its red right hand is armed to plague them again. Nor is it possible to conjecture how or where power, unrestrained by law, may seek its next victims. The States that are still free may be enslaved at any moment; for if the Constitution does not protect all, it protects none.

FOR FURTHER READING

Dan Carter, *When the War Was Over: The Failure of Self-Reconstruction in the South, 1865–1867.* Baton Rouge: Louisiana State University Press, 1985.

Harold M. Hyman, ed., *The Radical Republicans and Reconstruction, 1861–1870.* Indianapolis: Bobbs-Merrill, 1967.

Eric McKitrick, *Andrew Johnson and Reconstruction.* Chicago: University of Chicago Press, 1960.

Dorothy Sterling, ed., *The Trouble They Seen: Black People Tell the Story of Reconstruction.* Garden City, NY: Doubleday, 1976.

Viewpoint 36A

Blacks Should Have the Right to Vote (1866)

Frederick Douglass (1817–1895)

INTRODUCTION *The following essay by noted black abolitionist (and former slave) Frederick Douglass was first published in the* Atlantic Monthly *in December 1866. By then Congress had passed some reconstruction measures over President Andrew Johnson's veto, including the 1866 Civil Rights Act and extending the life of the Freedmen's Bureau. Douglass argues that such measures were not enough. The federal government cannot by itself protect the civil rights of blacks without becoming too powerful and despotic itself, he contends. State and local governments must take the lead in reconstructing the South and securing the rights of blacks, and these governments will only protect black civil rights if black men have the right to vote.*

Why are the decisions being made by Congress so important, according to Douglass? How does Douglass describe conditions in the South?

The assembling of the Second Session of the Thirty-ninth Congress may very properly be made the occasion of a few earnest words on the already much-worn topic of reconstruction.

Seldom has any legislative body been the subject of a solicitude more intense, or of aspirations more sincere and ardent. There are the best of reasons for this profound interest. Questions of vast moment, left undecided by the last session of Congress, must be manfully grappled with by this. No political skirmishing will avail. The occasion demands statesmanship.

Whether the tremendous war so heroically fought and so victoriously ended shall pass into history a miserable failure, barren of permanent results,—a scandalous and shocking waste of blood and treasure,—a strife for empire, as [British foreign secretary] Earl [John] Russell characterized it, of no value to liberty or civilization,—an attempt to reestablish a Union by force, which must be the merest mockery of a Union,—an effort to bring under Federal authority States into which no loyal man from the North may safely enter, and to bring men into the national councils who deliberate with daggers and vote with revolvers, and who do not even conceal their deadly hate of the country that conquered them; or whether, on the other hand, we shall, as the rightful reward of victory over treason have a solid nation, entirely delivered from all contradictions and social antagonisms, based upon loyalty, liberty, and equality, must be determined one way or the other by the present session of Congress. The last session really did nothing which can be considered final as to these questions. The Civil Rights Bill and the Freedmen's Bureau Bill and the proposed constitutional amendments, with the amendment already adopted and recognized as the law of the land, do not reach the difficulty, and cannot, unless the whole structure of the government is changed from a government by States to something like a despotic central government, with power to control even the municipal regulations of States, and to make them conform to its own despotic will. While there remains such an idea as the right of each State to control its own local affairs,—an idea, by the way, more deeply rooted in the minds of men of all sections of the country than perhaps any one other political idea,—no general assertion of human rights can be of

any practical value. To change the character of the government at this point is neither possible nor desirable. All that is necessary to be done is to make the government consistent with itself, and render the rights of the States compatible with the sacred rights of human nature.

The arm of the Federal government is long, but it is far too short to protect the rights of individuals in the interior of distant States. They must have the power to protect themselves, or they will go unprotected, in spite of all the laws the Federal government can put upon the national statute-book.

EVERY CITIZEN MUST HAVE THE FRANCHISE

Slavery, like all other great systems of wrong, founded in the depths of human selfishness, and existing for ages, has not neglected its own conservation. It has steadily exerted an influence upon all around it favorable to its own continuance. And today it is so strong that it could exist, not only without law, but even against law. Custom, manners, morals, religion, are all on its side everywhere in the South; and when you add the ignorance and servility of the ex-slave to the intelligence and accustomed authority of the master, you have the conditions, not out of which slavery will again grow, but under which it is impossible for the Federal government to wholly destroy it, unless the Federal government be armed with despotic power, to blot out State authority, and to station a Federal officer at every cross-road. This, of course, cannot be done, and ought not even if it could. The true way and the easiest way is to make our government entirely consistent with itself, and give to every loyal citizen the elective franchise,—a right and power which will be ever present, and will form a wall of fire for his protection.

———◼———

The South must be opened to the light of law and liberty.

———◼———

One of the invaluable compensations of the late rebellion is the highly instructive disclosure it made of the true source of danger to republican government. Whatever may be tolerated in monarchical and despotic governments, no republic is safe that tolerates a privileged class, or denies to any of its citizens equal rights and equal means to maintain them.

It remains now to be seen whether we have the needed courage to have that cause [for rebellion] entirely removed from the Republic. At any rate, to this grand work of national regeneration and entire purification Congress must now address itself, with full purpose that the work shall this time be thoroughly done. . . .

Frederick Douglass, "Reconstruction," *The Atlantic Monthly*, December 1866.

RECONSTRUCTION BY THE PEOPLE

The people themselves demand such a reconstruction as shall put an end to the present anarchical state of things in the late rebellious States,—where frightful murders and wholesale massacres are perpetrated in the very presence of Federal soldiers. This horrible business they require shall cease. They want a reconstruction such as will protect loyal men, black and white, in their persons and property: such a one as will cause Northern industry, Northern capital, and Northern civilization to flow into the South, and make a man from New England as much at home in Carolina as elsewhere in the Republic. No Chinese wall can now be tolerated. The South must be opened to the light of law and liberty, and this session of Congress is relied upon to accomplish this important work.

The plain, common-sense way of doing this work is simply to establish in the South one law, one government, one administration of justice, one condition to the exercise of the elective franchise, for men of all races and colors alike. This great measure is sought as earnestly by loyal white men as by loyal blacks, and is needed alike by both. Let sound political prescience but take the place of an unreasoning prejudice, and this will be done.

Viewpoint 36B

Blacks Should Not Have the Right to Vote (1867)

Andrew Johnson (1808–1875)

INTRODUCTION *Andrew Johnson, a white Southerner who served as president of the United States from 1865 to 1869 (following Abraham Lincoln's assassination), often found himself at odds with Republican leaders of Congress. One area of disagreement was black suffrage. Black leaders such as Frederick Douglass and many members of Congress argued that all blacks (or at least all black men), including ex-slaves in the South, should be given the right to vote. In the following viewpoint, excerpted from Johnson's 1867 State of the Union speech, he argues against black suffrage, arguing that it is an evil plot to give blacks political control over whites in the South and would ruin economic and social reconstruction in the region. Proponents of black suffrage were eventually successful in passing the Fifteenth Amendment to the Constitution in 1870.*

Is Johnson expressing a permanent or temporary resistance to the idea of black suffrage? What ideas does he have for helping the ex-slaves?

It is manifestly and avowedly the object of these [Radical Republican] laws to confer upon Negroes the privilege of voting and to disfranchise such a number of

Andrew Johnson, State of the Union address, December 3, 1867.

white citizens as will give the former a clear majority at all elections in the Southern States. This, to the minds of some persons, is so important that a violation of the Constitution is justified as a means of bringing it about. The morality is always false which excuses a wrong because it proposes to accomplish a desirable end. We are not permitted to do evil that good may come. But in this case the end itself is evil, as well as the means. The subjugation of the States to Negro domination would be worse than the military despotism under which they are now suffering. It was believed beforehand that the people would endure any amount of military oppression for any length of time rather than degrade themselves by subjection to the Negro race. Therefore they have been left without a choice. Negro suffrage was established by act of Congress, and the military officers were commanded to superintend the process of clothing the Negro race with the political privileges torn from white men.

The blacks in the South are entitled to be well and humanely governed, and to have the protection of just laws for all their rights of person and property. If it were practicable at this time to give them a Government exclusively their own, under which they might manage their own affairs in their own way, it would become a grave question whether we ought to do so, or whether common humanity would not require us to save them from themselves. But under the circumstances this is only a speculative point. It is not proposed merely that they shall govern themselves, but that they shall rule the white race, make and administer State laws, elect Presidents and members of Congress, and shape to a greater or less extent the future destiny of the whole country. Would such a trust and power be safe in such hands?

ARE BLACKS QUALIFIED TO VOTE?

The peculiar qualities which should characterize any people who are fit to decide upon the management of public affairs for a great state have seldom been combined. It is the glory of white men to know that they have had these qualities in sufficient measure to build upon this continent a great political fabric and to preserve its stability for more than ninety years, while in every other part of the world all similar experiments have failed. But if anything can be proved by known facts, if all reasoning upon evidence is not abandoned, it must be acknowledged that in the progress of nations Negroes have shown less capacity for government than any other race of people. No independent government of any form has ever been successful in their hands. On the contrary, wherever they have been left to their own devices they have shown a constant tendency to relapse into barbarism. In the Southern States, however, Congress has undertaken to confer upon them the privilege of the ballot. Just released from slavery, it may be doubted whether as a class they know more than their ancestors how to organize and regulate civil society. Indeed, it is admitted that the blacks of the South are not only regardless of the rights of property, but so utterly ignorant of public affairs that their voting can consist in nothing more than carrying a ballot to the place where they are directed to deposit it. I need not remind you that the exercise of the elective franchise is the highest attribute of an American citizen, and that when guided by virtue, intelligence, patriotism, and a proper appreciation of our free institutions it constitutes the true basis of a democratic form of government, in which the sovereign power is lodged in the body of the people. A trust artificially created, not for its own sake, but solely as a means of promoting the general welfare, its influence for good must necessarily depend upon the elevated character and true allegiance of the elector. It ought, therefore, to be reposed in none except those who are fitted morally and mentally to administer it well; for if conferred upon persons who do not justly estimate its value and who are indifferent as to its results, it will only serve as a means of placing power in the hands of the unprincipled and ambitious, and must eventuate in the complete destruction of that liberty of which it should be the most powerful conservator. I have therefore heretofore urged upon your attention the great danger—to be apprehended from an untimely extension of the elective franchise to any new class in our country, especially when the large majority of that class, in wielding the power thus placed in their hands, can not be expected correctly to comprehend the duties and responsibilities which pertain to suffrage. Yesterday, as it were, 4,000,000 persons were held in a condition of slavery that had existed for generations; to-day they are freemen and are assumed by law to be citizens. It can not be presumed, from their previous condition of servitude, that as a class they are as well informed as to the nature of our Government as the intelligent foreigner who makes our land the home of his choice. In the case of the latter neither a residence of five years and the knowledge of our institutions which it gives nor attachment to the principles of the Constitution are the only conditions upon which he can be admitted to citizenship; he must prove in addition a good moral character, and thus give reasonable ground for the belief that he will be faithful to the obligations which he assumes as a citizen of the Republic. Where a people—the source of all political power—speak by their suffrages through the instrumentality of the ballot box, it must be carefully guarded against the control of those who are corrupt in principle and enemies of free institutions, for it can only become to our political and social system a safe conductor of healthy popular sentiment when kept free from demoralizing influences. Controlled through fraud and usurpation by the designing, anarchy and despotism must inevitably follow. In the hands of the patriotic and worthy our Government will be preserved upon the principles of the Constitution inherited from our fathers. It follows, therefore, that in admitting to the ballot box a new class of voters not qualified for the exercise of the elective franchise we weaken our system of government instead of adding to its strength and durability.

I yield to no one in attachment to that rule of general suffrage which distinguishes our policy as a nation. But there is a limit, wisely observed hitherto, which makes the ballot a privilege and a trust, and which requires of some classes a time suitable for probation and preparation. To give it indiscriminately to a new class, wholly unprepared by previous habits and opportunities to perform the trust which it demands, is to degrade it, and finally to destroy its power, for it may be safely assumed that no political truth is better established than that such indiscriminate and all-embracing extension of popular suffrage must end at last in its destruction. I repeat the expression of my willingness to join in any plan within the scope of our constitutional authority which promises to better the condition of the Negroes in the South, by encouraging them in industry, enlightening their minds, improving their morals, and giving protection to all their just rights as freedmen. But the transfer of our political inheritance to them would, in my opinion, be an abandonment of a duty which we owe alike to the memory of our fathers and the rights of our children.

DANGERS TO THE NATION

The plan of putting the Southern States wholly and the General Government partially into the hands of Negroes is proposed at a time peculiarly unpropitious. The foundations of society have been broken up by civil war. Industry must be reorganized, justice reestablished, public credit maintained, and order brought out of confusion. To accomplish these ends would require all the wisdom and virtue of the great men who formed our institutions originally. I confidently believe that their descendants will be equal to the arduous task before them, but it is worse than madness to expect that Negroes will perform it for us. Certainly we ought not to ask their assistance till we despair of our own competency.

The great difference between the two races in physical, mental, and moral characteristics will prevent an amalgamation or fusion of them together in one homogeneous mass. If the inferior obtains the ascendency over the other, it will govern with reference only to its own interests for it will recognize no common interest—and create such a tyranny as this continent has never yet witnessed. Already the Negroes are influenced by promises of confiscation and plunder. They are taught to regard as an enemy every white man who has any respect for the rights of his own race. If this continues it must become worse and worse, until all order will be subverted, all industry cease, and the fertile fields of the South grow up into a wilderness. Of all the dangers which our nation has yet encountered, none are equal to those which must result from the success of the effort now making to Africanize the half of our country.

FOR FURTHER READING

W.E.B. DuBois, *Black Reconstruction in America.* New York: Free Press, 1998.

Eric Foner, *Reconstruction: America's Unfinished Revolution.* New York: Harper Perennial, 2002.

William C. Gillette, *The Right to Vote: Politics and the Passage of the 15th Amendment.* Baltimore: Johns Hopkins Press, 1965.

William S. McFeely, *Frederick Douglass.* New York: Norton, 1991.

Index